TWENTY-FIRST-CENTURY MOTHERHOOD

Twenty-first-Century
Motherhood

Experience, Identity, Policy, Agency

Edited by **Andrea O'Reilly**

COLUMBIA UNIVERSITY PRESS   New York

Columbia University Press
Publishers Since 1893
New York   Chichester, West Sussex
Copyright © 2010 Columbia University Press
All rights reserved

Library of Congress Cataloging-in-Publication Data
Twenty-first-century motherhood : experience, identity, policy, agency /
edited by Andrea O'Reilly.
p.   cm.
Includes bibliographical references and index.
ISBN 978-0-231-14966-2 (cloth : alk. paper) — ISBN 978-0-231-14967-9 (pbk. : alk. paper) —
ISBN 978-0-231-52047-8 (ebook)
1. Motherhood 2. Women—Identity 3. Women—Social conditions—21st century.
4. Mass media and women. 5. Women—Political activity. I. O'Reilly, Andrea, 1961–
II. Title: 21st century motherhood.

HQ759.T946 2010
306.874'309051—dc22

2010018535

Columbia University Press books are printed on permanent and durable acid-free paper.
This book is printed on paper with recycled content.
Printed in the United States of America

c 10 9 8 7 6 5 4 3 2 1
p 10 9 8 7 6 5 4 3 2 1

Contents

Acknowledgments

Serving as the editor of a book collection, particularly one as lengthy as *Twenty-first-Century Motherhood*, was a daunting and yet deeply rewarding experience; one that for me may be likened to arranging—and surviving—your child's birthday party celebrated by a houseful of sugar-crazed four-year-olds: a great deal of planning, hectic hours of supervision (or at least an attempt at such), and much clean up are guaranteed. But, as with my children's many birthday parties, I was fortunate to have many other mothers assist me in this task. I am deeply indebted to Lauren Dockett, Avni Majithia, Marisa Lora Pagano, Kerri Cox Sullivan, Anne McCoy, and Michael Simon at Columbia University Press; they directed, arranged, and tidied better than the most accomplished event organizer. All editors should be so fortunate. A big thank you to my research assistants, Sarah Trimble, Melissa Nurse, and Sara Malik, who skillfully and patiently took care of all the details and kept me sane throughout it all. A particular thank you is due to Randy Chase, my proofreader and indexer: no one can restore order to chaos better than Randy. I could not have completed this work without him. My deepest appreciation goes to the Social Science Research Council of Canada and its continued support of my research though various grants, most notably the Standard Research Grant and the International Opportunities Fund grant. Thank you to the members of the Association for Research on Mothering—my extended family who makes everything I do possible. Special thanks to Renée

Knapp at ARM, who makes me laugh when I want to cry. And to my "sisters," Lisa Brouckxon, Angela Bosco, Linn Baran, Christina Cudahy, Janice Giles, Frances Latchford, Jennifer O'Reilly, Adrienne Ryder, and May Friedman, thank you for the joy you bring to my life. My deepest gratitude goes to my children, Jesse, Erin, and Casey O'Reilly-Conlin, who love and support me despite the craziness of my writing life, and to my partner of twenty-eight years, Terry Conlin, who makes this writing life possible. Finally, thank you to the contributors of this volume, who made this task less daunting than it could have been and far more rewarding than I imagined it would be.

Introduction

ANDREA O'REILLY

Over the last twenty-five years the topic of motherhood has emerged as a central and significant topic of scholarly inquiry across a wide range of academic disciplines. A cursory review reveals that hundreds of scholarly articles have been published on almost every motherhood theme imaginable. The *Journal of the Association for Research on Mothering* alone has examined motherhood topics as diverse as sexuality, peace, religion, public policy, literature, work, popular culture, health, carework, young mothers, motherhood and feminism, feminist mothering, mothers and sons, mothers and daughters, lesbian mothering, adoption, the motherhood movement, and mothering, race, and ethnicity, to name a few. In 2006 I coined the term *motherhood studies* to acknowledge and demarcate this new scholarship on motherhood as a legitimate and distinctive discipline, one grounded in the theoretical tradition of maternal theory developed by scholars such as Patricia Hill Collins, Adrienne Rich, and Sara Ruddick. Indeed, similar to the development of women's studies as an academic field in the 1970s, motherhood studies, while explicitly interdisciplinary, has emerged as an autonomous and independent scholarly discipline over the last decade.

However, the numerous edited collections on motherhood have tended to be discipline specific or thematic in focus. This is surprising, given the explicit interdisciplinary and multidisciplinary nature of motherhood studies and the exponential growth of this field over the last two decades. Seeking to address this absence, this volume intends to provide an investigation of the salient motherhood topics across various scholarly disciplines. Specifically, this comprehensive interdisciplinary volume will examine the topic of motherhood explicitly from a twenty-first century perspective, making it the first collection of its kind.[1]

The idea for this volume arose from the tenth anniversary conference of the Association for Research on Mothering, which was held in Toronto, Canada, in October 2006. A central aim of this conference was to reflect upon the development of motherhood scholarship over the last two decades and to explore how motherhood themes and issues have changed with the advent of the twenty-first century. While many of the motherhood issues remain the same, the two hundred plus papers presented at the conference revealed not only that these issues are becoming increasingly more complex and complicated, but also that several new issues and challenges have emerged and will continue to appear as the twenty-first century unfolds. Accordingly, the aim of this volume is to study motherhood from a twenty-first-century perspective and to consider the challenges and possibilities of motherhood as the first decade of the new millennium comes to a close.

In the thirty plus years since the publication of Rich's *Of Woman Born,* motherhood research has focused upon the oppressive and empowering dimensions of mothering and the complex relationship between the two. Indeed, almost all contemporary scholarship on motherhood draws upon Rich's distinction "between two meanings of motherhood, one superimposed on the other: the *potential* relationship of any woman to her powers of reproduction and to children; and the *institution*, which aims at ensuring that that potential—and all women—shall remain under male control" (1986:13; emphasis in original). Following the above distinction, motherhood studies may be divided into three interconnected themes or categories of inquiry: motherhood as institution, motherhood as experience, and motherhood as identity or subjectivity. Within motherhood studies the term *motherhood* is used to signify the patriarchal institution of motherhood, while *mothering* refers to women's lived experiences of childrearing as they both conform to and/or resist the patriarchal institution of motherhood and its oppressive ideology. While scholars who are concerned with the ideology or institution investigate policies, laws, ideologies, and images of patriarchal motherhood, researchers who are interested in experience examine the work women do as mothers, an area of study paved with insights derived from Sara Ruddick's concept of maternal practice. The third category, identity or subjectivity, looks at the effect that becoming a mother has on a woman's sense of self; in particular, how her sense of self is shaped by the institution of motherhood and the experience of mothering, respectively.

Since the turn of the millennium a new theme in motherhood has emerged that I have termed *agency*. Motherhood scholarship, whether its concern is mothering as institution, experience, or identity, has tended to focus on how motherhood is detrimental to women because of its construction as a patriarchal entity within the said three areas. For example, scholars interested in experience argue that the gender inequities of patriarchal motherhood cause the work of mothering to be both isolating and exhausting for women, while those concerned with ideology call attention to the guilt and depression that is experienced by mothers who fail to live up to the impossible standards of patriarchal motherhood that our popular culture inundates them with. In contrast, little has been written on the possibility or potentiality of mothering as identified by Rich more than thirty years ago. This point is not lost on Fiona Green, who writes, "still largely missing from the increasing dialogue and publication around motherhood is a discussion of Rich's monumental contention that even when restrained by patriarchy, motherhood can be a site of empowerment and political activism" (2004:31). More recently, however, agency has emerged as a prevailing theme in motherhood scholarship. Specifically, the rise of a vibrant and vast motherhood movement in the United States over the last decade has paved the way for more meaningful exploration into the emancipatory potential of motherhood in the twenty-first century.

As the first to organize and examine motherhood research under these four constitutive themes, this volume will consider the impact of this new century on how motherhood is practiced and represented as experience, identity, policy, and agency. For the purpose of this volume, the more specific theme of *policy* will be used over the more general concept *institution*. Over the last two decades, most of the research on motherhood as institution has looked at how such is conveyed and maintained through ideology; less attention has been paid to how the institution of motherhood is, in the same way, enacted and enforced through policy, whether governmental, health, work, or educational. Thus, with the advent of the twenty-first century, a more policy-based perspective on the institution of motherhood is both judicious and essential.

The papers selected for the volume cover a wide range of disciplines and consider many diverse motherhood themes, including globalization, raising trans children, HIV/AIDS, the new reproductive technologies, queer parenting, the motherhood memoir, mothering and work, welfare reform, intensive mothering, mothers and/in politics, the influence of the Internet, third-wave feminism, and the motherhood movement. While all of the papers explicitly and directly address a motherhood concern central to the twenty-first century, the volume does not purport to fully represent twenty-first-century motherhood; instead, it offers a snapshot of the motherhood issues that have engaged scholars over the last decade. It should be noted that while this collection presents various regional, cultural, and racial perspectives—including Chicana, African American, Kenyan, Swedish, Canadian, American, Muslim, queer, low-income, trans, and lesbian—it remains largely North American in its perspective, as is the case with most motherhood research.

Overall, my aim in creating this volume has been to identify the salient themes of this new and exciting discipline of motherhood studies, and to investigate how these themes—experience, identity, policy, and agency—shape and are shaped by the new millennium. More specifically, the volume considers how the social, scientific, and technological developments of the last ten to twenty years, some of which were unimaginable even a decade ago—mothers and/on the Internet, interracial surrogacy, raising trans children, men mothering, intensive mothering, queer parenting, species-altering applications of new biotechnologies, androgenesis, the motherhood movement, mothering post-9/11, and the AIDS crisis—have forever altered the meaning and experience of motherhood for women and the societies in which they live.

The volume invites dialogue and debate on these important issues so that we, as mothers and as a culture, are able to fully comprehend and respond appropriately to such momentous changes. While in some instances these developments have been beneficial, in others they have been harmful; in any case, each set of outcomes requires new understandings of the experience and identity of mothering, and calls for new and innovative approaches to maternal agency and motherhood policy. While the changes examined here cannot be undone, it is my hope that this volume will enable us to better appreciate and respond to these developments by situating maternal experience, identity, policy, and agency in an explicitly twenty-first-century context.

EXPERIENCE

In her ground-breaking book *Maternal Thinking* (1989), Sara Ruddick, the first motherhood scholar to theorize the *experience of mothering* as opposed to the *institution of motherhood*, argues that mothering is a practice. "Practices," explains Ruddick, "are collective human activities distinguished by the aims that identity them and by the consequent demands made on practitioners committed to those aims" (1989:13–14). To engage in maternal practice, Ruddick continues, is "to be committed to meeting the demands that define maternal work. . . . The three demands—for *preservation, growth*, and *social acceptance*—constitute maternal work; to be a mother is to be committed to meeting these demands by work of preservative love, nurturance and training" (1989:17). In defining mothering as a practice, Ruddick enabled future scholars to analyze the experience and work, or practice, of mothering as distinct and separate from the identity of the mother. In other words, *mothering* may be performed by anyone who commits him- or herself to the demands of maternal practice. This perspective also enabled scholars to study the actual experiences of mothering as apart from, albeit affected by, the institution of motherhood. The word *mother*, as Mielle Chandler writes, is thus best understood as a verb; as something one does, a practice (2007:273). However, "mothering is not a singular practice, and mother is not best understood as a monolithic identity," because even among similar mothers "practices vary significantly" (Chandler 2007:273). In acknowledgment of these insights, the papers in this section approach mothering as a verb and are attentive to the multiplicity among and *within* maternal practices.

In the opening paper, "Chicana Mothering in the Twenty-first Century," Jessica Vasquez examines the experiences of mothering among Mexican American women in the early twenty-first century. Chicana mothering requires mothers to act as mediators between racial messages from the "outside world" and their children. As part of nurturing their children, minority mothers must consciously work to defuse negative external racial messages and replace them with affirmation. Just as racial and gender stereotypes pass from one generation to another within families, Vasquez argues, so can ideologies and resistance strategies. Mothers use their own experience as inspiration for teaching and molding their children. Vasquez concludes that the family is an important locus of study for an understanding of the transmission of both class and gender values with the Mexican American community.

Women's lives are at the center of social change in the Muslim world, as the competing pressures of modernization create different understandings of motherhood for Muslim women. "Muslim Motherhood: Traditions in Changing Contexts," by Gail Murphy-Geiss, argues that Muslim motherhood is changing in two main ways, resistance via "republican motherhood" and more moderate negotiation. These struggles are most pronounced among Muslim immigrants to the West. The author examines the long-lived traditional beliefs and practices regarding motherhood in Islam, and then looks to the linked social forces of modernization and globalization, which suggest an "alternative model" of Islamic motherhood in the twenty-first century, one that will both safeguard cherished Islamic values and integrate aspects of Western culture deemed desirable by many Muslim women.

The following paper, "Mothering in Fear: How Living in an Insecure-Feeling World Affects Parenting" by Ana Villalobos, investigates whether and how living in an insecure-feeling world with the possibility of sudden loss affects the ways in which women parent their children. Villalobos first establishes that there have been society-wide increases in subjective insecurity in the twenty-first century, resulting both from large-scale security threats such as 9/11 and from increasing access to communication technologies that allow broader audiences to witness personal incidences of loss, amplifying their effect on collective uncertainty. She then presents the mothering strategies a study group of contemporary women draws on to cope with perceptions of societal insecurity. Among these are classic protective mothering, in which mothers shield their children from information about or experience of negative occurrences, and what she calls *inoculation*, or the deliberate exposure of one's children to small doses of harm or risk in order to make them stronger and more capable of navigating a difficult and insecure world. This form of strategic parenting has implications for twenty-first century motherhood. Indeed, Villalobos' research suggests a possible shift in how women keep their children safe in a potentially hazardous twenty-first century world: from protection-by-*shielding* to protection-by-*exposure*.

In "Mother-Talk: Conversations with Mothers of Female-to-Male Transgender Children," Sarah Pearlman examines eighteen mothers' responses to learning that their daughters identify as transgender and intend to transition to male. The paper explores the participants' initial reactions and the various turning points in the process as their daughters transitioned to male. Pearlman finds that the degree of maternal acceptance relies on personal characteristics, educational background, political and religious beliefs, and recognition of a child's happiness following transition. Maintaining a relationship with their child was essential to these women, and each woman's sense of self as both a mother and an individual was enhanced by continuing to nurture a bond with her now trans son. Many accepted whatever connection was possible, a connection that often depended on terms set by their child. As one mother said, "I'm not going to lose my connection. Whatever level he will allow it, I will have it."

"Queer Parenting in the New Millennium: Resisting Normal," by Rachel Epstein, reflects on the author's fifteen years of research, education, activism, and

community organizing related to queer parenting. Currently there is much to celebrate on the queer parenting front in Canada, much of it affected by the debate
on and the realities of same-sex marriage. The author seeks to celebrate the gains
that have been made and the creative ways that LGBTQ people are making families, without denying sexuality or creating hierarchies of "normalcy." How can
queer families and parents get the recognition and protection they need without
creating "good" and "not so good" families and parenting arrangements? As parents, how do they maintain a radical critique of normalized versions of the family
while recognizing and fulfilling their desire to both protect and provide the best
for their children? The author urges queer communities not to collude with the
disavowal of sexuality from queer identities. She raises questions about how queer
communities can maintain and build on the radical history they have inherited as
sex and gender outsiders, as lesbians, as gay men, as bisexuals, as transsexual and
transgender people, as queer people . . . and as parents.

To end this section, Thenjiwe Magwaza discusses how the twenty-first-
century HIV/AIDS pandemic in Africa is forcing a redefinition of the concept
of motherhood, one that extends beyond the traditional boundaries of age,
sex, and gender. More specifically, Magwaza argues that the HIV/AIDS context is principally responsible for a significant shift in the understanding of the
concept and practice of motherhood within the African context. The paper is
based on a case study of six "mothers" of both sexes who range in age from fifteen to ninety years, and who are from selected South African households that
include children orphaned by AIDS. The main finding of the study is that the
participants' mothering practices and coping strategies are largely influenced
by a strong commitment to the well-being of the children and involve a high
degree of self-sacrifice on the part the "mothers."

IDENTITY

This section builds upon the previous section by likewise problematizing and
deconstructing the patriarchal construct of *mother* as a biological and essential category. Under the patriarchal institution and ideology of motherhood,
the definition of *mother* is limited to heterosexual women who have biological children, while the concept of good motherhood is further restricted to a
select group of women who are white, heterosexual, middle-class, able-bodied,
married, thirty-something, in a nuclear family with usually one to two children,
and, ideally, full-time mothers. Feminist scholars over the last two decades have

vigorously and rigorously challenged this patriarchal construct and called for new and expansive definitions of maternal identity. "Good" mothers, from the feminist perspective, include noncustodial, poor, single, old, young, queer, trans, and "working" mothers; likewise, the biological category of mother itself is expanded so as to allow for other nonbiological identities of maternity such as other-mothers—grandmothers and mentors—and fathers. Similarly, patriarchal motherhood limits family to a patriarchal nuclear structure in which a child's parents are married and are the biological parents, and where the mother is the nurturer and the father is the provider; conversely, families acknowledged from a feminist perspective embrace a diverse variety of compositions, including but not limited to single, blended, step-, matrifocal, and same-sex families. These new family formations have given rise to new social identities of motherhood; likewise, the new reproductive technologies over the last two decades have destabilized the biological category of motherhood. The papers in this section explore how the social, scientific, and technological advances of the twenty-first century have revolutionized the definition and representation of maternal identity. While the first three papers study the representation of maternal subjectivities in genres of the new millennium—motherhood memoirs and contemporary film—in the following studies new categories and practices of maternal identity are considered, including male mothering and androgenesis.

In the opening paper of this section, "Ambivalence of the Motherhood Experience," Ivana Brown reflects on and analyzes current representations of the maternal experience in popular literature on motherhood—in particular, memoirs, essays, and short stories published at the beginning of the twenty-first century. Brown argues that the recent wave of maternal memoirs can be characterized by the emphasis on the ambivalence involved in the motherhood experience. Using a sociological understanding of the concept, she analyzes maternal ambivalence as a social phenomenon that is produced by mothers' relationship toward the social institution of motherhood and the social expectations that are encompassed in the mother role; it is not rooted in mothers' relationships with their children. As Brown further argues, the authors of the memoirs also use their writings to uncover some of the untold realities of mothering, and to deal with their transition to motherhood as they negotiate and present their new identity and maternal status.

In the following paper, "Supermothers on Film; or, the Maternal Melodrama in the Twenty-first Century," Adrienne McCormick argues that Hollywood representations of mothers in the twenty-first century reveal the return of the maternal melodrama with a difference. The films under study—Joseph Ruben's *The*

Forgotten (2004), starring Julianne Moore, Robert Schwentke's *Flightplan* (2005), starring Jodie Foster, and Walter Salles' *Dark Water* (2005), starring Jennifer Connelly—involve supermothers who save their children by overcoming incredible odds. McCormick points out that these representations do not signal a new feminist era in Hollywood film, but are rather linked to Hollywood's penchant for idealizing certain kinds of motherhood over all others, with working mothers receiving the most negative treatment. In examining continuities between the melodramas of the 1930s–1940s and those of the contemporary period, McCormick shows that while both periods idealize motherhood as sacrificial, both also allow for contradictory readings that audience members can ponder in relation to their own lives. In the contemporary period, this is especially crucial for mothers in the audience, as they negotiate the debasement of "actual mothers" on the screen and the reinforcement of ideas of supermotherhood particular to the twenty-first century.

In her "Juno or Just Another Girl?: Young Breeders and a New Century of Racial Politics of Motherhood," Mary Thompson argues that the publication of *Breeder: Real-Life Stories from the New Generation of Mothers* (2001), co-edited by Ariel Gore and Bee Lavender, and the release of *Juno* (directed by Jason Reitman and written by Diablo Cody) in 2007 reflect a renewed twenty-first-century popular interest in young/teen mothers. Both texts celebrate young, counterculture women who elect to defy the social script of carefully delayed and well-planned pregnancy. A discussion of Sapphire's novel *PUSH* (1999) and Leslie Harris' *Just Another Girl on the IRT* (1992) aid in considering the invisible racial and/or class privileges of the counterculture stance. Finally, while *Breeder* explicitly recounts the experiences of young women carrying on the feminist struggle for reproductive rights and child care (*Juno* does so implicitly), it also reveals the problematic celebration of "choice" within feminism's third wave.

Andrea Doucet's paper, "Taking Off the Maternal Lens: Engaging with Sara Ruddick on Men and Mothering," is intended as a conversation between Sara Ruddick's view that "men can mother" and fathers' narratives. Drawing from her in-depth research project with 118 Canadian fathers who are primary caregivers of children, she explores fathers' narratives of caring for their children through Ruddick's threefold classification of mothering: preservation, growth, and social acceptability, which Doucet frames as three parallel parental *responsibilities*: emotional, community, and "moral." Encompassing theoretical work on gender equality and gender differences, as well as Doucet's own long trajectory of feminist research on the importance of men's involvement in childrearing, her paper addresses how fathers enact and speak about gender similarities and differences in parenting. Contrary to Ruddick and other feminist scholars who argue that men "can and do mother," Doucet argues that men do not mother per se because of the effects of deeply ingrained gendering processes, gender differences in friendship patterns, community wariness, and the long shadow of hegemonic masculinities. She concludes that listening to and theorizing men's narratives through a "maternal lens" can obscure the important reality that fathers enact wider conceptions of caring, which in turn has implications for theoretical and empirical understandings of mothering, fathering, masculinities, and parental responsibilities.

In "Reproducing Possibilities: Androgenesis and Mothering Human Identity," Deirdre Condit does the "unthinkable" and explores a new understanding of reproductive embodiment that is informed by the work of Shulamith Firestone and the writings of three materialist feminists who have come after her: Mary O'Brien, Nancy Hartsock, and Marge Piercy. Strongly felt throughout the paper is Condit's postmodern impulse to deconstruct identity, biology, and even materiality, despite the continuing conundrum of the "essentially" sexed body. Using Firestone's initial insights as a platform, Condit claims that an even more fully materialist reading of the dialectic of sex reveals that the problem of equality originates not with the fact that women's bodies reproduce, but rather with the fact that *the bodies of men do not*. Her argument holds that the lack of material reproduction in men significantly contributes to the fracture between men and women that has become sex oppression. Thus, while Firestone called for ectogenetic reproduction to free women to achieve equality, Condit explores the materialist implications of androgenetic reproduction as a means to free men, and thus generate a new avenue to equality.

POLICY

The third section explores governmental, work, medical, and health policy in various geographical and ethnic contexts during the first decade of the twenty-first century. The positions and experiences of mothers in contemporary societies are significantly affected by various forms of policy, which shape the choices that women have about their mothering. Indeed, whether they are medical, governmental, or workplace, policies have a significant impact on the lived experience of mothers, through their potential to be emancipatory or oppressive. Martha A. Fineman alludes to this oppressive potential: "Even social or cultural institutions such as motherhood that women occupy exclusively were what I call 'colonized categories'—initially defined, controlled, and given legal content by men. Male norms and male understandings fashioned legal definitions of what constituted a family, what was good mothering, who had claims and access to children as well as to jobs and education, and, ultimately, how legal institutions functioned to give or deny redress" (1997:224).

Although much has been written about motherhood as an ideology, and while specific aspects of mothering in isolation have been addressed in the literature, none of this has been grounded in the actual experience of mothering. Likewise, feminist theorists have looked critically at the effect of policy in a range of areas, but often in isolation from other aspects of a mother's lived experience. Fineman argues that there is a need to focus more positively on mothering, law, and public policy, maintaining that "in feminist legal theory, motherhood has primarily been presented as problematic for women." The invisibility of women's motherwork creates an incongruence between what policy says about mothers and what many women experience as mothers. The troubling result is a lack of support from society for the work that mothers do, which in turn can undermine women's equality.

Lorna Turnbull, in *Double Jeopardy* (2001), has identified several relevant themes that affect mothering. She highlights the rhetoric of law, policy, and politics that defines mothers as good or bad, the disadvantaged circumstances in which many women mother, the control that medicalization and professionalization exert over their mothering, the undervaluing of motherwork, and the position of relative inequality of mothers as it relates to a variety of areas such as income tax policy and the child welfare system. A review of *Canadian Feminist Literature on Law: An Annotated Bibliography* revealed that some areas of key concerns to maternal scholars include maternity and parental leave, workplace benefits, work-family balance, social welfare cutbacks, reproductive technologies, and increasing privatization of caregiving work.

This collection's section on policy will consider all of the aforementioned issues. The first two look at governmental policy with respect to both globalization and welfare reform in the United States, the next two examine workplace policy by focusing on academic mothers in the U.S. and breastfeeding and workplace practices in Kenya; the final two look at medical/scientific policy in relation to interracial surrogacy and the new biotechnologies.

Toward the end of the twentieth century an analysis of the interaction between welfare states and the international political economic context in which they operate began to emerge; however, analyses that consider the position of women remain rare, despite all of the new challenges women face in the twenty-first century. In "Mothers of the Global Welfare State," Honor Brabazon seeks to open this analytical space by using Sweden and Canada as examples. Brabazon takes the case of the availability of quality day care as a significant factor influencing women's employment—more specifically, mothers' employment. She combines (1) vertical analysis, examining the impact of neoliberal globalization on the particular interaction between market, state, and family that is characteristic of the welfare state, with (2) horizontal analysis, comparing these influences and interactions in two different countries representative of different welfare state models. While hers is an introductory analysis of complex subjects, Brabazon effectively distinguishes certain trends: the vulnerability of mothers' employment to global changes in the twenty-first century, and how the type of welfare state appears to have a significant influence on both the real and rhetorical pressures these changes create, and the responses of state and society to these pressures.

Next, Fiona Pearson examines "The Erosion of College Access for Low-Income Mothers." In 2005 the United States Congress reauthorized the Temporary Assistance for Needy Families (TANF) program, which had provided aid for low income parents and their children since 1996. Under this program, family members demonstrating need could receive public assistance for up to five years as long as adult participants actively engaged in work or educational activities. Many critics argued that the TANF program unnecessarily restricted participants' college educational opportunities before reauthorization. However, as Pearson argues, many of those limitations have remained in place since reauthorization, and so continue to effectively prevent participants from pursuing baccalaureate or graduate degrees. Such social welfare policies reflect trends that emphasize work in the formal economy over education, which may in part rest on the assumption that adequate institutional resources to meet low-income parents' educational needs lie elsewhere. This paper, based on interviews with nineteen TANF student participants, outlines the types of institutional resources that students have relied upon in the past to facilitate their educational goals. This study also demonstrates the ways that these resources have been challenged and restricted, particularly over the past eight years. The long-term implications of these findings must be further researched to determine how low-income students' access to college is changing as a result of current policy and budgetary decisions.

"Academic Life Balance for Mothers: Pipeline or Pipe Dream?" by Michele L. Vancour and William M. Sherman explores how the institution of motherhood, in both workplace policy and the ideology of intensive mothering, is experienced by academic mothers. Many of these highly educated professional women found themselves in a "tug-or-war" as they struggled to meet the overwhelming demands of two complicated roles, which both required their full-time psychological presence. Presented with extreme pressures to succeed in all aspects of their lives, women often make sacrifices that jeopardize their health and potential advancement; this trend may be more problematic for academic mothers with preschool children. In an attempt to better understand the phenomena academic mothers' experience, interviews were conducted at four teaching universities with seventeen female faculty members who have preschool-age children. The results of this research could potentially help women to achieve the delicate balance necessary to sustain intensive motherhood, an academic career, and a healthy lifestyle, and also support academic efforts for female faculty recruitment and retention.

In the next paper, Violet Naanyu explores the duration of exclusive breastfeeding with regards to work policies in different occupations in contemporary Eldoret, Kenya. The study, "Exclusive Breastfeeding and Work Policies in Eldoret, Kenya," examines the duration of exclusive breastfeeding during the first five months after birth, and goes on to investigate whether exclusive breastfeeding varies with demographic characteristics, mothers' occupation, distance to work, and work policies. The findings show that the duration of exclusive breastfeeding is similar for most mothers irrespective of occupation. Higher durations of exclusive breastfeeding are associated with increasing age, maternity leave, and distance to work. Surprisingly, she determines that access to breastfeeding-friendly work policies is not automatically associated with increased exclusive breastfeeding. In documenting the increasing complexity of mother-worker role conflict and utilization of family-friendly work policies in the twenty-first century, this paper calls for more research in this area.

Laura Harrison, in "Brown Bodies, White Eggs: The Politics of Cross-racial Gestational Surrogacy," argues that the feminist debates surrounding surrogacy have been fundamentally altered by technological shifts that have enabled gestational surrogacy, in which prospective "parents" can retain full genetic kinship ties to a child born by another woman. This technology has led to increasing numbers of women of color acting as surrogates, meaning that black or Latina women can give birth to a "white" child in what this essay refers to as "cross-racial gestational surrogacy." This essay will analyze surrogacy as a practice that has been transformed by technological innovation, incorporating an intersectional reading of this issue that interrogates how the multiple interstices of race, gender, and structural oppression come into dialogue with the "service" of surrogacy.

Scientists in the fields of genetics, robotics, informatics, and nanotechnology are leading a twenty-first-century revolution that could cure many currently incurable diseases, and open the door to a future in which we make a fundamental—and perhaps irreversible—break with human nature as we have known it. The work on these technologies in the United States is proceeding within an environment that is largely unregulated, with little public conversation about which technologies should or should not be allowed. In the paper that concludes this section, "What Will Become of Us? New Biotechnologies and the Need for Maternal Leadership," Enola G. Aird argues that the dominant values of American society are propelling us toward a future in which there will be no limits on the use of these new technologies, which will ultimately lead to a new eugenics and the commodification of human beings. She contends that maternal values, focused as they are on preserving the lives and dignity of children, may be our society's only remaining source of "braking" values—values that might enable us to slow down and set limits. This paper issues an urgent call to mothers—and others who subscribe to maternal values—to take a leading role in slowing down the biotech revolution before we reach a point of no return.

AGENCY

In *Of Woman Born* Rich writes: "We do not think of the power stolen from us and the power withheld from us in the name of the institution of motherhood" (1986:275). "The idea of maternal power has been domesticated," Rich continues, "In transfiguring and enslaving woman, the womb, —the ultimate source of the power—has historically been turned against us and itself made into a source of powerlessness" (1986:68). The aim of empowered mothering is to reclaim this power for mothers; to imagine and implement a mode of mothering that mitigates the many ways that patriarchal motherhood, both discursively and materially, regulates and restrains mothers and their mothering. In contrast to the patriarchal institution of motherhood, an empowered practice of mothering is one modeled upon maternal agency. More specifically, as patriarchal motherhood characterizes childrearing as a private and nonpolitical undertaking, maternal agency foregrounds the political-social dimension of motherwork. Even as feminist researchers concur that an empowered mothering that is modeled on maternal agency is better for mothers and their children, discussion remains on how this goal, as both practice and politic, may be achieved and sustained (Green 2006; O'Reilly 2007a, 2007b; Jeremiah 2006; Hewett 2006; DiQuinzio

2007; Stooke et al. 2010; Stadtman Tucker 2008). In other words, how do mothers individually and collectively refuse and resist the ideology and institution of patriarchal motherhood? What makes this possible? While researchers agree that "the process of resistance entails making different choices about how one wants to practice mothering" (Horwitz 2003:58), the larger question remains: What is needed at both the individual and cultural level to enable—or, more specifically, to empower—women to engage in this process of resistance? The papers in this section explore the achievement and implementation of maternal agency across a wide range of practices, both private and public, to include the motherhood movement, politics, childrearing, the Internet, and feminist mothering.

In the opening paper of this section, "From 'Choice' to Change: Rewriting the Script of Motherhood as Maternal Activism," Judith Stadtman Tucker argues that a growing awareness of the "motherhood problem"—the combination of cultural factors, social trends, and policy shortfalls that makes mothers and other caregivers disproportionately vulnerable to financial insecurity and makes the daily work of mothering harder than it has to be—presents an important opportunity for organizations and grass-roots activists intent on mobilizing mothers for social change. However, there is no clear consensus among leaders of the emerging mothers' movement about the best way to describe mothers' contributions to society or how to define and defend their rights. In particular, there is a shared conviction among movement activists that the present generation of mothers is indifferent or antagonistic to traditional feminist analyses of gender, power, and systems of oppression. In public statements, mothers' advocates blend and weave compatible and incompatible political theories and ideological frameworks to validate their agenda for change; liberal feminism, maternalism, and feminist care theory are among the predominant influences. The results of this exercise are often inconsistent and unpersuasive; consequently, this strategy may ultimately impede the movements' growth and visibility. This essay discusses some of the underlying obstacles to articulating a coherent politics of motherhood in today's cultural context, suggesting that the future success of the mothers' movement will depend on leaders' ability to develop and communicate an effective change narrative.

In "The Mothers' Movement: The Challenges of Coalition Building in the Twenty-first Century," Patrice DiQuinzio considers the implications of Bernice Johnson Reagon's analysis of coalition politics for the contemporary mothers' movement. DiQuinzio argues that the movement requires a clear understanding of both the difficulties and the value of coalition building and a strong commitment to doing the hard work of coalition building. Without this understanding and commitment, the mothers' movement risks focusing too much on nurturing and supporting others—and only some mothers at that—and thus jeopardizes its revolutionary potential. DiQuinzio draws from her own experiences of small instances of coalition building; using the examination of those differences among women and mothers that she personally finds very hard to negotiate, she illustrates the applicability of Reagon's analysis of coalition building to the mothers' movement. Through this, she is able to suggest some mothering issues and differences among women and mothers that provide ample opportunities for coalition building.

Marsha Marotta draws on her extensive explorations of the relationship between power and spaces in "Political Labeling of Mothers: An Obstacle to Equality in Politics." Marotta's work engages spaces as concrete, socially constructed, and political, as she provides a spatial context to consider the gender gap in voting and gender stereotypes in attitudes toward politics. She helps illuminate the links among culture, identities, and practices by examining such imposed labels as "soccer moms" and "security moms," as well as the self-packaging of mothers in Mothers Against Drunk Driving and the Million Mom March. Marotta shows how such labels illustrate the ways in which political discourse disseminates the ideology of the "good" mother, as well as how the labels help locate and keep mothers in what she calls "MotherSpace"–a particular space in politics and society that tends to reinforce notions of selflessness in mothers rather than advance equality and full participation as citizens. She argues that such practices place outer boundaries on mothers that ossify the meaning of motherhood, reduce the potential threat mothers pose when they do venture outside MotherSpace, and keep mothers at the margins of political power.

The next paper, by Camille Wilson Cooper, examines "Racially Conscious Mothering in the 'Colorblind' Century: Implications for African American Motherwork." The twenty-first century is remarkably unique given the widespread political, social, and educational claims that U.S. society is now—or should be—"colorblind." Yet a key paradox of the twenty-first century relates to the coexistence of racial transcendence and racial regression, which inevitably filters into African American mothers' consciousness. Cooper explores the ways in which living in an era that questions the salience of race may alter African American mothers' identity, experience, and politics. In particular, it considers whether colorblind ideologies and politics present better chances for African American families to achieve equality or if they veil racial oppression. The author contrasts the colorblind rhetoric and politics of twenty-first-century United States with the racially conscious mothering traditions of African American mothers; these traditions are closely tied to quests for racial liberation, cultural pride, and community uplift, which constitute acts of political resistance. The author further considers the extent to which these African American mothering traditions can and should be sustained given the contemporary milieu; she does this by describing some key opportunities and dilemmas that a nation aspiring to be colorblind presents to African American mothers and their families.

Next, in "It Takes a (Virtual) Village: Mothering on the Internet," May Friedman looks at the fascinating juxtaposition between the lived experience of mothering and the myriad ways that such work is documented on the Internet. Friedman argues that parenting has already become embedded in cyberculture and that, as such, any analysis of the pros and cons of the Internet as a parenting venue are facile; she notes that "despite the very real concerns present in understanding the ways that maternity is performed on the Internet, such an analysis *must* take place." The paper grapples with the chief flaws of online parenthood: (1) that within the context of cyberspace, patriarchal motherhood is once again the chief example of mothering practice; and (2), that the Internet itself is not a space that is equally accessed by all, but rather requires significant privilege in the guise of spare income and time. Having acknowledged these limitations, Friedman notes the ways that the Internet has allowed some mothers, particularly those with non-normative social locations, to connect and create a new form of community online. She explores important questions regarding the nature of community and activism and interrogates the possibility that, despite their unusual manifestations, both are firmly present within parenting cyberculture.

With the emergence of an international motherhood movement and the development of motherhood studies as an academic discipline, maternal scholars and activists have sought to define and develop a politic or theory of maternal empowerment . Maternal activists and researchers today agree that motherhood as it is currently perceived and practiced in patriarchal societies is disempowering if not oppressive for a multitude of reasons, ranging from the societal devaluation of motherwork to the endless tasks of privatized mothering and the impossible standards of idealized motherhood. Maternal activists and researchers likewise contest, challenge, and counter patriarchal motherhood by way of a plethora of theories of and strategies for maternal empowerment. The final paper, "Outlaw(ing) Motherhood: A Theory and Politic of Maternal Empowerment for the Twenty-first Century," will not so much revisit these ideas and strategies as request that scholars and activists alike rethink received or accepted notions of how and why motherhood functions as an oppressive institution for women. When asked, students, mothers, and researchers readily describe the exhaustion, guilt, boredom, anxiety, loneliness, and so forth of contemporary Western motherhood but are less forthcoming on why this is so. It is my view, and the argument of this paper, that modern motherhood functions as a patriarchal institution, one that has largely been impervious to change despite forty years of feminism, because of the gender ideology that grounds it: namely, gender essentialism and the resulting naturalized opposition of the public and private spheres. Only by unearthing and severing the ideological underpinning of patriarchal motherhood can we develop a politic of maternal empowerment and a practice of outlaw motherhood for the twenty-first century.

I became a mother to three children during the mid to late 1980s in a world radically different from the one explored in the papers in this volume, and while every decade brings change, I see the last two decades as being particularly transformative in relation to the meaning and experience of motherhood and mothering. Two decades ago, interracial surrogacy, androgenesis, and species-altering bio technologies were still the stuff of science fiction, and the looming AIDS/HIV crisis was only slowly being understood as increasing numbers of our gay friends and family members took ill and died. While the conservative backlash originated in the 1980s, the fallout took its greatest toll over the last decade in terms of welfare reform, cuts to social spending, loss in reproductive rights and freedoms, "downsizing," and so forth. Indeed, in the mid to late 1980s, "9" and "11" were still numbers, globalization was a concept largely known only to academics, and Islam was a religion unfamiliar to most in the West. Today you can do a Google search of the words *motherhood, mothering*, and *mothers* and come up with 438,000 hits; this is light years away from what was available to mothers ten to twenty years ago.

In 1983, when I first became pregnant, you would be lucky to come across a copy of Rich's *Of Woman Born* (1976) or Jane Lazarre's *The Mother Knot* at a used book store, that is, if they had not gone out of print; we certainly could not turn to the estimated 8,500 parenting blogs for comfort and community. Again, if we were fortunate we had a mother-friend from the same apartment block whom we could meet in the playground after dishes were done and weather permitting. The playdates, attachment parenting, "compulsory" breastfeeding, hyper-parenting, designer baby wear, and the "hurried child" of this century's new momism were all but unheard of twenty years ago. In addition, over the last decade and a half there has been a baby boom among lesbians, a reality worlds removed from the 1980s, when lesbians routinely lost custody of their children. Likewise, Chicana and African American motherhoods are now respected areas of scholarly research in the university, and they are increasingly regarded as valued and essential cultural practices of empowerment in the larger North American society.

The year 2008 witnessed a mother and an African American man competing for the leadership of the Democratic Party and a mother of five young children being nominated by the Republican Party for the position of vice president. In the first decade of this century the motherhood movement emerged as a formidable social movement, by and for feminists and mothers alike, one that provides an organized campaign to secure social and economic rights and recognition for mothers, making real what seemed a utopian fantasy a mere twenty years ago. So is it any better or easier to be a mother in 2008 than it was in 1984, when I first became a mother? At age 48, with my three children pretty much "raised" and with two friends close to my age becoming mothers this past year, I have found this to be a meaningful point of reflection lately. While I am relieved that I had my children before the rise of intensive mothering, I am also delighted that lesbian moms, single parents, common-law marriages, and "blended" families now outnumber patriarchal nuclear families. As the first decade of this new millennium comes to a close, I remain uncertain whether there is any conclusive answer to this timely question. Nonetheless, I am convinced that the issues facing mothers today are, for better or worse, more messy and muddled than they were two decades ago; if nothing else, this makes motherhood at the beginning of the twenty-first century a compelling topic, one that is truly worthy of "a volume of its own."

NOTE

1. The collection *Motherhood in the Twenty-first Century*, edited by Alcira Mariam Alizade, was published in 2006. However, this collection looks at the topic solely from the perspective of psychoanalysis.

WORKS CITED

Alizade, Alcira Mariam, ed. 2006. *Motherhood in the Twenty-first Century*. New York: Karnac Books.

Chandler, Mielle. 2007. Emancipated subjectivities and the subjugation of mothering practices. In *Maternal Theory: Essential Readings*, ed. Andrea O'Reilly, 529–541. Toronto: Demeter Press.

DiQuinzio, Patrice. 2007. Mothering and feminism: Essential mothering and the dilemma of difference. In *Maternal Theory: Essential Readings*, ed. Andrea O'Reilly, 542–555. Toronto: Demeter Press.

Fineman, Martha Albertson. 1995. *Mothers in Law: Feminist Theory and the Legal Regulation of Motherhood*. New York: Columbia University Press.

——. 1997. Feminist theory in law: The difference it makes. In *Feminist Legal Theories*, ed. K. Maschke, 216–236. New York: Garland.

Green, Fiona. 2004. Feminist mothers: Successfully negotiating the tensions between motherhood and mothering. In *Mother Outlaws: Theories and Practices of Empowered Mothering*, ed. Andrea O'Reilly, 31–42. Toronto: Women's Press.

——. 2006. Developing a feminist motherline: Reflections on a decade of feminist parenting. *Journal of the Association for Research on Mothering* 8.1/2:7–20.

Hewett, Heather. 2006. Talkin' bout a revolution: Building a mothers' movement in the third wave. *Journal of the Association for Research on Mothering* 8.1/2:34–54.

Horwitz, Erika. 2003. "Mothers' Resistance to the Western Dominant Discourse on Mothering." Ph.D. diss., Simon Fraser University.

Jeremiah, Emily. 2006. Motherhood to mothering and beyond: Maternity in recent feminist thought. *Journal of the Association for Research on Mothering* 8.1/221–33.

O'Reilly, Andrea. 2007a. Feminist mothering. In *Maternal Theory: Essential Readings*, ed. Andrea O'Reilly, 792–821. Toronto: Demeter Press.

——, ed. 2007b. *Maternal Theory: Essential Readings*. Toronto: Demeter Press.

Rich, Adrienne. 1986. *Of Woman Born: Motherhood as Experience and Institution*. 2nd ed. New York: Norton.

Ruddick, Sara. 1989. *Maternal Thinking: Toward a Politics of Peace*. Boston: Beacon.

Stadtman Tucker, Judith. 2008. Mothering in the digital age: Navigating the personal and political in the virtual sphere. In *Mothering in the Third Wave*, ed. Amber E. Kinser, 199–212. Toronto: Demeter Press.

Stooke, Roz, Pamela McKenzie, and Suzanne Smythe. 2010. Does all this make a difference? Supporting diverse forms of mothering in early learning programs. In *Mothers Who Deliver: Feminist Interventions in Public and Interpersonal Discourse*, ed. P. Reichert Powell and J. Fenton Stitt. New York: State University of New York Press.

Turnbull, Lorna. 2001. *Double Jeopardy: Motherwork and the Law*. Toronto: Sumach Press.

Experience | **PART 1**

Chicana Mothering
in the Twenty-first Century

*Challenging Stereotypes
and Transmitting Culture*

ONE

JESSICA M. VASQUEZ

This chapter examines the experiences of mothering among Mexican American[1] women in the early twenty-first century. Mexican Americans are a large and growing minority group as a result of both immigration and fertility rates. Chicana mothering requires acting as a guardian or mediator between children and racial messages[2] from the "outside world" (school, media, interracial social networks). Mothers are responsible for overseeing their children's growth and development; as minorities, this often requires their defusing negative racial messages and replacing them with affirmation.

The family remains a critical site of racial identity development because it is a locale where intergenerational biography-based teaching occurs. Just as racial stereotypes pass from one generation to another, either intentionally or unintentionally (Lieberson 1985), so too do ideologies and resistance strategies.

This project was supported through grants from the University of California at Berkeley, National Science Foundation, UC MEXUS, and the University of Kansas. I thank those who provided assistance on this project: Michael Omi, Ann Swidler, Shirley Hill, Joane Nagel, Joey Sprague and Christopher Wetzel. Direct correspondence to Jessica M. Vasquez, Department of Sociology, Fraser Hall Room 716, 1415 Jayhawk Blvd., Lawrence, KS, 66045, or to vasquez@ku.edu.

Mothers use their own experience as fodder for the transfer of knowledge and ideologies to their children. Investigating the concrete micro-interactions at home that mothers use to combat racial stereotypes is a necessary and timely subject for inquiry (see Bobo and Fox 2003).

This article considers how contemporary Chicanas engage in mothering in a racially charged and racially hierarchized U.S. society. More specifically, I ask how Chicana mothers resist the racializing images, tropes, and discourses aimed at their children by mainstream society. I find that Chicana mothers engage in three primary and potentially overlapping strategies as they rear their children. Mothers employ two strategies in the public sphere: "gendered encouragement" and "activism," both of which confront and resist racist and sexist derogatory stereotypes. The third strategy is centered on family life: inside the home, mothers are instructors of both ethnic traditions and gender ideologies.

The mothering strategies described here represent tactical responses to a twenty-first-century system of prejudice and discrimination that is not only interpersonal but also institutional. Over the past couple of decades, racism has become "structured" or "color-blind," that is, "white privileges . . . [have been] structured into the patterns of interaction in society so deeply that the overt defense of racial privileges became unnecessary" (Barlow 2003:31). While face-to-face, overt expressions of racism have not disappeared, civil rights protections and the ideology of multiculturalism have forced racism to go underground and become embedded in discourse and institutional practices (Bonilla-Silva 2003). Given this shift in racial ideologies and the systems of domination that evolved toward the end of the twentieth century, Chicana mothers have altered their parenting styles to address contemporary concerns. In practice this means that Chicana mothers protect their children by mediating between racializing institutions and their children's interests. Additionally, many Chicana mothers promulgate racial pride, ethnic traditions, and progressive gender ideologies, all of which elevate their historically subordinated ethnic and gender group's esteem in the minds of their children. Finally, the second-generation Mexican American mothers in my sample experienced upward mobility relative to their parents, and this gain in class status also informs their mothering styles.

FAMILIES AND RACE AT THE TURN OF THE CENTURY

"Motherhood is a culturally formed structure whose meanings can vary and are subject to change" (Segura 1994:211). Traditional femininity poses that a woman's fundamental role is to bear children and take primary responsibility for the domestic sphere. Feminist scholars problematize this formulation, arguing instead that the experience of motherhood is highly particular and invariably shaped by one's race, class, sexuality, and citizenship status (Rubin 1994; Scheper-Hughes 1992; Collins 1994). Despite this feminist critique, popular discourse in the early twenty-first century frames motherhood alternately as a romanticized endeavor (as opposed to effortful work) (Gardner 2008) or as such a fundamental and influential role that all mothers are bound to be critiqued for their shortcomings (Bailey 2006).

Prevalent twenty-first-century rhetoric of motherhood notwithstanding, motherhood must be understood in a context that extends beyond the nuclear family unit to include issues of race and class (Pattillo-McCoy 1999). Annette Lareau (2003) argues that families' socioeconomic statuses correlate with their "cultural logics of child-rearing." Different class-based child-rearing practices and philosophies lead to the transmission of advantages or disadvantages to children. While Lareau asserts that class is more powerful than race in shaping family life experiences, I argue that race remains a dominant force in shaping one's life experiences.

Since "every state *institution* is a racial institution" (Omi and Winant 1994:83, emphasis in original), examining the interplay between larger social structures and individual and family agency is crucial in examining the development of racial self-understandings. Schools are particularly important in these processes; they are primary sites of socialization outside the family. Much teaching and learning about social life and national culture takes place in schools (Valdes 1996; Tobin, Wu, and Davidson 1989; Davidson 1996). Pierre Bourdieu and Jean-Claude Passeron (1977; 1979) argue that the educational system has a chief role in social reproduction and in perpetuation of the extant social hierarchy. Schools legitimate the "cultural capital" of upper-class white students, while simultaneously excluding or marginalizing economically, culturally, and racially disadvantaged groups (Apple 1996; Bourdieu and Passeron 1977, 1979; Cummins 2001; Giroux 1981; Lareau and Horvat 1999). Precisely because schools are strong socializing institutions and educational degrees are positively associated with economic gain, they have also been sites of Mexican American political mobilization (Ochoa 2004).

Yet families also have formative power. Analyzing the practical knowledge, experiential wisdom, and personal perspectives mothers convey to their children is particularly interesting as we attempt to understand how the inner workings of families influence processes of racial identity formation. Families reinforce aspects of identity such as race, religion, or gender (Cohen and Eisen 2000) and mold educational aspirations (Kao 1998; MacLeod 2004). Families and "fictive kin" can also be a wellspring of survival strategies and interdependent support (Stack 1974). Again, this article seeks to understand how Chicana mothers can challenge, reshape, and overturn the racial lessons learned by their children in the dominant society's social institutions.

RESEARCH METHODOLOGY AND FIELDSITES

This article is part of a larger project on multigenerational Mexican American families in California. California has by far the largest Hispanic population in the United States (12.5 million), 10.4 million of which are of Mexican descent (data source: 2000 Census). I conducted sixty-seven in-depth interviews in twenty-nine three-generation families roughly split between northern and southern California. The bases for the northern and southern California fieldsites were the San Francisco Bay Area and Santa Barbara/Los Angeles counties.

I employed a theoretical sampling strategy, followed by snowball sampling. First I found and contacted families that fit my racial, ethnic, and generational profile by working through Hispanic chambers of commerce, Catholic churches, and high schools in various cities in my two selected fieldsites. Once I made contacts in the community, I proceeded with a snowball sampling strategy. The vast majority of the interviews were conducted in person and one-on-one. All respondents were either first generation (Mexican nationals who immigrated to the United States), second generation (the U.S.-born children of the Mexican immigrants), or third generation (the U.S.-born grandchildren of the Mexican immigrants). The vast majority of my interviewees were middle class. This article focuses on the experiences and parenting strategies of second-generation Chicana mothers (n=14).

CHICANA MOTHERING STRATEGIES

In this section I detail the three main mothering styles I identified through analysis of interview data: two are centered in the public sphere and one is focused on the private sphere. As mentioned at the beginning of this paper, the first parenting style is "gendered encouragement" and the second is "activism," both of which implicitly, if not explicitly, challenge negative stereotypes. Chicana mothers find it imperative to help their children overturn the negative stereotypes that are pervasive in public discourse and racialized images. The first parenting style, "gendered encouragement," involves both emotional support and practical advice that Mexican American mothers provide their children that is particularly sensitive to gender issues. Most Chicana mothers are alert and responsive to gendered expectations because in their own youths they suffered gender inequality. Their own parents encouraged opportunities for boys (including education) more than those for girls. As a result, these mothers are especially supportive of their daughters in their educational pursuits. Gender is not only a female issue, of course, and these mothers are simultaneously aware of the negative stereotypes cast on their male children and strive to counteract these prescriptions. The second mothering strategy, "activism," is called for when mothers observe or fear institutional or interpersonal discrimination against their children. The third mothering style revolves around home life: mothers are "teachers of culture," in terms of both ethnic traditions and gender ideologies. These mothering tactics are not mutually exclusive; mothers draw on these strategies and use them individually, successively, or in combination with one other.

Before we look at mothering strategies, it is important to note that these Chicana mothers espoused an ardent belief in the "American Dream." Chicana mothers perceive education as a means to attain the American Dream (namely financial gain, upward mobility, and the marks of overall success). Studies demonstrate a strong correlation between educational attainment, occupational status, and earning potential (Bowles, Gintis, and Groves 2005; Card 2001). These women's belief in education as a vehicle to attaining the American Dream is well founded; in fact, all of the families interviewed had followed a pathway of upward mobility through the three generations.

Lance Morelos' mother, like most second-generation Chicana mothers, saw education as offering a ladder for upward mobility. Lance recalls his mother's words:

> My mom, since I was in high school, would say, "I don't care if you get a degree in underwater basket weaving, get a degree." So we always lived in a very good area, which was predominantly a white area, in the smallest house, because they had the better schools. And [my parents] knew that. And so there would be nine of us in a three-bedroom house for a lot of years until my dad really started to prosper. The goal was "education, education, education." We all went to Catholic school. My parents were in debt most of their life because of it. . . . My mother always said, "Location, location, location." The best schools are the best opportunity.

Here education is touted as instrumental in achieving success, as well as symbolic of past and future accomplishments. As mentioned, the educational attainment in all the families interviewed rose with each succeeding generation. Ruby Castillo captures her family's three-generation upward educational trajectory:

> Education was not a big part of our family. Mom had 3rd-, 4th-grade education and dad had the same. . . . So in the family [education] was never really pushed, stressed, but I felt that I needed to pursue a higher education so I pushed myself. . . . Get an education. I saw that as a pathway to get out of poverty. . . . In my kid's generation, unfortunately, they don't know any struggles. I had to struggle if I wanted to get ahead, I had to take it upon myself to get educated and to get out and to work to buy my own clothes, etc. And I say that unfortunately, because I don't see their inner passion. For example, the son at University of California, Santa Barbara [is] so used to having everything . . . taken care of from food, roof over the head . . . [us] paying for [his] education. . . . When I saw his [application] essay, there was nothing about a struggle. [It was] "I want to be God, I want to be President," that type of essay.

Ruby had to seek out educational opportunities and funding sources on her own; she "pushed" herself to do so and now, at forty-six years old, she is a self-employed business owner. While part of the impact of her children's more coddled lifestyle may be the undesirable attribute of entitlement and loss of character-building challenges, her ability to coach her children throughout the college process speaks to the cultural and economic capital that a college degree bestows.

While belief in the American Dream is an ethos rather than a mothering strategy, it does inform how Chicana mothers consider and enact their responsibility as parents. These mothers have seen the American Dream achieved (or at least in progress) in their own families yet they are also wise to racist realities whereby people are differentially rewarded for the same work or are met with differing opportunity structures. It is in part the collision of a tightly held American Dream ideology and racial/ethnic discrimination and stratification that engenders the Chicana mothering strategies depicted here.

Gendered Encouragement

In Mexican immigrant families of the 1970s, male children were often offered opportunities and resources for school or other activities at the expense of female children. As a consequence of having been explicitly discouraged, these second-generation Chicanas developed a strategy of "gendered encouragement" when mothering their own children.

Yolanda Segura recalls how her father ridiculed her desire to go to college:

> I never finished my college education and part of that was because of opportunity and environment. . . . When I started to go to college right after high school, my dad sort of ridiculed it and was, you know, "What do you need that for? . . . You don't need that." And not having good study habits or really not knowing how to survive in college and not having the right people to guide me was what deterred me the most.

Yolanda particularly remembers how her race and gender influenced her experience. She recognizes that her parents enacted societal assumptions about Mexican immigrants and their families that in turn influenced her gendered upbringing as a "Mexican girl":

> There was always the people out there that just made assumptions about your skin color and your country; . . . that we weren't smart enough. . . . Certainly some of those [assumptions] were internalized by my parents bringing us up because there was this sense of you had to be humble and . . . being a Mexican girl . . . that you had your place in life.

Yolanda grew up in a traditional home and also describes her marital home as "very traditional." She is the full-time mother of three girls and her husband, a high-level executive at a large public relations firm, is the sole income earner. Not wanting to continue a cycle of gendered disadvantage, Yolanda was committed to encouraging her three female children in their academic lives. She adopted a parenting style that reflected the way she *would have liked to be* supported:

> For my kids, I want . . . to offer opportunities that I didn't get. . . . Because I had these strong male figures in my life that tried to push me down . . . I try to make [being a woman] as positive as possible. Not only being a woman but being a woman of color.

Yolanda hopes that by treating her children differently from how she was treated that she can modify their experience.

Chicanas' natal family life and exposure to negative stereotypes are not the only inspirations for mothering tactics. For example, Beatrice Madrigal instructed her daughter, Reyna, to get a college education in order to become economically independent. Beatrice struggled to support her family after her divorce because of her limited education. What came across most clearly in Beatrice's interview was not her sense of race but her gender awareness and strength as a woman. Reyna learned by example as she watched her mother become strong, independent, and assertive:

> [My mom] . . . taught us to be responsible people. . . . When she broke up with my father—I might have been like twelve—she started teaching us how to be really independent and not to rely on anyone. And to take care of yourself and . . . I think that is why I went off to college.
>
> JMV: Really?
>
> Reyna: Yeah, because she was a stay-at-home mom and when my dad left she had to go to work because my dad didn't give her any help or support. . . . That is what she has taught us: "Well, you need to work to take care of yourself. . . . You should go out to college." . . . She started talking about "so you don't have to rely on a man," and then she talk[ed] about what had happened to her.

The lesson that passed between the generations of Madrigal women was not about race or ethnicity, but about gender and economic independence. The lesson that Reyna learned was indeed the one her mother intended to relay. Beatrice remarks on how *her own mother* instructed her at the time of her divorce: "I fell apart for a week. And then my mother would say, 'You've got to get yourself back on your feet.' And I did. I didn't have no income coming in—their father didn't give me any money. And when he did it was like $25 for two . . . what can I do with $25 for two?" Indeed, the intergenerational lessons these Chicana mothers are passing along are about female endurance, independence, and a mothering strategy that is both strong and caring.

Chicana mothers also coached their sons in how to handle the negative stereotypes with which they are confronted. These mothers were very realistic in the goals of social decorum, good grades, and propriety they established for their children. Tyler Mendoza, a third-generation man, refers to his mother's efforts to motivate him to rebut society's low expectations:

> [She] always pushed school, school, school, school. So I had to do better in school[.] . . . C's were not that good, you get A's and B's. C's meant that you could do better. So, they always pushed from day one that I had to do better in school. I knew I had to try harder. . . . I had to try harder and prove that I wasn't one of those dumb lazy Mexicans or the ones that are going to drop out and get somebody pregnant.

Tyler's mother's guidance is clearly imbued with an awareness of the negative images of Mexican-origin boys: that they are dumb, lazy high school dropouts who will impregnate a teenage girl. Tyler's mother strictly counsels him in how to avoid that downhill path: get good grades and disprove negative stereotypes with upright behavior.

Similarly, Tina Acevedo's message to her son Tom about the importance of education is linked with encouraging him to invalidate negative stereotypes by living up to a higher standard. She instructs her son: "Hold your head up high, be on honor roll. Show people what you're made of. The stereotype that we're all dropping out of school or not showing up, that doesn't fit this family. That's not tolerated. We have a standard that we follow." This pragmatic recommendation administered to boys to stay in school reflects Chicana mothers' resistance against prejudiced notions about their Chicano sons. Regarding both daughters and sons, these Chicana mothers proffer practical advice that is both gender and race sensitive and serves to both caution and fortify their children.

Activism in Schools

High school–aged Mexican Americans complained of being (nearly) trapped in tracking systems. Those who escaped had parents who rigorously supervised their schooling and engaged the school administration when necessary.

Seventeen-year-old third-generation Andrew Rosenberg refers to the racialized sorting patterns that organize student placement in high school classrooms:

"Oh, he's Mexican—put him in that class." It's really . . . how it is. It's really bad. . . . But if you're Mexican and you walk into a class of all white people, it's like—oh, this is the GATE [Gifted and Talented Education] class. I don't belong here. When really a lot of those Mexicans who are in the normal classes should be in the GATE classes. And some of the people who are in GATE classes shouldn't be at all . . . most of them are just cheating their way through.

Andrew comments on the critical role that his mother's involvement in school activities had on his education:

I think my parents accelerated my education. They put me in a math program when I was a kid, so it made me really strong in math. They had me play sports—soccer. And they had me play instruments—I played piano and saxophone. [I've been] pretty lucky. . . . My mom was always on the PTA [parent-teacher association]. I feel like I could have just . . . been pushed to the bottom.

With parents—in particular, a mother—actively overseeing his schooling, Andrew escaped being racially tracked and relegated to remedial classes.

Students' relationships with school administrators mirror the racialized tracking system. Third-generation nineteen-year-old Veronica Guzman tells me about how she and her dark-skinned brother have a markedly different relationship with their high school vice principal than does their light-skinned, dark-blonde-haired sister:

> My sister, she's light skinned, she looks American, but she's a Mexican American. The vice principal thought she was white. They [the administration] didn't know that my brother and sister and I were related. And they would send information for her in English and for my brother they would send it in Spanish. She's blonde and according to them she's a *guera* [white woman] and he's *mexicano*, Mexican. The vice principal treated her differently because she was a blonde, she was a *guera*. When they found out she was Hispanic—a Mexican—it wasn't the same anymore.

After Veronica's mother, Gloria, spoke to the principal the situation improved. Gloria engaged in her children's school affairs with confidence and pride: "I am there because my mother could not be there because of her not knowing English." Her own immigrant mother's language deficit and inability to advocate on her behalf during her schooling incites Gloria to vigorously monitor and, when necessary, intervene in her children's education.

Mothering as activism in schools is one distinct way that these mothers help their children navigate racialized social institutions. These Chicana mothers see a role for themselves as advocates for their children in a primary U.S. institution in which they are embedded—schools. These mothers attempt to counteract institutional prejudice and discrimination by "cultivating" (Lareau 2003) or defending their children. Next we move on to how Chicanas mother in the domestic arena.

Mothers as Teachers of Culture

Mothers are active at mothering in both public and private spaces. Turning from the public to the domestic, this section examines mothers as teachers of culture. Mothers are teachers, or "carriers," of culture in two chief arenas: ethnic traditions and gender ideologies and roles. "Women are often constructed as the cultural symbols of the collectivity, of its boundaries, as carriers of the collectivity's 'honor' and as its intergenerational reproducers of culture" (Yuval-Davis 1997:67). In fact, women carry a particular "burden of representation" (Yuval-Davis 1997:45) as symbolic bearers of collective identity. As such, mothers are imagined to literally and figuratively "reproduce" cultures.

Chicana mothers see themselves as instrumental in protecting, passing on, and changing culture. They preserve and transmit cultural elements they appreciate and yet they see a responsibility to change those elements they find troubling, such as unequal gender roles (machismo, patriarchy, or the "cult of masculinity"). Cultural elements Chicana mothers want to retain include the value of family, a sense of roots or heritage, Mexican cuisine, and Catholicism.

> *Gloria Guzman*: "We come from a mariachi background. I noticed that Veronica was a natural dancer. [Veronica danced Ballet Folklórico—traditional Mexican dancing—for years.] . . . I did that too. My [grandmother], even though she was seventy, eighty, ninety, would dance folklórico. She would dance Jarabe Tapatío with my grandpa. [I want my children to] remember where they come from and not to forget who they are. And to speak Spanish."
>
> *Adele Mendoza*: "Mostly we'd be with family celebrating Christmas, holidays, birthdays, weddings, with aunts and uncles. We try to keep that going. The . . . tradition I carried on was probably the tamales. We do that every year. My mom taught me so we try to keep the family [making tamales for Christmas] at least one day out of the year."

Family, food, music, and dance all come across strongly in the narratives of Chicana mothers. Stay-at-home mothers have more time to spend actively "cultivating" their children than do working mothers and fathers. Yolanda Segura had the "luxury of being home" with her children while her Puerto Rican husband worked full-time. This had the effect of Yolanda actively transmitting more knowledge about Mexican culture to her children than her husband could spend representing Puerto Rican ways:

> I love being Mexican. . . . I love speaking Spanish. I love the culture and the food. And so I've passed it on to my [four] girls . . . and how important family is. My husband is . . . Puerto Rican–American; he was raised in the United States, very, very *Americano* in his ways. I was able to stay home with our girls so [I've passed on] all my traditions. And so they consider themselves *Mexicanas* first before they con-

sider themselves Puerto Ricans. They just don't know about [Puerto Rican culture] as much as they know about being Mexican.

Racial pride is a subtext of these narratives that work to promote cultural preservation and appreciation. Indeed, instilling in children cultural knowledge and a sense of racial pride is common among minority parents of various races (Feagin and Sikes 1994).

Motivated by racial pride, Elena Vargas cites not only cultural elements she wants retained but also reminds her offspring that much of the American Southwest was part of Mexico before the Treaty of Guadalupe Hidalgo was signed in 1848. Elena remarks:

> [I want] people [to] remember to keep speaking Spanish. To be proud of their culture and how it all started—that we were all Indians in the beginning in Mexico . . . how we lived here in California, this was our place. . . . And to remember . . . the importance of the family—that's more important than things and accomplishments. . . . It's so important to keep that family thing going and not forgetting where you came from. Keep speaking Spanish and buying Mexican food and making it at home and having trinkets and mementoes around and having pictures of your grandparents and pictures of Mexico. . . . Just keep that tradition going and not forgetting where your roots come from.

More explicitly, Elaine Morelos counsels her son Lance on the subject of racial pride. Her advice is not connected with the historical legacy of Mexicans in the U.S. Southwest that predates the annexation of those states; rather, her guidance is about fending off racial discrimination. Lance, whose natal family is "very proud" of their Mexican heritage, recalls his mother's pragmatic words:

> My mom used to say, "Everybody's shit stinks. Nobody is better than anybody else. And you remember that." I used to say, "Mexican? Oh, the upper-echelon?" I used to say that all the time when I was in high school and college. "Mexican? Oh, the upper-echelon?" And it used to kind of off-set people. Because if people saw that you were proud of your heritage, they'd let you alone.

As "symbolic center[s] of the . . . household" (Gillis 1997:236), Chicana mothers are concerned with representing and continuing Mexican culture. As such, they select cultural elements they find particularly meaningful and actively use them in their domestic life and attempt to pass them on to the next generation.

Mothers transmit not only "ethnic" culture—they also transmit "gender" culture (Chodorow 1978). We saw this in the earlier section on "gendered encouragement" when Chicana mothers attempted to balance gender power dynamics by especially encouraging their daughters in academic pursuits and consistently emboldening their sons to disprove deleterious stereotypes. Chicana mothers, through words and behavior, instruct their children on gender issues. Yolanda Segura teaches her children about racial diversity and challenges standard Eurocentric notions of beauty:

> I remember reading books to [my girls] . . . the traditional classics [like] Snow White. I would call it Snow Brown and I would [say] she lived in Mexico. . . . Whenever we would play Barbies, it would be "I'm Teresa, *no hablo* English [I don't speak English]." I always told my girls, "Look at how beautiful you are. Your color. . . . Be proud of who you are." . . . I would see billboards and it would be [white] models. I would tell my girls "I know no one that looks like that . . . this is the real world. This is what we look like."

Part of Yolanda's mission as a mother is to socialize her girls to be proud of their racial and cultural heritage and to be critical of mainstream beauty ideals that do not reflect their own image.

While Yolanda was rearing four daughters with the goal of positive self-images, twenty-eight-year-old Araceli Treviño was raising her two sons with the goal of dismantling strict gender roles. She calls herself a "nontraditional woman in a Mexican family," adding, "I don't cook." Araceli is trying to teach her two sons to be part of a vanguard of youth who will dismantle machismo:

> I don't want [my boys] to have the whole macho mentality. . . . I don't think there is anything wrong with having a boy that is really sensitive. I get frowned upon from so many Mexican guys that I hang out with. "He's going to be a sissy or he's going to be gay." And I'm like, "Just because he's sensitive or just because he doesn't want to tackle you doesn't necessarily mean gay." I want them to know that it's okay to own up to their feelings; it's okay to cry and it's okay to be sad.

Araceli is trying to equalize "feeling rules" (Hochschild 2003) and change masculine socialization through her gender-neutral child-rearing techniques (Beauvoir 1978; O'Reilly 2004).

Despite marked power asymmetries, Chicana mothers can counteract the racializing messages of public discourse and institutions. Mothers are profoundly important in shaping their children's experiences and understandings of race, ethnicity, and gender. Further, mothering strategies often reflect mothers' own experiences in their respective social locations and natal family systems.

The families discussed here all experienced significant upward mobility over the three generations interviewed, beginning with the immigrants. The second-generation Chicana women who are the focus of this article all came from poor families. This disadvantaged socioeconomic status in combination with growing up in a particular historical moment translates to their having been socialized by parents who were operating in a different context and with different priorities. As with poor families more generally, the priority of the immigrant generation was to address the daily needs of their families (Hill 2005:152). Once the second generation had achieved middle-class status (as did all the women described here), their tactics for personal, familial, and social advancement changed. No longer overwhelmed by economic needs, these Chicana mothers have been freed to turn their attention to challenging negative stereotypes, being activists on the part of their children, retaining cultural traditions, and endorsing anti-racist and anti-masculinist discourse and practice.

My findings add to Lareau's (2003) assessment that her middle-class respondents displayed a "concerted cultivation" logic of child-rearing wherein parents actively "develop" their children, often by utilizing parent-child conversations. Emphasizing the race and gender dimensions, Chicana mothers train their children to challenge negative stereotypes through the mothering techniques of "gendered encouragement" and "activism." Furthermore, mothers "teach culture" by transmitting—and sometimes revising—ethnic traditions and gender ideologies. These Chicanas use three primary mothering strategies that bridge public and domestic spheres in order to carefully chart a productive and ethnically-aware course into adulthood for their offspring. While commitment to preserving ethnic traditions varies, Chicana mothers are teaching lessons that show how ethnic background is an important dimension of social life, at the very least because of how their children are likely to be perceived and treated.

As with the change in racial ideologies, gender ideologies in the United States have also changed in the late twentieth and early twenty-first centuries, now offering rhetoric of gender equality. Chicana mothers consider their personal background, social context, and historical context—or "interpretive backdrop" (Vasquez 2005)—as they fashion their mothering strategies. Acutely aware of how their own parents stifled their educational opportunities and conscious of the bias in which men of Mexican origin are anticipated to fail in numerous aspects, these mothers responded with "gendered encouragement," supporting their children in gender-specific ways and teaching them to far exceed low expectations. Thus we see Chicana mothers promoting more egalitarian gender ideologies to both sons and daughters. Because "families are often the linchpin of gender inequality" (Hill 2005:152), with the changing mothering styles underway we may be in the midst of a sea-change wherein Mexican American youth of both sexes are socialized with goals of gender parity, racial equality, and educational achievement in mind.

NOTES

1. I use "Mexican American" and "Chicano/a" interchangeably.
2. Whether Mexican Americans, or Latinos generally, are a race or an ethnic group is a fraught question in the social sciences, politics, and within the group itself. I use "race" mainly because Latinos are often treated as a separate racial category and my interviewees referred to their experience as one of a subordinated racial group rather than one that is merely distinguished by ethnicity or culture.

WORKS CITED

Apple, Michael W. 1996. *Cultural Politics and Education*. New York: Teachers College Press.

Bailey, Eleanor. 2006. Why mothers always get the blame. *Mail on Sunday*, Nov. 10, 62.

Barlow, Andrew L. 2003. *Between Fear and Hope: Globalization and Race in the United States*. Lanham, Md.: Rowman and Littlefield.

Beauvoir, Simone de. 1978. *The Second Sex*. New York: Knopf.

Bobo, Lawrence D., and Cybelle Fox. 2003. Race, racism, and discrimination: Bridging problems, methods, and theory in social psychological research. *Social Psychological Quarterly* 66.4:319–332.

Bonilla-Silva, Eduardo. 2003. *Racism Without Racists: Color-Blind Racism and the Persistence of Racial Inequality in the United States*. Lanham, Md.: Rowman and Littlefield.

Bourdieu, Pierre, and Jean-Claude Passeron. 1977. *Reproduction in Education, Society, and Culture*. Trans. R. Nice. Sage Studies in Social and Educational Change 5. Beverly Hills: Sage.

——. 1979. *The Inheritors*. Trans. R. Nice. Chicago: University of Chicago Press.

Bowles, Samuel, Herbert Gintis, and Melissa Osborne Groves, eds. 2005. *Unequal Chances: Family Background and Economic Success*. Princeton: Princeton University Press.

Card, David. 2001. Estimating the return to schooling: Progress on some persistent econometric problems. *Econometrica* 69.5:1127–1160.

Chodorow, Nancy. 1978. *The Reproduction of Mothering: Psychoanalysis and the Sociology of Gender*. Berkeley: University of California Press.

Cohen, Steven Martin, and Arnold M. Eisen. 2000. *The Jew Within: Self, Family, and Community in America*. Bloomington: Indiana University Press.

Collins, Patricia Hill. 1994. Shifting the center: Race, class, and feminist theorizing about motherhood. In *Mothering: Ideology, Experience, and Agency*, ed. E. N. Glenn, G. Chang, and L. R. Forcey, 45–65. New York: Routledge.

Cummins, Jim. 2001. Empowering minority students: A framework for intervention. *Harvard Educational Review* 71.4:649–675.

Davidson, Ann Locke. 1996. *Making and Molding Identity in Schools: Student Narratives on Race, Gender, and Academic Engagement*. Albany: State University of New York Press.

Feagin, Joe R., and Melvin P. Sikes. 1994. *Living with Racism: The Black Middle-Class Experience*. Boston: Beacon.

Gardner, Marilyn. 2008. Was it easier being a mother in 1908? *Christian Science Monitor*, May 8, 17.

Gillis, John R. 1997. *A World of Their Own Making: Myth, Ritual, and the Quest for Family Values*. Cambridge, Mass.: Harvard University Press.

Giroux, Henry A. 1981. *Ideology, Culture, and the Process of Schooling*. Philadelphia: Temple University Press.

Hill, Shirley A. 2005. *Black Intimacies: A Gender Perspective on Families and Relationships*. Gender Lens series. Walnut Creek, Calif.: AltaMira Press.

Hochschild, Arlie Russell. 2003. *The Commercialization of Intimate Life: Notes from Home and Work*. Berkeley: University of California Press.

Kao, Grace. 1998. Educational aspirations of minority youth. *American Journal of Education* 106:349–384.

Lareau, Annette. 2003. *Unequal Childhoods: Class, Race, and Family Life*. Berkeley: University of California Press.

Lareau, Annette, and Erin McNamara Horvat. 1999. Moments of social inclusion and exclusion. *Sociology of Education* 72:37–53.

Lieberson, Stanley. 1985. Stereotypes: Their consequences for race and ethnic interaction. In *Research in Race and Ethnic Relations* 4, ed. Cora Bagley Marrett and Cheryl Leggon, 113–137. Greenwich, Conn.: JAI Press.

MacLeod, Jay. 2004. *Ain't No Makin' It: Aspirations and Attainment in a Low-Income Neighborhood*. 2nd ed. Boulder: Westview.

Ochoa, Gilda. 2004. *Becoming Neighbors in a Mexican American Community: Power, Conflict, and Solidarity*. Austin: University of Texas Press.

Omi, Michael, and Howard Winant. 1994. *Racial Formation in the United States: From the 1960s to the 1990s*. 2nd ed. New York: Routledge.

O'Reilly, Andrea. 2004. Mothering against motherhood and the possibility of empowered maternity for mothers and their children. In *From Motherhood to Mothering: The Legacy of Adrienne Rich's* Of Woman Born, ed. A. O'Reilly, 159–174. Albany: State University of New York Press.

Pattillo-McCoy, Mary. 1999. *Black Picket Fences: Privilege and Peril Among the Black Middle Class*. Chicago: University of Chicago Press.

Rubin, Lillian B. 1994. *Families on the Fault Line: America's Working Class Speaks About the Family, the Economy, Race, and Ethnicity*. New York: Harper Collins.

Scheper-Hughes, Nancy. 1992. *Death Without Weeping: The Violence of Everyday Life in Brazil*. Berkeley: University of California Press.

Segura, Denise A. 1994. Working at motherhood: Chicana and Mexican immigrant mothers and employment. In *Mothering: Ideology, Experience, and Agency*, ed. E. N. Glenn, G. Chang, and L. R. Forcey, 211–233. New York: Routledge.

Stack, Carol B. 1974. *All Our Kin: Strategies for Survival in a Black Community*. New York: Harper and Row.

Tobin, Joseph Jay, David Y. H. Wu, and Dana H. Davidson. 1989. *Preschool in Three Cultures: Japan, China, and the United States*. New Haven: Yale University Press.

Valdes, Guadalupe. 1996. *Con Respeto: Bridging the Distances Between Culturally Diverse Families and Schools*. New York: Columbia University Press.

Vasquez, Jessica M. 2005. Ethnic identity and Chicano literature: How ethnicity affects reading and reading affects ethnic consciousness. *Ethnic and Racial Studies* 28.5:903–924.

Yuval-Davis, Nira. 1997. *Gender and Nation, Politics and Culture*. Thousand Oaks, Calif.: Sage.

Muslim Motherhood | **TWO**

Traditions in Changing Contexts | GAIL MURPHY-GEISS

In 1971 Fatima Mernissi asked Moroccans what they saw as the biggest change that has occurred in the family and for women in recent years. Most pointed to changes in gender segregation, with observations such as "Women used to be protected" and "Women used to stay home" (Mernissi 1987:89). Indeed, women's lives are at the center of social change in the Muslim world. In particular, the competing pressures of modernization, often associated with Westernization, and the growing response of Islamist movements are leading to new, different, and at times conflicted understandings of motherhood for Muslim women. I argue that Muslim motherhood is changing in response to modernity, specifically in the forms of (1) resistance through republican motherhood, as well as (2) more moderate negotiation when deemed necessary or through pressure from younger generations. These tensions are most evident among Muslim immigrants to the West. Let us first look at the various traditional beliefs and practices regarding motherhood in Islam, most of which have been long affirmed, and continue to be widely accepted. Subsequently, the linked social forces of modernization and globalization will be introduced, along with the two primary responses noted above: resistance and negotiation. I conclude by proposing that

Muslim mothers of the twenty-first century will seek to navigate a path between these competing social forces, one "that could preserve Islamic values and blend them with the best of Western culture" (Akbar Ahmed 2007:119).

TRADITIONAL MOTHERHOOD: NATURAL AND RESPECTED

The Prophet Muhammad said, "Paradise lies at mothers' feet" (Minai 1981:162), and stated that one should show the greatest respect to first, one's mother, second, one's mother, third, one's mother, and fourth, one's father (Goodwin 1994:41). Traditionally, motherhood is the focus of a Muslim woman's entire life, inasmuch as her early years build toward this important role, and her later years either reap the benefits or suffer the consequences of her reproduction. In fact, in Islam, "woman" essentially means "mother" (Haddad 1985:285), for a woman who cannot conceive is considered *dhakar*, or male (Ghannam 2005:508). Since the only acceptable path to Muslim motherhood is marriage, we begin there.

Marriage

Marriage is the goal of every Muslim (al Farüqi 1988:64). Numerous Qur'anic verses and hadiths support this contention, as in "Marry the spouseless among you" (24:32–33).[1] Marriage then, is not only socially necessary, in that many Muslim societies frown upon single adult women and make no efforts for their care, but marriage is desired by Allah. Every Muslim girl is socialized to look forward to, or at least prepare for, her wedding. Although this is also true of males, the stigma attached to a single man is much less than for a woman, as he can always support himself and move freely throughout society.

Because marriage is considered to be "the single most important event" (Fluehr-Lobban 2004:98) in anyone's life, the choice of a mate is rarely left to the couple alone. Arranged marriage is the preferred mechanism for mate selection among Muslims, often involving both parents, extended family members, and sometimes matchmakers; the couple is often consulted as well. In some places, arranged marriages are more properly called "arranged introductions," after which the couple takes charge. Whether arranging or introducing, parents often want to cement larger family ties, which are thought to make for more stable unions than those with individual outsiders. They may also want to facilitate matches with people who have desired characteristics in regard to race, ethnicity, religion, age, educational level, and so on. Matrimonial online Web sites provide another matchmaking option, which can delimit the input of parents while still assisting young people in finding appropriate matches, of which parents will eventually approve (Ternikar 2004:19). So, while arranged marriages remain normative for most Muslims, realities exist on a continuum, and young people are increasingly seeking modifications. There is one widely told tale of a young couple in love. They wanted to marry, but her father insisted on making the arrangements. On the wedding night, the groom lifted her veil, to discover only then that the father had arranged the marriage they had desired. That this story is told at all indicates an effort to support the increasingly controversial notion that arranged marriages are ideal (Minai 1981:150).

Any marriage is more than a joining of two individuals; it is the joining of two families. This is especially true in Islam (al Farüqi 1988:64), as the focus is on the group rather than the individual. Patrilocal extended families are the norm in Muslim societies. Where many non-Muslims socialize their children for adult life outside the family, Muslim families expect male children to stay with the group, and female children are prepared to join the families of their husbands (Sherif 1999:211). Once there, her duties are three: (1) maintenance of the household, (2) the bearing and raising of children, and (3) obedience to her husband. Her husband's duties are to provide support of (1) his wife and (2) their children. In fact, if children aren't born soon, a husband may initiate a divorce or take a second wife, as childlessness is considered tragic (Hegland 2005:513).

According to Muhammad, Allah considers divorce to be "the most detestable of permitted things" (Denny 1985:305). For a mother, divorce can present unfortunate challenges regarding child custody. It is traditional for women to raise the children only up to a certain age (7–9 for girls and 9–11 for boys), after which they are claimed by the father (Fluehr-Lobban 2004:89). This attachment to a father's lineage is illustrated by the rule requiring a woman to wait some months to remarry after a divorce or after being widowed, in case she might be pregnant with her ex-husband's child. His family would have a right to claim that child as theirs (D. Bowen 2004:52).

Another traditional position in Islam is support for polygyny. According to Muhammad, multiple wives were allowed in order to relieve the burden on orphan girls, who were considered unmarriageable. Still, the teaching requires that these orphan wives be treated equitably, "If you fear that you will not act justly towards the orphans, marry such women as seem good to you, two, three, four; but if you fear you will not be equitable, then only one" (4:3). Polygyny, like marriage in general, was intended as a protection and a support for women and children (Wadud-Muhsin 1993:83), and was the only official accommodation for single mothers in Islam historically.

Children

Sons are preferred to daughters, though a mother with no daughters is also considered pitiable. Sons are socially crucial, in that they provide for the economic security of the family into the future—they will bring in wives who will bear children for the family line, and who will take care of the parents as they age. In Arab countries, the importance of male children is illustrated through the custom of addressing a mother by the name of her firstborn son, such as Umm Ahmad, or "mother of Ahmad." At the worst extreme, a girl's birth is the cause of mourning, during which husbands feel shame and women feel guilt (Goodwin 1994:43). In many cases though, a daughter provides more of a personal benefit, becoming part of her mother's circle of intimates until married, when she will bond with a new group of women, led by her new mother-in-law. Girls can also help to reduce a mother's workload around the home (Halvorson 2005:28). Both younger boys and girls are often emotionally close to their mothers, countering the more formal relationship each has with the father (Ghannam 2005:508).

In practice, family planning is discouraged in Islam simply because childbearing is considered so important for women; the more children a woman has, the more her status improves (Zurikashvili 2005:512). While childlessness is considered disastrous, even having only one child can be disappointing (Smith 1999:119). Other than social security and winning the respect of one's family, though, there is no inherent biological imperative in Islam to have many children (Wadud-Muhsin 1993:64). Fertility has often been encouraged more for social reasons that are only secondarily related to Islam. For example, Iraq discouraged, and in some places outlawed, birth control after the Gulf War to replace the many men who had died. On the other hand, Iran instituted a government-sponsored family planning program in 1990 in response to concerns about overpopulation. This required the reversal of an earlier Islamic stance discouraging contraception (Ramazani 1993:414). Thus it seems that at certain times and places, Islam may seem related to a procreative imperative that surpasses or reduces the family-planning dictates already normative in a culture.

Gender Roles: Separate but Equal

These traditional ideas about gender are based in the widely held assumption that women are naturally different from men, men being virile and aggressive and women being gentle and nurturing. Along with this is the idea that men are naturally made to rule, while women are designed to submit. Some of these

notions about gendered natures may stem from the fact that few relationships al-low men and women to know each other well. Through the customs of arranged marriages, segregation by sex, and the tight control of families, men and women are discouraged from interacting at all. The much-debated veil is one symbol of the larger gender segregation that defines gendered spaces distinctly, the male's being prominent and public, and the female's being less visible, at least to men (Mernissi 1987:94–97). These separate roles are seen as complementary—not competitive, but harmonious. This is illustrated in inheritance laws, many of which come directly from the Qur'an. Women may inherit, but always less than their brothers, because women are not responsible for supporting themselves or their families. Instead, women are supported by fathers, brothers, husbands, or sons, which allows women to dispose of their own money as they desire. Hence it is thought that women don't need as much. While men and women are equal in importance, they are not identical in role (al Farüqi 1988:26–27, 49).

So the family is the center of Muslim society, and the mother's role is at the center of the family, her natural and most important calling. These traditional ideas are ubiquitous throughout the Muslim world. Fluehr-Lobban (1988:97) summed it up this way: "Family is everything; there is no need to stress its impor-tance to those who are well aware of the fact." Certainly Islam's fellow Abrahamic faiths, Judaism and Christianity, are similarly patriarchal in their origins, and all three have been slow to change, especially with respect to the roles of women. As for Muslims in particular, debate over possible reform of laws that are Qur'anic can be delicate, as these teachings are believed to be the clearest from Allah (D. Bowen 2004:79). Many religions contain similar prohibitions against modern interpretations of holy texts, but there are particular realities for Islam today that are challenging these traditional teachings on motherhood in unique ways. Spe-cifically, the pervasive social forces of modernization and globalization create a climate in which Muslims want to continue affirming traditional roles while also reconsidering them.

ISLAMIST RESISTANCE TO MODERNITY

Muslims today are faced with tensions created by their attempts to maintain some of these traditional values and practices within the rapidly changing contexts of modernity. First, the wealth created by industrialization has not benefited many Muslim countries to the extent that it has advantaged the West. While this is not true in every case, even in oil-rich countries like Saudi Arabia, wealth is unevenly distributed; those linked to Western businesses do well, while others live in poverty. In addition, industrialization came more slowly to the Muslim world, though its effects hit more quickly, giving little time to respond (Schvaneveldt, Kerpelman, and Schvaneveldt 2005:88). While Americans and Europeans have had two centuries to adjust to the rapid production of factories, mass transportation, and increasingly accessible global communication, many in the Muslim world are moving overnight from little or no development to cell phone use and Internet access. This is especially important in regard to issues related to women. For example, while Christian feminists in the United States have been debating the role of women in the Church since the middle of the nineteenth century, Muslim feminism is younger, having first arisen in the first three decades of the twentieth century (L. Ahmed 1992:174). Even today, it is severely limited because of the "microscopic minority of educated Muslim women" who are adequately equipped to engage in theological deliberations about women in Islam (Hassan 2007:146). These comparisons are important for understanding the context in which much Muslim resistance to change occurs. It is also important to remember that Islam is not inherently opposed to change. In fact, its ability to adapt and flourish in many parts of the world and among people of diverse ethnic groups and in varied cultural and political settings is well known (Sanday 2002). Nonetheless, because the changes brought with modernity are associated with Western colonialism, many are resisted.

Islamism is one powerful site of this resistance. The 1967 loss of Egypt to Israel is usually considered the beginning of the movement. Some believed that defeat was the result of a loss of faith and practice of Islam, which had been compromised by modernization associated with the West. In addition, conditions throughout the Middle East created an environment that was ripe for discontent. Foreign investments had led to limited profits at home, most wealth being channeled primarily to Westerners and their few Arab liaisons. The growing number of poor people needed a sense of hope and, in many cases, simply resources for survival (L. Ahmed 2005:218). Islamists took the opportunity to serve people the governments were not, but aid came with the message that greater dedication to Islam was needed. So, as a reaction against Western imperialism and a sense of oppression under Western hegemony, Islamist leaders proposed a militant Islam as the answer to their problems. Anything Western became suspect. This of course included the feminist movement. Women seeking equal rights, equal pay, equal opportunities for education and employment, reproductive rights, and rights to sexual freedom were labeled as evil, and their ideas were condemned as unacceptable to Allah. Instead, Islamists taught that Muslim women could find liberation only in Islam. And while most Muslims are not extremists, Islamists leaders have been successful in mobilizing many mainstream Muslims in their battles for political power and against Western imperialism (Tohidi 2007:95).

The Veil

The revival of the veil is one common symbol of this Islamist movement taken up by ordinary Muslim women. Islamist governments, such as that of Khomeini in 1980, tried to require the veil and were largely successful, but many women donned it voluntarily in an act of solidarity with their Muslim brothers (L. Ahmed 2005:164). The debate regarding veils in France came about shortly thereafter, as immigrants began to shift their primary identity to Muslim as opposed to French (J. Bowen 2007:66). That kind of resistance and the desire to make a statement of pride about being Muslim exist even more so today. More and more young Muslim women are wearing *hijab* (head scarf) for the first time, even those whose mothers never wore it (Williams and Vashi 2007:285). Veiling exists on a continuum from the full-cover *burqa* to the basic covering of the hair (Haddad 2007:255), and across that entire continuum many women report positive feelings about veiling and even a sense of liberation. Some say they are not seen as sex objects and are able to move about society more freely in pursuit of progressive ends, like education and work (Read 2007:232). Recently new motivations are arising. Some are now using the veil to keep conservative first-generation immigrant parents at bay. They say their mothers are less likely to complain about their social lives, especially regarding dating, if they are veiled. In turn, such parents feel that the veil, as an obvious symbol of Muslim piety, safeguards their daughters from unwanted attention, and reassures the parents that their daughter is not becoming too Western. Ironically, daughters of more pro-assimilation parents are also veiling, often attempting to resist the efforts of their parents to blend into a new culture. This is primarily true of *hijab*, but a few are also donning *jilbab* (full-length robe), and more rarely, but in some places, even *nikab* (face covering) (Williams and Vashi 2007:283–285). It is important to note that there are some women (and men) who speak out against veiling, often led by Muslim feminists, who see the veil as a symbol of male domination, but also notable is the fact that whether veiled or unveiled, Muslim women support one another in their choice, realizing the complicatedness in various contexts, both across time and place (Read and Bartowski 2007:400, 409–411). Muslim women recognize the multiple meanings associated with veiling (L. Ahmed 2005:165), and understand that, for many, wearing the veil has increasingly become an activist expression of personal identity as well as, more culturally, an act of solidarity with the Muslim community (El Guindi 1999:145).

It should also be noted that a few Muslim women have recently decided to stop wearing the veil, out of fear for their children post 9/11. One American woman said, "It paints that target sign on my child. . . . It's my job to keep him safe. To raise him to be a devout Muslim and worship Allah. I don't believe I can do that in *hijab*. Not today" (Shawna 2008). While two-thirds of Americans admit to knowing little or nothing about Islam, 36 percent still claim to have an unfavorable opinion about the religion (Read 2007:231–232), and many American Muslims have been threatened and some have even been assaulted since 9/11. Still, overall there has been an increase in veiling worldwide, both before and after 9/11, though the reasons are multiple and differ depending largely on location and generation.

Republican Motherhood

Along with dress, women's roles have changed so as to be consistent with Islamism, and to aid in various revolutionary agendas. In some places, such as Iran, women were asked to carry weapons and fight as soldiers for the sake of Islam. More commonly, though, women have been asked to fulfill the special role that only women can: that of mother. The Islamist understanding of mother is not solely the traditional one outlined earlier, focused on her family alone as the basis for Muslim society. The Islamist mother is charged with being mother of the nation, contributing not only to the nurture of her family members in the private sphere of the home, but also to the creation of future citizens who will lead a more public Islam on the state and international levels. This model of "republican motherhood" is not new, as women have been called to serve the state in special ways during many revolutionary periods. The role of the republican mother in eighteenth-century America is one well-known example (Kerber 1980:245–250). As co-builders of the new nation, mothers were expected to harness their domestic abilities, until then focused mainly at home and increasingly at church, toward the development of educated citizens who were able to participate in a self-governed democracy. By extension, American women then challenged the ideology of separate spheres that defined their duties as solely domestic. These early feminists saw male hegemony as potentially destructive of the democracy they were all trying to create (Alexander 2006:242). The subsequent waves of the feminist movement expanded on those very challenges, not yet fully dismantling the ideology of separate spheres, but certainly blurring the boundaries in ways that would make virtually all public roles appropriate for women.

This model of the republican mother is similar to that present in contemporary Islamist rhetoric. Muslim motherhood is extolled as honorable, and encouraged as an important way to contribute to the larger society. Perhaps the most radical way such mothers can contribute is through bearing and raising sons who are willing to become martyrs for Islam. This ultimate motherly sacrifice is publicly glorified, as in this statement made by an Islamist leader at a Lashkar-i-Tayyabia convention in 2002: "Muslim sisters, you have the greater responsibility in the mission of jihad; men give money, but you give your sons" (Haq 2007:1023).

One major difference between eighteenth-century American republican motherhood and the contemporary Islamist version is the larger context. While the American goal was a democratic society, eventually requiring freedom and equality for all citizens regardless of first race and then gender, the goal of contemporary Islamists is a Muslim society, in which traditional gender roles are institutionalized, even sacralized as created and desired by Allah. And in the case of these Islamist mothers, the main enemy is not the patriarchy within their own communities, but oppression from the West, serving to unite Muslim men and women against a common foe. This shared goal seems to make for more compliance among Muslim women, accepting their role as traditional mothers, and seeing the expansion into republican motherhood as a complementary and welcome addition rather than as a challenge to gender differences as undemocratic. When there is resistance to this model, it is more out of love for children and the desire that they not die for Islam than a repudiation of traditional motherhood (Haq 2007:1028).

MUSLIM NEGOTIATIONS: NECESSARY AND GENERATIONAL

As mentioned earlier, few Muslims are militant Islamists, though many share the same concerns about the negative aspects of Western influences and particularly the decline of the family they see in Western society. The clash between the much-valued view of traditional motherhood in Islam and what might be the more acceptable aspects of modernity is an ever-present question, manifest in varied economic and political contexts brought about by globalization.

Situations of Necessity

Due to persistent instability in northern Pakistan, many men are away at war, and mothers are forced to raise children alone. Faced with increasing poverty, they are, by necessity, beginning to rethink the place of women in society. For example, trade and barter are diminishing as adequate for the support of a family, and cash incomes are becoming crucial to supplement farm production and home crafts. As a result, the birth of daughters is increasingly valued, as girls can contribute through employment as tailors or in local women's clinics, while also reducing a mother's work burden in the home (Halvorson 2005:29). Similarly, in post-Soviet societies, unemployment and widespread poverty are pushing women into the public realm of work for much-needed family income (Zurikashvili 2005:512). In both cases the intersection of political and economic realities is forcing a reassessment of traditional ideas about motherhood.

Even when such adjustments are made, motherhood continues to be the primary identity for Muslim women and work is pursued only when it does not interfere with domestic duties. In addition, girls who go to school are still expected to help with domestic duties once they get home. Work and education for women cannot undermine their most important roles as wives and mothers (Mohammad 2005:189). One American Muslim woman, whose work is the education of non-Muslims about Islam, notes her mixed feelings: "Sometimes I feel as if I am choosing between Islamic activism and raising my children." When she returns home from work, she makes a special point of spending uninterrupted time with her children so as to "make them feel like I have all the time in the world only for them" (al-Marayati 2005:110).

The Muslim ideological emphasis on the group over the individual combined with the fact that most Muslim families live in less developed places means that the extended family has remained normative for Muslims. In the rare cases where women have had to leave the home for school or work, there have always been other family members available to care for children and elders. Increasing industrialization in the developing world, as well as Muslim immigration throughout the West, is making this extended family model harder to sustain. The establishment of child care centers is now being discussed throughout the Arab world (Ghannam 2005:209), and a few facilities for the care of the elderly are now available in Iran (Hegland 2005:515). Some American Muslim mothers, when unable to stay at home with their children, say they are more willing to accept day care run by Muslims "in an Islamic way," but others will not accept even that and choose instead to live with less family income, or to accept the risk of not being able to reenter their professions, rather than accept child care from non-family members (Haddad, Smith, and Moore 2006:94). While the traditional extended family might enable Muslim women to pursue careers with no guilt or harm to the children (al Farūqi 1988:53), this family form is least possible in the West, where women most need or want to work outside the home.

Generational Forces

While some of these issues are particular to the younger generations, it is notable that mothers and daughters continue to share many of the same basic values. Schvaneveldt, Kerpelman, and Schvaneveldt's (2005) study of women in the United Arab Emirates set out to measure the generational differences in attitudes between daughters, all of whom were attending Zayed University, and their mothers. While they found some variations, such as the daughters' desire for later marriage, choice in mate selection, more use of birth control, and greater participation in work outside the home, differences tended to be small, and, in fact, similarities between the generations were even more significant. Most notably, mothers and daughters agreed about the importance of Islam in family life, which they did not want to change. Also, while both mothers and daughters saw some social change as welcome, they shared a resentment of Western domination, and agreed that Muslims can avoid the problems that come with Westernization through the maintenance of Islamic traditions.

There are generational differences as well. In a study of the Pukhtuns of Pakistan, Amineh Ahmed (2006) found generational negotiation around the tradition of arranged marriages. There it is the mothers who arrange the marriages of sons and daughters, which brings them honor in the community. Increasingly, though, young people are meeting outside of family connections. One story is told of a couple who met at a local party, but then kept in touch via the Internet, as he went back to school in Canada and she remained in Pakistan. The relationship developed, and they eventually arranged their own marriage secretly. When their mothers found out, they were devastated by what they saw as an inappropriate match in regard to social status, and also embarrassed that their "right" to arrange their children's wedding had been taken from them. Two years later though, they made peace with the situation, and hosted a belated ceremony to properly cement the match between the families and in the community (Amineh Ahmed 2006:125–127). Muslims are finding increasing opportunities for self-arranged marriages, but some negotiation with parents is likely to continue, as the community and family of origin remain important supports or hindrances for the long-term success of such relationships.

MUSLIM IMMIGRANTS TO THE WEST: ISOLATION VERSUS ASSIMILATION

In another manifestation of globalization, Muslims are migrating throughout the world and building large and growing minorities across the West. One of the most visible places has been Western Europe, where the number of Muslims has more than doubled in the past two decades (Osnos 2004:1). As Islamic and Western cultures collide, Muslim immigrants are driving Western people and governments to reevaluate their understandings of multiculturalism, and immigrants are rethinking what it means to be Muslim in non-Muslim contexts (Poggioli 2008:1).

Some Muslim countries encourage such migration as a way to increase national economic strength through income sent home as remittances. Indonesia has used the rhetoric of republican motherhood toward this end, saying women should emigrate to fulfill their calling to be "good mothers" in providing for the "national family" (Silvey 2005:134). Once a cohort of workers has established itself in another country, they are often followed by spouses, children, extended family members, and potential marriage partners for their children (Pels 2000:81). While experiences differ by country, the major question of assimilation versus isolation is central for all immigrants, and mothers are at the heart of this struggle. As keepers of the home and the primary socializing agents of children, mothers set the tone for bridging the cultural gaps in these new settings.

In every country, the great majority of Muslim women continue to prioritize their roles as wives and mothers. As a result, some will not work outside the home at all. Others seek part-time jobs to contribute to family income, but not at the expense of domestic duties. Many who do work prefer to have jobs in controlled environments such as factories, so as to avoid unnecessary or awkward encounters with unrelated men. For educated daughters in the next generation who want to pursue a career, parents often prefer highly respected professions, such as doctor or lawyer. The prestige of such a position can compensate somewhat for their more traditional views against women working outside the home (Mohammad 2005:193).

The promotion of traditional gender roles can come from outside one's immediate family as well. Because immigrants often settle near those from their home country, ethnic enclaves develop and thus enable easier integration, although primarily into that local ethnic community. This can make wider integration harder, or at least of less interest, as shared language and customs from home make for a level of comfort that discourages assimilation more broadly. The mothers in one Pakistani community in Great Britain reinforce their inward community focus by emphasizing their roles, first as socializers of their own children, but also as regulators of the same in others (Mohammad 2005:179). These communities then serve as proxies for the extended family networks that Muslims have long found so essential (Haddad, Smith, and Moore 2006:84).

Despite the desire among many Muslim immigrants to maintain traditional practices, some impact from the majority culture, especially on the younger generations, is inevitable. For example, in their study of family forms among Muslim immigrants to Australia, Yusuf and Siedlecky (1996) found that younger women desire fewer children than their parents, leading the researchers to expect a convergence to the Australian normative family size in just a few generations. In a study of Pakistani Muslim immigrants to the United States and Canada, Zaidi and Shuraydi (2002:511–512) found that while young women say they no longer believe in the "old-fashioned" system of arranged marriages, many still anticipate accepting such an arrangement because of the important role their parents continue to have in their lives. Tensions around arranged marriages among immigrants to the West are growing, though, and changes are likely. In fact, it would not be surprising if increased participation of women in education and the labor market will lead, as it did in the West, to later and self-arranged marriages, smaller families, and perhaps even higher divorce rates and single motherhood. On the other hand, it may be that Muslims' intense desire to avoid the Western model, to embrace the benefits of education and rights for women without also accepting the decline of their traditional family structures, is enough to resist previous trends.

Despite the tensions between traditional Islam and the forces of modernity, the overall feeling among Muslims is that the role of mother is essential for society and Islam. As the repository of ethical values, the incarnation of beauty and nurture, and the only one capable of giving birth, she is unparalleled. But influences both within and outside of Islamic societies are leading to new ideas, and in some cases change. The exact future for Muslim mothers is unclear. Will Muslim women be able to avoid the challenges of the dual role of American women, balancing both workplace and home? Will Muslim women ever see traditional gender roles as oppressive, or will they continue to value them as a positive alternative to Western decline? And will Muslim men be willing to change as well, helping with child care for example, as women have with revolutionary movements?

The most important question acknowledges both the various forces of modernity, some better and some worse, and the prevailing values of the great majority of Muslim mothers: Can Muslim women do what the second wave of the American women's movement neglected to do, and that is to find liberation for women while also affirming the importance and value of the mothering role? Maintaining a balance between these two seemingly oppositional forces will surely be the central challenge for Muslim women in the twenty-first century. The powerful forces of modernity and Islamism, along with the economic and political realities brought about by globalization, are unavoidable. Nonetheless, Muslim mothers, along with their sons and daughters, are increasingly seeking a middle way between the preservation of cherished Islamic traditions and the possible changes related to what they carefully deem to be positive elements of Western modernity.

NOTE

1. All quotes from the Qur'an are from Arberry 1955.

WORKS CITED

Ahmed, Akbar. 2007. *Journey Into Islam: The Crisis of Globalization*. Washington, D.C.: Brookings Institution Press.

Ahmed, Amineh. 2006. *Sorrow and Joy Among Muslim Women: The Pukhtuns of Northern Pakistan*. Cambridge: Cambridge University Press.

Ahmed, Leila. 1992. *Women and Gender in Islam: Historical Roots of a Modern Debate*. New Haven: Yale University Press.

——. 2005. The veil debate—again. In *On Shifting Ground: Muslim Women in the Global Era*, ed. Fereshteh Nouraie-Simone, 151–171. New York: Feminist Press.

Alexander, Jeffrey C. 2006. *The Civil Sphere*. New York: Oxford University Press.

al Farüqi, Lamya. 1988. *Women, Muslim Society, and Islam*. Plainfield: American Trust.

al-Hibri, Azizah. 1988. Muslim women and the American feminist movement. Paper presented at the Muslims in America Conference, Amherst.

al-Marayati, Laila. 2005. Working to help all the world's children. In *Muslim Women Activists in North America: Speaking for Ourselves*, ed. Katherine Bullock, 103–110. Austin: University of Texas Press.

Arberry, Arthur J., trans. 1955. *The Koran Interpreted*. New York: Macmillan.

Bowen, Donna Lee. 2004. Islamic law and the position of women. In *Islam and Social Policy*, ed. Stephen P. Heyneman, 44–117. Nashville: Vanderbilt University Press.

Bowen, John R. 2007. *Why the French Don't Like Headscarves: Islam, the State, and Public Space*. Princeton: Princeton University Press.

Brooks, Geraldine. 1995. *Nine Parts of Desire: The Hidden World of Islamic Women.* New York: Doubleday.

Denny, Frederick Mathewson. 1985. *An Introduction to Islam.* New York: Macmillan.

El Guindi, Fadwa. 1999. *Veil: Modesty, Privacy, and Resistance.* New York: Oxford University Press.

Fernea, Elizabeth Warnock. 1969. *Guests of the Sheik.* New York: Doubleday.

Fluehr-Lobban, Carolyn. 2004. *Islamic Societies in Practice.* 2nd ed. Gainesville: University Press of Florida.

Ghannam, Farha. 2005. Motherhood: Arab states. In *Encyclopedia of Women and Islamic Cultures,* vol. 2: *Family, Law, and Politics,* ed. Suad Joseph, 508–509. Leiden: Brill.

Goodwin, Jan. 1994. *Price of Honor: Muslim Women Lift the Veil of Silence on the Islamic World.* New York: Penguin.

Haddad, Yvonne Yazbeck. 1985. Islam, women, and revolution in twentieth-century Arab thought. In *Women, Religion, and Social Change,* ed. Yvonne Yazbeck Haddad, 275–306. Albany: State University of New York Press.

——. 2007. The post-9/11 *hijab* as icon. *Sociology of Religion* 68.3:253–268.

Haddad, Yvonne Yazbeck, Jane I. Smith, and Kathleen M. Moore. 2006. *Muslim Women in America: The Challenge of Islamic Identity Today.* New York: Oxford University Press.

Halvorson, Sarah J. 2005. Growing up in Gilgit: Exploring the nature of girlhood in northern Pakistan. In *Geographies of Muslim Women: Gender, Religion, and Space,* ed. Ghazi-Walid Falah and Caroline Nagel, 19–43. New York: Guilford.

Haq, Farhat. 2007. Militarism and motherhood: The women of the Lashkar-i-Tayyaba in Pakistan. *Signs* 32.4:1023–1046.

Hassan, Riffat. 2007. The issue of woman-man equality in the Islamic tradition. In *Women's Studies in Religion: A Multicultural Reader,* ed. Kate Bagley and Kathleen McIntosh, 143–149. Upper Saddle River, N.J.: Pearson Education.

Hegland, Mary Elaine. 2005. Motherhood: Iran, Afghanistan, and south Asia. In *Encyclopedia of Women and Islamic Cultures,* vol. 2: *Family, Law, and Politics,* ed. Suad Joseph, 513–515. Leiden: Brill.

Kerber, Linda K. 1980. *Women of the Republic: Intellect and Ideology in Revolutionary America.* Chapel Hill: University of North Carolina Press.

Mernissi, Fatima. 1987. *Beyond the Veil: Male-Female Dynamics in Modern Muslim Societies.* Bloomington: Indiana University Press.

Minai, Naila. 1981. *Women in Islam: Tradition and Transition in the Middle East.* New York: Seaview Books.

Mohammad, Robina. 2005. Negotiating spaces of the home, the education system, and the labor market. In *Geographies of Muslim Women: Gender, Religion, and Space,* ed. Ghazi-Walid Falah and Caroline Nagel, 178–200. New York: Guilford.

Osnos, Evan. 2004. Islam shaping a new Europe: Staking out their place in Europe. *Chicago Tribune*, Dec. 19. http://www.chicagotribune.com/news/watchdog/chi-0412190 554dec19,0,1178281.story (accessed Dec. 18, 2009).

Pels, Trees. 2000. Muslim families from Morocco in the Netherlands: Gender dynamics and fathers' roles in a context of change. *Current Sociology* 48.4:75–93.

Poggioli, Sylvia. 2008. In Europe, Muslim women face multiple issues. National Public Radio, Jan. 20. http://www.npr.org/templates/story/story.php?storyID=18234876 (accessed Oct. 15, 2008).

Ramazani, Nesta. 1993. Women in Iran: The revolutionary ebb and flow. *Middle East Journal* 47.3:409–428.

Read, Jen'nan Ghazal. 2007. Introduction: The politics of veiling in comparative perspective. *Sociology of Religion* 68.3:231–236.

Read, Jen'nan Ghazal, and John P. Bartowski. 2000. To veil or not to veil?: A case study of identity negotiation among Muslim women in Austin, Texas. *Gender and Society* 14.3:395–417.

Sanday, Peggy Reeves. 2002. *Women at the Center: Life in a Modern Matriarchy.* Ithaca: Cornell University Press.

Schvaneveldt, Paul L., Jennifer L. Kerpelman, and Jay D. Schvaneveldt. 2005. Generational and cultural changes in family life in the United Arab Emirates: A comparison of mothers and daughters. *Journal of Comparative Family Studies* 36.1:77–91.

Shawna. 2008. An introduction. Islam on my side: An anthology of Muslim American experience post 9/11. Feb. 26. http://islamonmyside.com/wordpress/?s=introduction (accessed Dec. 18, 2009).

Sherif, Bahira. 1999. Islamic family ideals and their relevance to American Muslim families. In *Family Ethnicity: Strength in Diversity*, ed. Harriette Pipes McAdoo, 213–221. Thousand Oaks, Calif.: Sage.

Silvey, Rachel. 2005. Transnational Islam: Indonesian migrant domestic workers in Saudi Arabia. In *Geographies of Muslim Women: Gender, Religion, and Space*, ed. Ghazi-Walid Falah and Caroline Nagel, 127–146. New York: Guilford.

Smith, Jane I. 1999. *Islam in America.* New York: Columbia University Press.

Ternikar, Farha. 2004. Changing marriage trends in the South Asian American community. Paper presented at the annual meeting of the American Sociological Association, San Francisco.

Tohidi, Nayereh. 2007. Muslim feminism and Islamic reformation: The case of Iran. In *Feminist Theologies: Legacy and Prospect*, ed. Rosemary Radford Ruether, 93–116. Minneapolis: Fortress Press.

Wadud-Muhsin, Amina. 1993. *Qur'an and Woman.* New York: Oxford University Press.

Williams, Rhys H., and Gira Vashi. 2007. *Hijab* and American Muslim women: Creating space for autonomous selves. *Sociology of Religion* 68.3:269–288.

Yusuf, Farhat, and Stefania Siedlecky. 1996. Family formation patterns among migrant women in Sydney. *Journal of Biosocial Science* 28.1:89–99.

Zaidi, Arshia, and Muhammad Shuraydi. 2002. Perceptions of arranged marriages by young Pakistani Muslim women living in a Western society. *Journal of Comparative Family Studies* 33.4:495–514.

Zurikashvili, Feride. 2005. Motherhood: The Caucuses. In *Encyclopedia of Women and Islamic Cultures,* vol. 2: *Family, Law, and Politics*, ed. Suad Joseph, 512–513. Leiden: Brill.

Mothering in Fear

THREE

How Living in an Insecure-Feeling World Affects Parenting

ANA VILLALOBOS

> I lived in New York City during 9/11. Still to
> this date I feel my shoulders flinch if any air-
> craft flies overhead very low or loud. . . . When
> I stroller down the sidewalk, or worse, let my
> three-year-old walk down the sidewalk, I am
> always afraid a passing car will jump the curb
> and hit him. I have bad thoughts about drive-
> by shootings. . . . I panic if I am in a store and
> he strays down an aisle and I can't see him—
> this is a fear of someone stealing my child.
> —Shirley Matheson, 27-year-old mother

Despite terrorism causing physical harm to a miniscule percent of the population, it causes an emotional response and *fear* of harm in a far larger percent. For example, more than two-thirds of Americans report being very or somewhat concerned about their own family, friends, or selves being the victims of a future terrorist attack (Huddy, Feldman, and Weber 2007:138).

A study in the Netherlands of the effects of stress from the 9/11 terrorist attacks even outside the United States examined the influence of maternal media exposure to those attacks during pregnancy (Smits et al. 2006). Presuming maternal stress adversely affects fetal growth, the researchers compared the birth weights of Dutch neonates who were in utero on September 11, 2001, with the weights of neonates in utero exactly a year later. After controlling for possible confounding factors, they found that the group exposed to the 9/11 attacks through the news media during pregnancy bore babies weighing 48 grams less than the nonexposed group (718).

If viewing the 9/11 attacks on the news caused such stress that women bore lower birthweight babies a continent away, what was its influence on mothers in the United States? More than half of Americans surveyed say the 9/11 attacks shook their general sense of personal safety and security (Huddy, Feldman, and Weber 2007:138). The question animating this essay is: how does living with that shaken sense of security affect the mother-child relationship? In particular, what mothering strategies do today's mothers utilize to cope with a perception of risk and threat in today's social environment? Ultimately, I discuss here a form of strategic parenting that is often overlooked in the academic literature but that was quite pronounced in my study.

METHODS

I interviewed fifty-one mothers of very young children, including two primary care–giving men.[1] Thirty-four of these mothers participated in a three-year longitudinal interview and observational study. The remainder participated in nonlongitudinal interviews, often with a single follow-up (n=17). These latter interviews specifically targeted terrorism and large-scale security threats and how these relate to women's approach to mothering. Altogether I conducted 168 interviews with mothers.

For the longitudinal study (n=34), I began with in-depth initial interviews during late pregnancy, prior to the birth of the babies, in order to understand these women's preexisting ideologies and orientations to mothering, and to gather extensive life histories. I then interviewed and observed the women with their babies in early infancy, followed by approximately one interview and observation per year until the child was three. I recruited these research participants primarily from five birth-preparation classes, and because it was my intention to seek ideologically disparate women, three of those birth classes were at a local hospital geared toward physician-assisted births, and two were at a lactation and doula center geared toward "natural births" with a midwife. Additionally, four of the participants were part of a social pregnancy group I located on the Web via a community forum, two participants responded to an ad I posted in another Web-based forum, and two were referred to me by others.

SOCIETAL INSECURITY

Before elaborating on the primary mothering strategy I discovered, I will discuss the perceived context of external threat and societal insecurity in which twenty-

first-century women mother, so that we may better understand the social context in which such a mothering strategy might emerge.

Whereas 9/11 brought a fear of terrorism to the American psyche, there are
numerous less dramatic but highly salient forms of "everyday" insecurity plagu-
ing many people today, such as fears of bankruptcy, downsizing, divorce, or medical catastrophes. There are also various parenting fears pertaining specifically to
one's children, such as gangs, drugs, Internet predators, and kidnapping. Not all
of this is new, and there are arguments about whether the twenty-first-century
world is really a scarier place than it was, say, thirty years ago, or if we just think
it is. But what is new is the magnitude of the fear, the subjective component of
insecurity that objective statistics may fail to capture. For example: "As crime
rates plunged throughout the 1990s . . . two-thirds of Americans believe[d] they
were soaring" (Glassner 2000:xi). If there is less crime now, why are Americans
more afraid of it?

We see this fear paradox again when we examine the labor market in the
early years of the twenty-first century, well after 9/11 but prior to the economic
crisis of 2008. Despite the "security" of a low unemployment rate, there was a
public perception of increasing job insecurity and almost half of workers were
"frequently concerned about being laid off" (Hacker 2007:18). This represents an
almost four-fold increase in concern since 1982.

There are numerous explanations for this recent amplification of risk perception, including media effects from the disproportionate coverage of dread-
ed events and disturbing trends in the news. However there is an additional,
less discussed way to resolve the contradiction between the public perception
of threats and scholarly evidence and statistics. This is through understanding
what I call *insecurity osmosis*: the social absorption of insecurity through witnessing other people's personal misfortunes.[2] In all eras, hearing about a friend's
bad luck has caused psychological ricochets, frequently prompting those who
heard such tales to wonder if they, too, would contract that illness, or lose their
job, or have their house burn down. However, in the twenty-first century, with
the rising accessibility of communication technologies, it follows that there
would be far greater insecurity osmosis occurring as the cumulative number
of cautionary tales people have witnessed or otherwise been exposed to rapidly
mounts. That is, as a result of the proliferation of e-mail, listserves, blogs, You-
Tube, Facebook, and other technologies for the easy mass-dissemination of formerly private information, many of today's incidents of woe have unprecedented
numbers of witnesses. I suggest that the increasing accessibility of these highly
personal stories of misfortune amplifies their effects on subjective insecurity and

the sense that the world is a place where bad things happen to ordinary people. For example, regarding marriage, many studies show the divorce rate has leveled off or declined since the early eighties (e.g., Whitehead and Popenoe 2005:1). Yet on a subjective level, sociologist Karla Hackstaff finds, "the felt prevalence of divorce is unmistakably greater" due to the "ripple effect" of repeated divorce exposure (Hackstaff 2000:135). This increase in the felt prevalence of divorce due to increased exposure to incidents of marriage loss (many via communication technologies) is precisely what I mean by insecurity osmosis.

In addition to society continuously amplifying personal fears of loss through the increased availability of tales chronicling such losses, these fears receive a jolt from large-scale national or global security threats such as 9/11. Recent research shows that "threat-induced anxiety tends to elevate risk perceptions" (Huddy, Feldman, and Weber 2007:136), meaning that many people overestimate risk in their personal lives in the months following large-scale security threats.

The twenty-first century has no lack of threat-induced anxiety to heighten people's risk perception. Another example is nuclear terrorism. In a January 5, 2008, presidential debate, the host, ABC News anchorman Charles Gibson, asked a question that he called "the central one" in his own mind regarding nuclear terrorism. Gibson prefaced the question with this statement: "The next president of the United States may have to deal with a nuclear attack on an American city. . . . The best nuclear experts in the world say there's a thirty percent chance [of such an attack] in the next ten years. Some estimates . . . [are] over fifty percent." This debate had 9.36 million viewers, so a large number of people simultaneously considered the potentially high probability of an upcoming nuclear attack on an American city. Dawn Butler, the twenty-year-old mother of two young children, explains how this fear can affect a family's geographical location. She says that two years ago, "I wanted us to move to Ithaca, New York [over two hundred miles from New York City], . . . but my husband felt it was too close to New York City—in his mind a definite target for a nuclear blast or, thanks to 9/11, a terrorist attack." So the family settled elsewhere.

Additionally, the phenomenon of global warming, which Al Gore brought to broad audiences in 2006 with his release of the film "An Inconvenient Truth," has caused people to question the continued inhabitability of our planet. Indeed, Beck (1999) distinguishes today's "risk society" from prior societies in which natural disasters were the primary concern precisely because today's technologies make the human species capable of self-annihilation for the first time in history. Likewise, Giddens writes: "For hundreds of years, people worried about what nature could do to us—earthquakes, floods, plagues, bad harvests and so on. At a certain point . . . we stopped worrying so much about what nature could do to us, and we started worrying more about what we have done to nature. The transition makes one major point of entry in risk society" (1999:3). Giddens adds that "'risk society' might suggest a world which has become more hazardous, but this is not necessarily so. Rather, it is a society increasingly preoccupied with the future (and also with safety)."

Myra Jacobson, a forty-one-year-old mother of a preschool-age daughter, discusses her perceptions of the "world out there" that her daughter will some- day be entering. She says, "I'm concerned there's not going to *be* a world. Global warming is number one . . . the environment is going to cease to exist. Add war, terrorism, random violence—people are just shot—road rage, diseases we can't eradicate. That's what [my daughter] is walking into."

Living in the twenty-first-century world, a world whose continued existence may come into question, must certainly affect how women mother. Though many mothers in my study did *not* express high levels of subjective insecurity despite the social primes I have listed above, the majority did, and it is this ma- jority that I address here. With the combination of insecurity osmosis, the eleva- tion of risk perception due to large-scale security threats, and the media's "if it bleeds, it leads" overemphasis on frightening stories, the twenty-first-century social environment leaves many women mothering in fear.

STRATEGIC MOTHERING

Shirley Matheson, a twenty-seven-year-old mother of a toddler boy, was in New York on September 11, 2001, and is currently living on the opposite coast. Be- cause she is "really worried about terrorism and crime," she says she tries to postpone her son's entry into the potentially dangerous world, to "slow things down" for him, and "let him be *a child*, without worries . . . a carefree existence." Additionally, she and her son spend "a lot of time nesting at home" together, away from the hazards of the world at large.

When threats occur, it is not at all uncommon for people to gravitate toward greater connection with their children. Specifically, after 9/11, those people "who felt personally threatened by terrorism . . . spent more time with their families" (Huddy, Feldman, and Weber 2007:132). Shirley's protective, highly involved form of strategic mothering forefronts the mother-child connection as an an- tidote to the world's ills. This strategy, referred to in the scholarly literature and popular press as "hover mothering," "intensive mothering," "the helicopter mom phenomenon," "hyper-parenting," or simply "overprotective parenting" (Hays 1996; Rosenfeld and Wise 2000; Warner 2005), is often taken to be paradigmatic of today's mothering.

However, not all mothers engage in protection-by-shielding or attempt to forestall the passage of time and shield their children from what they see as a "scary world." Shirley herself alludes to a very different parenting tactic she sees in her fellow mothers. She says: "I've noticed some moms in a hurry for their kids to grow up. Bicycles for third birthdays and wanting Bumbos [seats to prop babies into a sitting position before they are capable of sitting unassisted] so their babies can sit on their own are just two examples that come to mind."

Indeed, my study confirms Shirley's observation and reveals the existence of a wholly alternative form of protective parenting in the twenty-first century that does *not* shield children from frightening information or experiences, but rather intentionally *exposes* children to these for the sake of their emotional growth and edification. This is *inoculation*, or trying to prepare one's children for encounters with a diversity of forces, including menacing ones, by deliberate exposure to such forces in measured doses. Unlike Shirley's more connection-oriented strategy, inoculation is independence-oriented, and it is noteworthy that within my sample of mothers it is *more common* than Shirley's more classically protective form of parenting.[3]

Exploring the inoculation strategy is of great significance, even beyond its apparent prevalence. Foremost, a discussion of inoculation is a much-needed corrective in the sociology of family, where this strategy is generally overlooked.[4] This omission may be a result of the taken-for-granted belief that "protection" denotes shielding from rather than exposure to the world's perils, or of the widely shared scholarly perception that today's mother's are primarily "intensive" (Hays 1996). However, both of these are assumptions that may be outdated, particularly given changes in the social climate brought on by 9/11 and the increased salience of other new types of risk. Indeed, the inoculation strategy is most frequently utilized by women who see the world as *physically dangerous* due to terrorism, environmental degradation, crime, and large-scale security threats. Because these forms of risk are increasingly threatening to women, particularly since the attacks of September 11, 2001, this may be a distinctively twenty-first-century approach to mothering and could become still more prevalent as these fears of large-scale security threats increase.

It is also important to explore inoculation because even when this strategy *is* recognized—most typically in the popular press and among mothers themselves rather than by family scholars—it is often interpreted as neglectful and as reflecting a lack of concern for child safety and welfare. Amelia Hatch, a twenty-nine-year-old stay-home mother to a six-month-old baby, describes some "parents today" as trying to unduly "toughen their children up." She believes these parents are "setting your kid up to be emotionally traumatized. You're making them feel like, um, they've got to do it all on their own, and there's not always someone there for them. . . . I just think it's going to cause self-esteem issues and confidence issues down the road." Yet I will argue that exposing children to a certain level of risk can represent a very intentional, concerned parenting action intended as a *form of protection*. I will illustrate this through the case studies of two concerned mothers who utilize the inoculation strategy.

RISK AS PROTECTION

Julia Freitag, a thirty-three-year-old social worker, is well aware of "bad stuff" in the world, yet her means of dealing with that in child-raising is self-consciously set apart from what she calls "hover mothering." She believes a confident, relaxed mother will make children feel safe, whereas a nervous, worried mother will upset children. Speaking to a friend who is anxious about managing her two very young children on a long upcoming flight, she says:

> My piece of advice for you is: relax! It'll be all right and it'll be over in a few hours. Whenever we board a plane, I can point out the families at the gate who are going to have trouble with their kids during the flight. It's always the families with the nervous and worried parents. The more relaxed you are, the calmer your children will be.

In keeping with her relaxed attitude, and contrary to current middle-class parenting norms, Julia, who lives on a busy street in a large metropolitan area, allows her seven-year-old daughter to walk alone to the park to play, often for seven hours at a time on weekends, "pop[ping] in only occasionally for food or stuff she needs." Julia is not doing this because she views cars and strangers as safe, nor is she a hands-off, permissive mother—though she acknowledges that the stress of caring for her two much younger children may have *something* to do with it. Rather, she believes education about how to be a safe pedestrian, given fast, careless drivers, and about how to cope with would-be abductors will create the strength and confidence necessary for her daughter to effectively navigate the world. She says:

> We have set firm rules and explained them to her. Besides the obvious such as "Look, when you cross the street!" or "Don't walk up to a car!," some of our family rules are: "If there are no other children in the park, you need to come home." Single children are easier targets. I also believe in teaching her strategies of how to defend herself.

For example, if someone tries to drag the daughter off, she is instructed to yell, "I don't know you!," rather than kick and scream, so that witnesses will not simply dismiss her as a child having a tantrum and will more likely come to her aid. It is not always easy for Julia, who is keenly aware of risks, to let her daughter be vulnerable to them. She was "worried the first few times [my daughter] walked a couple of blocks by herself," but reports that she overcame this worry for her daughter's sake because "I refuse to deprive my child of her freedom."

Julia's philosophy is reflected by Lenore Skenazy, writing in the *New York Sun*; her April 3, 2008, editorial, entitled "Why I Let My 9-Year-Old Ride the Subway Alone," proclaimed the author's own inoculating approach to mothering. Skenazy left her nine-year-old son in a New York City department store, at his request, so that he could have a solo adventure and find his own way home. She writes:

> I didn't trail him, like a mommy private eye. I trusted him to figure out that he should take the Lexington Avenue subway down, and the 34th Street crosstown bus home. If he couldn't do that, I trusted him to ask a stranger. And then I even trusted that stranger not to think, "Gee, I was about to catch my train home, but now I think I'll abduct this adorable child instead." Long story short: My son got home, ecstatic with independence. Long story longer…: Half the people I've told this episode to now want to turn me in for child abuse. As if keeping kids under lock and key and helmet and cell phone and nanny and surveillance is the right way to rear kids. It's not. It's debilitating—for us and for them.   (Skenazy 2008:1)

Skenazy's editorial hit a public "hot button," and she quickly found herself on the "Today Show," "Talk of the Nation," Fox News, and MSNBC, among others, sometimes with the title "World's Worst Mother?" beneath her. While Skenazy received a flurry of letters in response to her editorial and subsequent media appearances, many accusing her of reckless endangerment, the majority of the letters were supportive, written by likewise inoculating parents who thanked her for breaking the silence on this formerly taboo type of child-raising.

Like Skenazy, Julia believes that overprotection stunts children's development. Julia says:

If I want to raise strong children, I will have to let them practice their skills of survival. I know so many families who will watch their kids like hawks, drive them everywhere, pick them up, control their teens by putting them in so many after-school activities that they don't get "any crazy ideas." But do they get *any* ideas that way? What will happen to these children if they leave to go to college? If they never had to look out for themselves, they are much more likely to get in trouble at that point without the adult supervision.

Julia has two parenting models in her mind: (1) sequestering children, which provides a level of immediate comfort and safety but which Julia believes ultimately puts children *more* at risk, or (2) inoculating children for their long-term good by teaching them to deal with a difficult world from the beginning.

Most parents posting at freerangekids.com, a website created in 2008 in which inoculating parents can connect with one another, agree. Stephanie Pringhipakis writes: "I think that *not* teaching children . . . how to be self-reliant and think for themselves is a lot more dangerous than exposing them gradually to certain calculated levels of risk-taking" (posted 10 Apr 2008, 1:34 am, emphasis added), and Rabbmari writes: "[I]f you don't give them room to make small mistakes, I fear they will make *big mistakes*" (posted 10 Apr 2008, 3:56 am, emphasis in original). Thus we see that inoculation decidedly does not reflect a lack of concern for child safety; it is a different model from protection-by-shielding, yet it expresses the same concern.

Indeed, Julia believes that letting children loose in society without survival skills is dangerous, and that misrepresenting reality to children will lead to problems later—when the curtain falls to reveal a shockingly different truth, one with which the children are ill-equipped to cope. As a way to avoid these problems, she values honesty.

I don't create a "safe haven" for my daughter by withholding bad news from her. She watched the space shuttle explode with me on the news [when she was two years old] . . . [and] knows about 9/11 and the resulting wars. . . . When her favorite preschool teacher was diagnosed with terminal cancer I did not give her the common "Yes, honey, she's really sick, but she'll be better soon" version many of her classmates got. I'm not lying to my child. I tell her about the bad stuff. She knows that I'm sad, angry, and upset about many things on this planet. But she also knows what wonderful things there are, and what we can do to protect them. I believe in empowering children, because they have to deal with our world when we're gone.

Another example of an inoculating parent is Sarah Gordon, a thirty-five-year-old mother of two girls, one fourteen months and one almost three years old, whose commitment is to live in and expose her children to a relatively "true-to-life" world. Sarah reflects on a recent incident, a stray bullet from a robbery near her house that left a little boy paralyzed. "I heard a number of parents in our neighborhood saying they were really shaken up that it happened so close to their homes. But I realized that I wasn't." Sarah attributes this to her stalwart prior recognition that such possibilities exist. "There are awful problems with crime just twenty blocks away from where we live and in the same city. The idea that we can close our eyes and not expect it to touch us is ridiculous. The idea that we can shield our kids from *random* violence is pie in the sky."

Trevor Butterworth, spokesman for the research center STATS.org, agrees. "The statistics show that [stranger violence to children] is an incredibly rare event, and you can't protect people from very rare events. It would be like trying to create a shield against being struck by lightning" (quoted in Skenazy 2008:1).

Because Sarah sees violence that would involve her children as random, and because she does not believe it is possible to shield them from such randomness, she brings her children with her into high crime areas of the city when she finds something worthwhile for them to experience there. Just as she believes violence is ever possible but never likely in her own "safe" neighborhood, she believes it is possible but still rare in "unsafe" neighborhoods, and she assumes that the vast majority of human interactions in such neighborhoods will be harmless and potentially enriching.

Sarah works as a photojournalist (which is why she is often in those high-crime areas) and says, "I love my work." Regarding her upbringing, she characterizes her parents as "incredibly stable and loving," and she grew up in a rural area where she could freely wander without much adult supervision or concern. "Yet there's a family predisposition to anxiety . . . and my mom was definitely overprotective." It is interesting to note that being "overprotected" as a child did not lead Sarah to an absence of fear or to a protracted innocence, but rather to an impression that there was something bad out there from which she had to be protected. She was "a very anxious child and young adult but with *nothing* to worry about."

In a personal rebellion against fear a decade ago, Sarah moved to Kazakhstan, which her friends and families decried as a "hotbed of extremism and terrorism."

During the years I was there, I did get mass e-mails from the U.S. embassy saying, "We have intelligence that suggests Americans should avoid gathering at ex-pat bars and hang-outs this week," or "There is increased chatter from the bin Laden cohort. Please alter your usual routes." But I had no run-ins with terrorism and had an amazing time there that forever changed me. Still, my family never stopped worrying and never stopped bothering me to return. I finally agreed to come back, and ended up settling in New York the first week of September in 2001. I got an internship downtown. And that's where I was on September 11th, watching the fireballs and the papers and people flying through the air. Running with the crowd when that first building started crashing down. Turns out going to Central Asia wasn't what put me close to a terrorist act. But it did give me a deeper, nuanced understanding of what's now affecting my own "safe" country. And it taught me: you just never know.

Her refusal to "close [her] eyes" to violence and negative occurrences, and her philosophical embrace of randomness and "not knowing," applies to her child-raising. Whereas Julia—who lets her daughter walk alone to the park—sees ignorance and inexperience in navigating fearful situations as the primary impediments to many children's survival in a sometimes frightening twenty-first-century world, Sarah sees over-anxiety about those fearful situations (and the subsequent paralysis in fully living one's life) as today's children's primary challenges.

Rather than seeking to avert that anxiety in her children by *avoiding* fearful situations, Sarah believes that exposing children to such situations alongside an adult who remains emotionally calm can help them learn to tolerate uncertainty and continue to be open to new experiences, even in fear. Sarah says she has "worked so hard in my life to shed anxiety as a ball and chain—through sheer willpower and putting myself in difficult but rewarding situations" that she is therefore "determined *not* to pass fear on to my kids."

This manifests in two ways in how she parents her children. First, she avoids overly regulating her children's environments based on least probability of harm because that would limit their exposure only to safe, known, or homogenous influences. Thus she is committed to "not altering [family] travel plans based on terrorist threats," and, as described above, to taking the children "to art and music shows in local neighborhoods that might not be the greatest. You'd be amazed at how walking around with two adorable kids suddenly starts great conversations with people who in the past have just looked at us like interlopers."

The second way she manifests her philosophical stance in parenting is by not letting her own anxieties interrupt the children's activities and explorations.

[This means] just standing back and letting [the kids] learn on their own about this world they're exploring, trying to let myself let them fall and hash things out with one another. I'm always there with a hug and kiss and words if they're upset. But I try really hard to let them process without imposing my grown-up fears. They want to try the slide? I might not be ready for it, or can see in my mind all the things that could go wrong, but I try to put that aside and sure enough it usually works out great and they have a new skill they're super proud about. *You just never know.*

Sarah credits a poem—appropriately, about fear—with partially forming her inoculating parenting philosophy. It represents why she sees fear itself as among the most fearful elements of twenty-first-century life for children, and further underscores that her use of inoculation in her mothering is due not to negligence or a lack of concern for her children's welfare, but rather to how she defines that welfare. The poem was written by one of her twelve-year-old students in Kazakhstan. The assignment was to draw a monster and then describe it. He handed in a small scrap of paper that read:

My Monster (not only)

Well, I think the monster which I want to describe isn't only mine
because these monsters live in all living creatures.
It's fear.
As a rule fearless people are mad, or little babies.
I really can't explain this feeling and I think I haven't to do it,
because you certainly understand me, don't you?
Sometimes the monster saves us,
but in most cases it just makes us a lot of troubles.
You understand that monsters like this haven't bodies
and so I really can't draw it
I think that who has this in mind, who has a very big monster,
is the very shyest and it doesn't make anybody more interesting.
So, let's become crazy and we'll be fearless.

Sarah adds:

I've kept that tucked into my passport case ever since he handed it in, trying to hold onto that glimpse into a child's vision for a fearless world . . . because I know fear is not productive. Better to channel it into concerns that you can do something about . . . [by] voting and being informed and what I'm trying to teach the girls now:

being observant and being friendly. And I don't mean to say I'm all that: *no fear* and bring on the bullets. . . . I think fear is a healthy, survival reflex that has its place. But when it starts to impinge on my curiosity and enjoyment of life then I try to remember: you just never know.

Thus we see two different examples of inoculating parenting. While they may be mistaken for negligence with the most superficial of glances, they each represent a different, deliberate parenting action taken to prepare children to successfully fare in a potentially hazardous twenty-first-century world. For Julia, who lets her daughter walk and play outside unsupervised, inoculation means giving her child the necessary information and experiences to learn to roam with minimized risk. Her underlying message is: "Freedom is a human right, but in order for me to let you free in a sometimes scary world, we will need to make it *less* scary through your education and empowerment." For Sarah, who takes her children with her to the "bad side" of town, inoculation means truly living in uncertainty and pushing back against the "irrational fear and distrust" that she blames for perpetuating "cycles of violence and hate and things to *really* be scared about." Therefore, her focus is less on strategically minimizing risk than on bucking the fear of it. Her underlying message is: "Disaster could strike at any moment, but while we're alive, rather than huddling in a hole to avoid potential harm, I want my family to *live* and appreciate the basic goodness of people and the beauty that makes life worth living."

Despite their differences, the common thread weaving these women's stories together is a belief that exposure to, rather than isolation from, fearful elements of society is the best way to raise a child capable of dealing with those elements when they inevitably present themselves in that child's life.

In summary, I have presented a form of strategic parenting common among my research participants yet frequently overlooked in the scholarly literature. As inoculation is associated with women for whom terrorism, environmental degradation, crime, and large-scale security threats are highly salient, and as these types of fears are on the rise, we might expect to see more mothers utilizing inoculation as the twenty-first century progresses. Furthermore, as I have shown through two very different case studies, despite engaging in parenting actions (or inactions) that may be interpreted as neglect or a lack of concern for child safety and welfare, the deliberate exposure of one's children to risk can be a highly concerned form of parenting, attempting to tool children to successfully fare in a sometimes frightening-seeming twenty-first-century world.

NOTES

1. While two of the primary caregivers participating in this research are male, I refer to informants collectively as "mothers" because utilizing such gender-neutral terms as "primary caregivers" or simply "parents" implies a false sense of gender equality in today's parenting and masks the enormous sociological influence of living in a primarily female-reared society.
2. Insecurity osmosis certainly includes, but is not limited to, stories experienced through the news media.
3. As my sample was nonrandomly selected, we should not make generalizations regarding the prevalence of the inoculation strategy in the population at large. However, as I may have over-sampled mothers who protect via shielding due to my recruitment at midwife-oriented birth classes, the fact that inoculation is *still* the most common strategy in my sample makes a more generalized prevalence in society more plausible.
4. One notable exception to this oversight is Allison Pugh's penetrating description of the practice among affluent African Americans of putting their children into activities with street-smart African American children from low-income families in order to promote their own children's cultural literacy and adaptability. This prioritization of "learning over social comfort" (Pugh 2009:256) is a form of what I call inoculation.

WORKS CITED

Beck, Ulrich. 1999. *World-Risk Society*. Cambridge: Polity Press.

Free Range Kids. 2008. For or against? April 10. http://freerangekids.wordpress.com/for-or-against/ (accessed April 14, 2008).

Giddens, Anthony. 1999. Risk and responsibility. *Modern Law Review* 62.1:1–10.

Glassner, Barry. 2000. *The Culture of Fear: Why Americans Are Afraid of the Wrong Things*. New York: Basic Books.

Hacker, Jakob S. 2007. *The Great Risk Shift: The Assault on American Jobs, Families, Health Care, and Retirement, and How You Can Fight Back*. Oxford: Oxford University Press.

Hackstaff, Karla B. 2000. *Marriage in a Culture of Divorce*. Philadelphia: Temple University Press.

Hays, Sharon. 1996. *The Cultural Contradictions of Motherhood*. New Haven: Yale University Press.

Huddy, Leonie, Stanley Feldman, and Christopher Weber. 2007. The political consequences of perceived threat and felt insecurity. *Annals of the American Academy of Political and Social Science* 614:131–153.

Pugh, Allison. 2009. *Longing and Belonging: Parents, Children, and Consumer Culture.* Berkeley: University of California Press.

Rosenfeld, Alvin, and Nicole Wise. 2000. *The Over-Scheduled Child: Avoiding the Hyper-Parenting Trap.* New York: St. Martin's.

Skenazy, Lenore. 2008. Why I let my 9-year-old ride the subway alone. *New York Sun,* April 7. http://freerangekids.wordpress.com/ (accessed April 14, 2008).

Smits, Luc, Lydia Krabbendam, Rob de Bie, Gerard Essed, and Jim van Os. 2006. Lower birth weight of Dutch neonates who were in utero at the time of the 9/11 attacks. *Journal of Psychosomatic Research* 61.5:715–717.

Warner, Judith. 2005. *Perfect Madness: Motherhood in the Age of Anxiety.* New York: Penguin.

Whitehead, Barbara Dafoe, and David Popenoe. 2005. *The State of Our Unions: The Social Health of Marriage in America.* Report by the National Marriage Project, Rutgers University.

Mother-Talk | **FOUR**

Conversations with Mothers of | SARAH F. PEARLMAN
Female-to-Male Transgender Children

> When you have a child, you don't know
> who you invite in the house.
> —Sicilian folk saying

Although there is now greater public acceptance of gay relationships and the morality of homosexual civil rights (Werum and Winders 2001), there is no transgender counterpart. Gender-variant people are the most frequently targeted group for persecution and continue to experience stigma, discrimination, and often violence (Drescher 2002). Parents of both homosexual and transgender children contend with numerous fears and concerns, most often focused on the potential for violence and threat to physical safety. However, while mothers of lesbian daughters may struggle with changed expectations and the loss of a heterosexual daughter, they still have a daughter. Parents of female-to-male (FTM) transgender children have a more complex, difficult, and prolonged course of adjustment, one compounded by greater stigmatization, self-consciousness, and shame as well as the *actual* loss of a daughter. Said one mother of a trans son, initially identified as a lesbian, "A lesbian is nothing. This is really big. Their mothers are upset because of who their child loves; my child hated herself, hated everything that identified her to the world."

There is very little literature on parents of transgender children, mostly chapters in books or articles by mental health professionals (Brown and Rounsley 1996; Jennings 2002; Lev 2004), anthologies composed of personal stories by parents and other family members (Boenke 1999), or books with chapters on parents, that include mothers, but written from the perspective of FTM individuals (Devor 1997). However, none focus exclusively on mother's experience of a daughter's sex reassignment, or the complexities of the mother-daughter relationship that can impact parental reaction to transition.

Addressing these issues is a qualitative interview study, conducted in 2000–2001, of 18 mothers who learned that their daughters identified as transgender and intended to, or were in the process of transitioning to male—or presenting as both female and male. The study was undertaken in order to understand the experience of the women interviewed, their reactions to the disclosure of intent to transition, and their process of coming to terms with a daughter's decision to change sex. Additional areas explored were the characteristics of mothers most likely to come to terms with sex reassignment and the various factors that influenced their adjustment.

The participants interviewed were women who parented during a time in which a cultural ideology, including child rearing values, encouraged individualism, personal gratification, and the right to individual identity and self-expression. Moreover, it became a time when there was language that captured the experience of mismatch between biological sex and gender identity, medical and surgical technologies that made sex reassignment possible, a surge of information and public awareness, and role models and peers—personal and online—in support of transition. Thus, it is no surprise that the numbers of women who recognize transgender identity and intend to transition has increased considerably (Hansbury 2004), insuring that, as the 21st century progresses, an increasing number of mothers will be confronted by a child's cross-gender identity, including mothers of younger-age children. Consequently, research studies on mothers of gender-variant children, including FTMs, will be an important contribution and expand the future development of motherhood studies.

THE STUDY

Method

Twelve interviews of mothers of FTMs were conducted, each lasting from one to two hours and audio-taped as each participant began to tell her story. Each interview began with instructions on completing a demographic questionnaire designed to provide information about each mother's background, age, relationship status, religious affiliation, work history, education, participation in social justice movements, the age of their child at disclosure, and the year when disclosure took place. This was followed by a narrative statement read by the researcher in which each mother was asked to tell the story of how she learned that her child identified as transgender and intended to, or was in the process of, transitioning to male. Following each participant's story, a series of open-ended questions were asked in order to understand (a) initial and later reactions to disclosure; (b) explanations of transgender identity; (c) recollections of a child's early gender-variant behaviors; (d) the milestone events and turning points which led to changes in feelings toward transition and resulted in reconciliation (defined as acknowledgement of the permanence of transition); and (e) factors that assisted with adjustment such as the relationship with their FTM child prior to and following transition and beliefs and values regarding motherhood and mothering practices.

A cover letter with instructions and the demographic questionnaire were mailed to the six remaining participants who could not be interviewed in person along with the narrative statement and a list of the same questions asked during the personally conducted interviews. These participants were requested to tape their responses to the narrative statement and the list of questions, and then forward the tape and the completed materials to the researcher. Verbatim transcripts of all interviews were then completed and analyzed to identify the various patterns and themes.

The demographic information and questions asked were informed by the literature on FTMs (Cromwell 1999; Devor 1997) and parents of transgender children (Brown and Rounsley 1996; Emerson and Rosenfeld 1996), narratives written by parents (Boenke 1999), and information distributed by parents' organizations as well as literature on parents' struggles to accept a child's homosexuality (Bernstein 1990; Pearlman 1992; Savin-Williams 1998). Also utilized were studies that correlated acceptance of homosexuality to tolerance of nonconformity and diversity, progressive political views, and personal history of social/political activism (Irwin and Thompson 1977; Pearlman 1992) and feminist psychoanalytic perspectives on mothering and the mother-daughter relationship (Chodorow 1978; Hirsch 1989).

Participants

The selection criteria included that each participant should be the mother of a daughter who identified as transgender, and was aware of her child's transgender identity for at least six months. Mothers were from Connecticut, New York, New Jersey, Maryland, Virginia, Illinois, Ohio, Washington, Alaska, and Vancouver, Canada. Two were from Australia. All were Caucasian and all but one was heterosexual.

At the time of their child's disclosure, 11 were married and seven had been divorced. Of the divorced women, one was single, four had remarried, one was partnered with another woman, and one was partnered with a FTM transsexual, a relationship that followed her daughter's disclosure. Fourteen participants had completed college and 10 had attained advanced degrees; 15 had similar professional backgrounds (nursing, counseling, social work, teaching, the arts); 10 were affiliated with churches or religious groups supportive of GLBT rights; and prior to disclosure, 13 had been involved in or identified with progressive movements or social justice causes, including feminism, the environment, civil rights, and/or peace movements. All were supportive of equal rights for women. Eleven were, or had been, members of PFLAG or transgender parents' organizations and seven were in leadership roles, national and local, and involved in active outreach and support of other parents as well as activities focused on transgender civil rights. Thus, participants shared a particular profile and certain characteristics, confirmed by the literature (Irwin and Thompson 1977; Pearlman 1992), that enabled them to ultimately come to terms with a transgender child. Consequently, the findings from this select group cannot be generalized to the population of mothers/parents of transgender children including minority (racial-ethnic) mothers.

FINDINGS

Disclosure and Transition

The age when daughters disclosed that they identified as male or transgender and planned or had begun the process of transitioning ranged from 15 to 36 years old. The time from initial disclosure to the interviews ranged from 6 months to 13 years. Twelve of the mothers learned that their daughters identified as transgender between 1996 and 1999; most learned around 1996. Ten disclosed from age 20 to 26; two disclosed at 15 and 18; the remaining six disclosed from 29 to 36. All but one was a biological child. Fifteen participants reported that their children had begun transitioning and were presenting as male at the time of disclosure. Of those 15 trans sons, all but two had already begun, or were about to begin, or planned on hormone therapy and eventual sex reassignment surgery.

Disclosure typically took place in-person just before, or soon after transition had begun through hormone therapy, or shortly after beginning hormone therapy, but before surgery. One trans son, a 15 year-old adolescent, disclosed while watching a movie on FTM trans identity. He said to his mother, "Mom, that's me. I am a boy. Inside I'm a boy." Two other mothers had daughters who deliberately presented as both female and male (bi-gender) in order to challenge gender norms. Both had facial hair but did not attempt to conceal breasts through binding. Only one was on hormones.

At the time of the interviews, 16 participants reported that their trans sons were presenting exclusively as male. Fourteen stated that their child was on hormone therapy and had completed, or were about to undergo, sex reassignment surgery, procedures that included chest reconstruction, hysterectomy, and liposuction. Two other trans sons had begun hormone therapy; another was about to begin taking hormones and planned eventual surgery. Mothers indicated that surgical delay was due to financial reasons (e.g., insufficient funds, no insurance). The amount of time elapsed since disclosure, the status of a child's transition, and successful male presentation were all factors that assisted mothers with coming to terms with sex reassignment.

The mothers in the study referred to their daughters as transgender, although some used the term, *transsexual* once sex reassignment surgery had taken place, but their language was varied and inconsistent. Most alternated between saying "daughter" or "son" and "she" or "he." Some referred to their child as a "daughter" prior to disclosure and "son" following transition. However, the majority expressed that they had difficulty thinking of their transgender child as a son. None of the mothers referred to their children as trans men and all had initial difficulty and most had ongoing problems with male pronouns. Some explained it as a matter of habit while others expressed that the change in pronouns signified the permanence of gender transition. All used the terms *child* or *children* despite the age or adult status of their offspring and, along with *trans men* and *trans sons*, these are the terms used throughout this chapter.

Thematic Findings

Disclosure: Mothers-in-Crisis

Although reactions varied in intensity, 11 of the 18 mothers described that disclosure precipitated a profound personal crisis characterized by shock, confusion, devastation, fear, and grief. The majority were completely surprised and most had never heard of female-to-male transgenderism. As one mother said, "He tried to explain it me. I didn't have a clue. I never heard of it. You're what! You're not really a she. You're a he. How could that happen? I was in horror." Eight mothers had observed that their daughter's appearance had become increasingly masculine. However, because they had initially identified as lesbian, mothers attributed the change in appearance to a butch lesbian identity or as experimentation with masculine presentation. Two mothers did guess. One related, "I said it first, 'You want to have a sex change.' She was very butch. You had to be blind not to know." Then she recalled,

> At age 15, she told me she wanted to be a boy and have a sex change. I was so angry. I said, "Well, yeah, well you do that, but right now you're a girl so get over it." I made it clear that I didn't want to discuss it.

Another told about her daughter's first attempts to disclose:

> She said through other people she had been meeting, she had begun to wonder about herself. When she finally did tell me, it was a horrendous shock. I had to hang up the phone. I was more devastated about it than I think about anything in my whole life. So foreign, totally gut wrenching. I was in a horrible state, crying and praying for several days.

The majority of these women described an extended period of emotional turmoil in which feelings of shame, helplessness, and profound grief emerged along with confusion on how to comprehend, manage, or convey to others the meaning of transgender identity and their daughter's transition. Most concealed it, some for a long time with marked concerns as to how others might react and how they would be regarded as mothers. As one said,

> I don't have daughter. I have a son. I don't have a she. I have a he. How do I go on not having a daughter? What do I do with those memories? How do I talk about my infant that was a female to people who only know that I have a son? I didn't tell anybody, not a living soul. They're not gonna understand. I don't understand. Gay was really nothing for me as a parent. You can hide a gay daughter. You can't hide a girl that becomes a boy. This was now an outward thing—a physical change, voice change, hair change. This now is not my child. What am I supposed to do?

Many openly challenged their daughter's decision to transition and clung to pretense and hopes that it was just a phase, that transition would not happen and just "go away." One told that she denied transition for a long time, perceiving it as a sex role or sex presentation change rather than as an actual gendered or physical body change: "We weren't dealing with it. We would have been happier to pretend that nothing is really happening to the body and it's just this kind of external change and role-playing." Consequently, denial served as an initial protective mechanism as mothers struggled to understand and come to terms with sex reassignment.

Although most participants described a period of protracted crisis, they were not immobilized. The majority searched for information and some sought social support. One told how she located an online group of mothers of FTM children: "I felt connected to other people who were going through the same experience. All seemed as shocked and stunned as I was." Another said that she was mostly concerned with how she could be helpful to her child, concealing her grief as she struggled to adjust. "I was still Super Mom for the first few months. I rarely allowed myself to feel what it felt like for me and what sorrow I had. I had to grieve and let go of my daughter." Yet, she sought information and support in order to figure out how she could be the "most supportive mother" and learn as much as she could, "trying to get up to speed on what this experience was about." Thus, a reoccurring theme were practices of maternal selflessness as mothers suppressed their own feelings and behaved according to what they perceived was in the best interest of their child ("Super Mom").

Finally, as mothers began to move past initial reactions, new perspectives emerged that ultimately reduced confusion and paved the way for later acceptance. As one related, "I understand now why she was so unhappy and had so many problems." A second said,

> She never felt like a lesbian. She didn't feel like she belonged in the lesbian community because she always knew she was really male and that she would transition. I wondered why she didn't embrace all of the lesbian stuff that there was. I gave her jewelry about lesbian things and she didn't wear it. She never was proud to be a lesbian because she never felt like she was. She always felt like she was male.

She later added, "You can dress like a male. You can walk around like a male. But you don't get treated like a male. If you're not male, you can't do what males do. If you're male, you want to be male." Two mothers of daughters who were in their early twenties expressed concern about the increase in the numbers of young women who lived in "radical" urban or academic environments and who were transitioning to male. They worried that transition was an act of rebellion, suggestibility, the influence of peers, or a jump on a "current bandwagon," and that there would be regrets as they grew older.

Disclosure: Other Reactions

Seven participants, although expressing numerous concerns, such as safety and threat of physical violence, conveyed a less intense reaction. They neither reported the same degree of devastation, nor appeared to be as focused on the loss of a daughter as the mothers described above. One, whose immediate response was mediated by familiarity and exposure to transgender people, stated, "I was probably as ready as a mother could be, social worker, Unitarian, interested in the issue, worked with hundreds of parents who had been through the kind of grief associated with finding out your kid is any kind of sexual minority." A second said,

> My husband and I probably dealt with this very comfortably and easily. We were not in any pain. He was always my son. We just didn't know it. It was a relief because we felt we had an answer to all the pain and suffering that this child had gone through. What was once a selfish uncaring female is now a happy, outgoing, unselfish, caring male. So for us it was an awakening, a rejoicing.

A third whose daughter was deliberately presenting as both genders believed it represented a political stance, experimental and perhaps impermanent, describing her as "something in the middle. No categories, no sex, no gender, just persons, a gender revolution. She always said there are more than two genders."

Finally, an Australian mother who had anticipated disclosure of lesbianism by her fifteen year-old adolescent told about her reaction, a response shaped by beliefs on mothering in which unconditional love, empathy, support, and protection of one's children were paramount.

> I was ready for lesbian. I'd prepared a speech that said "I love you, we always will." He said to me, "I am a boy inside." I didn't know what to say, so I used exactly the same speech I had prepared for a lesbian.

This mother recalled that she spent the whole night on the Internet, eventually finding people who could offer information and support. She quickly became her son's advocate, seeking permission for him to use his school principle's bathroom and to wear a boy's uniform. Within two years, she helped him obtain hormones and to legally change his name. During the interview she spoke about her family, saying that they

> changed all the phony photographs where he looked like a girl, so he looks like he's been a boy all his life. We made our youngest child "pronoun boy." He would correct us every time we said the wrong pronoun. It was great fun for a ten-year-old to correct his parents.

Yet, this same mother spoke about her own grief. "I've had my tears. I don't cry now. I'm happy for him. My job was to minimize the trauma, the hassles, and smooth the way, make his life as easy as I could. It's a mother's job."

In summary, there was neither one type of experience, nor one type of reaction, nor one explanation of differences in reactions. Familiarity with transition and exposure to transgender individuals, understanding the mismatch between biological sex and gender identity as the source of a child's suffering, intellectual understanding of the politics of gender, and maternal convictions that emphasized selflessness, empathy, and protection all served as factors that assisted mothers with coming to terms with transition. Overall, the majority of women interviewed set aside and masked their own feelings in order to respond to the perceived needs of their child, attesting to the pervasiveness of contemporary childrearing norms (Alwin 1990). They also began to take on the perspectives and opinions of their trans children.

Concerns

Recollections/Reconstructions

All of the mothers recollected gender-variant behaviors as far back as early childhood. Sixteen reported that their daughters preferred boys' activities and hated to be dressed in girls' clothing. One remarked, "He's always had these masculine qualities. She was a tomboy, she never dated, basically cross-dressed, and never wanted to wear a dress beyond the age of three." Others said that daughters had told them that they wanted to be boys, some believed they were boys, and a few had chosen boy's names. However, most mothers viewed their daughters as feminists or tomboys and some thought that masculine-like behaviors might be an early sign of lesbianism, thereby conflating gender and sexuality. One participant related the following:

I thought of my daughter being a lesbian by age two. She wouldn't play with dolls. She wanted to urinate standing up and called herself "Jack." Even though I was aware of transsexualism, a lightbulb never went off that this could be the case.

Two other participants said that there was something about their daughters' personalities and behaviors that were more stereotypically male: more independent, less need for closeness, or that they played like boys and had more interest in activities and ideas than feelings or emotions. Recollections of gender-variant behaviors during childhood and adolescence provided continuity of identity, lent credence to disclosure of male identity, and ultimately helped mothers make sense of transition.

Fears and Regrets

All of the participants had numerous fears and concerns, such as discrimination or psychological damage resulting from insults, harassment, stigma, and exclusion. However, hate crimes and physical violence were clearly the most prevalent fears and many mothers spoke of Brandon Tina as a powerful symbol representing the dangers to a transgender child. The two mothers of daughters who blended gender expressed specific concerns. One remarked that "she asks for trouble. She looks like a guy but she's built like a woman with a lot of facial hair on top of it." Safety, especially in public bathrooms, was a major issue, and mothers, once reconciled to transition, experienced great relief when they knew their child could successfully pass as male. Two of the three mothers whose children identified as gay males related the most intense fears, specifically about the threat of physical violence and contracting AIDS.

Many of the women interviewed expressed regrets that they had pushed their daughters to become more feminine and did not understand and were unaware of male identity. As one said, "I made her wear a dress. It must have been horrible for her. But I didn't know she didn't think she was female." "I probably could have picked up signs about the transsexual identity" stated a second. "I felt responsible for not making it easy enough for him to tell me," reported a third. Another questioned her parenting as well as the validity of her relationship with her daughter, saying,

I thought all these years that I had a daughter. I felt so bogus like it was all a lie. I was duped, mistaken. I didn't really know my own child. I felt so close to her. How could I not know such an intimate, important thing? What kind of a mother was I that I hadn't known she thought she was a boy. And I thought she was a happy kid.

Only one woman thought in terms of gender identity. "At age 14, I called a pediatric endocrinologist. There was a lot of male behavior. Deep voice, irregular periods. He said, 'He'll outgrow it, don't worry.' I never pursued it with another doctor. I regret that deeply." Remorse and self-blame were prevalent themes in mothers' accounts—attesting to the power of exacting motherhood standards. Consequently, many of those interviewed believed that they had failed as mothers by not comprehending a young daughter's male identity, or following through on gender identity concerns.

Other Adjustments: Sexual Orientation

Three mothers stated that their daughters had been married and identified as heterosexual; one said her child, an adolescent, identified as bisexual. However, 14 were mothers of daughters who initially disclosed as lesbian, providing support for Vitello's (2006) observations that lesbians are the population from which most FTMs emerge. Thus, the majority of participants told two stories: the first was about adjusting to a lesbian daughter; the second about learning that a daughter identified as transgender. At the time of the interviews, 11 of the 14 trans sons, initially identified as lesbian, remained attracted to women and were perceived, although not always self-identified, as heterosexual. Two were in a relationship with other FTM transgender individuals and one identified as bisexual. The three trans sons who originally identified as heterosexual remained attracted to men and were perceived, although not always self-identified, as gay men. Transition changed sexual orientation category, not sexual orientation, although some, initially identified as lesbian, had begun to describe themselves as bisexual.[2]

These changes were initially highly disturbing and disorienting to most mothers. One who talked about her daughter, previously identified as a lesbian, said, "He is actually a straight male. My feelings about this? Confusion. But if it works for them, that's what I care about." Another participant reported this: "You were a girl, you're gonna be a guy, you're gonna be bisexual. That means you're gonna go with guys. That makes you a gay man. Right?" Later in the interview, she remarked that her daughter was dating a FTM transgender individual. "I said to her, will you get an identity." Consequently, these mothers were confronted by both instability of sexual orientation and gender transition.

Turning Points and Explanations

Because 16 of the trans sons lived a distance away from their families, contact was infrequent and changes in appearance, especially once hormonal treatment had begun, was a shock to many mothers. As one said,

> I had left really a girl, a gay girl, and now have somebody with some facial hair and a big neck. But after a while, it's still your child. You get over the outward appearance and it just becomes your child again. It just took a little while.

"She looked like a man, her voice, the muscles. I began to see her as a man," described another. A third stated that her child "walked down the stairs one summer and he had the hairiest legs I'd ever seen and threw me into shock. He had man's legs. That was the moment that propelled me forward." For others, surgery was the turning point, convincing them of their child's resolve and reconciling them to the permanence of transition. As one mother expressed,

> It was a slow thing. She wasn't sure if she was going to have surgery. I felt like I was in limbo. I secretly hoped that this was a phase and that she was a lesbian. After the surgery, this was like the point of no return.

As observations of physical changes took place, perception and appraisal of a child's gender changed. Thus, a perceptual-cognitive switch occurred and some mothers began to perceive and experience their daughter as male. Although the majority (12) of the mothers interviewed had accepted their child's decision to transition to male, most still grieved the loss a daughter. Others expressed that they had persistent doubts as to the genuineness of male identity and *acted* accepting and supportive in order to minimize conflict and maintain a relationship with their trans son. As one mother said,

> There are still times when I have trouble with pronouns and when think of him as my daughter. Sometimes I wonder if I will ever see him as my son or I will always see him as my daughter who wants to be male.

Most of the mothers interviewed thought that genetics, specifically the amount of androgen secreted during early pregnancy, commonly referred to as the "androgen wash," affected brain development and explained transgenderism. As one participant said, "It's something in the brain, a chemical. You have to change what your outside is. She's not comfortable with who she is physically because her mind doesn't feel that way." Several spoke of their child as born in the wrong body while others believed that gender identity occurred on a continuum from female to male and a form of human variability. One commented that there was no one gender "dysphoria" experience or one transgender identity, but different experiences and different "levels of angst."

Losing a Daughter

For many mothers, it was the specific loss of a daughter and the special importance of the mother-daughter relationship that was the most painful aspect of transition. As one mother stated, "I really regret not having more children so I could still have a daughter." A second related the following:

> I didn't know how to feel. Here's my daughter, she's still alive, but there's this necessary part of grieving. I didn't want to lose her. I didn't want to stop saying I have a daughter. I feel like I'm grieving because I'm losing my daughter. My daughter is gone. She's died. She's just not there anymore.

Consequently, as mothers struggled to make sense of and communicate their experience of grief, several used the metaphor of death. One participant expressed that, "It was such a humongous loss. Not that I would ever wish it, but it would almost be better if she had died. People could understand what I was going through." A second agreed: "You don't have the words to sum up what this transgender experience is, so we used the words of dying. That pissed him off. But it was the only thing we had to grab onto." "She died, my mother-daughter relationship died, our concept of her has died," declared a third.

Several mothers reported that their daughters, although physically male, were the same as they were prior to transition. Others described specific relationship changes. As one mother said, "I think I relate to him differently. Less protective. I guess we were a little bit enmeshed." Conversations another mother used to have with her daughter no longer seemed appropriate: "We used to rag on men, joke about, talk about bio men. We would just laugh and have so much fun. But I'm looking at somebody that looks like a guy and it's just not the same thing." A third mother related that, "It was a whole new mind-shift realization of who she was. All my kids were girls, something on a very deep level, a soul level."

There were other adjustments as well. A fourth mother talked about the following dilemma:

I was doing quite well and then during her birthday, it was hard. I spent a lot of time looking for an appropriate card. A daughter card didn't seem like an appropriate card, son card didn't feel appropriate. I didn't want to give her just any kind of a card.

Adding to the experience of loss were new boundaries and rules on physical contact and access. As example, one mother related that, "When my daughter and I went traveling together, we would stay in the same room. I wouldn't be comfortable doing that. She's a guy now. I wouldn't do that with my son." A second reported the following: "We were in the bedroom talking and I started getting undressed. He said, 'Mom, I'm not the same daughter you used to have. You probably shouldn't undress in front of me.' I said, you're still my kid." Another expressed that touching had become "kind of uncomfortable. Not like before. Not much of a hug. Maybe a quick peck on the cheek."

What these mothers described resonated with both feminist psychoanalytic theories, in particular, object relations theory (Chodorow 1978; Hirsch 1989) as well as Adrienne Rich's (1976) work on mothering and the complexities of the mother-daughter relationship. To Hirsch, there is a "fundamental interconnection" (p. 130) between mothers and daughters that Rich calls a "powerful cathexis" (p. 226). Consequently, when a daughter transitions to male, interconnection and cathexis are disrupted as trans sons individuate, separate, and disentangle from mothers.

The majority of mothers, although accepting their child's decision to transition to male, still grieved—describing a residual sadness connected to daughter-loss that persisted, even among those most active in the transgender movement. As one participant said, "We lost a beautiful daughter. We have a great new son, but we really did lose a daughter. We're out there rah-rahing our new sons, organizing on our soapboxes, but we miss our daughters." Finally, several spoke of their relationship with their own mother and how it influenced their own parenting. Some described an emotionally close relationship that they wanted to repeat with their own daughter. Others sought to mother in ways that they wished they been parented by their own mother. Losing a daughter deprived them of continuing to re-experience their relationship with their own mother, or the opportunity to re-work how they themselves had been mothered—findings that are in accord with Chodorow's (1978) premise that women's wish to mother is motivated by the desire to relive the early mother-child bond, insuring the *reproduction* of mothering. Overall, for many of the women in the study, the dream of having a daughter and a deeply entwined relationship that would provide ongoing intimacy, companionship, mutual nurturance, and shared life values slowly faded.

Other Themes

The majority of participants disclosed to others selectively and with hesitation. As one said, "I haven't told that many. It's not that easy for me to do. I'm not comfortable saying it. It's my thing. It's me who doesn't want to go through the whole conversation." A second "let people know for us it was a blessing and not a situation that turned out to be a tragedy." Another "sent out change-of-gender cards, kind of a birth announcement." Disclosure to others was a critical factor in asserting acceptance of a daughter's transition as well as self-acceptance as a parent of a trans person. However, for many, telling others represented a "united family-front" in spite of unresolved feelings towards sex transition.

The majority of mothers saw their trans sons as happier and better adjusted once transitioned to male." The "essential difference is his inner sense of peace," described one. A second related

> I have a much happier son than I did a daughter. He is a wonderful example of a happy transitioned person. We had a child that was not very likable. We were estranged and when he transitioned, it actually healed our relationship.

Also, a number remarked on the respect and admiration that they had for transsexuals. Others expressed that their beliefs and values had undergone transformations and that their lives were enriched as a result of having a trans son. Mothers involved with trans people and/or the transgender movement, in particular, had become parental role models and parent surrogate figures for other trans individuals. As one said, "They don't have support from their own families and I'm there and supportive. Everyone wants me to be their mother."

Overall, the findings from the study including reactions to disclosure, fears and concerns, recollection of early gender-variant behaviors, informing others, and coming to terms with sex reassignment were supported by the literature on parents of FTMs (Boenke 1999; Brown and Rounsley 1996; Devor 1997; Emerson and Rosenfeld 1996; Jennings 2002; Lev 2004). However, acceptance of a transgender child can be not a matter of "either/or" but rather one of degree: a slow, uneven journey that takes resolve and hard effort, marked by the reemergence of anger, grief, and loss. It can mean resignation or ambivalence, or celebration of a trans son's happiness and bravery in choosing to live authentically. Confirming results by Irwin and Thompson (1977) and Pearlman (1992), the potential of a mother's acceptance rests on multiple factors: personal characteristics, educational background, and political and religious beliefs that value diversity and human rights. Also confirmed were convictions that emphasize maternal empathy and support, wanting a close relationship with their child, and recognition of a child's happiness (Pearlman).

The mothers interviewed in this study were a unique group of women. What was primary were their convictions on mothering and their relationship with their child, and the participant's sense of self as both mothers *and* individuals were enhanced by a continuing bond with their trans son and a major source of maternal self-worth. Consequently, findings concurred with Jean Baker Miller's (1984) work on the development of women's sense of self. Many mothers accepted whatever connection was possible, a connection that often depended on terms set by their child. As one said, "I'm not going to lose my connection. Whatever level he will allow it, I will have it. Whatever kind of relationship he wants to have, we will have." Another related that her trans son had told her, "If you can't be supportive, you won't be seeing too much of me." All mothers had to manage secrecy, concealment, and isolation, weather transgender insults, and sustain chronic fear of harm to their child. Most, although still grieving the loss of a daughter, became engaged in transgender activism trying to make a better world, not only for their own child, but for all trans people—empowering and transforming themselves in the process.

However, although challenging cultural beliefs on biological sex and gender identity, there was no questioning of patriarchal ideologies that demanded maternal effacement and selflessness at the expense of one's own experience and feelings. Neither was there critique of childrearing values that emphasized maternal attunement, gratification, and unconditional love—producing children who assumed understanding and support, no matter what their life choices—including sex reassignment. Mothers continued to place the needs of children before their own and although the advent of the 21st century expanded the terrain of maternal agency and activism to transgender rights, "super mothering" remained the norm and continues to prevail.

NOTES

1. Aaron Devor (2004) has formulated a fourteen-stage model of transsexual or transgender identity formation in which disclosure tends to take place just before or soon after the transition to male has begun.
2. Gianna Israel (2005) has noted that transition brings about reexamination and exploration of sexual identity.

WORKS CITED

Alwin, Duane. 1990. Cohort replacement and changes in parental socialization values. *Journal of Marriage and the Family* 52:347–360.

Bernstein, Barbara. 1990. Attitudes and issues of parents of gay men and lesbians: Implications for therapy. *Journal of Gay and Lesbian Psychotherapy* 1:37–53.

Boenke, Mary, ed. 1999. *Transforming Families: Real Stories About Transgender Loved Ones*. Imperial Beach, Calif.: Trook.

Brown, Mildred, and Chloe Rounsley. 1996. *True Selves: Understanding Transsexualism for Families, Friends, Coworkers, and Helping Professionals*. San Francisco: Jossey-Bass.

Chodorow, Nancy. 1978. *The Reproduction of Mothering: Psychoanalysis and the Sociology of Gender*. Berkeley: University of California Press.

Cromwell, Jason. 1999. *Transmen and FTMs: Identities, Bodies, Genders, and Sexualities*. Champaign: University of Illinois Press.

Devor, Aaron. 2004. Witnessing and mirroring: A fourteen-stage model of transsexual identity formation. *Journal of Gay and Lesbian Psychotherapy* 8:41–67.

Devor, Holly. 1997. *FTM: Female-to-Male Transsexuals in Society*. Bloomington: University of Indiana Press.

Drescher, Jack. 2002. An interview with GenderPAC's Riki Wilchins. *Journal of Gay and Lesbian Psychotherapy* 21:87–97.

Emerson, Shirley, and Carole Rosenfeld. 1996. Stages of adjustment in family members of transgender individuals. *Journal of Family Psychotherapy* 7:1–11.

Hansbury, Griffin. 2004. Transgender subjectivities: A clinician's guide. *Journal of Gay and Lesbian Psychotherapy* 8:7–18.

Hirsch, Marianne. 1989. *The Mother/Daughter Plot: Narrative, Psychoanalysis, Feminism*. Bloomington: Indiana University Press.

Irwin, Patrick, and Norman Thompson. 1977. Acceptance of the rights of homosexuals: A social profile. *Journal of Homosexuality* 3:107–121.

Israel, Gianna. 2005. Translove: Transgender persons and their families. *Journal of GLBT Family Studies* 1:53–67.

Jennings, Kevin. 2002. *Always My Child: A Parent's Guide to Understanding Your Gay, Lesbian, Bisexual, Transgender, or Questioning Son or Daughter*. New York: Fireside Press.

Lev, Arlene Ishtar. 2004. *Transgender Emergence: Therapeutic Guidelines for Working with Gender-Variant People and Their Families*. New York: Haworth.

Miller, Jean Baker. 1984. The development of women's sense of self. Work in Progress series. Stone Center for Developmental Services and Studies. Wellesley, Mass.: Wellesley College. http://www.wcwonline.org/pdf/previews/preview_12sc.pdf.

Pearlman, Sarah. 1992. Heterosexual mothers/lesbian daughters: Parallels and similarities. *Journal of Feminist Family Therapy* 4:1–26.

Rich, Adrienne. 1976. *Of Women Born: Motherhood as Experience and Institution.* New York: Norton.

Savin-Williams, Ritch. 1998. The disclosure to families of same-sex attractions by lesbian, gay, and bisexual youths. *Journal of Research on Adolescence* 8:49–68.

Vitello, Paul. 2006. The trouble when Jane becomes Jack. *New York Times*, Aug. 20, sec. 9, 1, 6.

Werum, Regina, and Bill Winders. 2001. Who's in and who's out: State fragmentation and the struggle over gay rights, 1974–1999. *Social Problems* 48:386–410.

Queer Parenting in the New Millennium

FIVE

Resisting Normal

RACHEL EPSTEIN

Almost fifteen years ago I wrote an article (Epstein 1996) suggesting the importance of paying attention to the complexity of the experience of lesbian parents and their children, in an effort to avoid creating a community "blueprint" of how our families should be or look. More and more "out" lesbians were choosing to bring children into their lives, and I was suggesting that paying close attention to our daily experiences, to our emotions, to our desires, and to the ways our beliefs and life experiences about biology, blood, parenting, family, and childhood impact the choices we make about how and with whom we parent—might help us avoid a "one-size-fits-all" approach to the whole enterprise.

Now, ten years into the new millennium, I'm taking the opportunity to reflect back on close to twenty years of education, activism, and organizing related to queer parenting, and, wouldn't you know it, raising similar questions. In doing so, I want to do two things. I want first to acknowledge and celebrate the changes

Thank you to Chris Veldhoven, Hershel Russell, and Lois Fine for commenting on a draft of this article. The opinions expressed in this article are those of the author and not necessarily those of the Sherbourne Health Centre.

that have taken place over the past twenty years in relation to queer parenting; and second to raise some questions about the current political context within which we are parenting—in particular, the debate about and realities of same-sex marriage. I worry that the struggle for and realities of same-sex marriage might be creating another "blueprint," a framework that privileges one way of parenting over another, that normalizes one way of parenting and marginalizes others. I worry that the pressures we experience as queer parents, pressures that are sometimes punitive, severe, and damaging to us and to our children, might lead us to embrace an institution that ultimately does not work in our best interests—a social institution that is about the regulation of sexuality, ours and that of other sex and gender outsiders. I want to urge that we not collude with the disavowal of sexuality from our identities as queers and particularly, from our identities as queer parents—hard as this may be sometimes in our desire to keep our children safe and well protected. Really I'm raising questions about how we maintain and build on the radical history we have inherited as sex and gender outsiders, as lesbians, as gay men, as bisexuals, as transsexual and transgender people, as queer people, . . . and as parents.

As queer parents we have historically faced many difficulties—many of us gave up our sense of entitlement to have children when we "came out"; gays and lesbians have had children taken away from them; some of us have not been able to be out to our children; some of us have been disowned by our families when we had children. And our children continue to feel the social stigma attached to our sexualities. They suffer because of the ways our identities have been squashed, shamed, and delegitimized. And of course we want to love and protect them, while teaching them to face challenges and fears with steadiness. So what does it mean, in the context of parenting, in the context of loving and aching to protect our children as much as we possibly can, to question the ways that the pressures we experience can lead us to desire "normal." "Normal," I would suggest, is not always better—for us, or for our children.

For me personally, the birth of my daughter in 1992, at a home birth surrounded by a dozen close friends/family, was a high point in my life. Since then I have been privileged, through my personal and work life, to have been closely connected to hundreds of queer parents, prospective parents, and families. I have had the benefits of an insider's view into many of the joys and challenges, dynamics and dilemmas of queer family life.

I am currently the proud co-parent of a fabulous eighteen-year-old girl, and stepparent to an equally fabulous boy who just turned twenty-five. In 1992 I began doing research on lesbian parenting, and my research and writing followed my life. When I was pregnant I interviewed lesbian couples about the day-to-day organization of their lives (2003); when someone close to me was denied access to a child as a nonbiological parent, I interviewed nonbiological lesbian parents (1995); when my daughter reached school age, I talked to other queer parents about their experiences with schools (1998; 2004); my long-standing admiration of butches led me to write about butch-identified biological mothers (2002). I was recently fortunate to be the editor of a wide-ranging and diverse collection of writings on queer parenting (2009). My other hat, as a mediator of interpersonal conflict, led to mediations and planning sessions with queer parents and prospective parents, attempting to work out the inevitable issues that arise whenever two or more people try to do anything together, let alone something as complex as parenting. The aim here is/was to keep people out of messy, painful, and expensive court battles, which often result in grief and loss for all. In 1997 Kathie Duncan and I began teaching the Dykes Planning Tykes (DPT) course in Toronto—a twelve-week course for queer woman considering parenthood. The course ran first through the Centre for Lesbian and Gay Studies' Queer Exchange, then through the Toronto Women's Bookstore, and in recent years is jointly sponsored by the 519 Community Centre and the Sherbourne Health Centre. DPT has also spawned similar courses for gay/bisexual/queer men (Daddies & Papas 2B [DP2B]), designed and facilitated by Chris Veldhoven, and for FTM (female-to-male) men (Trans Fathers 2B), designed and facilitated by Robin Fern. Through these courses I have watched hundred of babies be born or adopted into and grow up in queer families.

In 2001 I was privileged to be hired as coordinator of the LGBTQ Parenting Network, possibly the first program in Canada to receive funding to provide resources, information, and support to lesbian, gay, bisexual, transsexual, and transgender parents, prospective parents, and their families. The program began at Family Service Toronto and in 2005 moved to the Sherbourne Health Centre. Through the Parenting Network, we have developed information brochures, posters, and newsletters, and provided training workshops and presentations to schools, childcare centers, healthcare professionals, fertility clinics, family resource programs, and other professionals seeking to make their programs more accessible to LGBTQ families. We hold social and recreational events and forums, often in partnership with the 519 Community Centre, where queer parents and prospective parents meet informally to talk about things like schools, reproductive technologies, dynamics between biological and nonbiological parents, families of origin, interracial families, single parenting, co-parenting, step-parenting, racism, adoption, and issues for trans parents—both those who transitioned after having children and those who are considering parenthood post-transition. We coordinate support groups for single mothers, adoptive parents, trans parents, queer parents of color, and LGBTQ people dealing with issues of in/fertility and recently acted as consultants to Health Canada on the specific concerns of LGBTQ communities in relation to the 2004 Assisted Human Reproduction Act.

The Parenting Network also participates in creating a growing body of research on queer parenting in Canada. In collaboration with Dr. Lori Ross, a Toronto-based health researcher, we have investigated the experiences of queer women, pre- and post-conception, the state of LGBTQ adoption in Ontario, and the experiences, service, and research needs of African-Caribbean queer parents. We coordinated the Gay/Bi/Queer Fathers research cluster as part of the Father Involvement Research Alliance's SSHRC-funded national project, and, with funding from the Wellesley Central Health Corporation, explored the impact of the same-sex marriage debate on the school experiences of children and youth with LGBTQ parents.

The Parenting Network's work has been made possible through ongoing funding. Often unrecognized and less visible, there are many unfunded, grassroots LGBTQ parenting groups across the country. In large cities, small towns, and rural communities queer parents are connecting with one another to exchange information and support. In Montreal, the Lesbian Mothers' Association (LMA) has more than nine hundred members and has, on an entirely volunteer basis, provided major leadership in some crucial legislative and policy struggles, as well as providing social and practical support to its members. The LMA recently merged with the Papa-Daddy Group to form the Coalition des familles homoparentales (CFH) and for the first time has received some funding to support their work.

In Canada there is much to celebrate on the queer parenting front. Historically, in gay and lesbian communities, "coming out," identifying as other than heterosexual, recognizing one's desire for same-sex relationships, for many meant abandoning the prospect of having children. How many parents grieved when their children "came out" that there would be no grandchildren? How many gay- and lesbian-identified people themselves put the thought of raising children out of their consciousness as part of embracing newfound gay communities? While we have to take care not to assume that all queer or gender-variant people want to have children, or even want to think about it, developments over the past twenty years have made having children more possible as an option for more people. In both DPT and DP2B we spend time exploring the entitlement, or lack of it, that people feel in their desire to be parents. And that sense of entitlement is changing. Lesbians have been having children within queer identifications for more than twenty years. We are in the midst of what some refer to as a lesbian baby boom or, depending on gender, a gayby boom. Our courses are packed—people sometimes have to wait years to get in. For many the question has become not "*Can* I have kids?," but "*When* do I have kids?" More and more gay/bi/queer men are choosing to bring children into their lives—through co-parenting, fostering, adoption, and surrogacy. Trans people are becoming more organized and visible and are advocating for their rights, including the right to parent.

And, of course, some of the legislative and policy changes of the last decade have made queer parenting easier. It is now possible for lesbian/gay couples to adopt as couples through the Children's Aid Society (CAS). In Toronto the CAS has done much internal educational work to make lesbian/gay adoption more possible, and they regularly place children with lesbian/gay couples and singles. They are also taking steps to process applications by trans-identified prospective adoptive parents. Non-bio parents have access to second-parent adoptions and can be legally recognized as parents in most provinces and territories, with the exceptions of Nunavut and Prince Edward Island; and, with the exceptions of Saskatchewan, Prince Edward Island, Nunavut, and the Northwest Territories, two women using anonymous sperm donation to conceive can have both people registered as legal parents from the time of a child's birth. A court in London, Ontario, recognized three people (a lesbian couple and the man they are parenting with) as legal parents of a child. While there was some initial fear that the 2004 Assisted Human Reproduction Act seems to criminalize home insemination (we have since been repeatedly assured that this is not the government's intent), and there remain some practices related to reproductive technologies that discriminate against LGBTQ people, for the most part the law is getting better for queer parents in Canada.

However, things are not all easy. In 2001 a Canadian Leger poll (CLGRO Newsclippings on Adoption and Parenting Issues) indicated that more than 50 percent of the Canadian population felt that gays and lesbians should be denied the right to parent. This is a profound statistic, and one that has changed only slightly with time. We continue to parent in a social climate in which close to half the people around us believe we should not be allowed to be parents. And we are not far historically from the 1970s and 1980s, when women were at risk of losing custody of their children in court decisions that found lesbians to be unfit mothers (Pollack 1990). These decisions were based on a number of assumptions/myths about lesbian mothers—myths that are directed by extension, and often more vehemently, to gay fathers. These "myths" have demonized lesbian/gay parents in popular culture and are deeply embedded in mainstream consciousness. We, and now many heterosexual friends, colleagues, and professional associations, have spent decades rebutting them. They include assumptions that: lesbian/gay sexuality is immoral and that lesbians/gay men are promiscuous, sexually maladjusted, and likely to sexually harm children; children raised in lesbian/gay homes will develop inappropriate gender identities and gender role concepts and behaviors, and may themselves develop a homosexual orientation; healthy child development requires the presence and availability of biological fathers as "male role models" (or in the case of gay fathers, "female role models"); and children raised in lesbian/gay homes will be socially stigmatized and subjected to ridicule, teasing, and hostility from their peers.

Understandably, given the prejudicial legal climate, especially in the United States, much of the early research on lesbian parenting focused on rebutting these arguments. Women were at risk of losing their children; the stakes were high. There are now countless studies that "prove" that sexual abusers are not, for the most part, lesbians or gay men but are, in fact, heterosexually identified; that there is virtually no difference between the children of lesbians and those of heterosexual mothers with regard to gender identity, gender role behavior, psychopathology, or homosexual orientation; that lesbians mothers are actually more concerned than heterosexual single mothers with providing opportunities for their children to develop ongoing relationships with men (not to mention the more complex arguments that have been developed about the gendered assumptions embedded in "male/female role model" arguments); and that it is a dangerous, bigotry-fueled argument to suggest that *any* group that experiences systemic oppression should not have children because of the potential emotional damage to the children.

Every workshop I facilitate on issues of lesbian/gay parenting includes an exercise looking at these "myths" or "commonly held ideas" about queer parenting—and brainstorming about how to talk back to them. I've noticed, though, that the "commonly held idea" we tend to address least is the one that says "lesbians and gay men are oversexed, all they do is think about sex, talk about sex, write about sex, have sex—how could they ever be decent parents?" Lesbians and gay men who plan to parent get asked, in all seriousness, "But will you have sex in front of the children?"

How do we respond to these assumptions about our supposed obsessions with sex in the context of the questioning of our parenting abilities? I think one way we have responded is by denying or minimizing the sexual aspects of our lives in order to be seen as respectable, responsible, "good" parents. This is not surprising, given the same-sex marriage debate, which inundated us with media messages about the dangers to children of growing up with lesbian/gay parents. "First comes love, then comes marriage, then comes the gays and lesbians with baby carriages" goes the argument. Marriage and procreation become inextricably linked in the debate and the procreation aspect marked, by those who oppose same-sex unions, as a central problem. It's no wonder we feel pushed toward desiring respectability . . . our relationships, our families, our rights and desires to have children are being diminished every day in a very public national debate. So we see things like the article published in the *Globe and Mail* (Philp 2003) which featured a beautiful front-page photograph of a gay man holding a newborn baby. The article, a very sympathetic portrayal of gay men becoming fathers, describes some of the men who are considering parenthood:

> None fits the stereotype of the flamboyant drag queen or promiscuous, muscle-bound, bar-hopping gadabout . . . the pair are the image of domestic bliss, as traditional as a couple can be . . . they met, fell in love, proposed marriage on bended knee, wear wedding bands on their fingers, bought a house on a leafy street in west-end Toronto and now want to settle down and start a family. "I can't tell you how normal we are. Not all gay people are on Church St. wearing leather in the parade. We're in bed at 10:15 after watching the news, and we go right to sleep. We do everything that other couples do. So why wouldn't we want to have a child?"

While I understand the desire for respectability, for acceptance by the mainstream, and for the space to be left alone to live our lives, this quote scares and unsettles me. It scares me because I see the desire to be "normal" taking the form of a distancing from and a pathologizing of significant parts of queer communities. And it unsettles me because I see us desexualizing ourselves in order to be accepted.

Michael Warner, in his book *The Trouble with Normal* (1999), argues persuasively that the mainstream gay/lesbian movement, in response to the historic shame and stigma attached to gay/lesbian sexualities, has moved away from the politics of shame to a desexualized identity politics that claims lesbian/gay identities but disavows the sexuality that goes with them. In an attempt to create a "respectable, dignified gay community," there is a striving to be seen as "normal." The seeking of "normal," however, means there has to be the "pathological," the "not normal." The result is a distancing from and a pathologizing of non-normative sexualities—queer or straight. Instead of aiming to create a broad-based movement that claims diverse non-normative sexualities, the mainstream gay/ lesbian movement has adopted a stance of "we're gay, but this has nothing to do with sex" (1999:40) and the movement becomes desexualized, with sex and sexuality disavowed as "irrelevant."

The above quote from the *Globe and Mail* is illustrative of this framework. The author distances the gay fathers she is talking about from the "drag queens, the promiscuous, muscle-bound, bar-hopping gadabouts," and the gay fathers themselves distance themselves from those who "wear leather in the parade on Church St." These guys are in bed at 10:15 and "go right to sleep." Well, of course any parent knows that falling asleep at 10:15 is not unusual, nor is a lack of sex. What's troubling is the striving to be normal and the distancing from the "less desirable" segments of the gay community. The struggle for same-sex marriage institutionalizes this division between the "normal" and the "not so normal." Marriage sanctifies some relationships at the expense of others, and offers protection for sexuality that occurs within marriage, while invalidating and stigmatizing sexuality that takes place outside of marriage. With marriage we run the risk of creating "good gays" and "bad queers" (Warner 1999:114).

Neither does the marriage framework recognize the complex web of intimacies queer people often create. As Warner puts it:

> Queers have an astonishing range of intimacies . . . most have no labels, most receive no public recognition . . . many of these relations are difficult because the rules have to be invented as we go along . . . they can be complex and bewildering, in a way that arouses fear among many gay people and tremendous resistance and resentment from many straight people. Who among us would give them up?   (1999:116)

Straight culture, on the other hand, tells us "that people should be either husbands or wives or (nonsexual) friends. Marriage marks that line." Perhaps, suggests Warner, straight culture has something to learn from the "welter of intimacies" queer people create "outside of the framework of professions and institutions and ordinary social obligations" (116).

The idea that straight culture has something to learn from queers holds currency in recent debates about queer parenting as well. University of California sociologists Stacey and Biblarz published an article in 2001 in which they attempted to move away from the heterosexist "no difference, same as, just as normal as" arguments to look at what might actually be different or unique for children growing up with lesbian/gay parents. The differences they highlighted in children growing up with lesbian/gay parents included: less traditional gender-typing, higher self-esteem and better mental health, more egalitarian, shared parenting, more closeness and communication between parents and children, and increased awareness and empathy in children toward social diversity. These differences are interesting and show, as Stacey and Biblarz say, that "planned lesbigay parenthood offers a veritable 'social laboratory' of family diversity" (179). What is most significant, in my opinion, is the shift from the defensive position of proving that our families and our children meet some arbitrary and nonexistent heterosexual norm to the acknowledgment that there may be some possibilities created for children who grow up in queer households that are not organized around profoundly historically entrenched gender dynamics, and where there is an openness to sexual, and other kinds of, diversity. We should celebrate that our children are aware of and empathic toward social diversity—celebrate and expand this openness and create an environment in which they truly know that they can explore their own sexualities.

What I am suggesting is not simple. As queers we continue to be shamed and stigmatized as a result of our refusal to adhere to the sexual and familial norms of straight culture, and there is pressure on us always to conform, to have our children conform, and, particularly, to deny our sexuality in order to conform. The lesbian parent quoted below poignantly summarizes how we sometime experience these tensions and inner conflicts.

> We're clearly not aiming to fit in and we have this joint role of influencing our children with the message, "Be who you are." There is such pressure on us, as dykes, as weirdoes, as outsiders, and you know that anything that goes wrong with these children, somebody's going to blame it on your sexuality and how you're bringing them up. So that puts pressure on you to bring them up as perfectly fitting-in children. And you have to stop all the time and say, "No, no, no, no, no." And we're into pretty wild and raunchy sex and leather outfits and all this stuff and how do you go into the world and balance all this? For a while I decided "Okay, I'm going to give up that sex stuff, I'm going to become a nice safe academician, couldn't I just get a Ph.D. and I'd be a famous smarty cakes, right." And then I go, "No, no, this is the devil talking, you're about to make a really sick deal here, so put back on that leather jacket, get out to that dance, you know and let the kids see all of that." . . . I want them to do well academically, that's their survival . . . but they've got to be them in that, and wear whatever they want to wear, talk whatever way they want to talk, and be sure of who they are inside themselves. That's probably one of the hardest struggles. (BW 1992)

How will our children be sure of who they are inside themselves if they experience us denying who we are? By this I mean *all* of who we are—and by "we" I mean people, queer people, who celebrate the range of existing and the yet-to-come-into-being non-normative sexualities (gay and lesbian sexualities among them), people who are trying to, as Warner puts it, "bring about a time when the loathing for queer sex, or gender variance, will no longer distort people's lives" (1999:39). If what we are seeking is an end to the loathing of queer sex and gender variance, a strategy that disavows queer sexuality in favor of an institution that bestows rights and privileges on those who enters its doors, and denies rights and privileges to those outside the doors—those on the fringes, those who choose other ways to live their lives, those who define their sexual and intimate relationships outside of marriage, those who do not choose or prefer to live in a couple—seems a poor choice of strategy.

And yet I am deeply moved and fairly sure to cry at every queer wedding I attend. Why are we so touched by these ceremonies that are about an institution we do not necessarily endorse? Perhaps because we so crave and desire recognition for our intimate and sexual relationships and for our families. We have been so othered, so hated, so rendered invisible—we are hungry to be seen and recognized, made knowable and our lives possible. And there are material consequences to our lack of state recognition. As Judith Butler puts it:

> It means that when you arrive at the hospital to see your lover, you may not. It means that when your lover falls into a coma, you may not assume certain executorial rights. It means that when your lover dies, you may not be permitted to receive the body. It means that when your child is left with you, the nonbiological parent, you may not be able to counter the claims of biological relatives in court and may lose custody, and even access. It means you may not be able to provide health care benefits for one another. These are all very significant forms of disenfranchisement, which are made all the worse by the personal effacements that occur in daily life and invariably take a toll on a relationship. The sense of delegitimation can make it harder to sustain a bond, a bond that is not real anyway, a bond that does not "exist," that never had a chance to exist, that was never meant to exist. If you're not real, it can be hard to sustain yourselves over time. Here is where the absence of state legitimation can emerge within the psyche as a pervasive, if not fatal, sense of self-doubt. (2004:114)

It is certainly not this sense of self-doubt, this sense of not being "real," that we want to pass on to our children.

Butler goes on to raise questions similar to Warner's. Do we allow the state to monopolize the resources of recognition? Are there other ways of feeling possible, recognizable, even real? The way the marriage debate is being framed means that our striving "to become recognizable requires that we subscribe to a practice that delegitimates those sexual lives structured outside the bonds of marriage and the presumptions of monogamy . . . What would it mean," argues Butler, "to exclude from the field of potential legitimation those who are outside of marriage, those who live nonmonogamously, those who live alone, those who are in whatever arrangements they are in that are not the marriage form? . . . Such a practice is difficult, if not impossible, to reconcile with a radically democratic, sexually progressive movement" (2004:115).

The question then becomes: how do we both acknowledge our desire for intelligibility and recognition *and* maintain a critical and transformative relation to the norms that govern what is intelligible (Butler 2004:117)? In other words, how do we struggle for recognition of our relationships and families while struggling at the same time to transform what is recognizable? Warner poses the same challenge when he suggests that rather than aiming to win acceptance by the dominant culture, we aim to change the self-understanding of that culture—to broaden the range of sexualities and family forms that are recognizable and legitimate.

Suzanna Danuta Walters (2001), in a thoughtful essay on same-sex marriage, concurs with Butler and Warner that marriage "reinforces structural inequalities within families, . . . privileging state-regulated, long-term pairing over other forms of intimacy and connectedness." She raises questions about the conflation of *partnering* (a presumably sexual relationship between consenting adults) and *parenting* (a relationship of profound structural dependency). Citing the work of feminist legal theorist Martha Fineman (1995), she suggests that in order to create a less gendered social order, a distinction should be made between peer relations (partnering) and relations of dependency (parenting). This could have significant implications for the structuring of social policy: "Perhaps gays would do better to support legislation that removes marriage as a legal and economic category, while at the same time creating frameworks to socially, legally, and economically support relations of real dependency: parent to child, caretaker to caretakee, able-bodied to the disabled they care for, etc." (Walters 2001: 356n9).

With the victory of same-sex marriage in Canada and the ongoing struggles being waged in the United States it seems even more important that we maintain the distinction between partnering and parenting. The right conflates marriage and procreation—we don't have to. In fact we have a special talent for not confusing love and procreation, as it doesn't usually work that way for us—we rarely wake up pregnant. One of our greatest contributions has been the ways we create non-normative families. As Kath Weston (1991) has documented, many queer people have formed "families of choice," sometimes due to hostility and/or rejection from our families of origin. In our desires to have children we have made use of reproductive technologies, we have asked each other for sperm donations, and we have found people with whom we are not romantically or sexually involved but with whom we choose to parent. While many of us parent in couples, we also create families that have three parents, four parents, that are webs of complex biological and social relations, that challenge and expand notions of what it means to be a "parent," and what blood, biology, and family ties are all about. I don't think we want to allow this expansion of the meaning of family to be contracted by a yearning to be normal.

So, how do we resist "normal"? We can support legal struggles that recognize non-normative families, such as AA/BB/CC, the case in London, Ontario, that achieved recognition for three parents—a lesbian couple and the man they co-parent with. We can support other cases that work to extend parenting rights, separate from the rights of the couple—for example, the expansion of birth registration polices that are not based on marital or couple status, but on the social relationships of parenting. We can continue to work with adoption workers, fertility clinics, government agencies, health and social service providers, and schools and day cares to help them better understand our families—the meanings our communities ascribe to "chosen family," the fact that sometimes we come together in more than twos to parent, that there are lots of ways to think about the question of male or female "role models," and that there are bisexual and trans people who are and would make good parents.

And we can resist the politics of shame when it comes to our children. As queer parents we already know how important it is to not pass on shame to our children. Their best protection from the homophobia/transphobia and hatred they may experience at school and elsewhere is a lack of shame, a deep sense that they are just fine, that their families and their parents are just fine, and that if anybody disapproves, it's their problem. As queer people we carry shame with us in complex ways. As parents we are forced to notice the places we get caught, the places our shame sneaks up on us and makes us not want to tell people about our families, about how we brought children into our lives, about our relationships and our sexuality. Of course, most of the time it's none of their business, and we also want to teach our children to be strategic about where and with whom one chooses to "come out." But as parents we can't control when our children will come out for us, when we're picking berries, on an airplane, in the supermarket. We have to always be prepared to acknowledge our relationships and our families . . . otherwise our children learn that there is something not okay about us, and therefore not okay about them.

So let's extend what we already know about the destructiveness of shame, in order to combat the politics of sexual shame. Let's make sure our kids do not carry sexual shame, but rather that they learn from us that sexuality and gender are varied, fluid, complex, messy, exciting, scary, fun, and always changing. And sometimes this means holding our breath. I hold my breath when my daughter talks about her two moms as we're picking berries, or when I tell my hundred-year-old aunt that there is no father, just a sperm donor, or when I tell the Holocaust survivor we are interviewing in preparation for my daughter's bat mitzvah that she has two moms and see the look of miscomprehension? disapproval? cross her face. In the same way, I hold my breath when the conversation at the seder table turns to the joys of polyamory and my daughter and her teenage friends get fascinated; I hold my breath at Pride Day when my daughter and her friend stand, open-mouthed, taking in the nudity and the kinky sex and the myriad of ways people are celebrating themselves; I hold my breath when my close friend who was present at my daughter's birth and whom my daughter has always known as a woman, begins to grow facial hair and identify as trans, or when I realize that my children are witness to my own romantic/sexual life that doesn't follow a traditional trajectory.

I hold my breath and then I let it out because I realize our children can handle more than we think and because these are the people I love, the communities I love, and the communities and people and spaces that have allowed, and continue to allow, me to explore my own sexuality and to question traditional ways of doing family and relationships. I want my children to have the room to develop their sexualities, their families, their communities. I don't want them to live with a prescribed notion of what it means to be a sexual, alive, loving person. We don't need to present our children with a unified, singular, and static world. I recall my daughter and her friend asking me detailed questions about birth control and sexually transmitted diseases while we're cross-country skiing; or my daughter asking me to come to her school to talk about the "B" and the "T" from LGBT, because "they know about lesbian and gay but they need to know about bi and trans," or her asking me very matter-of-factly about which pronoun she should use to refer to a trans friend, or her telling me about the lingerie she plans to buy when she's older. I recall these moments and realize that our children can handle complexity and diversity when it comes to sexuality and gender.

My intention is not to suggest that it's all easy. It's not. Parenting isn't easy, and parenting with the added bonus of queerness is not always easy either. There are lots of difficult questions we have to answer, conversations to be had, and lots we don't know. But let's not fall into the trap of clinging to "normal" for the sake of our children. We owe them more than that.

Postscript: I asked my daughter to read and okay the above paragraphs about the incidents that cause me to hold my breath. Her response: "Do you mean we think those things are weird? Well, I don't."

WORKS CITED

Butler, J. 2004. *Undoing Gender.* New York: Routledge.

BW, personal interview, January 7, 1992.

Epstein, R. 1995. Flommies, imas, and mommies: Exploring the experience of nonbiological lesbian parents. Paper presented at the Canadian Sociology and Anthropology Association Learneds, Montreal, Quebec.

——. 1996. Lesbian parenting: Grounding our theory. *Canadian Women's Studies* 16.2.

——. 1998. Parent night will never be the same: Lesbian families challenge the public school system. *Our Schools/Our Selves* 9.1:60–64.

——. 2002. Butches with babies: Reconfiguring gender and motherhood. *Journal of Lesbian Studies* 6.2:41–57.

——. 2003. Lesbian families. In *Voices: Essays on Canadian Families*, ed. M. Lynn, 107–130. Toronto: Nelson Canada.

——. 2004. Our Kids in the Hall: Lesbian families negotiate the public school system. In *Mother Outlaws: Theories and Practices of Empowered Mothering*, ed. A. O'Reilly, 131–144. Toronto: Women's Press.

——, ed. 2009. *Who's Your Daddy? And Other Writings on Queer Parenting*. Toronto: Sumach Press.

Fineman, M. 1995. *The Neutered Mother, the Sexual Family, and Other Twentieth-Century Tragedies.* New York: Routledge.

Philp, M. 2003. Gayby boom. *Globe and Mail,* May 3, F4–F5.

Pollack, N. 1990. Lesbian parents: Claiming our visibility. In *Woman-Defined Motherhood*, ed. S. P. Knowles and E. Cole, 181–194. New York: Haworth.

Stacey, J., and T. J. Biblarz. 2001. (How) does the sexual orientation of parents matter? *American Sociological Review* 66:159–183.

Walters, S .D. 2001. Take my domestic partner, please: Gays and marriage in the era of the visible. In *Queer Families, Queer Politics: Challenging Culture and the State*, ed. M. Bernstein and R. Reimann, 338–357. New York: Columbia University Press.

Warner, M. 1999. *The Trouble with Normal: Sex, Politics, and the Ethics of Queer Life.* New York: Free Press.

Weston, K. 1991. *Families We Choose: Lesbian, Gays, Kinship.* New York: Columbia University Press.

Contemporary Mothering Practices in the Context of HIV and AIDS

SIX

A South African Case

THENJIWE MAGWAZA

In a family setting, research, literature, and social service providers mostly concentrate on adults living with the HIV virus or on AIDS-orphaned children. Although there is a growing literature on other family experiences, there has been minimal reporting on parenting children orphaned by the disease. Furthermore, only limited literature is available on the practices and experiences of mothering within this context. Elizabeth Thompson's (2000) work discusses the experiences and responses of mothers in AIDS affected families. Its focus is, however, on adult children, and the paper is drawn from a U.S.-based study. Another work on HIV/AIDS parenting is that of Kellie Stajduhar (1998). It makes reference to mothers' experiences in a study on family caregiving situations. However, there has been a paucity of similar research done on the African continent. One should note with appreciation a series of weekly reports by a South African Sunday newspaper, the *Sunday Times*. These reports, entitled "I know someone who has died of AIDS," present accounts of how families and close friends have dealt with the death of mostly young people affected by the AIDS scourge. None of the reports, however, has specifically focused on mothers.

Anyone who is infected by HIV and dies from AIDS has a host of family members, relatives, guardians, friends, and caregivers. Not only is the life of the infected individual challenged, but an entire circle of people are also profoundly affected. They, like the main victim, also need care, support, and a sympathetic audience able to listen to their tales of woe and despair (Macklin 1989:81–128). The family members' perspectives are necessary to get a holistic picture of the impact and effect of AIDS (Tiblier, Walker, and Rolland 1989; Thompson 2000). Given that it is women who are often expected to provide most support and care to AIDS victims and HIV-positive people, this paper presents one man and five women caregivers. Traditional African cultural notion and practice stipulate that first the mothers, then other women more than any other family member, ought to provide care. In turn, the term *mother*, irrespective of its traditional dictionary definition, has become associated with caregiving. It is important to understand how in particular mothers deal with the challenges of looking after children orphaned by AIDS.

The case study under discussion, taking its cues from the community under observation, refers to all six caregivers, including the male participant, as "mothers." Specifically, this paper aims to:

- Examine the construction and meaning of the term *mother*;
- Report on the questions that the extended motherhood concept and practice pose to an African traditional understanding in the twenty-first century;
- Present coping and survival strategies used by the "mothers" in their mothering practices.

BACKGROUND OF THE STUDY AND SAMPLE

This chapter emerges from a three-year-long study[1] (2004–2006) that focused on the aftermath of HIV/AIDS in a community of the region of KwaZulu-Natal, South Africa. The region is geographically positioned north of Durban, one of the major economic centers of the country. The location of the study is Inanda, a Bhambayi shack-dwelling and informal settlement.

The aim of the three-year study was to examine and record ways in which households cope under HIV/AIDS circumstances. Out of this study I observed that the concept "mother" was employed in a manner that challenges the African traditional understanding of the term, thereby forcing a redefinition of the concept. The term applies to a woman, biology, and age variables. I conducted eleven in-depth interviews with mothers or caregivers of children whose parents have either died or are in an advanced AIDS stage. Out of this number, for the purposes of this paper, I focus on six individuals. The other five participants were excluded because their characteristics are similar to those of the six on which I report. All the interviewed mothers were Zulu speakers, one of the main languages of the country. All the mothers were interviewed in Zulu in their own homes. Excerpts from the Zulu transcripts were later translated into English.

Methodology, Theory, and Analysis

A minimum of two sessions of semi-structured interviews, lasting from two to four hours, formed the basis from which the data for this paper were collected. The focus on the mothers' mothering practices and perceptions lasted about seven moths (March–October 2004). Prior to this I had had dealings with all the participants under the auspices of the project[2] on the aftermath of the HIV/AIDS scourge. Therefore, gaining their trust and confidence for the purpose of this study was not a difficult task. The nature of the interviews allowed the mothers a degree of flexibility both to lead and to define key topics they felt at ease to talk about. All participants gave permission for their information to be used for publication purposes, but without making public their family pictures and names. For this reason the narration employs pseudonyms.

The interviews were not tape-recorded, as there was general unease about "our voices and personal stories being shared with people we do not know." "We do not want our children to be taken to the world!"[3] These are some of the responses I received when I asked to use the participants' identity characteristics. In turn, hand notes were meticulously taken, which later needed to be validated at a second or third meeting with the mothers. Such subsequent meetings were considered crucial for this purpose.

Two ideological foundations inform the analysis of the study: a social constructionist perspective and the African-based indigenous knowledge systems (IKS) perspective. In using the social constructionist perspective, I argue that mothering choices indicate society's expectations of a mother: she is expected to give up everything in the interest of her children, irrespective of her personal beliefs, likes, and preferences. This study found that such personal sacrifice extends to making a decision not to have a sex partner. According to the social constructionist theory, the participants (mothers) also have a role to play in what happens in their lives. "A constructionist perspective maintains that individuals are meaning constructors and the significance of those meanings must be understood as contextually embedded" (Schwandt, as quoted in Thompson 2000:156). Despite the fact that five of the six mothers in the study did not give birth to the children they look after, they term their role as mothers and call themselves mothers, an indication that the practice of motherhood in Africa is changing in the twenty-first century. The activities of the mothers—be they a biological mother, a grandmother, a great-grandmother, a male guardian, or an institutional foster mother—demonstrate the special significance each mother attaches to his or her role.

The indigenous knowledge systems perspective, especially under the principles and philosophy of *ubuntu*[4] (humanity), was also used to conceptually analyze the collected data. All mothers cite the act of giving their life and energy to the task of mothering as an expression of holistic caring. This is a kind of caring that embodies care for the health, emotions, and general well-being of a person, a fundamental concept of the principle of *ubuntu*.

Besides the use of the social constructionist and *ubuntu* framework, grounded theory qualitative methods were employed for analytical purposes. In particular it is the underpinnings of Glaser and Anselm's (1967) grounded theory principles, which were later expanded by Strauss and Corbin (1994), that were employed for this purpose. The techniques of this theory are essential in knowledge production and exploratory studies. I regard this study as falling within the ambits of such studies. The theory maintains that research focus should be on the participants' main problems and the manner in which they try to solve them, rather than on preformed hypotheses. At the center of this approach is the act of "being sensitive," that is, being acutely aware of the interviewees' perceptions and choices. Glaser asserts that this method allows a researcher the liberty to discover what does go on during a research process, rather than assume what should be going on. For the purpose of this study, the qualitative holistic approach of the grounded theory was valuable in understanding and explaining the experiences of the mothers. Therefore, the details of information that emerged from the collected data inform the conceptual framework, analysis, and discussion of this paper.

Taking into account feminist methods of inquiry (Stanley and Wise 1983; Bowles and Klein 1983) as well, all attempts were made to allow and encourage the participants to lead the discussions. Further, in line with IKS principles and taking a lead from Charmaz (1988), Strauss and Corbin (1990), and Magwaza (2006), the mothers were encouraged to fully participate in the analysis of their own stories. According to these scholars, it is crucial that while data is being collected, it is concurrently analyzed with research participants. This practice ensures that the data analysis process does not start at the end of a data collection process, thereby limiting opportunities of getting research participants fully involved in the analysis process. While the mothers were being interviewed, their opinions on the significance and interpretation of what they were relating were sought. At the end of each interview session I went through the main points of the interview, with the further purpose of identifying the issues that emerged from it.

Guided by grounded theory, I identified and coded the issues into the following topics, which were later closely studied and refined as the research process developed. The main themes were:

- The concept and practice of mothering;
- Coping and survival strategies;
- Perspectives on prevalent cultural worldview and inherent practices.

Although some of the issues raised by the study are different from what Zulu society has for a long time understood, this exploratory study does not claim to represent all mothers facing the challenges of HIV/AIDS. Nonetheless, it makes compelling statements that should not be ignored in contemporary family studies within the context of HIV/AIDS.

Profile of the Six Mothers

This is a brief presentation of the six mothers selected for the purpose of this paper's discussion. Common characteristics are presented first, followed by a further explanation on each participant. The participants' ages range from fifteen to ninety years. All the interviewees are South Africans and Zulu speakers.

The chosen mothers have some points in common: none graduated from high school; each has chosen not to have a sex partner; although no one has a formal employment, all have some constant means of sustaining their families. All the participants care for children between the ages of three and sixteen years. On average, each participant cared for three children and was, at the time of the interviews, the main caregiver. The actual names of the participants are not used in this presentation, as they were promised. I make reference to them either by pseudonyms or by age.

Linda, a fifteen-year-old girl, is the eldest member of her family, which is composed of herself and her three- and eight-year-old brothers. After the death of her mother, when her youngest brother was only eighteen months old, the children briefly stayed with relatives. She says that they were compelled to return to their mother's shack when she was severely beaten following an accusation of stealing some money. Before taking full responsibility for her siblings she considered suicide, but states that "being a mother to the boys now gives me a reason to stay alive." Linda looked at me in disbelief and was rather surprised when I referred to her as a child. During our discussion, she was mostly on her feet ironing her older brother's school uniform. She herself had had to cut short her schooling, mainly to fend for her brothers. She gets some money selling candies and crisps on the street.

Thembi, an HIV-positive woman, is twenty-eight years old. She looks after three girls; two are children of a sister who died of AIDS. They are age eleven and thirteen years, respectively. The third child is a three-year-old whose father has recently passed away. Although she had recovered from returning bouts of sickness at the time of the interviews, her health condition made her decide to quit her last job as a shop assistant. She gets some money to sustain her family by cleaning the houses of two Indian families that live close by. As the money is too little to cover the family expenses, the elder girls sell fried fish during school breaks and after school. Thembi states: "As a patient and a parent with no proper income my life is a challenge. Although our needs outweigh our means, as both father and mother of these children I must be strong for them, especially when I am not well."

Lucky, a volunteer at the local AIDS hospice, is the only male "mother" among the six participants. He is thirty-three years old and cares for two nine-year-old boys, neither of whom is his own. One child is Lucky's nephew; the child's mother was Lucky's sister, who died the week I first met Lucky. The other child, as Lucky puts it, "was acquired under painful circumstances. At her death bed at the hospice, his mother asked me to adopt him. The death of the two mothers for these children compelled me to take them into my care." Although the thirty-three-year-old-man has not formally adopted the children, he receives a grant from government on their behalf. He is adamant about his role as a mother for the children.

Dolly, a forty-six-year-old woman, mothers five children in total. Two are the three-year-old twins of her daughter, who she strongly suspects died of AIDS, as indicated by the symptoms shown a few weeks before her death. The other three children are her own. She treasures the children as a manifestation of God's love for her. She says: "As a child, I always wanted to have many children and hoped to become a kindergarten teacher." To support her family Dolly sells fruit and vegetables on the street.

Zanele is a fifty-two-year-old woman who has been a widow for twenty-four years. Her husband was gunned down by robbers barely four years after they were married. She has decided not to remarry. Zanele and her husband had a hope for a big family. She tells me it would have been her "way of making up for the brothers and sisters I never had and the fact that I spent many years in foster homes." However, their wish did not come to fruition, as they only had two children from the marriage. Without a premeditated plan, her passion for a large family ultimately saw her looking after a minimum of five destitute children each year since her husband's death. This number has now gradually increased as the number of destitute children grows daily because of the HIV and AIDS pandemic. Her home has become a haven, especially for children orphaned by AIDS. At the end of 2006 her home, now regarded as an institution, sheltered sixteen children, and boasted two assistants and a security guard. Although Zanele receives a grant from the state and is supported by a number of donors, she refuses to refer to the children under her care as abandoned or orphaned. She emphasizes that she was called by God to "be a mother to the nine girls and seven boys, the big family I once earnestly pleaded with God to give to me."

Elsie, who never got married, is a great-grandmother to the three children she takes care of. When I asked how she copes, given her old age, she sighed; "I may be a ninety-year-old tired horse today, but all my life I have been looking after children, either my own or the relatives' children, and now my late daughter's. These children (*pointing at her great grandchildren in the room*) are the reason I am still alive." Like Zanele, she speaks of her caregiving as a mothering role. In the years 2003–2005, Elsie says, "three people have died from this house, dying of the new disease—that is my daughter and her two daughters. My great-grandchildren could be my ancestors' strategy of filling some gaps in my life, because if I did not have this family I would be on my own, just by myself." The "new disease" referred to by Elsie is generally understood as the HIV/AIDS scourge. The three people who died were her daughter and granddaughters. The three children Elsie cares for are three, nine, and ten years old, respectively. All live off the meager pension allowance she receives from the state.

THE CHANGING CONCEPT OF "MOTHERHOOD"

The term *mother*, *umama*, sparks a dynamic imagination among people, depending on who is using or receiving the term. In the African context, the term is likely to be associated with a woman, but it also comes with assumptions that the woman has given birth to a child. Due to the awe associated with the life-giving miracle, a mature woman will be respectfully addressed as *Mama*. Other than the biological understanding of the term, its next close use includes: a woman of your mother's age, a mother's sister, a mother-in-law, a church minister's wife. Also, providers of nurturing services, such as caregivers, are referred to as *(o)mama*. Sara Ruddick, in her book *Maternal Thinking* (1989), proposes that the act of mothering should be seen as affording care or nurture to children, a role she argues is independent of biological maternity and can be carried out by both men and women. This assertion has also been recently supported by other scholars, such as Doucet (2006), and constitutes a strong argument in favor of gay couples adopting children.

In an African context such a definition of mothering would cause some stirrings. However, in the case of this study I maintain that the practice of the six reported mothers supports Ruddick's standpoint, as it includes a child as well as a man assuming a mother's role. In most HIV/AIDS literature the fifteen-year-old mother, a participant in the study, would be referred to as a child household head, and not necessarily as a mother. And yet she not only performs the duties expected of a mother, but categorically calls herself a mother. As mentioned earlier, the man participating in this study also regards himself as a mother. I therefore submit that this study exposes the widening concept of mother from an African point of view, and challenges it also in general motherhood research.

The six mothers presented in this study have an attachment to the act of mothering in both a practical and a symbolic sense. For them it is not only the role of providing primary care to the children that is significant, but also the symbolic meaning of being there as a mother for each one of them. Calling themselves "mothers" is a significant reason for pride. All the mothers, in varied ways, regard their status as either the ancestors' or God's way of making up to them for a biological parenting that is either overdue or unlikely to happen.

Five of the six participants defined their mother status in nontraditional terms, thereby altering the limited understanding of motherhood. Fascinatingly, none of the definitions conform to the common African concept of motherhood. The fifteen-year-old and the male participants regarded the children they care for as gifts from God in lieu of the fact that they shall never have children of their own. Sadly, both stated that they are certain not to get involved in any romantic relationship, fearing contracting the human immunodeficiency virus. The twenty-eight-year-old HIV-positive mother who cares for three HIV-negative children, her own and her dead sister's, considers herself lucky to be a mother of three. She vows she does not want to have anything to do with men, as her previous boyfriend not only passed on the virus to her, but dumped her when he learned she was pregnant and HIV positive. Zanele, the woman with sixteen children at a funded institution, is a widow. She regards the children as a great gift from both God and her dead husband's ancestors; a token for the children she could have had, had her husband lived longer. Along the same thought pattern, the ninety-year-old great-grandmother also stated: "I had to have these boys as my own, as their mother. It is good they are well and healthy. They will carry the family name to the next generation. They are living proof that I had boy children."

From the above testimonies it is obvious that the HIV/AIDS context is largely responsible for such a significant shift in the understanding of the concept of motherhood within the African context. It can be argued that, for these mothers, the attitude and self-naming they adopt forms part of their coping strategy.

Practice of Mothering

The practice of mothering that the mothers construct and execute is informed by a number of factors, among others: Zulu cultural constructs, an individual symbolic significance attached to the mothering irrespective of orthodox values held within their community, the ideals of *ubuntu* (humanity), and a means of self-healing.

It could be argued that the traditional Zulu concept and practice of mothering lends itself to an extended usage. In fact, in a polygamous household, all father's wives were "mothers" to all the children, although there was a difference between the biological mother and the other "mothers." On the other hand, the mother's brother, *umalume* (uncle), was understood as a male mother and had a very special relationship with and responsibility for his sister's children. Orphans were readily adopted into the families of their father's brothers or, in their absence and under different terms, by the mother's brothers. Such traditional practices point to an extended understanding of "motherhood," one that is not based on the biological factors of being a woman and having given birth, but that emphasizes the nurturing and caring functions. In modern societies, however, the ties that linked traditional extended families have become loose, and the "motherhood" concept has become more restricted. Thus, my extended definition of mothering would cause a stir.

Unlike most residents of the Bhambayi village, four of the six mothers were found to distinguish themselves in caring for other people besides their own children. Other than their main mothering care duties, they mentioned that they regularly provide care for other people as well, that is, AIDS patients and the elderly.

Survival and Coping Strategies

A puzzling common trait of all six mothers is that they do not have sexual or romantic partners. With the exception of the fifteen-year-old participant, the reason offered as an explanation for the decision was the children's health, care, and welfare. The mothers felt good and grateful for their unattached status, which offered some guarantee of a disease-free life to protect the children's health. Their choice cannot be understood outside a socially constructed expectation that mothers should "sacrifice their own life in many respects for the children's benefit." This is a consequence of the traditional tenet that giving, preserving, and nurturing life is the highest human attainment. On the other hand, such self-sacrifice could also be understood as a coping strategy.

There is no doubt that mothering under the HIV/AIDS circumstances is a challenge. It is significant to note that three of the five other mothers cited the fifteen-year-old girl-mother as their inspiration, as she single-handedly looks after two children. She was referred to as a good model and one of the reasons that the mothers try to be strong during hard times.

Strength to persevere in caring for the children, especially without the support of formal employment, was drawn from a spiritual source. Religion has been reported to play a significant part in this instance.[5] In particular, sources of strength were guidance from the Christian religion and the ancestors. Four mothers mentioned that one of the dominant demands in their prayers was to live long enough to see the fulfilment of God's or the ancestors' plan for the children. Aware of the high rate of death in areas of HIV prevalence, all the mothers wish for a long life, concerned for the children. It was found that the wish was also prompted by the sad realization that few members of the family[6] were interested in caring for the children. Also, all the participants had some affiliation with a support group, whether formal or informal. This was identified as necessary, for the need to talk about one's situation eases the difficulty of facing HIV/AIDS factors in their lives.

A common feature among all the mothers was that, although they were not in formal employment, they were all involved in some trade activity aimed at complementing their main source of income. All the participants, except the youngest and oldest mothers, were in regular contract employment. In addition to this kind of employment, most mothers were involved in some kind of income-generating activity: selling anything, from loose single cigarettes to fruit and vegetables, or candies, crisps, and fried fish. The needs of the growing children in their care were cited as reasons for such economic enterprises.

Challenging the Zulu Traditional Worldview

A number of traditional cultural Zulu values are challenged by these families. The concept of what constitutes a family—that is, a married heterosexual pair group in a stable relationship, with the man being the head of the household—is strongly questioned.

Magwaza (2003), reporting on an African Zulu mothering practice, notes that the mothering duty is ideally considered a communally shared practice, probably developing from traditional polygamous settings where each wife was also the mother of all the children in the household. Neighborhood mothers, mothers' sisters, and grandmothers are often within reach to offer help. It was found that for all the mothers in the study this ideal option was deliberately shunned, indicating an altered experience of motherhood for them. On being asked about communal mothering all the mothers were adamant that they did not favor the practice. Instead, there is a conscious support network among three of the mothers in the study. They maintain that their support group is a better option, and has worked well for them. This decision was made out of fear that, should the network be extended to include mothers with no experience of AIDS deaths, their families might be hurt. Stigma and insensitivity toward families that have suffered AIDS deaths continues to be a concern within South African society.

This paper has demonstrated that the concept of motherhood is undergoing profound changes even within a predominantly traditional African society. The realities of HIV/AIDS, with the consequent high numbers of AIDS orphans, are cited as some of the main reasons for the change. In support of this argument the paper has employed the experiences of six "mothers" of households of children orphaned by AIDS. Of significant note is the fact that only one of the six mothers is the biological mother of any of the children under her guardianship. Also, employing the principles of the grounded theory of research, the stories of the six mothers have been used to formulate the main argument of the paper: in the twenty-first century the conception of family and the practice of mothering are under drastic review in families that have been directly affected by the human immunodeficiency virus and AIDS.

NOTES

1. I wish to acknowledge the South African National Research Foundation (NRF) and the University of KwaZulu-Natal for resources made available for the success of this study and this paper. Any opinions, findings, and conclusions or recommendations expressed in this material are those of the author. The funding organizations do not accept any liability in regard thereto. My gratitude also goes to Prof. Canonici, my mentor, for input made toward the final draft of this essay.
2. The aim of this project was to generate knowledge on how to deal with HIV/AIDS, and in particular caregiving. Its intent was to work according to cultural understandings of the communities involved that had been achieved through research and consciously making an effort at understanding the context in which the knowledge(s) and understandings operate.
3. This was an exclaimed response from one of the mothers—with disgust in her voice, an indication of the regard for people outside this mother circle.
4. This is a philosophy that is largely based on the need to respect and care for other people and in particular strangers, visitors, and generally vulnerable people.
5. Philippe Denis and Nokhaya Makiwane (2003) make reference to this fact following a study on the coping strategies of some South African families directly affected by HIV/AIDS.
6. In the African context, the term *family* refers to an extended family.

WORKS CITED

Bowles, Gloria, and Renate D. Klein, eds. 1983. *Theories of Women's Studies.* London: Routledge and Kegan Paul.

Charmaz, Kathy. 1988. The grounded theory method: An explication and interpretation. In *Contemporary Field Research: Perspectives and Formulations*, ed. Robert. M. Emerson, 109–126. Boston: Little, Brown.

Denis, Philippe, and Nokhaya Makiwane. 2003. Stories of love, pain, and courage: AIDS orphans and memory boxes. *Oral History* 3.1/2:66–74.

Doucet, Andrea. 2006. *Do Men Mother?: Fathering Care, and Domestic Responsibility.* Toronto: University of Toronto Press.

Glaser, Barney G. 1978. *Advances in the Methodology of Grounded Theory: Theoretical Sensitivity.* Mill Valley, Calif.: Sociology Press.

Glaser, Barney G., and A. Anselm. 1967. *The Discovery of Grounded Theory: Strategies for Qualitative Research.* Chicago: Aldine.

Macklin, Eleanor, ed. 1989. *AIDS and Families.* New York: Harrington Park.

Magwaza, Thenjiwe. 2003. Perceptions and experiences of motherhood: A study of black and white mothers of Durban, South Africa. *Jenda: A Journal of Culture and African Women Studies.* http://www.jendajournal.com/issue4/magwaza.html (accessed Nov. 19, 2006).

——. 2006. IKS methodological pilgrimage: Processes and procedures. In *Freedom Sown in Blood: Memories of the Impi Yamakhanda,* ed. Thenjiwe Magwaza, Yonah Seleti, and Mpilo P. Sithole, 15–26. Thohoyandou, South Africa: Ditlou.

Ruddick, Sara. 1994. *Maternal Thinking: Toward a Politics of Peace.* Boston: Beacon.

Stajduhar, Kellie I. 1998. Palliative care at home: Reflections on HIV/AIDS family caregiving experiences. *Journal of Palliative Care* 14.2:14–22.

Stanley, Liz, and Sue Wise. 1983. "Back into the personal"; or, Our attempt to construct "feminist research." In Bowles and Klein 1983:20–60.

Strauss, Anselm, and Juliet Corbin. 1990. *Basics of Qualitative Research: Techniques and Perspectives for Developing Grounded Theory.* Newbury Park, Calif.: Sage.

Thompson, Elizabeth A. 2000. Mothers' experiences of an adult child's HIV/AIDS diagnosis: Maternal responses to and resolutions of accountability for AIDS. *Family Relations* 49.2:15–164.

Tiblier, Kay, B., Gillian Walker, and John S. Rolland. 1989. Therapeutic issues when dealing with families of persons with AIDS. In Macklin 1989:81–128.

Identity | **PART 2**

Ambivalence of the
Motherhood Experience

SEVEN

IVANA BROWN

Being a mother is conventionally associated with happiness. For many mothers, however, mothering is filled with conflict, anxiety, and ambivalence. Yet maternal ambivalence often remains unacknowledged. When acknowledged, ambivalence about motherhood is often considered deviant or problematic (Parker 2005; Hollway and Featherstone 1997). Despite that, at the beginning of twenty-first century ambivalence about motherhood has been quite widely explored in popular culture. In this article I examine representations of the motherhood experience in maternal narratives published at the beginning of the twenty-first century in the United States. I specifically focus on depictions of maternal ambivalence. The goal of this analysis is to contribute to a better understanding of ambivalence in the context of current social conditions of motherhood. I use motherhood memoirs as publicly accessible sources that provide an excellent window into expanding public discourse on motherhood. Further, as a part of popular culture, they help to define acceptable forms that maternal ambivalence can take for their readers. The analysis of these narratives shows that the motherhood experiences of twenty-first-century mothers are strongly infused with ambivalence, which is largely located in the social conditions and expectations of contemporary motherhood.

THEORETICAL PERSPECTIVES ON MATERNAL AMBIVALENCE

Imagine a mother in the middle of the night singing a lullaby to a screaming baby. "*Rock-a-bye, Baby . . .* " While the melody is soothing and the mother is lovingly holding the baby, the words could be seen to express a desire to hurt the child (Taylor 1996; Parker 2005). According to psychotherapist Rozsika Parker, the author of the treatise on maternal ambivalence *Torn in Two*, this scene represents safely contained and creatively expressed maternal hatred coexisting with love for her baby (2005:73). In general, ambivalence refers to the coexistence of conflicting and opposing thoughts or feelings; in the case of mothers, these are usually described as a coexistence of love and hatred. Parker's analysis builds on and extends the psychoanalytic theories of ambivalence developed by Sigmund Freud, Melanie Klein, Donald W. Winnicott, and others. While their focus was largely on the infant's development and the infant's love/hate feelings toward the mother (Suleiman 2001:116), Parker looks at the mother-child relationship from the perspective of the mother and her ambivalence toward the child. She argues that while it may be hard to accept, all mothers experience complex and conflicting feelings about their babies.

Psychoanalytic theories see both love and hate as rooted in the unconscious and coexisting side by side. The presence of maternal ambivalence, however, is not always problematic. For a mother, unmanageable awareness of conflicted feelings where she expects to feel love can, according to Freud, turn against one's self and result in self-torment and depression (in Parker 2005:19). In contrast, managing ambivalent feelings and dealing with the ensuing anxiety and fear of loss can promote a sense of concern, responsibility toward the child, and differentiation of the mother's self from the baby (Parker 1997:22), thus benefiting the mother-child relationship.

Cultural expectations of the idealized mother, who never has negative feelings toward a child, can cause the ambivalence to grow into anxiety (Parker 1997:34) and ambivalence is also behind much of the guilt mothers feel about motherhood. Ambivalence is made unmanageable because of every woman's desire to be a good mother according to the current social definition (Parker 1997:34). In acknowledging the effects of social and cultural context on mothers' relationships to their children and the existence of maternal ambivalence, Parker moves a purely psychological understanding of ambivalence into a sociological perspective. In such a perspective, it is the sociocultural conditions of mothering and the image of the "good mother," which women internalize, that result in the ambivalent love/hate feelings new mothers have toward their infants (Lupton 2000).

Sociologists then locate ambivalence in particular historical, social, and cultural conditions and conflicting social norms and expectations oriented toward the same role (Merton 1976).1 As social actors, mothers may experience ambivalence because of conflicting social norms and expectations about what it means to be a mother. Standards of mothering, understanding of childhood, relationships between mothers and fathers, the role of the extended family and community in childrearing, participation of women in the labor force, and family economic resources are among the social and cultural factors influencing mothers' experiences of motherhood. For example, depending on their social class, mothers may be expected to devote all their time and energy to their children but also remain women with their own interests or careers (Peskowitz 2005; Hays 1996). Such conflicting expectations create not only a personal conflict but also a more complex and social structural contradiction "embedded in sets of structured social relations (e.g., class, age, race, ethnicity and gender) through which opportunities, rights, and privileges are differentially distributed" (Connidis and McMullin 2002:565; see also Pillemer and Luescher 2004). In other words, people experience ambivalence according to their position in social structures and according to the resources that they have available to resolve it.

I contend that we can best understand maternal ambivalence if we look at both its psychological and its social components, which emerge from contradictions at the subjective level (cognitions, feelings, motivations) or from contradictions at the level of social structures (statuses, roles, and norms), respectively (Luescher and Pillemer 1998). Thus, while maternal ambivalence is usually studied in the psychological context of the relationship with the child, I see it also as socially and culturally produced, and shaped by the circumstances that define women's lives. This sociological understanding of ambivalence with the awareness of its psychological component shapes my approach to the analysis of maternal ambivalence in the memoirs under study here.

REPRESENTATIONS OF MOTHERHOOD EXPERIENCES IN POPULAR LITERATURE

The end of the twentieth century saw a sharp increase in interest in the motherhood experience in both popular and academic literature. Indeed, more than seven hundred books on motherhood were published in the U.S. book market in the last two decades of the twentieth century (Douglas and Michaels 2004:8). A significant part of this wave is represented by the books, sometimes referred to as "mommy lit" (Hewett 2006), that focus on motherhood experiences and opinions about mothering in contemporary society from the perspective of mothers as writers.

In this analysis I focus on "mommy memoirs," a subcategory of "mommy lit" that includes nonfictional essays and memoirs. I analyze only books published on the American book market between the years 2000 and 2004, in order to capture the essence of motherhood experiences on the verge of the new century. The analyzed books are listed at the end of this article. I selected titles over a two-year period using repeated keyword searches of the online bookstores Amazon. com and Barnes&Noble.com. I included only books that described the authors' own motherhood experiences without offering explicit advice to their readers. While the selected books differ in length, structure, and method of presentation, their authors mostly write about pregnancy and the early years of mothering (although some include longer time spans). Unlike many existing sociological and other academic studies of motherhood, these books are aimed at wide audiences, written in an accessible language, and emphasize the authors' subjectivity and experience. The memoirs and essays I analyze feature the maternal experiences of women from varied backgrounds and with diverse expectations about motherhood. Their authors promise the reader refreshing and honest views on motherhood and the adjustments that women have to make when taking on this role, a signature trait of the mommy lit genre (Hewett 2006:121).

Upon reading these books it became clear to me that providing an honest view of motherhood meant including both the joyful and the painful experiences associated with mothering. Ambivalent feelings about motherhood are thus quite central to these writings. As the issue of maternal ambivalence is not featured prominently in motherhood advice books and our society sees maternal ambivalence as possibly deviant and problematic (Parker 2005; Hollway and Feathstone 1997), I found these public acknowledgments of maternal ambivalence particularly intriguing. Simultaneous admissions of ambivalence by several authors within a relatively short period becomes especially intriguing when we consider the sociocultural context of the high expectations placed on contemporary mothers (Hays 1996) and the idealization of the motherhood experience (Douglas and Michaels 2004) that keeps conflicted and negative aspects of motherhood hidden behind a mask (Maushart 1999). The mask of motherhood keeps maternal ambivalence a secret that most women do not usually reveal until later on in life (Maushart 1999:111). The goal of the present analysis is to locate and analyze the aspects of the motherhood narratives infused with ambivalence in order to contribute to better understanding of motherhood experiences and maternal ambivalence at the beginning of the twenty-first century.

The current wave of maternal writing, with its critical lens on the motherhood experience, follows a tradition of the motherhood writing that goes back to the beginning of the twentieth century, with maternal experience appearing mostly in fiction and poetry (Hewett 2006). Motherhood memoirs and the theme of ambivalence became prominent in the works of several feminist writers on motherhood in the 1970s, such as Adrienne Rich's *Of Woman Born*, Ann Oakley's *Becoming a Mother*, and Jane Lazarre's *Mother Knot*. These mothers/writers felt guilty about the lack of enjoyment they found in motherhood and child care and their ambivalent feelings about being a mother. However, they saw the conflict and the negative side of mothering as being rooted in the social conditions of a patriarchal society—in which mothers are left to take care of their children in the isolation of the nuclear family and without sufficient structural support systems—rather than in their relationship with their children. From this distinction also stems Rich's differentiation between mothering as an experience and practice and motherhood as a socially and culturally formed institution (O'Reilly 2004). This distinction remains the basis of most of today's maternal theory and research (O'Reilly 2004:2).

While the twenty-first-century writers use less radical political language than their predecessors, the difference between the social expectations of motherhood and the experience of mothering remains a source of their maternal ambivalence. Cultural assumptions about the naturalness of mothering to women (and the biological mother in particular) and the need for children to be mothered remain prevalent in popular consciousness. This belief in women's natural role as mothers, combined with the pressures to be a good mother who follows the ideology of intensive mothering (Hays 1996:6–9) while balancing work and family responsibilities, makes the work of mothering today even more exhausting than in previous decades. I suggest that social pressures and requirements to mother in such an intensive way and the necessity to combine multiple roles and identities are reasons for the resurgence of interest in maternal experience and for the renewed interest in the conflicted nature of maternal ambivalence at the beginning of the new century.

REPRESENTATION OF MATERNAL AMBIVALENCE IN CURRENT MOTHERHOOD WRITING

Although ambivalence takes different forms for different authors, several common themes emerge in the analyzed narratives. The themes I discuss were defined through a "grounded theory" approach (Glaser and Strauss 1967), and the analyzed issues were reflected in the majority of the analyzed books. Among the most common themes are divergences between expectations and the reality of motherhood, formation of maternal identity, difficulties in combining work and child care, and mothering according to prevailing social expectations. I also discuss how the authors manage ambivalence, and the relationship between maternal writing and ambivalence.

Expectations and Reality of Motherhood

These narratives have two things in common: first, depictions of the transformative power of pregnancy and motherhood, and second, descriptions of the ambivalence the writers felt about this transformation, their identities, and their lives as mothers.

The most common thread among the analyzed memoirs is the dramatic and life-changing nature of the transition to motherhood; surprise caused by its overwhelming character, the unexpected ambivalence that most authors feel about their new role of mother, and identity conflicts between the motherhood self and their "pre-baby" identity. According to recent sociological research, many new mothers experience motherhood in a similar way (Miller 2007; Lupton 2000; McMahon 1995:132–135). Maternal memoirs bring these conflicted feelings about motherhood to the forefront. The titles of the analyzed books suggest that most of their authors were not so overwhelmed by love and joy over their new babies that they did not realize the difficulties of being a new mother. The titles of the books that focus on the transition to motherhood mention "shock" (Buchanan 2003), "misconceptions," "lies" (Wolf 2001), and the "not-so-perfect life" (Fox 2003). Writers with older children use titles that include words such as "difficult times" (Cheever 2001) and "unbalanced" mom (Belkin 2002). Brockenbrough's (2002) title warns her readers, "It could happen to you!"

For many authors, motherhood was quite different from what they expected. Once they became mothers and the mask of motherhood was removed (Maushart 1999), the reality they faced was very different from their expectations (Lupton 2000; Miller 2007). Divergences between expectations and reality contributed to the ambivalence about their new role. While not all of their expectations had been positive and many approached motherhood with doubts and misgivings (Slater 2002; Wolf 2001), their new life made them feel confused, surprised, and overwhelmed. Buchanan describes her feelings shortly after her daughter was born as very uncertain, different from ever before:

It seemed that my entire world had shifted in the course of one exhausting day, joyous, eventful day. . . . I waited for that mythical maternal instinct to kick in, waited for someone—a mother, my mother, any mother—to acknowledge that yes, everything does feel different and new and difficult and that's okay. (2003:xii)

Changes that start with the birth of the baby quickly spread to mother's entire life. Brockenbrough describes some of the overwhelming changes in her life this way:

When you have a baby, you trade your nice and orderly life for one that is chaos and kisses. You can't hurry, because babies have schedules of their own. You can't rest, for the very same reason. . . . You don't plan for the life you want to have. You live it, as best as you can. And even if you're not going fast, it still feels like you've taken flight. (2002:201–201)

For some, the motherhood experience confirms their biggest worries and ambiguities about becoming a mother in the first place. Wolf (2001), for example, noticed that while she enjoyed the presence of her baby, the motherhood experience was dramatically and mostly negatively changing her life:

My life as a mother had become just what I feared. My delight in our child was absolute. At the same time I experienced a tightening of the world's circumference; I was chained to the couch nursing; I was stunned with fatigue; I was a vast primate of the flesh. I had become all the things I was most afraid I would be. Also, we had moved to the suburbs. (2001:208)

Even though the majority of writers tried to prepare for motherhood, most of them found their preparations insufficient, as often noted in academic writings (Miller 2007:351; Lupton 2000). Expressing frustration over her inability to prepare for motherhood, Slater (2002) asked a few days after her daughter was born:

What does motherhood mean? So far, all I can say is this. Whatever you plan for, it will not happen. You plan for you labor but the baby is breach. You plan to call her Sara but she comes out all Kate. . . . I planned for a crisis and instead I get calmness. (2002:146)

Some of the ambivalence thus lessens the surprise caused by the intense and overwhelming nature of the motherhood transition. Once they became mothers, these mostly educated, professional women realized that motherhood was different from their expectations. Cultural images of idealized motherhood contribute to this divergence between expectations and reality and contribute to the ambivalence experienced by new mothers (Lupton 2000; Parker 2005).

Forming a Motherhood Identity

Overall, two main tendencies appear in the authors' descriptions of the transition to motherhood: some feel like mothers immediately after their baby is born, while others discover that acquiring the motherhood identity and developing a bond with the baby takes time (Miller 2007). This latter group of women often goes through a period of uncertainty and ambivalence about motherhood and believes that one has to learn how to become a mother. It is interesting that both of these feelings are somewhat unexpected by the mothers who go through them.

Among the authors who did not expect to easily form the motherhood identity is Allison Crews, a teenage mother writing "When I Was Garbage," in Gore and Lavender's collection of essays (2001). As a pregnant fifteen-year-old, she was under a lot of pressure from her friends and family to give up her baby for adoption. Despite these pressures, she wanted to keep and raise her baby. She felt a connection with the baby and felt like a mother as soon as her son was born: "I held my tiny infant son in my shaking arms . . . He was so much more than I could have dreamed, so much more than a fuzzy little ultrasound worm." Pumping breast milk while her son was in incubator, she thought: "I had an abundance of precious golden milk that only a mother could make. *I was a mother*" (36). The physiological readiness to be a mother thus in this case trumped her social unpreparedness.

Cheever (2001) experienced motherhood in a similar way, although she became a mother in a very different social position: when she was thirty-eight and financially comfortable. But as a professional woman, she did not expect to enjoy motherhood. Her feelings changed as soon as she had a baby:

> In the moment that I held my baby daughter in my arms . . . I changed so fast that I felt dizzy. I instantly loved and wanted to protect her. Loving her became the focus of my existence. . . . As my baby grew, my love for her grew right along with her. (2001:19)

Such feelings of love and instant attachment are part of a "good mother" image prevalent in our society (Miller 2007). However, as psychologists tell us, love is not experienced unopposed and even mothers who quickly bonded with their babies experienced ambivalent feelings about mothering and struggled to understand them. Cheever describes the complex nature of love and emotions mothers feel toward their babies as follows:

> Love raised a lot of questions. The other side of love isn't hate. . . . It's being paralyzed. It's a flash of helpless anger which grabs you up for one murderous minute and then drops you, panting, back into ordinary life. When I could comfort my daughter . . . I was in ecstasy. . . . When she cried out in pain, long shrieky cries and I couldn't make a difference, I wanted to flee; I wanted to die.   (2001:20)

Mothers who do not immediately experience attachment and love for their babies struggle with this cultural image of instant love and their own feelings of confusion and ambivalence about their own ability to mother (Miller 2007). Buchanan, for example, describes the moments after her daughter was born and she saw her for the first time:

> The first thing I remember thinking . . . was "Who is this little stranger?" She didn't look like me, she didn't look like my husband; . . . I couldn't connect this little person with the faceless kicks and jabs I had felt inside me for so many months. . . . I was still surprised to discover that my first emotion was not the intense love I'd heard described but, instead, a sense of overwhelming responsibility.   (2003:53)

In a similar vein, Lauren Slater describes the long and gradual process she underwent before she developed socially expected feelings of love for her baby. Almost a month after childbirth, she comments on her maternal feelings and finds it unexpected that she feels the same way as she did before she had the baby:

> I am a mother but I don't look like a mother. I don't feel like a mother. . . . I've grown accustomed to the word, but it stays at a distance from me. I thought I would be smashed flat, or heaved high, mythically altered for this, the most mythic roles but, shock of all shock, here I am, still me. And the baby? I have come to like her a little bit. That's it. A little bit.   (2002:148)

Many authors also feel that in order to become mothers, they need to undergo a total transformation of who they are and create a new motherhood self. Wolf (2001) was uncertain that she could undergo such a transformation successfully:

> So many older women kept advising me that the mother-self to come would be a better self. I found this less than reassuring. . . . that maternal "I" did not exist yet. I did not yet know if I could successfully transform my current self into her.   (2001:106)

Particularly in the early stages of motherhood, it is not easy to incorporate the new identity into a woman's existing self, contributing to ambivalence about their new motherhood identity. For example, Cusk (2001) feels that her "old" self and her "motherhood" self are quite separate, although she tried to unify them:

> To be a mother, I must leave the telephone unanswered, work undone, arrangements unmet. To be myself I must let the baby cry, must forestall her hunger or leave her for evenings out, must forget her in order to think about other things. To succeed in being one means to fail at being the other. . . . At first . . . I am driven to work at the newer of the two skills, which is motherhood; and it is with a shock that I see . . . the resulting plunge of my own significance.   (2001:57)

The authors express most ambivalence about acquiring the motherhood identity when they feel that it is threatening their pre-baby selves. Cusk (2001) writes about moments when she perceives herself and her baby not even as two separate beings but instead a well-coordinated "motherbaby," sustained through around-the-clock nursing, which for Cusk becomes a way to slowly delete her old self-identity (2001:93ff.). The loss of pre-baby identity is reinforced by society, which, as Buchanan suggests, pushes mothers out of their own self-identity into invisible mom-identity, making mothers invisible to the rest of the world (2003:66). This loss of pre-baby self, reinforced by low social valuation of mothers, contributes to the ambivalent feelings the writers feel about motherhood (Crittenden 2001).

Balancing Work and Motherhood Identities

For many contemporary women, their identities are strongly entrenched in their careers. Many authors thus feel the loss of their "pre-baby" self expressed through their work, which they abandoned or cut back on due to the demands of child care. For these educated and career-focused women, the effect of motherhood on their identity is quite significant, and the resulting changes in their lives and selves are surprising and not always welcome (Peskowitz 2005).

In order to preserve their pre-baby identities, most of our writers continue to work outside the home, or adjust to working from home. Since many of them were writers before they had children, this means mostly writing from home. Many authors find the role conflict between their identities as a writer and as a mother hard to balance. Many feel so overwhelmed by child care and housework that they find it hard to continue writing. For instance, Sherry Thompson (in Gore and Lavender 2001, "Mother Tongue") describes her struggle to include writing in her everyday life, filled with child care, but is not ready to give up the writing:

> It is not always easy to integrate my artistic aspirations with my regular mama life. It is difficult to write with a small boy and an infant daughter. . . . And I wonder why I don't let something go, lighten my load and make the journey easier. . . . I know the only something I could get rid of would be my oddly strung bits of words and rhythm; yet I cling to them like a drowning woman.   (Thompson in Gore and Lavender 2001:73)

It is part of her ambivalent motherhood experience that she feels that despite the difficulty of finding time for writing, the motherhood experience provides a new source of creativity for her writing (see Parker 1997).

> It is only here, in the midst of sandwich crusts, dirty diapers, trips to the doctor, bedtime stories, lost sandals . . . that I have found my poetic voice. . . . My children appear just under the surface of poems. . . . I know that the quality of work is only possible because of the authentic, transformative experience of motherhood.   (Thompson in Gore and Lavender 2001:75)

Many authors, however, feel a serious conflict between working and motherhood but perceive a social pressure to succeed in both. Not being able to combine these two identities leaves the writers feeling guilty and insufficient (e.g., Wolf 2001; Fox 2003). June Day (in Gore and Lavender 2001, "Movements") feels that motherhood has impeded her ability to work and write:

> My daughter is almost two. I have not produced any significant art or writing since her birth. . . . My guilt over being "unproductive" tires me out. I shouldn't feel this. . . . Cultural expectations are the source of my problem. It isn't enough just to be a mother, even though it's difficult and important work. Good mothering isn't considered successful or even sufficient. One must have a MotherPlus Plan—maybe have the MotherPlus law career or be a MotherPlus novelist. It fills me with guilt, always coming up short.   (in Gore and Lavender 2001:90)

When mothers return to work outside of the home, some express a feeling of being torn between their work and their children (Peskowitz 2005). One day, staying longer at work because her writing had been going well, Wolf returned home late. While she felt sorry for her hungry baby, she was also angry that she had had to interrupt her work:

> Interruption was now my life. I was crying because I could not win. Because, as a worker, I was turning away from my work at exactly the most important moment; yet, at the same time, as a mother, I had already stayed too long at the fair. (2001:211)

Wolf later argues that this identity conflict and loss of self occur because of the low social status of motherhood in the current society. Many of the writers of these books do not take easily the demotion to the low status of motherhood and the consequent devaluation of their social position once they become mothers (Crittenden 2001; Peskowitz 2005). That makes their transition to motherhood and acceptance of their maternal identity even more difficult.

Social Expectations of Motherhood

In describing the process of becoming a mother and their mothering experiences, many authors observe that while they have gradually adjusted to their new identity, it is the social expectations on how to be a good mother that make it difficult to fully enjoy motherhood. In other words, many of these women refuse or find it hard to be mothers following the standards of "new momism,"[2] a term coined by Douglas and Michaels (2004). Similar to Hays' ideology of "intensive mothering," new momism is "a set of ideals, norms, and practices, most frequently and powerfully presented in the media, that seem on the surface to celebrate motherhood but which in reality promulgate standards of perfection that are beyond your reach" (Douglas and Michaels 2004:4).

Both of these concepts describe how, in twenty-first-century middle-class society, a mother is required to be the central caregiver to the child, put the child's needs ahead of her own, and support beliefs that "no woman is truly complete or fulfilled unless she has kids, . . . and to be a remotely decent mother, a woman has to devote her entire physical, psychological, emotional and intellectual being, 24/7, to her children" (Michaels 2004:4). Normative pressures then lead women to internalize and follow these standards, which are not always easy to implement (Maushart 1999; Hays 1996). An inability, or unwillingness, to follow these set norms, as well as their unexpected rigidity, is behind some of the ambivalence that many new mothers feel about their motherhood role, as evident in the analyzed books.

For many, the problem is that such intensive mothering leaves very little space for a mother's personal identity or the fulfillment of her own needs. Several writers present these concerns (e.g., Wolf, Buchanan, Cusk). Faulkner Fox, for example, writes about the effect of "attachment parenting," one of the strictest methods of intensive mothering popular since the 1990s, on mothers she met around her:

> If practiced fully, [attachment parenting] required that you carry your baby with you all day in a sling, nurse on demand all day and all night, let baby doze on her own schedule during the day (in your arms), and let her sleep with you all night long. . . . based on the exhausted faces and bodies I saw around me—at La Leche League meetings, in the midwife's office, at library sing-alongs—full adherence to attachment parenting could nearly kill a woman. Certainly, I feared, it could kill a woman who wanted to be a writer, a woman who needed time alone.   (2003:217)

Fox also understood that part of her dissatisfaction with being a mother and a wife had roots in the current definition of motherhood as a social institution that requires mothers—*but not fathers*—to give up their identities and devote themselves totally to their children (Peskowitz 2005).

To resist the pressures of new momism, she felt it was necessary for her to maintain a balance between her children and her work, and to devote time separately to both of them. Fox writes:

> Something to do with motherhood was causing me trouble, but as long as I managed to work at least few hours a day, it wasn't time spent with my children. When one of them was crying or whining, I certainly felt stress, but for the most part, my children were an enormous ballast. Their joy was infectious, and as long as I didn't have to see other mothers, I usually felt just fine.   (2003:194)

As Fox makes clear, it was the presence of other mothers, who serve as mirrors and judges of mothering (Parker 1997) and enforce the social norms on "good" mothering, that made her uncomfortable about her own mothering and fulfillment of the motherhood role. Fox thus clearly locates the ambivalent feelings she has about motherhood outside of the mother-child relationship and her feelings for her children, positioning them instead in the social space of norms and expectations on mothers (Parker 2005:63).

Managing Ambivalence

While most of the authors of the narratives I read found motherhood surprising and expressed their ambivalence about it, they all found ways to cope with this ambivalence. Fox's efforts to balance her work and time with her children, as well as her decision to pursue interests that supported her "pre-baby" self, are examples of the strategies employed by mothers to manage ambivalence. Creating a support network of friends played important role in strategies employed by some writers (Buchanan 2003), while yet others found support in their extended families, which helped out when necessary. Brockenbrough, for example, says she would not be able to manage motherhood without the support of her husband, friends, and family:

> They say it takes a village to raise a child. I'm not sure that's exactly it. Right now, I feel like it's taking a village to raise me. My brothers and sisters and in-laws have all taken turns holding the baby on too many occasions to count.   (2002:145)

Most of the authors found some adjustment and balance among their various identities as their children grew older. They also became more skilled in the mothering tasks and accepted their motherhood identity. For example, Cusk observes:

> Increasingly, motherhood comes to seem to me not a condition but a job, the work of certain periods, which begin and end and outside of which I am free. My daughter is more and more part of this freedom, something new that is being added, drop by daily drop, to the sum of what I am. . . . For the first year of her life work and love were bound together, fiercely, painfully. Now, it is as if a relationship has untethered itself and been let loose in our house.   (2001:209)

But even once they had adjusted to motherhood, most of the authors remained critical about the social institution of motherhood and the social position of mothers as they continued to deal with conflicts between their work and families and social expectations of "good" mothering. In response to these social pressures, many retreated from the institutional requirements of motherhood and instead focused on mothering and their relationship with their children, supporting thus the argument that maternal ambivalence is socially based and not affected by their relationship with the child.

MATERNAL WRITING AND AMBIVALENCE

I suggest that the authors discussed here use their memoirs as social accounts (Orbuch 1997:455) to help them deal with the transition to motherhood, a major event in their lives, and to negotiate and present their new identity and status. Writing can also be interpreted as a creative outcome of ambivalence (Parker 1997), allowing the authors to acknowledge their maternal ambivalence in a socially acceptable way. While some of these books are written in a humorous tone (Brockenbrough 2002; to a lesser extent, Gore and Lavender 2001; Buchanan 2003; Belkin 2002), a socially acceptable display of maternal ambivalence (Parker 1997:17; Hewett 2006), most use serious (Cheever 2001) and even socially critical tones (notably Wolf 2001; Fox 2003). Except for their writing, the authors feel that as a result of social pressures to be a good mother, admitting ambivalence is still not an option (Buchanan 2003:60–61). Buchanan argues that it should be acceptable to acknowledge that while mothers are thankful for their children, there are aspects of child care and mothering that are not always enjoyable (63). Many writers perceive a lack of openness in talking about motherhood issues, mostly the darker ones (Maushart 1999), and some of them justify their own writing as satisfying the need for more discussion and openness about maternal ambivalence (Wolf 2001; Fox 2003).

The writers try to convey to their readers that motherhood experiences are not limited to happy and enjoyable moments, which is quite different from the messages women receive about motherhood before they become mothers. These books thus represent a generational response to a societal lack of acknowledgment of conflicted feelings about motherhood and the identity crisis that motherhood can evoke (Hewett 2006). By writing about their own mixed feelings about motherhood, not only do the writers break the silence about maternal ambivalence but they are also creating a public discourse that makes ambivalence a part of the motherhood experience, making it more manageable for other mothers (Hewett 2006:135; Parker 2005). Fox, for instance, clearly expressed in her writing that helping other women deal with their mixed feelings is one of the reasons she wrote her book:

> This book is my story, and it's idiosyncratic, but I've been compelled to write it out of a sense that the isolation, conflict, and love I've felt as a wife and mother are anything but

limited to me. I've wanted to tell the truth—in writing—in the hope that my story could help other women feel less alone, less crazy, and possibly less guilty.   (2003:14)

While at first glance we might assume that ambivalent feelings are based in a mother's relationship with her children, my reading and analysis of twenty-first-century maternal memoirs suggests that maternal ambivalence is largely socially and culturally based. Most of the ambivalence presented in the memoirs stems from the social and cultural conditions of mothering, whether it's a lack of preparation for motherhood, social isolation, loss of identity, or a conflict between work and child care. Very little of the authors' ambivalence is located in their direct relationship with their child. Even when they express surprise over the lack of attachment to the child and the length of time to experience maternal bonding, they hardly mention hate, aggression, or annoyance toward their children but rather express surprise over unrealistic social expectations of instant bonding. Social expectations requiring new mothers to completely devote themselves to their children and leave little space for their own needs and identities significantly add to the maternal ambivalence expressed in the analyzed memoirs.

Psychologist Rozsika Parker (2005:63) somewhat critically points out that many social researchers (and writers) are careful to keep the distinction between the overwhelming, isolating, and stifling work of child care, and the emotionally rewarding relationship with the child. Such positioning suggests that authors are not completely honest in their writing because of persisting idealization of mothers and social taboos regarding the relationship between a mother and a child. I believe that this distinction and the relatively low emphasis on the psychological relationship between mother and child in the analyzed memoirs do not take away the urgency this generation of mothers feels about the social conditions of their mothering. The simultaneous appearance of these memoirs and their success suggests that mothers—both as writers and as readers—feel a need to communicate and reflect on their motherhood experiences (Hewett 2006:135), as well as explain and justify their ambivalence about motherhood. In these memoirs, ambivalence is presented as a complex combination of feelings, beliefs, and attitudes that arise in reaction to social norms and expectations of mothering and are located in concrete social-structural and cultural conditions of mothering. By acknowledging these feelings publicly, the writers create a space for expressing ambivalence within the motherhood discourse and allow their readers—mothers—to frame their motherhood identity and ambivalence within this space. The message "It could happen to you!" is thus meant to help the readers to normalize their own possible feelings of inadequacy and ambivalence about motherhood and make maternal ambivalence a "normal" part of the motherhood experience.

Writing of the maternal narratives provides the authors with a space for reflection and social criticism of the current conditions of motherhood. They use their memoirs to challenge exiting cultural definitions and practices related to motherhood as a social institution as well as existing gender relationships and familial forms. In some cases, the authors point to alternative arrangements and possibilities of mothering, attempting to change the status quo (Fox 2003; Slater 2002; Cheever 2001; Gore and Lavender 2001; Wolf 2001). Understanding and expressing their own feelings of ambivalence thus becomes a source of not only personal (Parker 1997), but also social, and possibly, political change (Hewett 2006).

What makes the issue of ambivalence significant and different for this generation of writers is that after decades of increasing gender equality and opportunities for women, these mothers find themselves facing maybe even more oppressing norms of what constitutes "good mothering" than their predecessors (Hays 1996; Douglas and Michaels 2004). At the same time, they continue to mother in the conditions of a nuclear family or increasingly as single mothers without sufficient structural support, and as women who have developed or would like to develop careers while raising their children. After being brought up with the images of "having it all," when they become mothers, they face a different reality from what they expected: the reality that combines the joys of motherhood with loss, conflict, and anxiety (Peskowitz 2005; Stone 2007). Motherhood forces them to reevaluate their relationships, values, and ideas about motherhood, parenthood, gender, and their position as women, mothers, and writers in the society of the twenty-first century.

NOTES

1. The first sociological theory of ambivalence was presented by Robert Merton and colleagues in the 1960s; see, e.g., Merton and Barber 1963 and Merton 1976.
2. While none of the authors discussed here uses this term, their descriptions of the social definitions of a "good" mother in many respects coincide with this definition.

BOOKS ANALYZED

Belkin, Lisa. 2002. *Life's Work: Confessions of an Unbalanced Mom*. New York: Simon and Schuster.

Brockenbrough, Martha. 2002. *It Could Happen to You! Diary of a Pregnancy and Beyond*. Kansas City: Andrews McMeel.

Buchanan, Andrea J. 2003. *Mother Shock: Loving Every (Other) Minute of It*. Emeryville, Calif.: Seal Press.

Cheever, Susan. 2001. *As Good as I Could Be: A Memoir of Raising Wonderful Children in Difficult Times*. New York: Washington Square Press.

Cusk, Rachel. 2001. *A Life's Work: On Becoming a Mother*. New York: Picador USA.

Fox, Faulkner. 2003. *Dispatches from a Not-So-Perfect Life; or, How I Learned to Love the House, the Man, the Child*. New York: Harmony Books.

Gore, Ariel, and Bee Lavender, eds. 2001. *Breeder: Real-Life Stories from the New Generation of Mothers*. Seattle: Seal Press.

Slater, Lauren. 2002. *Love Works Like This: Moving from One Kind of Life to Another*. New York: Random House.

Wolf, Naomi. 2001. *Misconceptions: Truth, Lies, and the Unexpected on the Journey to Motherhood*. New York: Doubleday.

WORKS CITED

Connidis, Ingrid Arnet, and Julie Ann McMullin. 2002. Sociological ambivalence and family ties: A critical perspective. *Journal of Marriage and Family* 64:558–567.

Crittenden, Ann. 2001. *The Price of Motherhood: Why the Most Important Job in the World Is Still the Least Valued*. New York: Holt.

Douglas, Susan J., and Meredith W. Michaels. 2004. *The Mommy Myth: The Idealization of Motherhood and How It Has Undermined Women*. New York: Free Press.

Glaser, Barney G., and Anselm L. Strauss. 1967. *The Discovery of Grounded Theory: Strategies for Qualitative Research*. Chicago: Aldine.

Hays, Sharon. 1996. *The Cultural Contradictions of Motherhood*. New Haven: Yale University Press.

Hewett, Heather. 2006. You are not alone: The personal, the political, and the "new" mommy lit. In *Chick Lit: The New Woman's Fiction*, ed. Suzanne Ferriss and Mallory Young, 119–139. New York: Routledge.

Hollway, Wendy, and Brid Featherstone. 1997. *Mothering and Ambivalence*. London: Routledge.

Lazarre, Jane. 1976. *The Mother Knot*. New York: McGraw-Hill.

Luescher, Kurt, and Karl Pillemer. 1998. Intergenerational ambivalence: A new approach to the study of parent-child relations in later life. *Journal of Marriage and Family* 60:413–425.

Lupton, Deborah. 2000. "A love/hate relationship": The ideals and experiences of first-time mothers. *Journal of Sociology* 36.1:51–63.

Maushart, Susan. 1999. *The Mask of Motherhood: How Becoming a Mother Changes Our Lives, and Why We Never Talk About It.* New York: Penguin.

McMahon, Martha. 1995. *Engendering Motherhood: Identity and Self-Transformation in Women's Lives.* New York: Guilford.

Merton, Robert. 1976. *Sociological Ambivalence, and Other Essays.* New York: Free Press.

Merton, Robert, and Elinor Barber. 1963. Sociological ambivalence. In *Sociological Theory: Values and Sociocultural Change,* ed. Edward A. Tirayakian, 91–120. New York: Free Press.

Miller, Tina. 2007. Is this what motherhood is all about? Weaving experiences and discourse through transition to first-time motherhood. *Gender and Society* 21:337–358.

Oakley, Ann. 1979. *Becoming a Mother.* Oxford: Martin Robertson.

Orbuch, Terri L. 1997. People's accounts count: The sociology of accounts. *Annual Review of Sociology* 23:455–478.

O'Reilly, Andrea, ed. 2004. *From Motherhood to Mothering: The Legacy of Adrienne Rich's Of Woman Born.* Albany: State University of New York Press.

Parker, Rozsika. 1997. The production and purposes of maternal ambivalence. In Hollway and Featherstone 1997:17–36.

——. 2005 (1995). *Torn in Two: The Experience of Maternal Ambivalence.* 2nd ed. London: Virago.

Peskowitz, Miriam. 2005. *The Truth Behind the Mommy Wars: Who Decides What Makes a Good Mother?* Emeryville, Calif.: Seal Press.

Pillemer, Karl, and Kurt Luescher, eds. 2004. *Intergenerational Ambivalences: New Perspectives on Parent-Child Relations in Later Life.* Contemporary Perspectives in Family Research 4. Oxford: Elsevier.

Rich, Adrienne. 1986. *Of Woman Born: Motherhood as Experience and Institution.* 2nd ed. New York: Norton.

Stone, Pamela. 2007. *Opting-Out: Why Women Really Leave Careers and Head Home.* Berkeley: University of California Press.

Suleiman, Susan Robin. 2001. Writing and motherhood. In *Mother Reader: Essential Writings on Motherhood,* ed. Moyra Davey, 113–137. New York: Seven Stories Press.

Taylor, Verta. 1996. *Rock-a-by Baby: Feminism, Self-Help, and Postpartum Depression.* New York: Routledge.

Supermothers on Film

EIGHT

or, Maternal Melodrama
in the Twenty-first Century

ADRIENNE McCORMICK

Hollywood's maternal melodramas from the 1930s through the 1950s reveal a great deal of national and cultural conflict over the roles of mothers in U.S. society. Analyses of films such as King Vidor's *Stella Dallas* (1937), Michael Curtiz's *Mildred Pierce* (1945), and Douglas Sirk's *Imitation of Life* (1959)—to name only a few—explore the constraints of gender, class, race, and consumerism on mothers in the early to mid twentieth century. Critical responses explore how these films punish mothers for their shortcomings, while simultaneously constructing visions of ideal motherhood. Though representations of mothers have always been present in film, the early years of the twenty-first century reveal an explosion in representations of supermothers, women who again must prove their mettle despite numerous failings. Films such as *The Forgotten* (Joseph Ruben, 2004), starring Julianne Moore; *Flightplan* (Robert Schwentke, 2005), starring Jodie Foster; and *Dark Water* (Walter Salles, 2005), starring Jennifer Connelly, all involve supermothers who save their children against incredible odds. The visible powers they struggle against are no longer economic or social, but include terrorists, aliens, and the supernatural. All of these mothers succeed in overcoming unimaginable challenges to save their children.

Taking continuities with the maternal melodramas of the early twentieth century as a starting point, I argue that these new maternal melodramas of the twenty-first century punish the mothers onscreen, while reinforcing ideals of supermotherhood. This tension reveals cultural anxieties about white U.S. mothers in particular and what their advances in the workplace mean to the heterosexual compact. Supermotherhood in twenty-first-century films is further complicated, however, by the presence of mothers onscreen who fail to live up to any ideals of motherhood. Films such as *Freedomland* (Joe Roth, 2006); *Or, My Treasure* (Keren Yedaya, 2004); and *Kept & Dreamless* (Vera Fogwill and Martin Desalvo, 2005) feature mothers who fail their children in various ways. These three films—from Hollywood, Israel, and Argentina, respectively—reveal how ethnic, racial, and cultural differences intersect with traditional gender roles and highlight the limits placed around what it means to be a supermother. Taken together, the filmic representations of twenty-first-century motherhood examined in this paper—supermothers and mothers who fall short of that moniker—reveal continuing cultural anxieties about how women combine motherhood, work, and sexuality—inside or outside the heterosexual institution of marriage. Putting their representations in dialogue with one another illustrates the abiding power of the ideal of sacrificial motherhood; suggests complex possibilities for how spectators respond to idealized, debased, and failed mothers; and reveals fissures in representations of ideal motherhood that point to actual mothers' struggles in the twenty-first century.

MATERNAL MELODRAMA IN THE TWENTIETH CENTURY

Maternal melodramas from the early decades of the twentieth century, and classic feminist film critics as they responded to them, serve as a starting point for a trajectory that bridges the century in its filmic portrayals of mothers. Hollywood has always been a barometer for U.S. cultural anxieties, and its representations of sacrificial mothers are particularly rich.

In the 1930s class mobility features largely in positioning mothers in Hollywood film. *Stella Dallas* (King Vidor, 1937) is perhaps one of the earliest and best known of these films, and typifies maternal sacrifice. The film both punishes and idealizes Barbara Stanwyck's Stella Dallas, a mother who sacrifices her daughter by ostracizing her so that she may achieve a successful marriage into upper-class society. When Stella Dallas stands outside of the wedding ceremony at the film's conclusion, looking in from the rain, and then walks away in triumph at her daughter's success, the film idealizes sacrificial motherhood by suggesting that all mothers should strive to be so noble, yet it also punishes the actual mother onscreen by suggesting that a poor mother should give her children up when upward class mobility is at stake. Mary Ann Doane's analysis of *Stella Dallas* emphasizes that Stella's "distanced spectatorial position is synonymous with her own negation as a mother. . . . Her sacrifice, her very absence from the scene, nevertheless insures her transformation into an Ideal of Motherhood" (Doane 1992:78). In "Something Else Besides a Mother," Linda Williams makes a similar point, arguing that the "device of devaluing and debasing the actual figure of the mother while sanctifying the institution of motherhood is typical of 'the woman's film' in general and the sub-genre of the maternal melodrama in particular" (Williams 1987:300). The spectator contends with these contradictory representations, vacillating between identification with the mother who sacrifices for her child and distancing from her as a debased character whose failure to transcend class barriers accounts for her need to make those sacrifices in the first place.

While class is still at issue, the 1940s reveal mothers grappling also with the ramifications of leaving the traditional domestic space, or refusing to reenter it after the war. In *The Desire to Desire: The Woman's Film of the 1940s,* Mary Ann Doane identifies the 1940s as the decade when mothers are reduced to an opposition that polarizes motherhood's "two excesses," being too close to a child—a condition linked to the dangers of isolationism—and being too distant from a child, and thus neglectful (Doane 1992:82). Joan Crawford's Mildred in *Mildred Pierce* (Michael Curtiz, 1945) epitomizes this polarization, as she struggles with class constraints to raise her two daughters. The key conflicts in the film circulate around women's roles as mothers in the domestic sphere and whether and when it is appropriate for them to step into the public economy. Pierce can be read as a progressive, feminist character in that she works baking pies, as a waitress, and eventually as a restaurant owner to support her daughters as a single, divorced mother. But she also reveals social anxieties about women working outside of the home after the culmination of World War II; Pierce bankrupts her business and fails in the public sphere by spoiling her elder daughter too much, and overlooks her duties as a mother and fails in the private sphere by being out on a date when her younger daughter begins showing signs of pneumonia. Her younger daughter's subsequent death can be read as Pierce's punishment for neglecting her job as mother (being too distant), and her elder daughter's downfall can be read as her punishment for being too much of a mother (being too close).

The bad mother/good mother and public/private polarities run throughout the film. The closing tableau epitomizes its struggles with women's roles in the post-WWII context. This scene shows Pierce as she walks out of the police station—where her elder daughter has just been charged with murder—into the sunrise with her estranged ex-husband. In the foreground, two women on their knees scrub the courthouse steps. In a 1945 context, this final image can be seen as reinforcing the contemporary ideology that women should leave their wartime jobs and return to the home. In "Feminist Film Theory: *Mildred Pierce* and the Second World War," Linda Williams argues, however, that this oversimplifies the film, and discredits the complexity of the female spectator's ability to process contradictory messages about womanhood, and about motherhood in particular. Williams argues that the final tableau can also be read as showing "a middle-class couple in a state of momentary and uneasy equilibrium," in that both have been "chastised for failing to fill their proper roles; their story cannot be subsumed into, or made secondary to, the untold story of the two women on their knees" (Williams 1988:28). Rather, the combined images show a complex range of constructions of femininity and motherhood in the film, with which the spectator must grapple.

In the 1950s, we see mothering written through the tensions of changing race and gender relations in the decade of the nascent civil rights movement, as evidenced in films such as Douglas Sirk's *Imitation of Life* (1959). On one level, Lana Turner's Lora and Juanita Moore's Annie again embody the extremes of the neglectful and the idealized mothers. Turner's role as a neglectful mother is counterpointed by Moore's role as the mother who is always present and supportive, but with race in the mix, there is little to celebrate as Moore fills in the sacrificing mammy role of racial stereotype. Motherhood here is complicated not only by class and gender role expectations, but by racialization and racism. Lora fails to mother Susie adequately by placing her career before her daughter, whereas Annie is the ever-present mammy, there to support Susie—Lora's daughter—in her adolescent struggles. Being cast in the mammy role, however, highlights Annie's failure to mother her own daughter Sara Jane, in an iconic refiguring of slavery's domestic tensions. John Stahl's 1934 version of *Imitation of Life*, starring Claudette Colbert, portrayed a white woman and an African American woman working together as partners to make a fortune from selling pancakes.

Jackie Byars contrasts the two films, emphasizing how they reveal shifting cultural responses to motherhood and work. In the depression-era economy, Colbert's Bea is ambitious because she has to be to support her family. In the late 1950s, Turner's Lora is ambitious because she wants to be, and that ambition threatens the patriarchy (Byars 1991:248). Race further complicates the different representations of the mothers' roles as workers, in that Lora's work is seen as problematic, while Annie's labor is invisible and assumed to be natural (Heung 1987:28–29). The film's conclusion demonstrates the degree to which the film represents uneasiness with white women's labor outside the home. When Annie dies at the film's end, her daughter returns and is comforted by Lora, so the film ends with a representation of the white career woman finally assuming a maternal role. Jackie Byars argues that this narrative closure supports dominant ideologies about motherhood and reveals the film's contradictory messages: "At a time when women were entering the workforce in unprecedented numbers, this film pits both residual and emergent notions of family structure and gender against the dominant ideology, which prevails in the narrative solution" (1991:249). Lora is returned to an appropriate maternal position at the film's end. But alternatives have been presented as well, Byars argues, and concludes that members of filmic audiences "negotiate ourselves" as we engage with these contending ideas (1991:258).

Jumping ahead two decades and writing on representations of mothers in the 1980s, E. Ann Kaplan argues that the questions raised regarding class, gender, and racial tensions for mothers in the 1960s and 1970s led to a backlash in filmic representations: "North American culture feels threatened by the legacies of the women's, gay, and other liberation movements of the sixties. As a result, it counters with images of couples happily united around the biological baby" (Kaplan 1994:269). Kaplan sees a trend in the late 1970s and 1980s of absenting the mother through films such as *Three Men and a Baby* and *Look Who's Talking*, where the fetus/infant replaces the woman as subjective agent. Furthermore, the mid-to-late 1980s reveal a "concern discourse" about white mothers in the workplace, manifested in films that began to "present satisfaction in mothering and the choice of mothering over career," which we can see in Diane Keaton's *Baby Boom* (Charles Shyer, 1987), for example (Kaplan 1994:260).

What is consistent across all these decades of the twentieth century is the positioning of film as a key site for the working through of cultural anxieties, especially in regard to white women as they balance motherhood, work, and their positions as sexual beings. Thus, maternal melodrama has a long and complex history against which to read the recent resurgence of filmic representations of motherhood.

HOLLYWOOD SUPERMOTHERS
IN THE TWENTY-FIRST CENTURY

"Supermother" films coming out of Hollywood in the twenty-first century thus far feature mothers having to prove their mettle once again, no longer against insensitive husbands, racism, limited employment opportunities, and the like, but rather against terrorists, the supernatural, and aliens from outer space, to name but a few of their contemporary challenges. The difficulty of finding a job for a black woman or a white divorcee in the 1930s through the 1950s has been replaced with the difficulty of protecting one's children against alien abduction or supernatural murder at the turn of the millennium, and doing it without help. In *Flightplan*, the father is dead. In *Dark Water*, he is more present, but in the process of being divorced. In *The Forgotten*, his memories of being a father have been erased. What we are left with are mothers—all white, all middle class, all employed, all outside of the traditional heterosexual institution of marriage—having to save their young children.

As Doane and Williams observed in relation to maternal melodramas in the 1930s and 1940s, these films continue to either absent or degrade the actual mother, while at the same time elevating ideals of motherhood. As contemporary maternal melodramas, *Flightplan*, *Dark Water,* and *The Forgotten* all debase the mothers in the films, in that they must fend off accusations of insanity and/or delusion. Jodie Foster's Kyle Pratt is debased throughout the film by accusations of delusion, while she is actually a cog in a terrorist plot to extort money from an airline. These charges of mental imbalance come from the captain and crew of the plane that she is flying home on to the United States after her husband's apparent suicide; they try to convince Pratt that her daughter is not lost on the plane, but actually died with her father and never boarded the plane. Contemporary film provides enough examples of scenarios where the audience must determine whether a character is delusional or not, that we do not automatically assume that her daughter was in fact physically with her when she boarded the plane. The close connection of women and hysteria further contributes to the film's debasing of Pratt as a mother and a woman. Eventually, she stymies the terrorist plot orchestrated by a flight marshal (who has kidnapped her daughter) and a flight attendant (who erased her daughter's name from the manifest) in order to extort money from the airline. Through these plot lines, the film reveals the continuing tension between a sacrificial ideal of motherhood, as Pratt risks her life repeatedly to find her daughter and thwart the terrorist plot, and a tendency of filmic representations to degrade and debase mothers onscreen, as this film does with its representations of the delusional mother.

One of the key tensions that this opposition signals is the role of the professional woman as mother, a tension that U.S. culture still has not resolved in the twenty-first century. Jodie Foster's character in *Flightplan* was originally written for a man, to be played by Sean Penn ("Trivia," Internet Movie Database). When

Foster sought the role, everything stayed the same—the job of propulsion engineer, and even the name Kyle Pratt. In casting Pratt as a mother rather than as a father, the film puts into play the familiar figure of the madwoman. As such, she cannot be taken seriously by the other characters in the film when she insists her daughter has disappeared, raising the question of whether propulsion engineers can indeed even be mothers, and, by extension, whether mothers can be propulsion engineers.

The debasement of the actual mother appears in *Dark Water* as well, where we see Jennifer Connelly's Dahlia suffering from severe headaches. Women's physical infirmity also has a long history in representation and has been used historically to keep women from venturing too far into the public sphere. Dahlia's husband portrays her headaches as evidence of a mental imbalance, in an attempt to win custody of their young daughter, Ceci, and punish Dahlia for breaking the heterosexual compact. Of these three film's supermothers, Dahlia is punished most radically for stepping outside the bounds of the nuclear family. After separating from her husband, Dahlia must move her daughter to a dilapidated and haunted flat on Roosevelt Island (formerly known as Welfare Island) between Manhattan and Queens, because that is what she can afford. Her failure to provide better economic support for her daughter is echoed in the specter of another neglectful mother, who is never directly referenced in the film. The ghost who haunts Dahlia and her daughter was a girl who drowned in the building after being abandoned by both of her parents. The ghost befriends Ceci, and ultimately threatens her life. In the pivotal scene, the ghost is drowning Dahlia's daughter, so Dahlia screams, "I'll be your mother. Take me!" In death she becomes the idealized sacrificial mother both to the dead girl and to her own living daughter—who can still see and hear her, but only in that building, where Dahlia will remain for eternity, the film implies, mothering the abandoned ghost daughter. Thus, Dahlia is absented as an actual mother, in that she dies at the film's end to save her daughter. She connects closely with Williams' articulation of the absence of the actual mother, and the elevation of ideal motherhood that we have seen coming from Hollywood throughout the twentieth century.

In this film, the anxieties that are most apparent circulate around a mother who slides from the middle class, heterosexual ideal into poverty, loss, and abjection. The film is suffused with questions of maternal power. Can Dahlia support Ceci? Can she protect her? Did the ghost's mother abandon her, or was she more directly responsible for her drowning? Water references throughout the film are amniotic, but not in a nurturing sense. These waters drowned the neglected girl, seep through the ceiling from the apartment above (where the girl lived before being abandoned), and threaten to drown Ceci as well. They are imbued with great powers and great fear, typifying the abject, especially in its associations with maternal power (Kristeva 1982:72). Culturally, the film struggles with the role of the divorced mother and her punishment for failing to support her child. Psychologically, the film explores the abject mother, from whose defiling grasp Ceci must escape—into the arms of her father—in order to survive. For the female spectator, we see a familiar vacillation—between identification with the sacrificial mother and distancing from her abjection.

The split between the ideal and the debased mother is evident in *The Forgotten* as well. Julianne Moore plays Telly Paretta, who is being counseled for having fabricated the existence of her nine-year-old son, Sam. In fact, she is the only mother—indeed, the only parent—involved in an alien experiment on Earth who stymies the aliens' attempt to prove that the human maternal instinct in particular can be beaten, erased, excised from human consciousness. The fathers in the film are easily manipulated—through the extraction of their memories—to believe that they either never had children or made them up. But Telly refuses to believe it, and is thus diagnosed as delusional. This tendency in supermother films to saddle the mother with a questionable mental state is clearly gendered. This is the key feature that distinguishes contemporary representations of supermothers from those of superfathers. For superdads such as Denzel Washington in *John Q* (Nick Cassavetes, 2002), and Tom Cruise in *War of the Worlds* (Steven Spielberg, 2005), race and class present formidable challenges to their being seen as adequate protectors of their children. But through desperate measures, they prove their worth as superfathers—Washington by procuring for his son a heart transplant, and Cruise by successfully shepherding his children through an alien invasion to the safety of their mother's parents' brownstone in Boston. These fathers are never called crazy, and thus reveal that Hollywood's representations of supermothers are much more ambivalent than its representations of superfathers.

The ambivalences in *The Forgotten* also circulate around traditional gender roles, mostly in terms of the nuclear family. When Telly starts digging around for answers, the aliens go so far as to erase the memory of her from her husband's mind. This perhaps explains the pivotal role of Ash, the father of one of Sam's friends, to whom Telly appeals for help. They reconstruct another "traditional" family unit, in their joint efforts to find their children. However, at the end of the film, it is Telly alone who faces the alien, and she alone who remembers anything. The focus is on the mother, in a move that essentializes her role and portrays her as the quintessential supermother. In the film's final sequence, we see the main alien figure in the experiment trying to retrieve Telly's earliest memory of her son, in order to make his experiment succeed. He chooses the moment of birth. But this does not work, because even after he removes that memory, Telly still remembers that she "had life inside" of her. She thwarts his study by going back to her connection with her fetus pre-birth, in a scene that celebrates the primal connection of mother and "unborn child." The film's celebration of that connection is not mirrored in its look at the heterosexual compact. As the only person who remembers anything, Telly approaches Ash in the film's final scene, as they watch their children play together, restored to their neighborhood playground. They meet as if for the first time. The film does not explore whether Telly will form a sexual relationship with Ash or be able to resume her nuclear family unit with Sam's father, played by Anthony Edwards. So while she has succeeded as a supermother, her ability to maintain that role in the traditional nuclear family is still very much in question.

The accusations of mental instability against the white mothers I am concerned with here shadow the successes and the resourcefulness of their representation as supermothers, and provide evidence of the anxiety over motherhood that still pervades contemporary U.S. culture, especially when white mothers work outside the home, seek other-mothering arrangements to provide care for their children, and leave the heterosexual unit. But the films cannot be read as simple demonizations of these mothers, since films do not articulate easily consumable narratives either empowering women to change their lives or conversely influencing them to support the status quo. Maternal melodramas across the century reflect changing social tensions, and produce complex possibilities for women spectators and even, perhaps, the spectator as mother. A key question these films raise is: How is the spectator as mother positioned by supermother films?

If she's not white, her position as spectator will have to cross racial representations to see whether there is any space carved out in these supermother fantasies for mothers who are women of color. Carol B. Duncan argues that when black women characters are featured in contemporary film—notably in science fiction—they are "usually represented as 'heroic mothers' whose portrayal draws on the long-standing mammy stereotype and occasionally as hypersexualized victims" (Duncan 2004:79). They are seen as "ethical and moral compasses whose wisdom mediates their relationships to white, male protagonists" (Duncan 2004:80). Examples that jump most readily to mind are Angela Bassett in *Strange Days* (Kathryn Bigelow, 1995) and Gloria Foster as the Oracle in *The Matrix* (Andy and Larry Wachowski, 1999). When we see black mothers who are not "moral compasses," they fail to balance motherhood, work, and sexuality—

as the white mothers do—and are more likely to appear as failed mothers than as supermothers. Halle Berry's Leticia in *Monster's Ball* (Marc Forster, 2001) develops a sexual relationship that avoids victimization, but only after her portrayal as an abusive mother to her son and his subsequent death. With few exceptions, portrayals of black mothers in the 1990s and early twenty-first-century film tend to demonize them—especially if they are single—modeling mainstream American culture and its devaluing of single black motherhood.

Once again, we see the trio of motherhood, work, and sexuality as an impossible combination. For the black heroic mothers Duncan writes about, they combine work and motherhood, but are not allowed to express their sexualities. They are either single or asexual, baking cookies in the kitchen. When Leticia develops a sexual relationship, her child is dead. The white supermothers also combine work and motherhood, but have to prove their abilities as mothers through the tremendous feats they must accomplish. Their sexual lives are also in flux, as they move from the heterosexual institution of marriage as a result of death, divorce, and alien intervention. Given the significant cultural differences between representations of black and white supermothers, the continuities between the two are striking. Both black and white mothers "fail" to balance motherhood, work, and sexuality, revealing the broad strokes with which ideal motherhood continues to be painted in U.S. culture. So while the contexts in which black heroic mothers and white supermothers play out their lives are quite different, spectators are similarly positioned as they must negotiate the different ways different mothers "succeed" and "fail."

FAILED MOTHERS IN THE TWENTY-FIRST CENTURY

Running counter to the supermother representations I explore above are a set of other mothers whose representations reveal additional anxieties in response to mothers who refuse to work outside the home, who work in fields that are not appropriate for idealized mothers, and who have complex sexualities outside of the heterosexual institution of marriage.

In *Freedomland* (2006), Julianne Moore plays Brenda Martin, a working-class, white, single mother whose failure as a mother stems from her prioritizing of her sexual needs over her mothering responsibilities. Martin claims that her five-year-old son has been abducted by a black man during a carjacking. This is the narrative she fabricates in order to hide the fact that Cody, her son, drank a whole bottle of cough syrup with codeine in it in order to punish her for leaving him alone while meeting her black lover. Racial tension, class, and the intersection of gender and mothering all converge to position and punish Brenda Martin for prioritizing a sexual liaison with a black man over the well-being of her son, and then trying to shirk the responsibility of her actions by blaming the stereotypical black male criminal for what she has done; this evokes the case of Susan Smith, who drowned her sons in South Carolina in 1994 before claiming that her car had been stolen by a black man.

Kaplan observes, "Images of a radically transformed family are needed to help us move toward new institutional forms for the postmodern era—forms that would finally accept, and make possible, white women combining sex, work, and motherhood" (Kaplan 1994:269). Martin fails dismally in this regard, losing her sexual relationship, her job as a childcare provider in a local day care for impoverished children, and her son. That she is a white woman in a predominantly black community heightens the particular tensions of her failure, in a society that is accustomed to the elevation of white motherhood and the debasement of black mothers. The film thus presents the spectator with another set of contradictory representations; Brenda Martin can be interpreted as bridging racial barriers in her work with children and women of color and her relationship with a black man, but she also displays the worst form of racism in her evoking the specter of the stereotypical black male criminal. Furthermore, the film reveals continuing anxieties about single white mothers, and their inability to adequately protect their children while trying to fill the role of the breadwinner and maintaining sexually active lives.

As we look at Hollywood and independent films in the first decade of the twenty-first century, Kaplan's call for "images of a radically transformed family" seems to have come to fruition, but these images are by no means simple or celebratory. The space for representing white women as sexual beings, workers, and mothers is more evident in films that portray mothers as failures in terms of the dominant ideologies of idealized sacrificial motherhood. *Freedomland* provides us with a Hollywood example, but there are also two pertinent films from Israel and Argentina, respectively, both of which portray a single mother struggling to raise a daughter while refusing traditional work options and displaying overt sexuality. Keren Yedaya's *Or, My Treasure* (2005) portrays a failed mother in Ronit Elkabetz's Ruthie, a street prostitute trying and failing to find different work. It is her daughter, seventeen-year-old Or (which means "light" in Hebrew), who is the supermother, attending high school, working as a dish-washer, collecting bottles for refund money, and giving sexual favors to the landlord to keep from being evicted. In one scene, Or bathes Ruthie when she comes home bleeding after being assaulted on the job. Or mothers Ruthie in the film, caring for her physically and trying to get her to leave prostitution. She even lines up a job for Ruthie to work as a maid. Yedaya's formal decisions—she uses no score and a stationary camera—create a nonsentimental structure that balances the highly charged content of the film, in which Ruthie chooses sex work over domestic labor or the traditional family unit. This forces the spectator into the situation of choosing how to read her actions, and whether to judge her for failing as a mother or to suspend judgment in the light of her struggles as a prostitute and a woman with sexual desires of her own.

The space constraints in the film put Ruthie's sexuality squarely in Or's (and the spectator's) visual frame. Or sleeps in the one bedroom they have, and Ruthie sleeps on the couch in the den. When Ruthie has sex with her boyfriend, Or comes home to the two of them in bed together. There are no consequences for Ruthie for her nonpaid sexual activities, a significant difference between the failed mother and the supermother. However, there are severe consequences for Or for her sexual activities. The film portrays her sexual development as a curious adolescent. Her boyfriend—with whom she is sexually active—is made to stop seeing her by his parents, who are also neighbors to Ruthie and Or, as well as being Or's employers. The boyfriend's mother states that Or is too easy, a conclusion she comes to as much from Ruthie's occupation as from Or's behavior. So while the film manages to portray a woman combining work, sex, and motherhood, Ruthie's sex work is violent and sporadic at best, sex for her is fraught with questions of money, and her role as a mother is severely hampered by work and sex. Reading Or as a mother to Ruthie, her ability to mother is likewise compromised by age, her sexual relationships are tainted with sexual double standards, and her work options are limited to low-paid labor or sex work. She chooses the latter as she slowly enters her mother's profession.

This depiction of the failed mother, read in conjunction with Hollywood's supermothers, reveals Doane's "two excesses" still at work in contemporary filmic representations of mothers (Doane 1992:82). If being too close to a child signaled the dangers of isolationism in the 1940s, perhaps being too distant from a child in the twenty-first century signals the dangers of globalization and the tensions of geopolitical relations that both yoke cultures together as never before and yet alienate them at the same time—largely through power differentials. Ruthie's johns are guest workers in Israel, though Yedaya does not draw attention to this in the film (Klawans 2005:35). Set in Tel Aviv, *Or, My Treasure*, in its rejection of a "narrow-focused social melodrama" and "its ability to combine a sense of alienation with a constant feeling of compassion, holds up a mirror to contemporary urban Israeli society" (Klein 2005:73). Since both mother and daughter choose to prostitute themselves, the film forces the spectator to grapple with presumptions about the costs of desire for women, and mothers in particular. When Or chooses to start working as a prostitute—after being ostracized by her boyfriend's parents—we see the pervasive punishment that women and mothers in particular experience when they step outside the traditional heterosexual compact and take their labor into their own hands. These costs do not stay with the women as mothers themselves, but are passed down to their daughters as well. In a globalized economy, the film suggests, women with few options have little to barter beyond themselves.

In Vera Fogwill and Martin Desalvo's *Kept & Dreamless* (2005), another mother and daughter struggle to make ends meet during Argentina's economic collapse. Vera Fogwill's Florencia is a cocaine addict, and her daughter—nine-year-old Eugenia—does what she can to ensure their survival. Florencia also combines work, sex, and motherhood: she works as a maid for an acquaintance, in a striking parallel to Ruthie's attempt to find legitimate work; she has sex with an occasional boyfriend, also in the den of her apartment; and she mothers Eugenia when she is not asleep or passed out. What is significant about Florencia's approach to work is that it is not a job that turns her luck around, but more the bond she forms with her formerly estranged friend—who likewise leaves a lot to be desired in her mothering. Prior to working as a maid, Florencia spouts anti-capitalist rhetoric, defends not working, and ekes out an existence on graft as she cons money for fake abortions from her own estranged, middle-class mother. The film portrays a complex network of women who enable each other's survival. The spectator again swings between frustration over Florencia's refusal to work, and admiration for her resolve to put bonds with family above a desire to enter the middle class.

Sexuality in the film is likewise repositioned. Bodies and nudity are natural and shared. Eugenia becomes the audience's surrogate spectator in this regard, commenting to her mother's boyfriend, "I can see your dick. But don't worry. I've seen lots of dicks. I'm tired of them." Eugenia reveals that she takes her mother's sexuality as a matter of course. It is not something shameful, but has become merely boring. Florencia likewise views sexuality and reproduction as common elements of life. When she tells Eugenia she is pregnant again, and that she wants to keep it despite her mother's insistence upon an abortion, she says, "I'm not afraid of what she says might happen to me." The audience is never told what that is, but can surmise that it has to do with economics. Florencia's decision affirms her role as a mother despite her class position and drug addiction. The film ends with her bathing her new son, her estranged mother having returned offering help without strings attached or judgment.

Motherhood suffuses *Kept & Dreamless,* and despite her drug addiction and refusal to work, Florencia subverts traditional ideals of sacrificial motherhood and provides emerging alternative understandings of what is valuable in mothering. She bathes Eugenia and washes her hair in a tender scene early in the film, and tickles her and talks to her about philosophical issues. In contrast, Florencia's friend and employer Celina is depressed and unhappy in her marriage, despite being very financially well off. She is constantly angry with her two daughters. Florencia's mother Sara uses money as power over Florencia, and Olga the neighbor is estranged from her children, largely due to their selfishness. Another plot in the film follows Eugenia's father and his mother as they are evicted from their home. The film's portrayal of her mothering is also complex, in that she harangues her son for his shortcomings, but stands by Eugenia when she visits them at the film's end, showing her how to use a tampon when her first period comes and reassuring her in that moment of passage. Mothers abound in the film, and portray a true range of mothering possibilities—unlike anything the spectator sees in Hollywood's supermother extravaganzas.

Where *Or, My Treasure* spins into a dystopia of punishment for mothers as sexual beings, *Kept & Dreamless* weaves not a utopia, but an alternate vision of society that would value mothering in multiple places, value women's work on multiple levels, recognize women as sexual beings without demonizing them as such, and rethink how women's work, mothering, and sexualities are both valued and devalued against a backdrop of South American political and economic instability in the globalized twenty-first century.

SUPPORTING MOTHERS

The examples from Israel and Argentina reveal directors portraying what appear to be antitheses to idealized sacrificial mothers. The women struggle to provide the basics of food and shelter, often leaving these to their daughters to sort out. Yedaya's film challenges a social structure that provides few options to women, but Fogwill and Desalvo's film proactively posits different social avenues to survival—outside of traditional work and family structures. In both films, the spectator is charged with the task of evaluating what it means to mother, and how mothering intersects with state interests and responsibilities.

Comparing these films to Hollywood productions, we see both more and less being asked of mothers in U.S. contexts. The supermothers discussed above surmount great challenges, but the films themselves do little to complicate the binary of idealized and debased motherhood. And this is a fairly consistent pattern. Two additional examples reveal that Hollywood has yet to rise to Kaplan's challenge to construct new ways of representing motherhood that are equal to the complexities of the twenty-first century, and that allow women to combine work, motherhood, and sexuality. Uma Thurman's Beatrix Kiddo in *Kill Bill Volumes 1* and *2* seems like a great opportunity to rethink the maternal melodrama. But even Tarantino's work cannot escape the quandary of how to break this mold. On one hand, Beatrix/"The Bride" reinforces traditional ideals of motherhood by giving up her job as an assassin when she learns she is pregnant, because you cannot be an assassin and a mother. On the other hand, we could read her as a new kind of figure, both mother and assassin, when at the end of *Volume 2* she decides to kill Bill—her former lover and the father of her child—rather than reunite with him. The spectator is left once again with a woman who has to eclipse or eliminate one part of her life. For Beatrix, that part is Bill, who represents her sexual being.

Another example can be found in Niki Caro's *North Country* (2005), which brings together issues of white motherhood, work, and sexuality in Charlize Theron's character Josey Aimes, who becomes one of the first women to seek work in the Minnesota iron mines. But once again, the character cannot work, mother, and have sex outside of marriage without being punished. Aimes withstands sexual harassment on the job and a withering court case, but the film is most interesting for its attention to her role as a single mother, and how she sticks with her job and her commitment to fight the harassment so that she can be a good provider and role model for her kids. She combines work and motherhood, but sacrifices a sexual relationship in that the film leaves no room for her to pursue one with the Woody Harrelson character, Bill White. The film is noticeable for how it does *not* create a romance between Aimes and White, though the possibility for it is hinted at throughout. Do we read this as yet another failure of filmic representation to produce a woman character who combines work, sex, and motherhood? Or do we read this as the film refusing to recuperate its heroine back into traditional heterosexuality? Thinking back to the end of *Mildred Pierce,* the spectator is once again faced with a complex spectrum of possibilities. The positioning of Theron as a mother in the film in many ways supersedes her positioning as a litigant in a famous sexual harassment lawsuit, situating her as yet another supermother of sorts.

While we can definitely see a continuity in the twenty-first-century Hollywood films with the sacrificial ideals of motherhood that many films in the 1930s and 1940s exhibited, we can also see continuity in terms of contradictory readings that audience members can take with them in order to intervene against those sacrificial ideals, as they respond to representations of actual mothers and what happens to them in these films. And here Dahlia is perhaps most instructive. While Foster's Kyle Pratt, Moore's Telly, Thurman's Kiddo, and Theron's Aimes all hold their children in their arms at the end of their respective films, Dahlia remains separated from her daughter at the end of *Dark Water*. Her story is the most circumscribed by class limitations in the Hollywood films, and brings to mind Miriam Peskowitz's argument in *The Truth Behind the Mommy Wars*: that media-constructed images of mothers at war with each other over their differences tend to cover over their similar struggles to find support for their mothering, support that is lacking at all economic levels but most brutally—and perhaps most life-threateningly—for those who live at or below the poverty line (54) and outside of the traditional nuclear family. Reading Dahlia—and putting her in dialogue with Ruthie and Florencia—requires that we think about maternal sacrifice and the support that mothers need, not only when fighting the supernatural, but when seeking the basics of food and shelter as well. While *Flightplan*'s Kyle Pratt and *The Forgotten*'s Telly Paretta leave the mother in the audience with little but awe at the supermothering powers displayed before her, Dahlia and her counterparts in Ruthie and Florencia leave the mother in the audience expecting more—more support, more options, more tangible ways for mothers to survive, work, love, be sexual, and practice mothering outside traditional heterosexual family units.

WORKS CITED

Byars, Jackie. 1991. *All That Hollywood Allows: Re-Reading Gender in 1950s Melodrama*. Chapel Hill: University of North Carolina Press.

Doane, Mary Ann. 1992. *The Desire to Desire: The Woman's Film of the 1940s*. Bloomington: Indiana University Press.

Duncan, Carol B. 2004. Black women and motherhood in contemporary cinematic science fiction. In *Mother Matters: Motherhood as Discourse and Practice*, ed. Andrea O'Reilly, 79–86. Toronto: Association for Research on Mothering.

Heung, Marina. 1987. "What's the matter with Sara Jane?": Daughters and mothers in Douglas Sirk's *Imitation of Life*. *Cinema Journal* 26.3:21–43.

Kaplan, E. Ann. 1994. Sex, work, and motherhood: Maternal subjectivity in recent visual culture. In *Representations of Motherhood*, ed. D. Bassin, M. Honey, and M. M. Kaplan, 256–271. New Haven: Yale University Press.

Klawans, Stuart. 2005. Adult content. Review of *Howl's Moving Castle, Madagascar, Or (My Treasure)*, Human Rights Watch International Film Festival. *The Nation,* June 20, 34–36.

Klein, Uri. 2005. Review of *Or (My Treasure)*. *Film Comment*, July–August, 73.

Kristeva, Julia. 1982. *Powers of Horror: An Essay on Abjection.* New York: Columbia University Press.

Peskowitz, Miriam. 2005. *The Truth Behind the Mommy Wars: Who Decides What Makes a Good Mother?* Emeryville, Calif.: Seal Press.

Trivia. n.d. Internet Movie Database. http://www.imdb.com/title/tt0408790/trivia (accessed Dec. 14, 2006).

Williams, Linda. 1987. "Something else besides a mother": *Stella Dallas* and the maternal melodrama. In *Home Is Where the Heart Is: Studies in Melodrama and the Woman's Film*, ed. Christine Gledhill, 299–325. London: BFI Books.

——. 1988. Feminist film theory: *Mildred Pierce* and the Second World War. In *Female Spectators: Looking at Film and Television*, ed. E. Deirdre Pribram, 12–30. London: Verso.

FILMS

Baby Boom. Dir. Charles Shyer. United States: Meyers/Shyer, 1987.

Dark Water. Dir. Walter Salles. United States: Post No Bills Films, Pandemonium Productions, Touchstone Pictures, and Vertigo Entertainment, 2005.

Flightplan. Dir. Robert Schwentke. United States: Touchstone Pictures, 2005.

The Forgotten. Dir. Joseph Ruben. United States: Revolution Studies and Visual Arts Entertainment, Inc., 2004.

Freedomland. Dir. Joe Roth. United States: Revolution Studios, 2006.

Imitation of Life. Dir. Douglas Sirk. United States: Universal Pictures, 1959.

Imitation of Life. Dir. John M. Stahl. United States: Universal Pictures, 1934.

Kept & Dreamless [*Las mantenidas sin sueño*]. Dir. Vera Fogwill and Martín DeSalvo. Argentina: Avalon Productions, 2005.

Kill Bill Vol. 1. Dir. Quentin Tarantino. United States: Miramax Films, A Band Apart, and Super Cool ManChu, 2003.

Kill Bill Vol. 2. Dir. Quentin Tarantino. United States: Miramax Films, A Band Apart, and Super Cool ManChu, 2004.

Mildred Pierce. Dir. Michael Curtiz. United States: Warner Brothers, 1945.

North Country. Dir. Niki Caro. United States: Warner Brothers, Industry Entertainment, Participant Productions, and Nick Wechsler Productions, 2005.

Or, My Treasure. Dir. Keren Yedaya. Israel: Bizibi, 2004.

Stella Dallas. Dir. King Vidor. United States: Samuel Goldwyn Company, 1937.

Juno or Just Another Girl?   **NINE**

Young Breeders and a New Century of   MARY THOMPSON
Racial Politics of Motherhood

The critical success of the 2007 film *Juno* came as something of a surprise. If "we" agree that teen pregnancy is a problem, then why this popular and critical fascination with pregnant sixteen-year-old Juno MacGuff? Described as "too odd and too smart to be either a case study or the object of leering disapproval" (Scott 2007), Juno is "the daughter most parents ought to be proud to have" (Kine 2007:49), and critics caution that the film is without a reproductive rights agenda, as Juno simply "makes her choices as she sees them and, no matter what our personal beliefs, we respond to her pluckiness and snappy humor" (Thomson 2007:C1). While I agree that *Juno* is an enjoyable film, I am curious as to the renewed cultural interest in pregnant teens in this century, and I am equally suspicious of claims that the text is free of ideology or that we are simply responding to a smart, plucky heroine.

This essay investigates the twenty-first-century racial politics of motherhood through a reading of recent representations of counterculture teenage mothers

An earlier version of this essay appeared in *Genders* 43 (2006).

in the film *Juno* and in the edited collection *Breeder: Real-Life Stories from the New Generation of Mothers* (Gore and Lavender 2001). Specifically, this essay reads against the celebration of "choice" lauded in these depictions by considering the ideology of the "new momism," as well as the racial and class privileges behind notions of "choice." To accomplish this reading, I look to earlier texts, the 1993 film *Just Another Girl on the IRT* and the novel *PUSH* (Sapphire 1996), not just for how they remind us of the genealogy of the term *breeder* as a racist label for black mothers from slavery through welfare reform, but also for how they reveal "choice" as a function of racial privilege. My argument is that, while *Breeder* and *Juno* uphold ideals of "choice," the texts also reveal that young, countercultural women—typically assumed too financially unstable to parent—can claim legitimate motherhood through an intersection of ideologies of consumerism and race privilege. By performing their legitimate claim through race- and class-based "good" choices, however, mothers in *Breeder* and *Juno* mask how these privileges "trump" the disadvantages of youth in the cultural struggle to define "good mothers."

In the introduction to *Breeder*, co-edited by Ariel Gore and Bee Lavender, Gore recounts how as a younger person, she and fellow punks harassed pregnant women at the grocery store by yelling "breeder" at them, cynically questioning the wisdom of "bringing children in to *this* world," and sneering, "how deluded is *that*?" (2001:xiii). Now that she is a mother herself, Gore's perspective has changed. In an interview in *Clamor*, she describes the collection's themes as "love and death and surviving and mothering soulfully in this world—the one we swore we'd never bring children into, the one that spawned our cynicism and the one that, ultimately, nurtures our hope" (Adney 2001:67). With Lavender, Gore co-edits the zine and Web site *Hip Mama*; she sees their work as filling the need for alternative and empowering representations of motherhood. She states, "As the daughters of the 1970s feminist movement, we cherish our reproductive freedom. And as willing breeders, we refuse to be oppressed by the institution of motherhood" (2001:xiii). Resisting what she calls the "diaper commercial" version of carefully planned motherhood, she boasts, "In a culture where women often delay childbearing as long as nature and science will allow, we chose to have our kids *while*, not *instead of*, following our dreams" (2001:xiii).

Recurrently throughout the collection, norms of family structure are questioned and redefined. The text offers stories of single mothers, teen mothers, and lesbian mothers who rely on artificial insemination or adoption, as well as families whose structures are disrupted by suicide, manic-depression, bulimia, autism, and infertility. These stories affirm alternative family structures and question the assumed normalcy of the hetero-normative, two-parent family, reflecting one author's observation, "We are re-creating family" (2001:100). In addition, stories about birth control pills, pregnancy tests, neonatal care units for premature babies, and breast pumps that allow new mothers to work nine-to-five jobs reveal the technologizing of motherhood, while other stories challenge medicalized motherhood by narrating the experience of women giving birth at home or unassisted. In other stories, the cultural narrative of pregnancy as a happy time is interrogated for how it delegitimizes some women's experiences, and several stories challenge the image of mothers as asexual and/or passive by reflecting sexual mothers and mothers who seek to teach women's empowerment to their children. As the editors intend, *Breeder* is a celebration of the idea of "choice" and the variety of reproductive choices being made by young women.

Not explicitly a third-wave feminist text, *Juno* (screenplay by Diablo Cody and directed by Jason Reitman) offers a similar story of female empowerment through personal choice. Sixteen-year-old post-punkster Juno MacGuff (Ellen Page) discovers herself to be pregnant after orchestrating a sexual encounter with her childhood best friend, Paulie Bleeker (Michael Cera). Foregoing a "hasty abortion" after learning that the fetus has fingernails, Juno elects to have the baby and give it to the "lovely couple" of suburban and tasteful McMansion-dwelling adoptive parents, Vanessa and Mark Loring (Jennifer Garner and Jason Bateman). Confronted by a series of tough choices (including whether or not to go through with the adoption process when the Loring's marriage unravels), Juno is nevertheless feted by the film for an ironic self-awareness that enables her to navigate her options. The film concludes happily with the baby in Vanessa's apt care and with Juno's recognition that she has loved Paulie all along. Not only does she choose when and with whom to have sex, she decides what to do with her pregnancy before involving her parents, and, even more significantly, she selects the family who will adopt her child. Still naïve and "dealing with things way beyond [her] maturity level," Juno is nevertheless in control of her sexuality and reproductive options.

Despite the seemingly feminist celebration of choice that characterizes these texts, my contention is that the representation of motherhood in both *Breeder* and *Juno* can actually be read in highly conventional ways—that are dissatisfying from a feminist perspective—because of the texts' participation in the "new momism." A critique of attachment parenting, Douglas and Michaels' *The Mommy Myth* (2004) analyzes the phenomenon the authors dub the new momism, an ideological backlash against feminist gains in the arenas of child care and the family. Over the past three decades, the authors contend, media allegations of an "internal social threat" posed by mythic welfare queens and mothers who kill their children (à la Susan Smith) have intensified a cultural obsession with motherhood as exemplified by the relentless representations of celebrity mothers. At once a subject of media focus, motherhood has also become a site of consumer culture activity; good motherhood, according to the new logic, means being a good consumer. All mothers—including stay-at-home moms, working moms, moms with special needs children, moms who buy only organic foods, and many others—have become markets, fueling a national hypernatalism, maternal self-surveillance, and cultural vigilance. Douglas and Michaels argue:

> The new momism gained momentum in the 1980s because of media panics about endangered kids, the lack of institutional supports for families, and because of right-wing attacks against working mothers. But let's not also forget that a key tenet of the new momism—that it was crucial to invest in as many goods and services for your child as possible—was very, very profitable. The spread of cable TV, which brought distant UHF stations and kid-specific channels like Nickelodeon, Disney, The Cartoon Network, Fox Family, and MTV into the home, made targeting mothers and kids much easier, and more incessant. The ever-ballooning standards of good motherhood were inflated even further by the simultaneous exhortations to buy more, buy better, buy sooner. (2004:269)

Today's woman, according to the ideology of the new momism, is not complete without a child to whom she sacrifices herself as primary caregiver (2004:4). While seemingly a celebration of motherhood, this message—neither new nor progressive—conveys intensified levels of patriarchal surveillance and internalization. Douglas and Michaels reveal that the new momism offers false assurances to mothers through proper consumer choices, while suffocating them with products and foreclosing avenues of escape from a relentless message to define successful womanhood in terms of ceaseless self-surveillance, sacrifice, and consumption.

Being a counterculture mom (even a particularly media-hip one) does not make one immune to the new momism, and unavoidably *Breeder* and *Juno* participate in the new momism ideology, which in turn informs the popular reception of their texts. *Breeder* and *Juno* reflect, for example, the new momism dictum of maternal self-sacrifice. Despite the editors' claims that the authors in *Breeder* chose "to have our kids *while,* not *instead of,* following our dreams," several if not most of the narratives portray women who at best must postpone their plans for educations and careers. The few authors who balance childrearing with careers are nevertheless pulled by the same forces that insist they make other personal sacrifices in the interests of their children. Similar sacrifices to children are presented in *Juno*, as the protagonist sacrifices her body to the gestation of the child she then gives to Vanessa, who in turn sacrifices her marriage in order to adopt the child her husband does not want.

In addition to reflecting ideas of maternal self-sacrifice, these texts uphold the new momism's emphasis on maternal primacy. The subtitle of *Breeder*, for example, indicates that its focus is on mothers—not feminist parenting more generally. In *Juno*, the primacy of mothers is represented through their being the capable parents: Juno makes the "correct" decision to put the child she cannot adequately care for up for adoption; her stepmother, Bren, leaps to her defense against a prejudicial ultrasound technician; and Vanessa realizes that she will be a better parent without her husband. Despite alternative lifestyles, the mothers in both *Breeder* and *Juno* still enjoy, uphold, and celebrate maternal privilege, and it is this privilege, I believe, that appeals to their audiences. While these texts affirm mothers, their focus on parenting as *mothering* reinscribes the "natural" primacy of women in child care and locates their power in this role. Fathers do make appearances (a stay-at-home dad in one story in *Breeder* and the passive geeky Paulie in *Juno*, as well as Juno's own father) but pale in comparison to the abundance of super-capable mothers undertaking attachment parenting.

While *Breeder* and *Juno* disrupt certain conventional images of motherhood and materialism, the underlying tenets of the new momism—sacrifice, maternal primacy, and consumerism—are reflected in their stories and reveal their protagonists to be "good choice"–makers and therefore good mothers. Gore and Lavender reveal the consumer-based identities of the authors in *Breeder* in the following terms:

> Women of my generation grew up in a blur of ERA demonstrations and disco dancing. We were commune babies, latchkey kids, the daughters of women who changed what it meant to be female in America. . . . We became riot grrrls, sometime slackers, student-loan queens. We published zines, pioneered the new high-tech economy, revitalized the American tradition of political protest.   (2001:xii)

The "hippies and punks" included in the pages of *Breeder* represent an ideological counterculture to middle-class American values, but as riot grrrls, college students, and technology pioneers, they are also clearly marked as counterculture *consumers* (of music, media, education, technology, etc.). The brief essay by Kimberly Bright at the beginning of the collection works well to illustrate the shared consumer characteristics of the authors and intended readers. Bright's "Breeder Rites of Passage" lists a series of "firsts" presumably shared by the authors, including "college: obscure liberal arts school on scholarship," "trip to Europe (Montmartre, Soho, Prague)," "psychotherapy; detox center or Prozac prescription," "motherhood," "Volvo purchase," and "mortgage (funky cottage, townhouse, or bungalow in artsy neighborhood" (2001:2). Although young consumers, the authors are validated as politically correct, thoughtful consumers who make politically superior choices about in vitro fertilization, adoption, home births, and parenthood, education, and careers, etc.

Similarly, the mothers in *Juno* (both biological and adoptive) exhibit consumer-based identities by which viewers can recognize their claim to motherhood. The adoptive mother, Vanessa, clearly asserts her "good choice"–making power through her recognizable middle-class material possessions, including her tasteful home, clothing, jewelry, and car. Juno, on the other hand, is a discriminating fan of alternative and punk music (underscored by the indie-infused soundtrack of the film), graphic novels, and slasher-films, and also has plans to attend college. Both Vanessa and Juno are framed by the film to enable the audience's appreciation of their "good choices" in consuming and in mothering. However, as feminist readers and viewers of *Breeder* and *Juno*, we might consider how the construction of "good choice"–makers implicitly relies upon the production of "bad choice"–makers and informs our understanding of these mothers.

In *Beggars and Choosers*, Ricki Solinger raises an alarm against the way the feminist discourse of rights has been supplanted by the marketplace discourse of choice in understanding women's entitlement to control of their reproductivity. As Solinger asks, "How can users of such a term avoid distinguishing, in consumer-culture fashion, between a woman who can and a woman who can't afford to make a choice?" (2001:6), suggesting the discourse of choice's power to efface the real material differences between women/mothers. As a result, we lose sight of how one group of women's access to choices depends upon other women being denied choices. She uses the example of how foreign adoption by U.S. parents depends upon the effacement of the biological mothers in countries whose parenting "choices" usually are profoundly limited by economic oppression. In fact, we see this erasure when Juno jokingly chastises the Lorings for not adopting a child from China, where, she ironically speculates, ubiquitous unwanted babies are shot from t-shirt guns at sporting events.

Ultimately, the discourse of choice establishes categories of "good choice"–makers and "bad choice"–makers that reinforce the belief that motherhood is the earned privilege of the middle class. Here Solinger points to recent punitive public policy and welfare reforms that judge women of color (predominantly) as "bad choice"–makers who are not entitled to their children or to making decisions about them because they are too poor and/or got pregnant too young or too often. As Dorothy Roberts (1997), Hortense Spillers (1997), Patricia Hill-Collins (2000), and Angela Davis (1981) have argued, these are the women to whom the title "breeder" has been most scornfully applied, resulting in the strongest social censure and the most damaging social policies. As in previous decades, today's urban-dwelling, resource-less, African American, teenage mothers on welfare are still the reproductive Other of legitimately reproducing middle-class mothers; they are, as Douglas and Michaels observe, the "internal threat" that the new momism is defined against. As Solinger has observed, the increasing commodification of pregnancy and motherhood has resulted in some women having "more legitimate relationships to babies and motherhood status" while other women are defined as "illegitimate consumers" (2001:7). While age can be one factor in determining a woman's legitimate claim to motherhood and reproductive rights, the combined factors of race and class continue in the twenty-first century to hold greater sway.

Taken in the context of Solinger's work, the texts of *Breeder* and *Juno* seem less like progressive celebrations of feminist choices and more like assertions of relative class and race privilege. While some of the authors in *Breeder* identify themselves as nonwhite, they are not the economically disadvantaged authors; and while five out of the thirty-six authors discuss being on welfare, public assistance is represented as being on par with other challenges (such as when to discretely pump one's breasts). None of the authors' situations explicitly reflects the intersecting constraints of racism and class oppression. Overall, the text is a celebration of the relative freedom to choose when to go to college, when to have careers, and when to have children—choices that reveal the class and/or race privilege of most of the authors.

Juno similarly reflects an assertion of white middle-class women's legitimate claim to motherhood. Despite coming from a working-class background, Juno's race, wit, and plans to attend college mark her as a woman who is clearly on her way to earning the privilege of motherhood—even the fact that she chooses Vanessa, whose race and class mark her as a superior adoptive mother, works in framing the audience's appreciation of Juno as an ideal choice-maker. Juno is an informed, savvy, self-aware, and self-actualizing consumer, but above all else she is white. While Katha Pollit (2008) has critiqued the film from a feminist perspective, arguing that it privileges adoption over abortion, I believe that a feminist critique is also required of how the legitimization of white women's claims to birthing and adopting babies rests on the tacit delegitimization of other (non-white, non-middle-class) women's choices.

The affirmation of reproductive choice and motherhood as a middle-class and white privilege comes into relief when *Breeder* and *Juno* are compared to texts about African American teen pregnancy and motherhood. Two texts from the 1990s, Sapphire's novel *PUSH* (1996) and Leslie Harris' film *Just Another Girl on the IRT*, help to frame our understanding of whose choices are being celebrated and why. While it might be tempting to read the difference between these texts historically and argue for some kind of "progress" in tolerance for young women's reproductive choices, my argument is that the racial difference of the protagonists of these texts explains the difference in critical and audience reception.

Precious Jones, the African American protagonist of *PUSH*, is an illiterate sixteen-year-old incest-survivor living on welfare in Harlem with two children by her father. Prior to the novel's action, Precious has had her first child at age twelve, but it is her second pregnancy that prompts her expulsion from junior high and her enrollment in an alternative school, where she learns she has contracted HIV from her father. Exposing the realities behind the stereotype of the "welfare mother," Sapphire's novel reveals social institutions enforcing and protecting patriarchal and (white) racial privilege. Keenly aware that her compromised literacy is part of her social voiceless-ness and disenfranchisement, Precious observes that her existence is like that of the otherworldly vampires she sees on television, whose presence is not recorded by mirrors and photographs:

> I big, I talk, I eats, I cooks, I laugh, watch TV, do what my muver say. But I can see when the picture come back I don't exist. Don't nobody want me. Don't nobody need me. I know who I am. I know who they say I am—vampire sucking the system's blood. Ugly black grease to be wipe away, punish, kilt, changed, finded a job for. (Sapphire 1996:31)

Precious' recognition that she and her children are victimized not only by her parents but also by the medical providers, educators, law enforcement, and policy makers who enforce her marginalization "pushes" readers to consider how the delegitimization of some women's claim to motherhood is directly related to racist and class-based stereotypes.

Unlike the pleasure evinced by viewers and critics for Juno's choices, readers express feelings of alienation, frustration, disgust, and pity when forced to see the world from the margins, through the eyes of Precious. However, in the classroom, this outrage is often directed more at Precious than at the interlocking systems of oppression (and the reader's own participation in them). Students express their dislike of Precious' lack of options and control (why doesn't she leave Harlem?) and support (why don't the teachers/police officers/social workers/nurses help her?), her lack of self-knowledge (how can she not know she's pregnant?), her lack of control over her body's reactions (why does she respond sexually to being raped by her father?), and her lack of control over the future (why doesn't she resist being tracked toward a GED and a dead-end job?). Most shocking, however, is the realization that Precious is often not even aware of the choices from which she is excluded. Early in the novel, when she arrives at the alternative school, Precious asks a staffer, "What alternative is?" [sic] (1996:26), which becomes an emblematic question. Even when we as readers can identify our own complicity with the social policies that constrain Precious, it is still hard not to be skeptical of her ability to be a "good mother" even when presented with her obvious love and care for her children. How can she get an education, find a job, and break the cycle of welfare? How can she survive AIDS? These concerns are often expressed in terms of class and economic issues, but the unspoken issue of race is clearly interwoven.

Even more revealing of the contrast in cultural attitudes about black and white women's childbearing is a comparison of the films *Juno* and *Just Another Girl on the IRT*. Predating *Juno* by fifteen years, *Just Another Girl* also generated considerable critical buzz for its young lead actor, its subject matter, and its author/director, and just as *Juno* has been credited as the female version of *Knocked Up*, critics interpreted *Just Another Girl* as a gendered reply to Spike Lee's films. In this story of teen pregnancy, sixteen-year-old African American Chantel (Ariyan Johnson) plans to graduate from her Brooklyn high school early and go on to medical school. Like the character Juno, Chantel narrates her story, revealing that she is naïve but intelligent, self-aware, and an agent of her own fate—choosing between sexual suitors and deciding against abortion and adoption when she learns she is pregnant. Here is where the thematic similarities end, however. Chantel slips into denial of her pregnancy, spending her boyfriend's money on clothes rather than the abortion he wants; when the baby arrives, she instructs him to throw it in the trash (which he does not do) before eventually realizing that she wants the child. The film flash-forwards to its conclusion, a rushed but upbeat acknowledgment by Chantel of the difficulties she encounters separating from her baby's father and living in her parents' home with her baby while attending community college. Like Juno, Chantel has learned something about herself through this experience, but unlike Juno's romantic realization that she is in love with the baby's father, Chantel's realizes her political double-consciousness, which enables her to see that she is "just another girl on the IRT" (a black single mother) to the outsider, but she is not reducible to the negative value she herself once attributed to that image.

The critical response to the Leslie Harris' film is remarkably different from the response to *Juno*. Labeled reproductively "ignorant" (Berardinelli 1993) and an "incorrigible sexual tease," whose "appalling naivete [. . .] probably typifies that of thousands of inner-city teen-agers year after discouraging year, making them perpetual candidates for unwed motherhood and sabotaging their dreams" (Arnold 1993), Chantel is unflatteringly assessed by critics as being served her "comeuppance" in the film (Hinson 1993). I find these reviews troubling for their negative judgment of Chantel's sexuality (a desirous female sexuality that in *Juno* reflects the protagonist's positive agency) and for their clear marking of Chantel's choice to mother as disastrous—that is to say, illegitimate. Despite the film's ending, which attempts to signal clearly to the viewers that Chantel is undefeated, critics persist in viewing her situation as doomed. Even black feminist critics Michelle Wallace and bell hooks found *Just Another Girl* to be a failed film for representing black women as "bad choice"–makers—Chantel is a failed black consumer who does not make the "good" choice to spend her money on an abortion.

To return to the critical praise for *Juno* that introduced this essay, we can see how a collusion of consumer- and race-based ideologies positions the viewer to acknowledge Juno's choice-making faculties, while the abilities of Chantel Johnson—no matter how she defends them—are not to be trusted, according to the critics. While this difference could be explained by an imagined progress over the past decade in thinking about young women's reproductive agency, there is more evidence that suggests that the twenty-first century surveillance of motherhood and "respect" for the choices of counterculture mothers arises from late-twentieth-century anxiety over so-called illegitimate mothers. The positive audience and critical reception of the seemingly unconventional young, counterculture motherhood found in *Breeder* and *Juno* rest upon untroubled class- and race-based notions of who has a legitimate claim to motherhood. The unexamined cultural legitimacy given to white and middle-class young women's mothering choices is revealed more clearly when considering the negative reception of young black mothers in *PUSH* and in Leslie Harris' film. This comparison reveals that when having "choices" is accepted as synonymous with having reproductive rights, it becomes difficult to recognize limitations on the reproductive "choices" of non-white and low-income/poor women and easier to mistake the women themselves as "bad choice"–makers.

WORKS CITED

Adney, Kaile. 2001. Interview with Ariel Gore and Bee Lavender. *Clamor* (July/August): 67–68.

Arnold, Gary. 1993. A bumpy ride on the "IRT": Filmmaker misses express to top. *Washington Times*, April 2, E3.

Berardinelli, James. 1993. *Just Another Girl on the IRT.* Reelviews.net. http://www.reelviews.net/movies/j/just_another.html (accessed Jan. 30, 2008).

Bordo, Susan. 1993. *Unbearable Weight: Feminism, Western Culture, and the Body.* Berkeley: University of California Press.

Davis, Angela. 1981. *Women, Race, and Class.* New York: Random House.

Douglas, Susan J., and Meredith W. Michaels. 2004. *The Mommy Myth: The Idealization of Motherhood and How It Has Undermined Women.* New York: Free Press.

Gore, Ariel, and Bee Lavender, eds. 2001. *Breeder: Real-Life Stories from the New Generation of Mothers.* Seattle: Seal Press.

Hill-Collins, Patricia. 2000. *Black Feminist Thought: Knowledge, Consciousness, and the Politics of Empowerment.* 2nd ed. New York: Routledge.

Hinson, Hal. 1993. *Just Another Girl on the IRT. Washington Post*, April 2.

hooks, bell. 2001. *Feminism Is for Everybody.* Cambridge, Mass.: South End Press.

——. 1994. What's passion got to do with it? An interview with Marie-France Alderman. In *Outlaw Culture: Resisting Representation*, 46. New York: Routledge.

Kine, Starlee. 2007. About a girl: Jason Reitman's 'Juno' grows up before your eyes. *Film Comment* 43.5 (Nov./Dec.): 49–50.

Miller, Lisa. Interview with Sapphire. desires.com/2.4/Word/Reviews/Docs/sapphire.html (accessed Sept. 2003).

Pollit, Katha. 2008. Maternity fashions, junior size. *The Nation*, Jan. 21, 10.

Roberts, Dorothy. 1997. *Killing the Black Body: Race Reproduction and the Meaning of Liberty.* New York: Vintage.

Sapphire. 1996. *PUSH.* New York: Vintage.

Scott, A. O. 2007. Seeking Mr. and Mrs. Right for a baby on the way. *New York Times*, Dec. 5.

Solinger, Rickie. 2001. *Beggars and Choosers: How the Politics of Choice Shapes Adoption, Abortion, and Welfare in the United States.* New York: Hill and Wang.

Spillers, Hortense. 1997. Mama's baby, Papa's maybe: An American grammar book. In *Feminisms*, 2nd ed., ed. Robyn Warhol and Diane Price-Herndl, 384–405. New Jersey: Rutgers University Press.

Thomson, Desson. 2007. Expect the unexpected from *Juno. Washington Post*, Dec. 14, C01.

Wallace, Michelle. 2004. The search for the good enough mammy: Multiculturalism, popular culture, and psychoanalysis. In *Dark Designs and Visual Culture*, 275–288. Durham: Duke University Press.

FILMS

Juno. Dir. Jason Reitman. Perf. Ellen Page, Michael Cera, Jennifer Garner, Jason Bateman, Allison Janney, J. K. Simmons. United States: Fox Searchlight Pictures, 2005.

Just Another Girl on the IRT. Dir. Leslie Harris. Perf. Ariyan Johnson, Kevin Thigpen, Ebony Jerido. United States: Miramax, 1993.

Taking Off the Maternal Lens | **TEN**

Engaging with Sara Ruddick | ANDREA DOUCET
on Men and Mothering

My interest in men and mothering began in 1990 when, as a newly arrived and very pregnant Ph.D. student at Cambridge University, I came across the work of Sara Ruddick. A number of aspects of Ruddick's work stood out for me. First was her opinion that "the most revolutionary change we can make in the institution of motherhood is to include men in every aspect of childcare" (Ruddick 1983; see also Chodorow 1978; Dinnerstein 1977). Second, I was very intrigued by the assertion of Ruddick, and many others, that "men can and do mother" (Ruddick 1995; see also Robinson and Barrett 1986; Crittenden 2001; Ehrensaft 1984, 1987; Kimball 1988; Hrdy 1999; Jackson 1995; Risman 1987, 1998, 2004). Finally, in addition to wanting to engage with this provocative claim of Ruddick's about men and mothering, I was intrigued by her way of framing mothering around three core maternal demands, "preservation, growth and social acceptability," and her view that "to be a mother is to be committed to meeting these demands by works of preservative love, nurturance and training" (Ruddick 1995:17).

Ruddick's assertion that men could mother stayed at the back of my mind as I balanced my doctoral work at Cambridge with caring first for one child, who arrived in my first year of studies, and then for twins as I was completing my dissertation. I thought about it especially when my husband took our first daughter, when she was a toddler, to a "moms and tots" playgroup and even more so when, after attending the group only three times, he decided that he would not go anymore. In exploring his rationale for not persisting with this social experience that might benefit our daughter, he recounted how, each time he entered the church basement with our daughter, he felt like he was entering a very closed club reserved for mothers only. He was weary of being viewed with a strange combination of suspicion and congratulatory amazement. It occurred to me then, for the first time, that, contrary to Ruddick's view, perhaps gender could matter in some community sites when it comes to just *who* is doing the mothering.

The issue of men and mothering came back to puzzle me as I neared the end of my full-term twin pregnancy. Feeling like I was suspended in time, I sat through the last ten weeks of a long and large phase of carrying two infants within me, watching my husband care for our daughter, who was then four years old. They played constantly while I sat in the window, full belly weighing me down, reading tomes of feminist theory on gender equality and gender differences. I watched him cook her meals, bathe her, comfort her, read to her, and lovingly tuck her into bed at night. I often asked myself: Was this father "mothering" this child?

This question of men and mothering continued to hover around me as I recovered slowly from an emergency caesarean, breastfed twin babies for ten months, and grieved each stage as they physically let go of me and the centrality of my maternal body in their little lives. In the years that followed, I spent a lot of time walking with the twins, pushing them in their double pram, and then stroller, first in Cambridge, England, and then later in Halifax and Ottawa, Canada. With each passing season and with each year, I noticed how there were more and more fathers standing in schoolyards and walking with children in parks in the early morning hours. Who were these fathers? How did they come to be here? Why were there suddenly so many of them? Were they being warmly welcomed into the local versions of the "moms and tots" group that had coldly excluded my husband a decade earlier? I constantly wondered: Were these men mothering?

Amid these constant instances of participant observation of Canadian fathers in Halifax and Ottawa, I received funding and institutional support to undertake a study of fathers who are primary caregivers. Over a four-year period, I interviewed more than one hundred fathers from many sectors of the Canadian population about their fathering experiences. The fathers who participated in the study self-identified as primary caregivers of their children, falling into one of three categories of experience: "stay-at-home fathers," "single" fathers (sole-custody, joint-custody, and widowers), and, as part of my effort to include fathers of ethnic minority groups as well as gay fathers, several "shared caregiving fathers." The study included fifteen fathers from visible ethnic minorities, four Aboriginal fathers, and nine gay fathers. The majority of fathers participated through semi-structured interviews while fourteen women also participated in the study through interviews with their partners/husbands who were stay-at-home fathers (see Doucet 2006).

In conducting my interviews with fathers, I drew on Ruddick's three maternal demands, although I framed these as "responsibilities." This translation was facilitated by my reading across other works on mothering, where it was consistently argued that, if mothering has one essential core, it is that it is synonymous with the responsibility for children (Fox 1998, 2001; Lazarre 1976; McMahon 1995; Miller 2005; Rich 1986; Scheper-Hughes 1992). The issue of responsibility was also paramount in my mind because when I had written about men and women and their divisions of labor in the years preceding this study, I had noted that while there was international consensus that men had increased their contributions both to domestic tasks and time invested in child care and housework, there has been remarkably little change in the responsibility for domestic life. I wanted to talk to men who were taking on the primary care of children for significant periods of time because I felt that their reflections might hold part of the key to solving the puzzle of women and domestic responsibility (see Doucet 2000, 2001). Building on Ruddick's three maternal demands of "protection," facilitating children's social "growth" and the consolidation of the "social acceptability" of mothers, my research on men as primary caregivers explored three parallel sets of responsibilities: emotional, community, and "moral." These are briefly described below.

PROTECTIVE CARE (EMOTIONAL RESPONSIBILITY)

In *Maternal Thinking* Ruddick defines "preservation" or "protective care" in the following way: "it simply means to see vulnerability and to respond to it with care, rather than . . . indifference, or flight" (1995:19). This is a state of mind, and its associated practices are well captured in several decades of feminist scholarship on "care" and the "ethic of care" (Fisher and Tronto 1990; Gilligan 1982; Graham 1983; Noddings 2003). As evinced by political theorist Joan Tronto in her description of caring, emotional responsibility involves "knowledge about others' needs," which the carer acquires through "an attentiveness to the needs of others" (Tronto 1989:176–178). In wanting to denote both the tasks of caring and the responsibility for caring, I utilized the term "emotional responsibility" to capture the essence and work of protective care and the responsibility for its enactment (that is the "response-ability").

I investigated the issue of emotional responsibility by asking men about their typical days and weeks with their children, and I asked men and women in couple interviews about their approaches to childrearing in concrete and practical terms. My study of men as primary caregivers provides a partially affirmative answer to the question of men and mothering by highlighting how men care and nurture in ways that very much resemble what are often considered maternal ways of responding. The overwhelming picture painted by both mothers and fathers is that the practices of mothering and fathering have much in common. Joining a large body of research produced over the last two decades, my research with primary care–giving fathers argues that fathers can be just as nurturing and responsive to their children as mothers are and that fathers who are actively involved with their children can develop skills that enable them to partake in this task of "preservation."

Nevertheless, at the edges of these somewhat symmetrical practices, gender differences play out in several important ways. Most notably, there are differences between mothers and fathers in their overall style of nurturing, with fathers emphasizing fun, playfulness, physical activities, sports, the outdoors, practicality in emotional response, and the promotion of independence and risk-taking with older children. The examples of men roughhousing infants, getting the children outdoors, being physical and active, and promoting children's independence recurred overwhelmingly in fathers' and mothers' narratives. While some fathers certainly do not fit this mold in all instances, the overwhelming majority of fathers do. An example of how fathers and mothers differ in terms of dominant approaches to emotional responsibility is well summarized by Penny, who said in her couple interview with husband Carl: "There are differences, such as nursing, which only I can do. And in the stereotype that has actually borne out in our situation of you being more rough and tumble and me being the more cuddly one."

FACILITATING CHILDREN'S SOCIAL "GROWTH" (COMMUNITY RESPONSIBILITY)

A second responsibility that I explored in my work on fathers builds on Ruddick's second maternal demand, how mothers facilitate children's social "growth." According to Ruddick (1995:19): "The demand to preserve a child's life is quickly supplemented by the second demand, to nurture its emotional and intellectual growth. Children grow in complex ways, undergoing radical qualitative as well as quantitative changes from childhood to adulthood." She also recognizes that others are interested in these growth processes: "Many people other than mothers are interested in children's growth—fathers, lovers, teachers, doctors, therapists, coaches. But typically a mother assumes the primary task of maintaining conditions of growth" (1995:20).

Building on Ruddick's point that others are interested in children's growth, my work investigates in detail these others that partake in ensuring children's growth, and mothering also involves coordinating, balancing, negotiating, and orchestrating these others who are drawn into children's lives. Reframing this maternal demand as a responsibility, my work posits that mothering entails the taking on of community responsibility. This implied a robust conception of domestic life, pointing to how the care of children occurs not only within households, but also between households, and between households and other social institutions (i.e., schools, doctors' and dentists' offices, workplaces, and community venues).

Do fathers meet the maternal demand of facilitating children's growth? Do they take on community responsibility? The answer to this question is a mixed one. The fathers in my study gave varied names to community responsibility, including "the higher care," "administration" (as opposed to "maintenance"), and "seeing the need" (as opposed to "filling the need"). While mothers, in both joint-custody and stay-at-home-father families, still oversaw most of the organizing, networking, and orchestration around children's lives, there have been tremendous changes within households and communities, with fathers taking on a greater share of this work and responsibility. Most notably, some sole-custody fathers and stay-at-home fathers took on most of this responsibility and devised their own strategies for accomplishing this part of parenting. Fathers also developed their own parenting networks, through their involvement in children's sports and in community activities and by connecting with other fathers who are taking advantage of increased fathering programs in community settings; that is, fathers constructed their own distinct paternal networks alongside female-dominated ones.

My research does not dispute the already large library of international research that makes the case that the majority of unpaid work in communities, and the overwhelming bulk of community responsibility, remains in the hands of women. Nor does it counter Anita Garey's astute claim that "homework, volunteer work and extracurricular activities are ways in which mothers link their children to the public world—and are symbolic arenas in their strategies of being mothers" (Garey 1999:40). Nevertheless, my research demonstrates that fathers also "link their children to the public world" through their central role in extra-curricular activities such as sports and recreational activities. As community re-sponsibility requires the linking of children's needs into the wider relationships within which caring work is planned and negotiated, the ways in which men create and maintain relationships and friendships with other men and women become particularly significant. The tendency for men to have—or to believe in men's propensity to have—sparse social networks, to form friendships mainly through sports and paid work, and to possess homophobic tendencies that tinge men's relations with one another come to the fore in fathers' reluctance to con-nect with other fathers (Kimmel 1994; Seidler 1992, 1997; Walker 1994).

Issues of time and space also emerged as important considerations in re-searching fathers and community responsibility. With regard to spatial consid-erations, fathers connected more easily with mothers in gender-neutral settings such as coffee shops or parks and less well in female-dominated playgroups or in women's homes. Time is important in that the passage of time has lessened the perception that there are large differences between fathers and mothers on community terrain. Efforts at the greater inclusion of fathers in the early years of childrearing is evident in more father-focused and father-inclusive program-ming by community, health, and parenting centers in Canada; it is further pres-ent in the Canadian government's recent doubling of parental leave allowances, which has resulted in an increase in the numbers of fathers taking this leave (Perusse 2003).

This heightened presence of fathers in the social landscapes of parenting might indicate an increase in fathers networking around their children and thus taking on a greater community responsibility. Currently, however, my argument remains that considerable gender differences continue to mark this aspect of maternal responsibility.

THE "SOCIAL ACCEPTABILITY" OF FATHERS AS MOTHERS (MORAL RESPONSIBILITY)

Sara Ruddick's third maternal demand is that of the "social acceptability" of mothers to the wider community: "The third demand on which maternal prac-tice is based is made not by children's needs but by the social groups of which a mother is a member" (1995:21). Drawing on this notion of the "social acceptabil-ity" of mothers, my work on men and mothering explored how men came to take on what I term the "moral" responsibility for children. This is a conception of "moral" rooted in symbolic interactionism and ethnomethodology, which is very much tied up with the "shoulds" and "oughts" of what it currently means to be a good mother or a "proper" mother and a good father or a "responsible" father.

Framing "social acceptability" as a set of "moral responsibilities" and the "shoulds" and "oughts" of parenting, my research demonstrates that women feel judged for not caring enough while fathers who are primary caregivers feel judged for not earning enough. Recurrent comments of feeling like they have "failed as a man" or that they are "not being a good man" underpin many of the narratives of fathers who have given up earning or have pushed earning into a secondary place in their lives.

Caring for others is intricately connected to "people's identities as moral beings," which are constantly "being constructed, confirmed and reconstructed—identities as a reliable son, a generous mother, a caring sister or whatever it might be" (Finch and Mason 1993:170). Similarly, fathers work to find a sense of what it means to be a "good father" from within a social and cultural location and "with reference to other people" (Finch and Mason 1993:61). While judged as earners, fathers are also differentially judged as carers, a space where they can be viewed as incompetent or through a community lens that is marred with suspicion. In spite of the enormous changes in the social conditions under which men parent, there are still residues of a social fear around close relations between men and children, particularly between men and the children of others. Such suspicions differ between rural and urban areas, and are differently expressed for low-income fathers and gay fathers. Nevertheless, what is striking is how the gendered quality of such scrutiny cuts across class, ethnicity, and sexuality. Both women and men commented on this.

The "social acceptability" of men as mothers was affected by issues of social class and sexuality in various ways. Being economically successful and exhibiting definitive signs of heterosexuality assisted fathers so that they felt capable as carers and, more importantly, felt that they were judged as capable by others. In this vein, low income or unemployed fathers faced a form of "double jeopardy" whereby they felt judged both as a "*failed* male," for not being a primary or successful breadwinner, and as a *deviant* man, in their role as primary caregiver. Meanwhile, gay fathers often faced what theorists have termed "multiple jeopardy" because gender, sexuality, and, in some cases, social class worked against them.

While, as persuasively argued by Martha McMahon (1995), many women experience profound "moral transformations" when they become mothers, my study on fathers as primary caregivers found that such transformations can also occur for them. The fathers in my study found that their "hard edges had softened," they recognized the value in caring work, and they articulated a commitment to taking on what has traditionally been a balancing act for women—that of straddling family responsibilities with paid employment. While some authors have argued that such moves symbolize mothering practices and identities (see Risman 1987, 2004; Coltrane 1986), my argument is that fathers are not mothering and they are not mothers. Rather, fathers are reconfiguring fathering and masculinities and what it means to be a man in the twenty-first century.

MEN, MOTHERING, AND MATERNAL LENSES

In observing and listening to the stories of fathers (and a small group of mothers) over the past fifteen years, I have come to believe that studying fathers' caregiving through the lens of men and mothering ultimately limits our understandings of fathers' caring. Listening to, and theorizing, men's narratives and practices through the questions "*Do they mother?*" or even "*Can they mother?*" implies that we are looking at fathering and fathers' experiences of emotional, community, and "moral" responsibilities through a maternal lens. Other ways of nurturing are thus pushed into the shadows and obscured. For example, with regard to the issue of emotional responsibility, a maternal lens misses the ways in which fathers promote children's independence and risk-taking, while their fun and playfulness, physicality, and outdoors approach to caring for young children are sometimes viewed only as second-best, or invisible, ways of caring. Similarly, in terms of "growth" or community responsibility, the use of a maternal lens means that we miss the creative ways that fathers are beginning to form parallel networks to those that have traditionally been brought into existence by and for mothers. My work on fathers as primary caregivers highlights how important it is to remove the maternal lens when studying fathering.

As this paper began with Sara Ruddick's inspiration, it is fitting that I conclude with an acknowledgment of respect for her work. In drawing on her writing on men and mothering, it is critically important to locate her claims within the larger moral, epistemological, philosophical, and political aims that inform her eloquent and persuasive writing about mothering. One of her aims is to demonstrate that the moral and epistemological perspectives developed through maternal practices could form the basis for a peace politics and a broad social critique. As she puts it, "maternal thinking is a 'revolutionary discourse' that has been marginal and peripheral but that, as a central discourse, could transform dominant, so-called normal ways of thinking" (Ruddick 1995:268) and lead to a possible "world organised by the values of caring labour" (Ruddick 1995:135).

Ruddick's larger project resonates with earlier work by Chodorow (1978) and Dinnerstein (1977), who shared similar concerns about the fundamental imbalances that occur in a society when one gender does the metaphoric "rocking of the cradle" while the other gender "rules the world."

One of Ruddick's further aims has been that of challenging and disrupting the binary distinction between mothers and fathers and the taken-for-granted ideological and discursive lapsing between mother/carer/homemaker and father/provider/breadwinner. In her words: "The question I want to address is whether there is anything in the 'nature" of children, women, or men that requires a sexual division of parental labor even in post-patriarchal societies" (1997:207).

My work shares such philosophical concerns with Ruddick. Where we differ, however, is in the different projects that we both set out to explore. My work as a sociologist and as a feminist qualitative researcher has aimed to understand—at the level of everyday experience as articulated in fathers' and mothers' narratives—the issue of men and mothering and the specific question of whether men do mother. While my previous work on fathering and mothering took place only as a hypothetical conversation with Ruddick, it was through the international gatherings facilitated by the Association of Research on Mothering, and more specifically the tenth anniversary conference "Motherload," that I have had the honor and privilege of finally meeting and beginning a set of email conversations with Sara Ruddick. Through our email exchanges, she has reaffirmed her ideas on genderless care and has concurred on the importance of empirically examining what it is that "men and women really do" through engaging in research where "you have to look at men, listen to them, hear the details of their experience as men who mother, allow the differences and similarities with women" (Ruddick, email exchange, 2006). In building on her ground-breaking philosophical work, this is indeed what my research from men's perspectives has attempted to do.

WORKS CITED

Chodorow, Nancy. 1978. *The Reproduction of Mothering: Psychoanalysis and the Sociology of Gender.* Berkeley: University of California Press.

Coltrane, Scott. 1996. *Family Man: Fatherhood, Housework, and Gender Equity.* New York: Oxford University Press.

Crittenden, Anne. 2001. *The Price of Motherhood: Why the Most Important Job in the World Is Still the Least Valued.* New York: Holt.

Dinnerstein, Dorothy. 1977. *The Mermaid and the Minotaur: Sexual Arrangements and Human Malaise.* New York: Harper.

Doucet, A. 2000. "There's a huge difference between me as a male carer and women": Gender, domestic responsibility, and the community as an institutional arena. *Community Work and Family* 3.2:163–184.

——. 2001. "You see the need perhaps more clearly than I have": Exploring gendered processes of domestic responsibility. *Journal of Family Issues* 22.3:328–357.

——. 2006. *Do Men Mother? Fathering, Care, and Domestic Responsibility.* Toronto: University of Toronto Press.

Ehrensaft, Diane. 1984. When women and men mother. In *Mothering: Essays in Feminist Theory*, ed. Joyce Trebilcot. Totowa, N.J.: Rowman and Allanheld.

——. 1987. *Parenting Together: Men and Women Sharing the Care of Their Children.* London: Collier Macmillan.

Finch, Janet, and Jennifer Mason. 1993. *Negotiating Family Responsibilities.* London: Routledge.

Fisher, Bernice, and Joan Tronto. 1990. Towards a feminist theory of caring. In *Circles of Care: Work and Identity in Women's Lives*, ed. Emily K. Abel and Margaret K. Nelson. New York: State University of New York Press.

Fox, Bonnie. 1998. Motherhood, changing relationships, and the reproduction of gender inequality. In *Redefining Motherhood*, ed. Sharon Abbey and Andrea O'Reilly, 159–174. Toronto: Second Story Press.

——. 2001. The formative years: How parenthood creates gender. *Canadian Review of Sociology and Anthropology* 38.4:373–390.

Garey, Anita Ilta. 1999. *Weaving Work and Motherhood.* Philadelphia: Temple University Press.

Gilligan, Carol. 1982. *In a Different Voice: Psychological Theory and Women's Development.* Cambridge, Mass.: Harvard University Press.

Graham, Hillary. 1983. Caring: A labor of love. *A Labor of Love: Women, Work, and Caring*, ed. Janet Finch and Dulcie A. Groves, 13–30. London: Routledge and Kegan Paul.

Hill-Collins, Patricia. 2000. *Black Feminist Thought: Knowledge, Consciousness, and the Politics of Empowerment.* 2nd ed. London: Routledge.

Hrdy, Sarah Blaffer. 1999. *Mother Nature: A History of Mothers, Infants, and Natural Selection.* New York: Pantheon Book.

Jackson, Marni. 1995. *The Mother Zone: Love, Sex, and Laundry in the Modern Family.* New York: Holt.

Kimball, Gayle. 1988. *50-50 Parenting: Sharing Family Rewards and Responsibilities.* Lexington, Mass.: Lexington Books.

Kimmel, Michael S. 1994. Masculinity as homophobia: Fear, shame, and silence in the construction of gender identity. In *Theorizing Masculinities,* ed. Harry Brod and Michael Kaufman, 119–141. Thousand Oaks, Calif.: Sage.

Lazarre, Jane. 1976. *The Mother Knot.* New York: McGraw-Hill.

McMahon, Martha. 1995. *Engendering Motherhood: Identity and Self-Transformation in Women's Lives.* New York: Guilford.

Miller, Tina. 2005. *Making Sense of Motherhood: A Narrative Approach.* Cambridge: Cambridge University Press.

Noddings, Nel. 2003. *Caring: A Feminine Approach to Ethics and Moral Education.* 2nd ed. Berkeley: University of California Press.

Pérusse, Dominique. 2003. New maternity and parental benefits. *Perspectives on Labour and Income, Statistics Canada* 4.3:12–15.

Rich, Adrienne. 1986. *Of Woman Born: Motherhood as Experience and Institution.* 2nd ed. New York: Norton.

Risman, Barbara J. 1987. Can men mother? Life as a single father. *Family Relations* 35: 95–102.

——. 1998. *Gender Vertigo: American Families in Transition.* New Haven: Yale University Press.

——. 2004. Gender as a social structure: Theory wrestling with activism. *Gender and Society* 18.4:429–450.

Ruddick, Sara. 1983. Maternal thinking. In *Mothering: Essays in Feminist Theory,* ed. Joyce Treblicot, 213–230. Totowa, N.J.: Rowman and Littlefield.

——. 1995. *Maternal Thinking: Towards a Politics of Peace.* 2nd ed. Boston: Beacon.

——. 1997. The idea of fatherhood. In *Feminism and Families,* ed. Hilde Lindemann Nelson, 205–220. New York: Routledge.

Scheper-Hughes, Nancy. 1992. *Death Without Weeping: The Violence of Everyday Life in Brazil.* Berkeley: University of California Press.

Seidler, Vic. 1992. Rejection, vulnerability, and friendships. In *Men's Friendships,* ed. Peter M. Nardi. London: Sage.

——. 1997. *Man Enough: Embodying Masculinities.* London: Sage.

Walker, Karen. 1994. "I'm not friends the way she's friends": Ideological and behavioral constructions of masculinity in men's friendships. *Men and Masculinities* 2.2:38–55.

Reproducing Possibilities

ELEVEN

*Androgenesis and
Mothering Human Identity*

DEIRDRE M. CONDIT

Feminists have to question, not just all of
Western culture, nevertheless, the organization
of culture itself, and further, even the very
organization of nature.
—Shulamith Firestone, *The Dialectic of Sex*

If women's social roles are dictated by nature,
feminism itself becomes impossible, for
resistance to nature is, in one sense at
least, impossible.
—Elizabeth Grosz, "Sexual Difference
and the Problem of Essentialism"

[I]f men could become pregnant, they would
not be men (indeed no one would be a man,
as we understand that term).
—Cass Sunstein,
"Neutrality in Constitutional Law"

Radical feminist Shulamith Firestone revolutionized feminist theory when she argued for ectogenetic reproduction as the route to equality in her 1970 treatise, *The Dialectic of Sex*. Drawing on Marx's dialectical method and de Beauvoir's feminist existential reading of reproduction, Firestone pointed to women's reproductive anatomy and function as the source of women's oppression within patriarchy. Pregnancy, said Firestone, burdened women and kept them from the bodily freedom experienced by men (1970:8). In her view, overthrowing sex difference, through the possibility of technological methods of artificial, extra-uterine reproduction—so-called ectogenesis—was the only means for women to achieve a much-desired synthetic 'equality' from the dialect of sex.

In the forty years since the publication of Firestone's landmark treatise, medical science has continued to inch toward the realization of some form of ectogenetic reproduction, as a series of essays by Singer and Reynolds (1983) indicates.[1] Despite this, feminist considerations of both Firestone's thesis and the possibilities of ectogenetic reproduction are surprisingly thin and continue to be strikingly one-sided. Many radical feminists, such as Mary O'Brien (1981) and Mary Daly (1978), were outraged at Firestone's claim that women's biology is to blame for women's oppression and were appalled by the notion that women should give up the ability to reproduce in order to become "equal to men." Their fierce critiques effectively squelched further feminist theorizing in this area and condemned Firestone's thesis as heresy (Jaggar 1988:93). Ironically, though reading snippets of her work is necessary for students of the "canon" of feminist theory, few attend seriously to the fundamental tenets of Firestone's radical claims (Stabile 1997:508).[2] Only a handful of feminists have taken Firestone seriously, and of those, most have taken a nearly uniform, narrow, and what Lublin has labeled a generally "technophobic" response to both her work and the feminist issues posed by developing reproductive technologies. Only a very few feminists, like Marge Piercy in her extraordinary novel *Woman on the Edge of Time* (1976), have tried to engage Firestone on her own terms.[3]

The recent postmodern turn from the matter of bodies toward concern for "bodies that matter," in Butler's (1993) turn of phrase, has drawn feminists even further away from the subject of embodied reproduction. Butler warns against taking "an easy return to the *materiality* of the body." She cautions that in a postmodern world, matter invokes "a sedimented history of sexual hierarchy and sexual erasures which should surely be an *object* of feminist theory. To return to matter requires that we return to matter as a *sign* which in its redoublings and contradictions enacts an inchoate drama of sexual difference" (1993:48). Thus, while we can all readily see the reproducing body, we must not keep it quite in focus in our theorizing. To do so, to talk of the reproducing material body as if it were an extant thing, somehow outside of what language tells us it is, is to re-ensnare woman in her naturalized, materialized, "womanhood." In doing so, we re-essentialize she whom we have struggled so long to free from her essential bindings.

This fear of being found to be "essentialist" is ubiquitous in recent feminist theorizing. As Grosz explains, "Essentialism entails the belief that those characteristics defined as women's essence are shared in common by all women at all times; it implies a limit on the variations and possibilities of change—it is not possible for a subject to act in a manner contrary to her nature. Essentialism thus refers to the existence of fixed characteristics, given attributes, and a-historical functions that limit the possibilities of change and thus of social reorganization" (1994:84). Thus the debate about the body, snuffed out by the threat surrounding the sex difference question, has increasingly been resolved by feminists simply denying that there is anything biologically determinative, knowable, or, in the language of postmodern feminism, pre-socially meaningful, about the body generally, and women's bodies in particular. To allow otherwise, it seems, is to deny the possibility of ending women's oppression. The rare exception to this total theoretical evacuation is a handful of works by radical-cultural, eco-feminists and others, who have argued contrarily that women's biology is not only determinative, but in some cases even superior to that of men's.[4] Nevertheless, even many of these feminists find they must recant or "soften" their theory upon accusations of "essentialism." Many have simply retreated to safer, more nebulous, alternative discourses predicated on theories of women's differing "cultures."

Consequently, while there is a burgeoning focus on "the body" in feminist theorizing, paradoxically, women's bodies are increasingly absent within that literature. The result is that though most patriarchal and conservative claims for men's domination and women's "differences" typically originate with the notion of biological sex difference (Grosz 1994:84; Ghiglieri 1999; Baumeister 2007), feminist theorists are engaged in dialogue elsewhere. A recent fledgling foray into a feminist conversation on embodiment, science, feminism, and law, held at Emory University, clearly demonstrated our continuing discomfort with the question of materially embodied "difference." The very title of the conference, "An Uncomfortable Conversation on Sociobiology, Evolutionary Psychology, and Feminist Legal Theory," was evocative of this theoretical anxiety.[5]

My purpose here is not to revisit Firestone's method extensively or to dwell much upon the conclusions she draws about the role of biological reproduction in the social and political oppression of women. Rather, I propose to do the "unthinkable" and explore a new understanding of reproductive embodiment that is informed by Firestone and the materialist works of three feminists who have come after her. These include well-known Firestone critic Mary O'Brien, a more recent feminist materialist, Nancy Hartsock, and renowned feminist science fiction writer Marge Piercy. Their works provide a platform for constructing a theory of androgenesis and for exploring the feminist implications of the embodied reproducing male. Using Firestone's method anew, I search for a more fully materialist reading of the dialectic of sex to reveal that the problem of equality originates not with the fact that women's bodies reproduce, but rather with the fact that the bodies of men do not. I will suggest that perhaps it is the *lack* of material reproduction *in men* that significantly contributes to the sex-difference fracture that has become manifest as sexed oppression. Thus, while Firestone called for ectogenetic reproduction to free women to achieve equality, I explore the materialist implications of androgenetic reproduction to free men and conceivably thereby generate a new avenue to human equality.

Though reproduction has always been at the heart of the "woman question," as Plato demonstrated nearly twenty-five hundred years ago in the fifth book of his *Republic*, it was not until Firestone penned her startling work that feminist theorists began to entertain the question: What if we do it *without* women? Up until that time, alternative reproductive theorizing had focused primarily on what to do with children once born, or how to avoid birthing them at all.[6] Only a smattering of works had speculated on alternative reproductive methods. We can find examples in the Greek myth of Athena's paternal birth from the head of her father, Zeus, or in Mary Shelley's *Frankenstein*, wherein man's technology generates a monstrous lifelike creature. Squier's work (1994) points to an active discussion of ectogenesis in popular culture and some scientific research during the 1920s in both the United States and Europe. However, for the most part it was not until Firestone that feminists seriously engaged the connections between women's inequality, their biology, and the possibility of ectogenetic reproduction.

As an intellectual student of Marx, Engels, and Simone de Beauvoir—to whom *The Dialectic of Sex* is dedicated—Firestone applies Marx's method to *re*production and attempts a materialist analysis of women's oppression—or what she calls "sex class" (1970:2). Marx and Engels' brilliance stopped short at the application of their method to human reproduction, according to Firestone. Picking up where they left off, she finds that it is the *dialectical* relationship between the categories "male" and "female" that creates the struggle of sex difference. This struggle translates into "the first division of labor based on sex, which developed into the [economic-cultural] class system" (12). In her reading of biology, sex class is the "most fundamental" division of labor, for its origins are in nature.

The basic, biological moment confronted by Firestone in *The Dialectic of Sex* is that only women conceive, gestate, and give birth to our offspring. She recognized that this embodied, differing capacity for reproduction marks women and men as distinct and, as a result, she concluded that the only means for achieving equality would be to overthrow that distinction. To do so she opted for a technology of reproduction outside of the female body, thus the resort to the fantasy of ectogenesis. The problem with this reasoning is that although Firestone wanted to provide a Marxist reading of reproduction, her reading simply was not materialist *enough*. Her reasoning stalled at the evident point of women's bodies because her reading was more overtly biologist and insufficiently materialist in method. As Grosz explains, biologism

> is a particular form of essentialism in which women's essence is defined in terms of women's biological capacities. Biologism is usually based on some form of reductionism: social and cultural factors are the effects of biologically given causes. In particular, biologism usually ties women closely to the functions of reproduction and nurturance, although it may also limit women's social possibilities with evidence from neurology, neurophysiology, and endocrinology. Biologism is thus an attempt to limit women's social and psychological capacities according to biologically established limits. (1994:84)

By this way of reading reproduction, biology *is* destiny. When Firestone claims that woman's biology is her destiny she does so because she reads reproductive biology *outside of social interaction*. However, this is *not* a materialist interpretation. The beauty of Marx's analysis was that it understood that the material world and the social world are mutually porous; each influences the other—hand and glove shape each other, as it were. In the case of reproduction, biologic capacity to reproduce in women's bodies influences and shapes the possible social environments into which that reproduction is introduced. Equally important to understanding the material impact of biological, embodied reproduction, however, is the reciprocal influence exercised by the social environment on biology. Biology is a component of destiny, but that does not mean that biology itself carries inherent meanings. Biology is a material phenomenon. If we change the biology, we change the material reality.

It is ironic that while she admonishes Beauvoir to "go back to [the] first principles" of biology, Firestone herself commits a similarly egregious error (1970:16). In Firestone's view, Beauvoir fails to consider sufficiently the impact of biology, looking only to how one "becomes a woman" after the point of biological difference. Firestone, however, fails to look beyond the biological fact of women's embodied reproduction to solve the sex difference dialectic. Her limited materialism neglected to take into account the enormous implications of reproducing *in* the body and what that holds for the creation of identity; rather, she valued only the converse as the more "natural" state of being. In her view, women's biology *inherently* crippled women and thus made them *incapable* of equality with men. As O'Brien (1981), Spelman (1988), and Murphy (1989) rightly note, Firestone begins with the male body model and never gets beyond it. The result is a devaluation of all things female; an ironic confirmation of patriarchal principles even as she desired to dismantle them.

What, then, *is* reproduction, from a materialist perspective? It is the *interaction* of the material, reproducing body with the social world that simultaneously lies beyond the body and encompasses it. In Marx's language, *how* we reproduce shapes how we think about reproduction, and so too the converse. Never being able to reproduce in the body has profound and distinct material consequences for men. Firestone says it makes them free; but the freedom they experience is *only* the freedom of not reproducing. She romanticizes this freedom into an idealized, abstracted male identity, one that belies the material conditions into which their "freedom" is born. This celebration of the materially atomized state of the nonreproducing male body precluded further consideration of the implications of such an embodied state of being. She never asked the question: Is it good for men to be like this? To the contrary, Firestone rightly perceived that because women were not biologically like men they did not live like men. But her harsh disdain for pregnancy and childbirth (1970:189–190), her conflation of child bearing with child rearing (73–78), and perhaps even her own status as not-yet-having-given-birth prevented her from exploring the possibility that reproducing in the human body is both necessary *and desirable* for human life. The result is that in Firestone's philosophy, patriarchy is transparent, and women's biology culpable.

Despite its many feminist critics, Firestone's theory of ectogenesis has taken hold in popular culture. Our growing fascination with ectogenesis is evident in the spate of recent science fiction works that feature ectogenetic reproduction. Works in this genre include David Weber's highly successful Honor Harrington series and Sheri Tepper's extraordinary *Fresco* (2000). As Lublin notes, however, because feminist theorists are almost uniformly "technophobic" in their response to most reproductive technologies and to the concept of ectogenesis, their voices are not much evident in the conversations that surround the topic (1998:23). Moreover, feminist technophobia combines with both the fear of being labeled "essentialist" and postmodernism's inability to "focus" on the "matter of bodies" (Butler 1993:ix), which means that feminist theory has largely neglected questions of the materiality of the body and materialist analysis as a means for thinking it through. The works of the three feminists listed above are exceptions to this rule. Their works have strongly influenced my desire to provide a new, more fully materialist reading of the reproducing body, and it is to their various lessons about material reproduction that I now turn.

Canadian materialist feminist Mary O'Brien is among the most forceful of critics of Firestone's work. In *The Politics of Reproduction* (1981) she applies a nuanced reading of men's reproductive identity, and concludes that men create patriarchy because they are alienated from the product of their reproductive labor (51). In her view, man is alienated from his seed in the copulative act, and so creates abstract principles to compensate for the fact that he has no sense of continuity or connection with time and nature (33). Because man is "negated not as lover, but as parent," men as a class experience a "nullity" which they "clearly cannot bear, and history demonstrates the lengths to which men have gone to ameliorate the uncertainty of paternity, both conceptually and institutionally" (43). Alienating their reproductive identity, through the act of heterosexual intercourse, therefore situates men differently with respect to reproduction than it does women, who do not alienate the product of their reproductive labor. This material fact creates not only different anticipatory responses to children (*of* my body versus *in* my body), but also results in differing attachments toward children. Thus for O'Brien, patriarchy is the material consequence of the fact that men cannot reproduce in their own bodies, *despite their evident desire to do so* (147).

However, in my own materialist analysis of the nonreproducing body, I suspect the problem is even more complex than a psychological angst expressed as the desire to dominate reproduction. Patriarchy may indeed be the attempt to control reproduction, but it may also be what happens when people do not reproduce in themselves and have no expectation of ever being able to do so. That is, not reproducing, and identifying from birth as a not-reproducer, may create what we have come to know as patriarchal consciousness—a consciousness that is distanced from others, abstracted, and disaffected. Perhaps it is *this* state of material life that leads to what O'Brien and others describe as the liberal, individualized "self" that denies the importance of intimacy, connection, and unity. It may be that one comes more easily to the domination of others when one has not nurtured beings in and with one's own self. To understand this, we need to look at how the cultural, social, and biological amalgam of reproducing in the body, expecting to reproduce in the body, and nurturing within the body affects the consciousness of the people in our species who do just that—women. We need look then to the work of Nancy Hartsock, who has tackled this question head-on. If, as Nancy Hartsock so winningly asserts, reproducing *in* women's body's concurrently *shapes* women's epistemic worldview *differently*, then *not* reproducing in the body should have equally powerful, though markedly different effects.

Hartsock's materialist analysis of reproduction is both persuasive and appealing. Drawing heavily on Marx and O'Brien, her work asserts that both masculinity and femininity are the *consequences* of materialist reproduction. She claims that women lead materially different lives from men not only because of male oppression, but because *only* women reproduce the species and do so in an embodied manner (1995:71). Women *qua* biologically female persons both experience reproduction and are socially prepared to experience reproduction throughout most of their lives—what she calls "sensuous human activity, practice" (73). While not all women reproduce, most are born and socialized to the expectation that they will do so. As a result, all people socially identified as biological "women" are influenced and shaped by women's biological reproduction, *even if they never themselves experience a pregnancy* (O'Brien 1981:50).

Hartsock acknowledges that the converse is true as well: women who experience a pregnancy are not uniformly shaped by the extant cultural expectations that surround each woman who does so (1995:75). Indeed, the cultures and contexts within which material reproduction occurs have enormous impact on how particular pregnant women interpret and experience their pregnancies. Nevertheless, this does not negate the profound material effect that the biological experience itself has on those who undergo it. Rather, it claims that among the influential components of human identity formation, giving a human being the demarcation of biological sex in the category "female"—those who can/will/should/could/might reproduce through pregnancy in their bodies—translates into an experientially different life-track from those demarcated as "male"—those who can't/won't/shouldn't/couldn't reproduce through pregnancy in their bodies. This is true, I would argue, even for people who internally identify with a gender schema that is unaligned with their external, biological material being.

It is therefore the capacity for, the material experience of, and the various cultural fantasies about reproducing the species within their bodies that makes women "women." As Hartsock notes, materially, the experience is an activity uniquely experienced by the delimited category of "women." The institution by which women come to reproduction, motherhood, and the preparation for motherhood—which "almost all female children receive as socialization, [and] results in the construction of female existence as centered with a complex relational nexus" (1995:77)—*must*, from a materialist view, make women different people from men. Reproducing the species makes people who do it different from people who do not, while it does not necessarily also make all who do so the same. Moreover, and perhaps more important for our purposes here, is the fact that *not* reproducing the species within one's own body, and *never having the slightest idea that one could reproduce in one's own body*, must inevitably make nonreproducing people at least somewhat different from those who do or could.

The material, reproductive embodied distinction stubbornly manifests itself as the demarcation between those who comprise the first group, women, and those who comprise the second group, men. As Hartsock elucidates, "One aspect of this relational existence is centered on the experience of living in a female rather than a male body. There are a series of boundary challenges inherent in the female physiology—challenges that make it impossible to maintain rigid separation from the object world. Menstruation, coitus, pregnancy, childbirth, lactation—all represent challenges to bodily boundaries" (1995:78). Hartsock concludes that the effect of this embodied difference is that women and men become different kinds of people. Women develop a sense of self-connection to the world; men develop a "sense of self as separate, distinct, and even disconnected." This means, "girls come to define and experience themselves as continuous with others. . . . Girls enter adulthood with a more complex layering of affective ties and a rich, ongoing inner set of object relations" (79). The disconnection experienced by men translates into patriarchal consciousness, which then results in women's subordination. If it is reasonable to conclude, then, that men oppress women, at least in part, because they cannot themselves reproduce, then, in the interest of women's freedom from oppression, *let us help men do it!*

Hartsock and O'Brien lead us to understand that Firestone's reading of reproduction had it exactly upside down. Her argument, that we should take reproduction out of women's bodies—particularly within the context of the patriarchal system of sex difference that had grown as a result of women's-only reproduction—would inevitably lead not to women's equality but rather, quite possibly, to even greater oppression of women. This is the exact result most feared by her critics (Murphy 1989:68). Under Firestone's analysis, even in the face of ectogenesis changing women's lives, men would not have undergone any material change. Even worse, however: the human capacity for caregiving, which plausibly is fundamental to and materially derived from embodied reproduction, would also have been eliminated. Rather than being made equal, we could well become an entire species of alienated, disconnected beings. Mary Shelley's *Frankenstein* reminds us that life created outside the gestating "maternal" body is certainly something, but it is not *human*. Recent biological research also tells us that gestation within a moving, talking, warm, humming, symbiotic "maternal" body may simply be biologically necessary for developing human embryos to become, well, human (DiPietro 2002; Schaffer 2009; Reynolds 2005).

Suppose we now consider a converse to Firestone's thesis. If the material condition of reproduction influences one's identity away from oppressive institutions and toward caregiving and nurturing, it would thus seem both necessary and desirable to change men by encouraging them and assisting them in becoming reproducers as well. Furthermore, it turns out, after forty years of research in this area, that the technologies aimed at reproducing outside the female body in a machine may actually be more suited for reproducing inside the male body. For example, research by Cornell University's Center for Reproductive Medicine and Infertility in New York City has experienced greater success in transplanting artificial womblike devices back into the bodies of adult mice than when they have been maintained in other non-animate mediums (Pilcher 23; Reynolds 2005). Uterine transplant research has experienced some preliminary success, according to *Transplant Connect* (2007) and stem-cell research is touted for its promise of organ generation—all pointing to the development of embodied methods by which men might one day be able to reproduce within their own bodies.

The third theorist upon whose work I draw is Marge Piercy, with her highly esteemed feminist utopia *Woman on the Edge of Time*, published six years after *The Dialectic of Sex*. Though most feminists point to her fictional experimentation with ectogenetic reproduction, I am more interested in her experimentation with the technological altering of male biology, and the effects on human consciousness she projects such a change might have.

To many, the idea of male pregnancy is a startling proposition. Nevertheless, the benefits of androgenetic reproduction could be many. In some ways, we will not know what they might be until we try. In her novel, Piercy provides us a vision of what an altered male biology, reconstructed to permit the kind of boundary-free interconnection that occurs between children and women (as alluded to by Hartsock), could be like. As the tale recounts,

> Barbarossa . . . picked up the crying baby. "They can hear you ten miles out on the shelf farm, you hairy little beast!" He sat down with the baby on a soft padded bench by the windows and unbuttoned his shirt. . . . He had breasts. Not large ones. Small breasts, like a flat-chested woman temporarily swollen with milk. Then with his red beard, his face of a sunburnt forty-five-year-old man, stern-visaged, long-nosed, thin-lipped, he began to nurse. The baby stopped wailing and begun to suck greedily. An expression of serene enjoyment spread over Barbarossa's intellectual schoolmaster's face.   (134)

Though he did not give birth to his baby here, Barbarossa's transformed self as the result of his embodied ability to nurse hints at the possibility had he done so. The vision Piercy affords us is one in which, as Cass Sunstein notes above, men as we know them no longer exist (1992:35n129). Instead, what we have is a world in which nurturing and caregiving are our most fundamental values, and sex/gender has essentially become irrelevant.

It is unclear to me whether androgenesis is a *necessary* condition to over-come patriarchy, but I think it might be. Constructivist and postmodern femi-nists, arguing against the pre-social body (in order primarily to elide the sex dif-ferences problem, might I add), have emphasized the possibility of men learning to become caregivers after children are born. Indeed, feminists from Millett to Crittendon have been imploring men to do this for at least the past half-century but with only meager success. It may be that the numbers of men engaging ac-tively in child care remains remarkably low because they are not born into or raised with the expectation that they can one day have an intimate, nurturing, bodily experience with their offspring. The feminist demand that they "get en-gaged" simply misses the materialist point made herein.

There could be other benefits from androgenesis as well. Radical feminists have long argued that men want to control women's bodies because they want the capacity to reproduce. If men reproduce, this takes away the need for patriar-chal access to children. They would no longer need to control women to control their own reproduction. This may be the vision of equality we should seek. Some radical feminists have suggested that if men could reproduce without women, they would eliminate all women (Jagger 1988:93; Murphy 1989:68). However, if the dividing line were material reproduction, when men have babies, women and men would no longer exist. Thus, the "male" incentive for eliminating all women should be gone as well. Finally, if a materialist reading of the reproduc-tive experience and process is correct, men should be changed creatures. Thus, the impulse to oppress should itself have given way.

In an androgenic world there would still be differences between women and men; men would be able to reproduce by choice only (presumably it would re-quire some kind of positive, volitional act on the part of a would-be male mom), whereas the same might not be true for women. Many pregnancies are unwant-ed today, but this too may be the result of a patriarchal, material, nonreproduc-ing worldview that would disappear as well. When men have the capacity to get pregnant, it may lead them to think about pregnancy differently and thus take its possibilities more seriously.[7]

Perhaps the most vexing problem when considering androgenesis, and ironi-cally the most materially intransigent, is that part of the "false consciousness" of sexed-being is that we become invested in our sexed/gendered identities. Many women see the ability to reproduce as women's "special power" (Piercy 1976:134). The response to the idea of men encroaching on women's turf is potentially in-timidating. Similarly, men are heavily materially invested in being nonreproduc-ers. Overcoming the patriarchal ideology that structures masculine identity, in order to get men to reproduce, may be a very sticky wicket. An elaborate, ongoing cyber-hoax at www.pregnantman.com (or http://www.malepregnancy.com/) suggests that some men are intrigued by the possibility already. Piercy once again gives us a vision of both the possible and its potential terrors:

> On the window seat, Barbarossa cuddled his baby to his breast, all the stern importance melted from his features. She could almost hate him in the peaceful joy to which he had no natural right; she could almost like him as he opened like a daisy to the baby's suckling mouth.   (135)

Shulamith Firestone might not have liked this conclusion, for it turns her argument on its head. However, it was her insight and her bold decision to confront the question of biological reproduction that led me to explore the politics of androgenesis. Hartsock (1995) argues for a more comprehensive feminist materialist analysis of women's lives; finally confronting the question of biology is certainly a necessary step toward that end. Entertaining the possibility of androgenesis moves us toward an even richer discussion as well.

NOTES

1. There is obviously disagreement about whether ectogenetic reproduction can ever be realized technologically. For a discussion of the state of the technology, see Reynolds 2005.
2. See any historical survey work on feminist theory as evidence, e.g., Tong 1998; Jaggar 1988; Donovan 1991; and Kolmar and Bartkowski 1999.
3. It is important to note that although Piercy took up Firestone's thesis in her seminal science fiction work, *Woman on the Edge of Time*, many feminists argue that she did so as a means of critique rather than in support of Firestone's thesis. See for example Nancy Lublin, where she concludes that Piercy's take on Firestone is "one of cynicism: Firestone's hopes and dreams provide the foundation for an interesting science fiction, but an unlikely reality" (1998:32).
4. The difficulties in creating feminist theory taxonomies are many. Linda Alcoff (1988) uses this phrase and I find it has merit. Tong (1998) utilizes a similar taxonomy. Some radical feminists, however, object to the phrase. It is used here only to demarcate woman-centered feminists.
5. The two-day conference, organized and hosted by Martha Fineman, was held at Emory University School of Law, Atlanta, Georgia, on Dec. 1–2, 2006.

6. See, for example, Plato on the former; Beauvoir (1972) on the later.

7. See Pottinger's *The Fourth Procedure* (1995), Tepper's *Fresco* (2000), and Reitman's film *Junior* for such visions.

WORKS CITED

Alcoff, Linda. 1988. Cultural feminism versus post-structuralism: The identity crisis in feminist theory. *Signs: Journal of Women in Culture and Society* 13:3.

Baumeister, Roy F. 2007. Is there anything good about men? Address presented at the American Psychological Association. http://www.psy.fsu.edu/~baumeistertice/GoodAbtMenAPATalk.doc.

Beauvoir, Simone de. 1952. *The Second Sex*. Trans. H. M. Parshley. New York: Vintage Books.

Butler, Judith. 1993. *Bodies That Matter: On the Discursive Limits of Sex*. New York: Routledge.

Corea, Gina. 1987. *Man-Made Women*. Bloomington: Indiana University Press.

Crittenden, Ann. 2001. *The Price of Motherhood: Why the Most Important Job in the World Is Still the Least Valued*. New York: Holt.

Daly, Mary. 1978. *Gyn/ecology: The Metaethics of Radical Feminism*. Boston: Beacon.

DiPietro Janet. 2002. Prenatal/perinatal stress and its impact on psychosocial child development. In *Encyclopedia on Early Childhood Development*, ed. R. E. Tremblay, R. G. Barr, R. De V. Peters, 1–5. Montreal, Quebec: Centre of Excellence for Early Childhood Development. http://www.child-encyclopedia.com/documents/DiPietroANGxp.pdf.

Donovan, Josephine. 1991. *Feminist Theory*. New York: Continuum.

Firestone, Shulamith. 1970. *The Dialectic of Sex: The Case for Feminist Revolution*. Toronto, Canada: Bantam.

Ghiglieri, Michael P. 1999. *The Dark Side of Man: Tracing the Origins of Male Violence*. Reading, Mass.: Perseus.

Grosz, Elizabeth. 1994. Sexual difference and the problem of essentialism. In *The Essential Difference*, ed. Naomi Schor and Elizabeth Weed. Bloomington: Indiana University Press.

Hartsock, Nancy. 1995. The feminist standpoint: Developing the ground for a specifically feminist historical materialism. In *Feminism and Philosophy*, ed. Nancy Tuana and Rosemarie Tong, 69–90. Boulder, Colo.: Westview.

Jaggar, Alison. 1988. *Feminist Politics and Human Nature*. Lanham, Md.: Rowman and Littlefield.

Junior. Dir. Ivan Reitman. Perf. Danny Devito, Arnold Schwarzenegger, Emma Thompson. United States: Universal Studios, 1994.

Kolmar, Wendy K., and Frances Bartkowski. 1999. *Feminist Theory: A Reader*. Mountain View, Calif.: Mayfield.

Lublin, Nancy. 1998. *Pandora's Box: Feminism Confronts Reproductive Technology*. Lanham, Md.: Rowman and Littlefield.

Millett, Kate. 1970. *Sexual Politics*. Garden City, N.Y.: Doubleday.

Murphy, Julien S. 1989. Is pregnancy necessary? Feminist concerns about ectogenesis. *Hypatia* 4.3:66–84.

O'Brien, Mary. 1981. *The Politics of Reproduction*. Boston: Routledge and Kegan Paul.

——. 1995. Reproducing Marxist man. In *Feminism and Philosophy*, ed. Nancy Tuana and Rosemarie Tong, 91–103. Boulder, Colo.: Westview.

Piercy, Marge. 1976. *Woman on the Edge of Time*. New York: Fawcett Crest.

Plato. 1968. *The Republic of Plato*. Ed. and trans. Alan Bloom. New York: Basic Books.

Pottinger, Stanley. 1995. *The Fourth Procedure*. New York: Ballantine.

Reynolds, Gretchen. 2005. Artificial wombs. *Popular Science,* Aug. http://www.popsci
.com/popsci/futurebody/dc8d9371b1d75010vgnvcm1000004eecbccdrcrd.html.

Rose, Hilary. 1987. Victorian values in the test-tube: The politics of reproductive science and technology. In *Reproductive Technologies: Gender, Motherhood, and Medicine*. Cambridge: Polity Press.

Schaffer, Amanda. 2009. This goat did not come from an artificial womb. *Double X,* June 4. http://www.doublex.com/print/2136.

Shelley, Mary Wollstonecraft. 2003. *Frankenstein; or, the Modern Prometheus*. 1831. Ed. Susan J. Wolfson. New York: Longman.

Singer, Peter, and Deane Wells. 1984. *The Reproduction Revolution: New Ways of Making Babies*. Oxford: Oxford University Press.

Spelman, Elizabeth V. 1988. *Inessential Woman: Problems of Exclusion in Feminist Thought*. Boston: Beacon.

Squier, Susan Merrill. 1994. *Babies in Bottles: Twentieth-Century Visions of Reproductive Technology*. New Brunswick: Rutgers University Press.

Stabile, Carol. 1997. Feminism and the technological fix. In *Feminisms*, ed. Sandra Kemp and Judith Squires. Oxford: Oxford University Press.

Stanworth, Michelle. 1987. Reproductive technologies and the deconstruction of motherhood. In *Reproductive Technologies: Gender, Motherhood, and Medicine*. Cambridge: Polity Press.

Sunstein, Cass R. 1992. Neutrality in constitutional law (with special reference to pornography, abortion, and surrogacy). *Columbia Law Review* 92:29–44.

Tepper, Sheri S. 2000. *The Fresco*. New York: HarperCollins, 2000.

Teresi, Dick, and Kathleen McAuliffe. 1998. Male pregnancy. In *Sex/Machine: Readings in Culture, Gender, and Technology*, ed. Patrick Hopkins. Bloomington: Indiana University Press.

Tong, Rosemarie. 1998. *Feminist Thought*. 2nd ed. Boulder, Colo.: Westview.

Transplant Connect. 2007. Study reports on the feasibility of uterine transplant. Jan. 2. http://www.transplantconnect.com/news_detail.php?id=41.

Policy | **PART 3**

Mothers of the Global Welfare State

How Neoliberal Globalization Affects Working Mothers in Sweden and Canada

HONOR BRABAZON

While comparative welfare state literature of the twentieth century focused on the institutional characteristics of welfare states and on comparative frameworks on a national or cross-national level (Daly 2000), analysis of the interaction between welfare states and the international political economic context in which they operate is necessary in the twenty-first century, although such work is only now emerging (Esping-Anderson 1996; Åkerman and Granatstein 1995; Mishra 1999). Examinations specifically considering the role of women (and especially mothers) in welfare states remain rare. This paper seeks to open this analytical space. It explores the relationship between neoliberal globalization (understood as an international phenomenon) and the interaction between market, state, and family that is characteristic of the welfare state (understood as a national process). It does this through an examination of current changes to daycare programs, which constitute a significant factor influencing women's labor market participation and thus women's equality. The analysis is not only vertical but also horizontal. As I am seeking to extend the *comparative* welfare state literature, two countries will be contrasted along this global-national line of analysis. Canada and Sweden have been chosen as representatives of the liberal and social-democratic welfare state models, respectively, since high levels of women are employed in these welfare state types.[1] While this is a broad scope for a short paper, the goal is not to attempt to reach decisive conclusions but rather to present a taste of the possibilities that future comparative welfare state analysis in the twenty-first century—one that links the national and international levels with an eye to gender—could yield, particularly that with a focus on working mothers.

The paper will begin at the national level by establishing the theoretical background of welfare states, outlining the importance of day care to gender equality, and tracing the historical development of day care programs in relation to the development of the welfare state in Canada and Sweden. Next, it will move to the international level, examining the theoretical and practical nature of neoliberal globalization, its impact on Canada and Sweden, and the policy responses to it and interactions with it in each country as these affect day care and women's employment. Throughout this process, the paper will seek to identify trends relevant to a twenty-first-century comparative welfare state analysis that considers both national and international contexts.

BACKGROUND

Theoretical Context

While there is generally a bifurcation in the literature between mainstream and feminist analysis, both perspectives have provided insights necessary for a complete analysis of women in welfare states and the influence on women of welfare states' reactions to global pressures at the turn of the millennium. Esping-Andersen (1990) has created a generally accepted mainstream typology focusing on relations between the market and state realms of the welfare state, and thus dividing welfare states into three categories based mainly on their level of *decommodification*, or the degree to which one's well-being is tied to one's citizenship rather than one's status in the market (Morgan 2001). Feminist scholarship has emphasized the importance of the family realm of the welfare state, and Sainsbury (1999) has offered a similar typology based on welfare states' level of *defamilization*: the degree to which one's well-being is tied to one's citizenship rather than one's status in the family. Both typologies emphasize the extent to which benefits are allocated based on citizenship (*social citizenship* based on the development of *social rights*), and both thus see the welfare state as shaping social stratification, whether stratification by gender, class, or other lines. It is the intersection of all three realms (market, state, and family) where class (loosely mainstream analysis) and gender (loosely feminist analysis) interact (Daly 2000a). Care services such as day care programs are found at this intersection (Daly 2000a; O'Connor 1993), and the changes to welfare states examined here highlight the continued relevance of gender-class linkages in shaping the reactions of welfare states and the impact of these reactions on women in the twenty-first century.

It is the more recent version of Esping-Andersen's typology (1996), which represents a degree of synthesis of mainstream and feminist research, that will be used here for simplicity. The typology comprises three welfare state types: a social-democratic type with strong state involvement, preference for universal benefits accorded based on citizenship, integration of economic and social policy, and support for gender equality via a dual-earner norm;[2] a liberal type subordinating state involvement to the market, favoring means-tested benefits, and generally leaving questions of gender to individual "choice" and to the market; and a conservative type in which the state maintains traditional class and gender roles and benefits are accorded usually through the earner and only when family-based solutions are exhausted. In these three models, responsibility for care is given to the state, market, and family realms, respectively.

Day Care and Women's Labor Market Participation

The location of care responsibility described above is crucial to women's labor market participation and can be altered by day care policies. The balance of female/male employment is delicate and not static. It is part of the larger balance between market, state, and family in terms of resource and responsibility distribution in general and in relation to care provision specifically (Daly 2000). Moreover, women's employment is contingent on gender ideology, which increases its vulnerability to change.

Factors influencing women's labor force participation can be direct or more broad and systemic. Direct factors can be divided into three categories: those affecting the supply of women's labor (generally policy arrangements); those affecting the demand for women's labor (generally the structure of the labor market) (Daly 2000); and those affecting the ideological norms for women's societal role. Day care represents an intersection of all these factors: by taking on women's traditional role of caring for children, day care frees women to enter the labor force (supply); as traditionally female work, day care employs mainly women (demand); and by facilitating women's gender role shift toward both earning and caring, day care implies an ideological shift to some degree toward gender equality. Broad systemic factors influencing women's employment include those related to the structure of the welfare state type or to the specific national context (for example, the presence of class struggle), which are also drawn out in discussions on day care (such as its universality), as will be seen below.

Daly (2000) describes the context in which women in liberal and social-democratic welfare states work in relation to these factors, identifying high levels of public service-sector employment as characterizing *demand* for women's employment in both Canada and Sweden, while identifying very different policy and ideological orientation as characterizing *supply* of women's employment in each. Specifically, in social-democratic states, child care is de-privatized by generous childcare services based on a gender-neutral dual-earner norm. In liberal welfare states, child care is privatized based on an ideology of women's "choice" between earning and caring roles and the liberal idea of market supremacy. In practice, however, women in liberal states enter the labor force by necessity of a second family income in the absence of generous benefits, rather than by choice, and must find inferior private market care alternatives on their own (Daly 2000).[3]

Thus, while women in both Canada and Sweden exhibit high levels of labor market participation at the beginning of the twenty-first century, they do so under very different "constraining" or "natural" circumstances, respectively, reflecting their different welfare state types (Daly 2000). The facilitating role day care can play, however, is clear in both cases. It is in this context that we can understand the development of day care in each country and also the impact of changes to day care on women's employment in each country at the turn of the millennium.

The Development of Day Care

The development of the day care programme in Sweden and Canada reflects each country's welfare state type and has increased women's employment along the lines outlined above. It is important to note that the development of day care in both countries was not only a feminist struggle, but also an ideological and (in Sweden) a class struggle. The welfare state in both Sweden and Canada began addressing childcare needs from a similar ideological perspective, that of woman as housewife-mother, with maternity insurance and other policies, such as joint taxation reinforcing, this. As a result of the different welfare state model, the ideological shift in Canada—from a male breadwinner norm to the dual-earner norm—necessary for the full implementation of universal day care was slower and eventually truncated.

Sweden's social-democratic welfare state, oriented toward union and class equality, influenced the feminist and ideological struggles there. In Sweden, both direct cooperation between feminists and labor and the discourse of universality and social rights, due to strong union-led class struggle, were significant. In the 1940s, for example, when the first limited state childcare subsidies were introduced, long before strong feminist advocacy for day care (Benner and Vad 2000), the concept of universal day care as a social right was pursued by both labor and government as a class-equalizing measure based on the idea of "giving each child a fair start" (Lundqvist 2004). In the mid-1960s, "state feminism," a characteristic of the Swedish welfare state that facilitates women's organizing within existing organizations such as unions, led to the formation of an important coalition, Group 222. The group fostered the ideological shift from male-breadwinner to "choice"—the right to choose between paid and household work—supporting policies such as the care allowance, which could be used if a mother pursued either option. Then in the late 1960s and 1970s, cooperation between Group 222 and Sweden's trade union confederation (LO) led to a shift from "choice" to dual-earner norm when LO joined feminists seeking an expanded female labor force in order to reduce a labor shortage (Mahon 1999).[4] Major investments in day care followed (Morgan 2001; Mahon 1999). Social-democratic party dominance and the destratifying, universal nature of the social-democratic welfare state ensured that the new childcare programs were universal in nature, leading to the extension and broad institutionalization of the dual-earner norm and ultimately to a commitment to universal day care for children ages one to four in 1991 (Lundqvist 2004; Benner and Vad 2000). Thus, as in many elements of the Swedish welfare state that promote gender equality, support for universal day care has been closely linked to support for class equality, because of the destratifying goals of each.

Largely as a result of Canada's nature as a liberal welfare state, however, these defining class-based features have been absent from the feminist and ideological struggles here. As in most liberal welfare states, women's organizations are not integrated into mainstream organizations like unions, so the fight for child care has lacked broad strength, particularly for a universal agenda. The labor movement is weak, and Canadian politics shirks class-consciousness in favor of regional-consciousness. Furthermore, an outdated system of executive federalism in which the federal government collects increased revenue while the provinces are responsible for increased services (including day care) (Åkerman and Granatstein 1995) adds an additional layer of conflict not found in Sweden. The first day care subsidies in 1966 were thus the result of traditionally-Canadian intergovernmental conflict rather than an ideological shift away from "choice" or toward class equality. The subsidies were part of a larger reform package called the Canada Assistance Plan, which involved neither the labor nor the feminist movement in its creation and which set the current convention of means-tested subsidy-based day care funding that is typical of a liberal welfare state. After the 1970 Royal Commission on the Status of Women's recommendation for universal child care and modest federal programs in the 1970s (also aimed at regional appeasement), it was only in the 1980s, when strong union-feminist coalitions were finally built, that policy support for a universal dual-earner model was seriously considered. It was not fully accepted, however, before the rise of neoliberalism at the end of the century and its rewinding of these ideological developments (Mahon 1999).

As these programs developed in each country, primarily employing women and providing child care to working parents, the demand for and supply of women's labor increased, as did women's labor force participation. Since the early 1990s, however, the steady increase in women's employment has been reversed, slowed, and informalized to varying degrees (Daly 2000; Almey 2007). This is, interestingly, the period of cutbacks to day care programs in both countries in response to the very domestic and international pressures that have set the context for the labor force participation of mothers in the twenty-first century.

PRESSURES

"Globalization," or global capitalism, forms "the essential context of the welfare state" in the twenty-first century (Mishra 1999:15) and is a concept of many facets and definitions. This paper understands the current version of globalization not only as a market-driven economic phenomenon but also as a political phenomenon driven by, and facilitating, the internationalization of the ideology of neoliberal capitalism: crudely, that of an unregulated market with a bare minimum of social protection in order to facilitate the privatization of economic activity under a banner of market supremacy and individual choice (Mishra 1999). Neoliberal globalization comprises a compendium of political, economic, cultural, social, and other changes resulting both from international pressures and from domestic actors invoking these international pressures rhetorically (Panitch and Gindin 2003). Both have pushed welfare states toward a recommodification of labor (Mishra 1999) and, as this paper will suggest, a refamilization of care. The most significant pressures here are those encouraging reductions to social spending such as day care programs. These pressures are economic, political, and ideological and affect the Canadian or the Swedish system in the new millennium in different ways and to different degrees depending on the type of each welfare state.

The heart of the welfare state has been the ability to tax and spend freely, but neoliberal globalization has increased the influence of perceived or real external constraints on these freedoms. With the increased mobility of capital, attracting and retaining foreign investment becomes more important. Business uses this as leverage to demand debt and deficit reduction through expenditure cuts (not tax increases) so that governments can minimize inflation and thus secure business investment. This logic of global capitalist competition is taken up in political discourse by neoliberal politicians and other actors as justification for immediately and massively cutting back and privatizing social services, and otherwise pursuing their business agenda (Mishra 1999). This is the primary pressure on the Canadian welfare state, which by nature already accepts a liberal logic and whose social programs are less entrenched and thus more vulnerable to cuts (Esping-Andersen 1996).

In the Swedish case, the pressure for cutbacks to ensure global competition is also significant but is further complicated by unemployment. Unemployment has stressed the Scandinavian growth and employment model that forms the basis of the Swedish welfare state. Sweden could balance full employment and high social expenditure as long as domestic credit and investments could be controlled by the government and consensual wage moderation could be guaranteed by employers and employees. With financial liberalization in the 1980s, much Swedish capital leaked abroad, undercutting domestic investment and job generation.[5] More unemployed meant less income tax revenue, more draw on the social welfare system, and thus a more expensive welfare system with less available funding (Esping-Andersen 1996). Sweden's financial stability was compromised, and pressure to reduce spending took hold (Benner and Vad 2000). Although the logic of cutbacks is farther from traditional Swedish discourse than Canadian discourse, Sweden *has* been ideologically pressured by the neoliberal (capitalist) rhetoric of "increasing efficiency" and "increasing work incentive," which has increased pressure to scale back the public sector and its services (Esping-Andersen 1996; Mishra 1999).[6]

Finally, in both states regional integration applies further pressure for cutbacks by enhancing the threat of easy production relocation to "better" business climates and making competition appear more crucial (Esping-Andersen 1996). These economic, political, and ideological pressures of neoliberal globalization, although slightly different in each country depending on its welfare state type, have created an impetus and justification for cutbacks to social programs—including day care—in both countries as a response.

RESPONSES

Much like the pressures, the policy responses to neoliberal globalization in each state also appear to be strongly linked to the different welfare state type of each. While responses in each country so far have been marginal, relatively speaking (Esping-Andersen 1996), direct policy changes (especially in Canada) are clear, and broad systemic changes (especially in Sweden) reveal hidden stresses and potential fissures in the future of day care programs and potentially in women's employment as the twenty-first century continues.

In Canada both the federal and many provincial governments have embraced neoliberalism as in many other liberal welfare states, deliberately adopting deregulatory, market-driven responses to global pressures, beginning in the 1980s (Boix 1997; Esping-Andersen 1996). In terms of direct policy changes, day care cutbacks have decreased both supply and demand for women's labor, and the liberal ideology of family "choice" has been enforced.

Massive cutbacks to both transfer payments for day care spending (Esping-Andersen 1996) and spending itself have been the result (OCBCC 2001; Mahon 1999). The Canada Assistance Plan, which first established federal funding transfers for day care, has been abolished (Mishra 1999), replaced only by block payments of nonearmarked funding—which has resulted in a net drop in federal funding since 1996 (CCAAC 2004). Provincial transfer payments in one province, Ontario, were cut by the last neoliberal government by 47 percent (Kitchen 1997), removing a total of $160 billion from child care, which resulted in fee increases, layoffs, reduced spaces, and reduced wages (OCBCC 2001). After similar cutbacks in the province of Manitoba, an estimated 175,000 children did not have access to day care programs (Prentice 2000).

By the turn of the millennium, Canada had moved from having the lowest proportion of working women among major industrialized countries thirty years earlier to having the second highest; yet, as the new millennium has progressed, Canada has continued to drastically cut back support for working women. According to Statistics Canada, about 70 percent of women in Canada with children under twelve years old work, but there are licensed childcare spaces for only 12 percent of these children outside of Quebec (Bailey 2004; FAFIA

2008).[7] From 2001 to 2006, childcare fees increased while the number of regulated spaces rose slowly. In 2007 the number of regulated childcare spaces grew by 3 percent, which is the smallest increase yet this decade (FAFIA 2008). Effective in April 2007, the federal neoliberal government eliminated its commitment to reach $1.2 billion annually in funding for childcare services. Instead, it has allotted $250 million to a Childcare Space Transfer to provinces and territories, which effectively represents an 80 percent reduction from the previous commitment (FAFIA 2008; CCAAC 2006b). Child care is affordable for high-income families and (with subsidies) for some low-income families, but for others the fees are extremely difficult to pay, reaching up to $10,000 per year outside the province of Quebec—this is among the highest prices for child care in the world and exceeds the annual cost of university (Maxwell 2003; Anderson 2008). For example, child care in Manitoba can cost half the salary of a clerical or service-industry worker (Prentice 2000). A 2006 Organization of Economic Cooperation and Development (OECD) report ranks Canada last of fourteen countries for public investment in early childhood education and care services (below the OECD's recommended benchmark) and last of the twenty OECD member states in terms of accessibility of child care, despite a stronger fiscal position in Canada than in the other G7 countries (CCAAC 2006a; FAFIA 2008).

These cuts have influenced both the demand for and the supply of women's labor. Michalopoulos and Robins (2000) have found that day care prices have a statistically significant effect on employment in Canada. An increase of one dollar per hour would decrease full-time employment by about 5.1 percentage points. Since women often earn less than male partners and since it is still more widely accepted (and expected) for women to stay home with children than men, the jobs forfeited are primarily women's. CCAAC 2006b draws from the *National Child Care Study* (1988) when it observes that it is "overwhelmingly mothers who make child care arrangements and scramble when they fall apart." While the number of women in the labor force may continue to rise (Bailey 2004: Daly 2000), this is not always secure, full-time employment, and women's employment patterns clearly differ from those of men (ACTEW 2007; Almey 2007). According to Statistics Canada, in 2006, 26 percent of all women in paid labor worked part time, while the same was true of just 11 percent of men. Thirty-five and a half percent of women aged twenty-five to forty-four who work part-time do so because they are caring for children, compared with just 4 percent of men of that age. The number of women who are self-employed is growing relative to the number of men, which may also be linked to childcare responsibilities. In 2006 35 percent of self-employed workers were women, an increase from 31 percent in

1990 and 26 percent in 1976 (Almey 2007). Self-employed women tend to earn less than their male counterparts (ACTEW 2007). Also, unemployed women are more likely than unemployed men to have left their last job because of family or personal reasons (Almey 2007). Women are more likely than men to have breaks in their work trajectory, largely from taking time off to care for their children (ACTEW 2007). This often reduces or slows their opportunities for income raises and promotion, plus mothers are the most likely to refuse work, transfers, or promotions due to family responsibilities (CCAAC 2006b).

When mothers who are unable to afford child care cannot stay at home, private care alternatives, usually by untrained providers in unregulated, substandard conditions, must be sought (Kitchen 1997). In 2003 40 percent of children under five years old received nonparental care. Fifty-six percent of this was provided in someone else's home, 22 percent in the child's home, and just 20 percent in a day care center (CCAAC 2003). A patchwork of informal arrangements is often created, for example combining mothers foregoing or reducing paid work, parents working opposite shifts, or calling on relatives or neighbors (CCAAC 2006b).

In addition to the price of care, according to Michalopoulos and Robins (2000), a Canadian mother's wage rate also has a significant effect on her use of child care. When childcare workers' wages (already below the national average) are decreased due to cutbacks, these workers (97 percent of whom are women in Canada) have to make childcare choices for their own children (Government of Canada 2003). Moreover, when parents seek cheaper, unregulated alternatives, they are usually employing women, often un-unionized, at even lower wages. While the wages of trained childcare workers increased slightly between 2001 and 2006, child care remains one of the lowest paying jobs in Canada (FAFIA 2008). Both wage cuts and insufficient wage increases for women further push them to care for their children themselves, making it more difficult and less likely for them to maintain full-time employment (Mahon 1999). Less public funding has also led to layoffs, putting even more women out of work. In one small town in Ontario, Eliott Lake, sixteen employees were laid off at the only day care center as a result of cutbacks (OCBCC 2001).

In addition to cutbacks, there has also been a strong shift in Canadian social programs and services away from universal programs (Mishra 1999; Esping-Andersen 1996) (indeed health care is the only universal program left and the services it covers continue to be delisted), suggesting that the universal day care program promised by successive federal governments starting in 1970 (Branswell 2003) is not forthcoming.

Furthermore, the continuation of cutbacks despite consistent federal budget *surplus* once the deficit "crisis" was over (Mishra 1999) suggests not only economic but also ideological motivation. Universal day care is possible yet seems not to be desired by neoliberal governments. Instead, they have promoted a return from near-acceptance of and policy support for a dual-earner norm in the 1980s back to the preceding ideology of "choice." This can be the "choice" of paid or household work or the more reactionary idea that parents should not have "chosen" to have children if they could not afford child care (Kitchen 1997). Sometimes the ideological shift takes us back further to the male-breadwinner norm, refamilizing child care as women's responsibility, not the state's or the market's. Childcare services were identified by Supreme Court of Canada Justice Rosalie Abella in the 1984 Royal Commission on Equality in Employment as "the ramp to women's equality" (FAFIA 2008). A strong majority of Canadians and opposition parties support the creation of a national childcare program. Neoliberal governments, however, seem committed to using and entrenching women's unpaid labor in the home—and to opening the way for corporate childcare agencies, which have begun to appear in Canada, to capitalize on the childcare crisis (FAFIA 2008). This has been recognized as a direct ideological attack on women (Kitchen 1997), since universal programs built on a dual-earner framework are most conducive to the real and equal participation of women in the workforce, and indeed in society more broadly, as discussed above.[8]

Because of the broader systemic changes that are reducing the power of the women's movement, the direct cutbacks and ideological battle have been difficult for the movement to fight. As Canadian policymakers accept the neoliberal ideology encouraging reprivatization of care and recommodification of labor, what talk of equality and social citizenship has existed is becoming marginalized in Canadian political discourse. Since it is with the help of this language that women were first brought into the policy debate (Mishra 1999), the women's movement itself is becoming marginalized. Furthermore, the women's movement in Canada has largely been funded by the federal government, and cutbacks have reduced the budget of the leading women's umbrella organization and others by over 50 percent (Åkerman and Granatstein 1995; Mishra 1999), further dulling the movement's resistance to direct and ideological change in Canada entering the twenty-first century.

In Sweden, direct policy changes have been less drastic, as in other social-democratic welfare states, but it is the *direction* of direct policy changes combined with the *direction* of broad systemic changes that most ominously suggests that women in the Swedish labor force are not immune to global capitalism.

In terms of direct policy changes, Sweden, like other social-democratic welfare states, has made fewer cutbacks, has reinvested in part following acute crises, and has avoided systemic change toward neoliberalism, embracing neoliberal policies reluctantly (Boix 1997; Åkerman and Granatstein 1995; Mishra 1999; Benner and Vad 2000).

Pressure to reduce taxes and state expenditure as outlined above led to cutbacks in many areas, including day care (Åkerman and Granatstein 1995; Mishra 1999; Esping-Andersen 1996). Esping-Andersen (1996) has identified day care expansion as Sweden's one pressing social service need, yet cutbacks in the 1990s resulted in user fee increases, modest expenditure development, and reductions in personnel, which in turn resulted in fewer day care places—reducing access to care and employment in care, as well as quality of care (SOU 2000). As in many social-democratic welfare states, after the deficit was eliminated the government tried to increase public service funding, but in the case of day care, funding was not fully restored to the areas from whence it was cut (Benner and Vad 2000). Like most of the programs cut back, day care work is dominated by women, and many women lost jobs as part of the strategy to reduce the deficit (Benner and Vad 2000). In such a situation, women have been forced to make employment choices similar to those described by Michalopoulos and Robins above; the supply of and demand for women's employment decreased, as did women's employment (Daly 2000a). Ideology played less of a role here since the dual-earner norm has long been ingrained in Swedish society and is institutionalized in other areas such as taxation, and the cuts in Sweden were minimal compared with Canada, but the direction of change may have future implications as the next century unfolds.

This change in direction is supported by reforms made to day care and several other programs since the 1990s (Mishra 1999). Alterations shifting orientation from a citizenship to a more social insurance model have been allowed (Mishra 1999; Esping-Andersen 1996), including a maximum taxation level for day care fees, thereby making day care Sweden's only non-income graded social service (Lundqvist 2004; Esping-Andersen 1996; Benner and Vad 2000).[9]

This directional change can also be seen on a broad systemic level. In Sweden the most significant broad systemic challenge to resistance to childcare cutbacks has been a weakening of the traditional framework underlying the Swedish welfare state—the characteristic corporatist consensus between organized labor, the state, and employers. Increased internationalization empowered employers who disengaged from, and therefore eroded, the traditional Swedish welfare state framework (Mishra 1999).[10] Simultaneously, with new types of non-standard and postindustrial employment, class boundaries have slowly begun to blur and non-unionized employment to increase (Nelander 2004). Since strong labor had used the corporatist framework to institutionalize universality as a measure to reduce class inequality, and this by extension had led to measures designed to reduce gender inequality as well (such as day care programs), labor has an interest in and has been an active defender of universality and measures of destratification based on both market and family status (Benner and Vad 2000). Although Swedish unions remain strong, their bargaining power has decreased relative to employers', and future defense of universality may be more difficult (Mishra 1999).

The influence of each country's welfare state type on its responses in the area of day care to the pressures of neoliberal globalization is thus significant. The liberal Canadian welfare state is closer to the neoliberal ideal and embraces neoliberalism and neoconservative family values, making deeper cuts to programs like day care. The social-democratic Swedish welfare state resists cutbacks and systemic changes toward neoliberalism, but Swedish day care programs are more endangered by long-term threats to labor since there has been strong historical support from labor for universal destratifying programs like day care, characteristic of the social-democratic model. In both cases, as day care has decreased, so too has women's employment.

This paper has attempted to introduce a new global level of analysis suited to the twenty-first century into the comparative literature on welfare states, and particularly that on the role of mothers in welfare states. It has used the example of day care as a significant factor influencing women's (and specifically mothers') employment—vertically to examine how neoliberal globalization affects women's employment and thus their role and position in the welfare state, and horizontally to compare this impact on Canada and Sweden as representatives of two different welfare state types. While this is merely an introductory analysis, some general trends are apparent. First, the nature and extent of global pressures, responses to them, and the impact of these responses on day care and women's employment appear to be linked directly to the type of welfare state in each country. Second, women's employment (and likely gender equality by extension) in neither country seems to be institutionalized to the extent that it is immune to national responses to global pressures, although women in Sweden seem less affected. Third, just as the role of class/labor struggle characteristic of each welfare state type was important in shaping the discourse guiding, the force behind, and the type of gender policies entrenched, so too does the role of class/

labor struggle characteristic of each welfare state type seem to be important in shaping the discourse guiding, the force behind, and the type of gender policy *retrenchment*. Finally, it appears that the effects of changes in each country have only begun to be felt, as deeper fissures appear to have been created in their welfare state structures.

The purpose of this paper is not, however, to draw decisive conclusions so much as to introduce a new space for future debate: a comparative analysis of the interaction between welfare state types on the national level (and especially mothers in these welfare state types), combined with the economic and political context within which they operate on the international level. Further research in this area is needed as the welfare states of the new millennium take form. How they define the role of mothers in the labor force will prove critical in shaping the position of women in the twenty-first century.

NOTES

1. Where there is divergence among liberal states (e.g., extent or continuity of participation), Canada is closest to Sweden (Daly 2000a). As small states, both are likely to have loosely similar significance in the international scene as regards processes of neoliberal globalization (Åkerman and Granatstein 1995). Women's labor market participation is an indicator of women's equality (Daly 2000). The author appreciates a generous discussion on some of the history in the paper with Åsa Lundqvist in 2004.

2. While Sweden's welfare benefits and programs are broadly universal, their extent is often determined, augmented, or administered through labor force participation (Lundqvist 2004; Mukhtar-Landgren 2004).

3. In the conservative welfare states typical in continental Europe, traditional gender roles are favored and care is mostly privatized, provided only on a part-time basis. Other important factors influencing supply of women's labor include taxation policies that favor women as earners of their own income.

4. The introduction of individual taxation and parental leaves is also related to this ideological shift away from the male-breadwinner norm.

5. Simultaneously, Sweden's centralized bargaining tradition came apart. This will be discussed in more detail below.

6. Unemployment is one of the key campaign issues that brought a center-right coalition government to power in a narrow win in 2006, defeating the Social Democrats, who had governed for all except ten of the past eighty-nine years.

7. While only 22 percent of Canada's children live in Quebec, the province offers 45 percent of the regulated childcare spaces in Canada (FAFIA 2008).

8. This argument can be further supported by most governments' choice to cut back on programs like day care, which directly affect mostly women, more than programs like unemployment insurance, with more universal constituents. The resurgence of "choice" can also be seen in the current neoliberal federal government's 2006 childcare credit.

9. Other such changes include a reduced and more earnings-based pension system and an increase in exit restrictions for benefits such as unemployment insurance, leading to increased reliance on means-tested welfare programs.

10. Increased internationalization led to financial deregulation and more export-oriented industry in the 1980s (Esping-Andersen 1999). With the increased option of obtaining cheaper labor abroad, employers were empowered to push for labor market flexibility, withdraw from employer-employee organizations, invest abroad, and threaten to invest abroad if taxes were not reduced and spending cut back (Mishra 1999; Esping-Andersen 1996). This disengagement of capital has been the leading cause of the erosion of the traditional framework, although internal conflict also weakened organized labor relative to employers (Mishra 1999).

WORKS CITED

ACTEW (A Commitment to Training and Employment for Women). 2007. Keeping women current: Women and the Canadian labour market. http://www.actew.org/projects/pwpsite/snapshots/canadian_women.html (accessed Nov. 16, 2008).

Åkerman, Sune, and Jack L Granatstein. 1995. *Welfare States in Trouble: Historical Perspectives on Canada and Sweden*. Uppsala: Swedish Science Press.

Almey, Marcia. 2007. Women in Canada: Work chapter updates. http://www.statcan.ca/english/freepub/89F0133XIE/89F0133XIE2006000.htm (accessed Nov. 12, 2008).

Anderson, Lynell. 2008. Quality, affordable child care? Not in Canada . . . thanks to market failure. Canadian Centre for Policy Alternatives, editorial, June 23. http://www.policyalternatives.ca/Editorials/2008/06/Editorial1912/ (accessed Nov. 12, 2008).

Bailey, Sue. 2004. 71% of women in labour force. *Winnipeg Free Press*, March 10.

Benner, Mats, and Torben Bundgaard Vad. 2000. Sweden and Denmark: Defending the welfare state. In *Welfare and Work in the Open Economy*, ed. Fritz Scharpf and Vivien A. Schmidt. Oxford: Oxford University Press.

Boix, Carles. 1997. Privatizing the public business sector in the eighties: Economic performance, partisan responses, and divided governments. *British Journal of Political Science* 27:473–496.

Branswell, Helen. 2003. Need for child care vastly outstripped by availability, report shows. Toronto: Canadian Press News Service, February 10.

CCAAC (Child Care Advocacy Association of Canada). 2003. Briefs and reports. http://www.ccaac.ca/parent_voices/main-EN.html (accessed Nov. 11, 2008).

——. 2004. The Child Care Advocacy Association of Canada Reacts to federal budget: Baby steps won't take us far. Press release, March 25.

——. 2006a. International report condemns Tory approach to child care. Press release, Sept. 20. http://www.ccaac.ca/pdf/media/OECD_Report.pdf (accessed Nov. 11, 2008).

——. 2006b. Caring about employability. http://www.ccaac.ca/pdf/resources/briefs/EmployabilityBrief.pdf (accessed Nov. 12, 2008).

Daly, Mary. 2000. A fine balance: Women's labor market participation in international context. In *Welfare and Work in the Open Economy*, ed. Fritz Scharpf and Vivien A. Schmidt. Oxford: Oxford University Press.

——. 2000a. *The Gender Division of Welfare*. Cambridge: Cambridge University Press.

Esping-Andersen, Gösta. 1990. *The Three Worlds of Welfare Capitalism*. Cambridge: Polity Press.

——. 1996. *Welfare States in Transition: National Adaptations in Global Economies*. London: Sage.

FAFIA (Feminist Alliance for International Action). 2008. *Women's Inequality in Canada*. Submission of the Canadian Feminist Alliance for International Action to the United Nations Committee on the Elimination of Discrimination Against Women on the Occasion of the Committee's Review of Canada's 6th and 7th Reports. www2.ohchr.org/english/bodies/cedaw/docs/ngos/FAFIACanadaCEDAW2008_2.pdf (accessed Nov. 12, 2008).

Government of Canada. 2003. Job futures. http://www.jobfutures.

Kitchen, Brigitte. 1997. "Common sense" assaults on families. In *Open for Business, Closed to People: Mike Harris's Ontario*, ed. Diana Ralph, Andre Regimbald, and Neree St-Amand. Halifax: Fernwood.

Lundqvist, Åsa. 2004. Personal discussion, Lund, Sweden, May 18.

Mahon, Rianne. 1999. "Both wage earner and mother": Women's organizing and child care policy in Sweden and Canada. In *Women's Organizing and Public Policy in Canada and Sweden*, ed. Linda Briskin and Mona Eliasson. Montreal: McGill-Queen's University Press.

Maxwell, Judith. 2003. *Caregiving—What's It Worth?* CBC Commentary, Sept. 2. Canadian Policy Research Networks. http://www.cprn.org/doc.cfm?doc=381&l=en (accessed Nov. 10, 2008).

Michalopoulos, Charles, and Philip K. Robins. 2000. Employment and child-care choices in Canada and the United States. *Canadian Journal of Economics* 33:35–470.

Mishra, Ramesh. 1999. *Globalization and the Welfare State*. Cheltenham: Elgar.

Morgan, Kimberly. 2001. Gender and the welfare state: New research on the origins and consequences of social policy regimes. *Comparative Politics* 34.1:105–124.

Mukhtar-Landgren, Dalia. 2004. "Gender and welfare." Lecture, Lund University, Lund, Sweden, May 24.

Nelander, Sven, LO. 2004. Personal interview, via telephone from Lund to Stockholm, Sweden: May 17.

O'Connor, Julia. 1993. Gender, class, and citizenship in the comparative analysis of welfare state regimes: Theoretical and methodological issues. *British Journal of Sociology* 44.3:501–518.

OCBCC (Ontario Coalition for Better Childcare). 2001. Downloading: The funding crisis in childcare. http://www.childcareontario.org/library/downloadingfs.html.

Panitch, Leo, and Sam Gindin. 2003. Global capitalism and American Empire. In *Socialist Register, 2004: The New Imperial Challenge*, ed. Leo Panitch and Colin Leys. London: Merlin Press.

Prentice, Susan. 2000. *A Decade of Decline: Regulated Child Care in Manitoba, 1989–1999*. Winnipeg: Canadian Centre for Policy Alternatives.

Sainsbury, Diane. 1999. *Gender and Welfare State Regimes*. Oxford: Oxford University Press.

SOU (Swedish Government Reports). 2000. *Two of a Kind*. Stockholm: Gritzes.

The Erosion of College Access for Low-Income Mothers

THIRTEEN

A. FIONA PEARSON

> Where can you go without an education?
> —Candy, twenty-year-old student and mother
> of one, studying secondary education

> Going back to school is much more
> important than just getting a job.
> —Keisha, twenty-five-year-old student and
> mother of three, studying medical technology

U.S. Americans are surrounded by messages—in the news, in literature, in school, and at work—that emphasize the role of education in achieving the American dream. It is therefore no surprise that most U.S. Americans believe in the promise of higher education. Such beliefs are reflected in college enrollments, which increased 20 percent between 1996 and 2004 (U.S. Department of Education 2006). In a recent poll, 87 percent of respondents stated that a secondary school graduate should go on to college before taking a job after high school (Immerwahr 2004). Clearly a vast majority of U.S. citizens accept the idea that attaining a college degree is necessary for ensuring lifelong success. Despite such beliefs, the educational pathway to college for low-income mothers receiving welfare has been increasingly difficult. Recent changes to U.S. federal and state policies, including U.S. welfare and childcare assistance programs, have restricted low-income mothers' college access, undermining their attempts to pursue commonly held educational goals.[1] The study presented here, based on interviews with seventeen low-income mothers, examines the effects of institutional policies and resources on low-income mothers' access to postsecondary education as we enter the twenty-first century. In particular, this research seeks to reveal the ways current political, governmental, and educational institutional systems are facilitating or obstructing the potential success of thousands of low-income parents, a disproportionate percentage of whom are mothers of color, who are struggling to move themselves and their families out of poverty via a postsecondary education.

THE PROMISE OF EDUCATION

The correlation between education and income has been well documented in both theoretical and statistical analyses. According to figures released by the U.S. Census Bureau, in the year 2000 African American women who possessed a high school degree earned $20,638 annually and $36,524 annually with a baccalaureate degree. Latinas with a high school degree earned $19,540 and $31,507 with a baccalaureate degree. Comparable figures for white women were $21,047 and $35,438 for a high school and college degree respectively (U.S. Census Bureau 2004). Not only may attaining degrees affect income levels, but simply enrolling in postsecondary classes has been shown to increase an individual's earning potential. Kane and Rouse (1999), in their summary analysis of research examining the relationship between years of education and income, found that for every year's worth of college credit attained by individuals, income increased by 5–8 percent, whether or not the individual actually attained a degree. Individuals completing an associate's degree could expect to see their annual incomes increase by 15–27 percent. In general, the income increases of women attending college are lower than those of men, but women earning two-year nursing degrees were found to experience annual earning increases equal to or more than those experienced by men earning a two-year degree.

Attaining a college education not only increases the likelihood of improving one's economic prospects and social agency, it simultaneously increases the likelihood that one's children will attend college. Ellwood and Kane (2000) found that the children of college-educated parents are on average 75 percent more likely than those of non–college-educated parents to attend some kind of postsecondary institution. When Ellwood and Kane examined income differentials, they found that the same patterns existed for all income brackets. Not only do parents' experiences matter, but research has also determined that parents' attitudes toward education will significantly influence their children's likelihood of finishing high school and attending college (Crosnoe, Mistry, and Elder 2002). These findings clearly demonstrate the significance of parents' educational experiences and attitudes on children's academic and later economic success.

In reference to low-income mothers, Harris (1996) found that having some postsecondary education reduces by 41 percent the chance that a woman will return to welfare. Simply put, the more highly educated a mother is, the less likely she is to later require public assistance in order to support herself and her family. Further, when compared to individuals who have not attained a high school diploma, individuals with at least a college degree are ten times less likely to have a family income under the poverty level (U.S. Census Bureau 2004) and mothers are half as likely to have an infant who dies at birth (National Center for Health Statistics 1998). Clearly, infant mortality is highly correlated with poverty, but because education and poverty are so inextricably connected, the potential beneficial effects of improving low-income mothers' educational access cannot be ignored (Shaw et al. 2006). Finally, education, and the corollary economic benefits it provides, increases low-income mothers' social and cultural capital, empowering them to influence debate regarding family and educational social policy (Polakow et al. 2004). The evidence is clear: mothers, families, and society benefit when low-income mothers are provided with a higher education.

METHODS

Below are described the experiences of seventeen mothers who were receiving welfare assistance via the Temporary Assistance for Needy Families (TANF) program as they pursued their college degrees in 2004. Because all individuals interviewed for this study self-identified as African American or black, this sample does not reflect the racial or ethnic diversity evidenced in the TANF population across the nation—in 2004 only 39 percent of all TANF participants identified as African American. However, this sample does reflect the racial/ethnic makeup of the TANF population in the county in Georgia where this research was conducted, where 97 percent of TANF participants were categorized simply as "black."[2]

In semi-structured, in-depth interviews, I asked all sample participants to share information regarding their educational experiences. Influenced by Dorothy Smith's (1987, 2006) method of inquiry, institutional ethnography, I focused my analysis on the institutional processes that facilitated or obstructed these mothers' access to college. In particular, I focused on how TANF policy shaped students' experiences and opportunities, but I also highlighted in my analysis the effects of institutions that participants referenced in their interviews. Although each student mother I talked with expressed very different institutional needs, the following three institutional-level themes consistently emerged: TANF policy, financial aid, and childcare access. As these findings demonstrate, institutionally located resources facilitated or prevented students from receiving the aid they needed in varying and sometimes complex ways.

FINDINGS

Welfare Reform and Postsecondary Education in the Twenty-first Century

In 2002 the Center for Women Policy Studies cited Georgia as being more generous than most states in allowing TANF program participants to pursue postsecondary education. However, as I soon found out, educational access for mothers receiving welfare was steadily decreasing, as local program administrators responded to the state and federal emphasis on securing jobs, not attending college. At the time of these interviews, students were allowed to consider hours spent pursuing a baccalaureate or master's degree as meeting their core work activity requirements for only twelve months. After that time, they were expected to locate paid or approved unpaid work, logging in a minimum of twenty hours a week. They could use hours spent pursuing a college degree to fulfill their final ten hours a week work activity requirement—to receive benefits, participants must work for a minimum of thirty hours a week total (U.S. Department of Health and Human Services 2006b). States, however, are now imposing stricter requirements than those presented in these guidelines and many states do not consider pursuing a baccalaureate or master's degree as a valid work activity for any length of time.

Current welfare reform was initiated in 1996 when President Clinton signed Congress's Personal Responsibility and Work Opportunity Reconciliation Act (PRWORA). As a result of this legislation, the Temporary Assistance for Needy Families program (TANF) replaced the sixty-one-year-old federal assistance program Aid for Dependent Children and Families (AFDC). AFDC was initially formed in the 1935 under the name Aid to Dependent Children (ADC) as part of Franklin D. Roosevelt's New Deal policies implemented in the latter years of the Depression. The ADC program, which emerged from the Mother's Pension Movements of the 1920s, allocated funds to female-headed households so that mothers, many of whom were WWI widows and the vast majority of whom were identified as white, could stay home and care for their children (Abramovitz 2000). As the century wore on, however, and as civil rights legislation and increased federal investment in poverty reduction programs in the 1960s allowed more and more low-income women of color to apply for and receive AFDC benefits, both public sentiments and political rhetoric regarding the program became increasingly racialized and negative (see Neubeck and Casenave 2001; Gilens 1999). Anti-welfare rhetoric in the 1980s and 1990s culminated in the passage of PRWORA, when members of Congress and the Democratic president himself optimistically announced that "welfare as we knew it" had ended. The newly established Temporary Assistance for Needy Families (TANF) program promoted marriage; emphasized paid work over education; and, as the word "temporary" implies, imposed strict time limits. Perhaps most importantly, low-income mothers would be expected to work in exchange for cash benefits and other public assistance, including limited access to child care; no longer was welfare an entitlement program. These changes to welfare law, in part resulting from more than thirty years of gendered and racialized rhetoric maligning low-income African American women's mothering (Roberts 1997), would dramatically alter the daily routines of thousands of individuals then receiving welfare benefits.

More recently, in a late-night U.S. congressional session at the end of 2005, the Temporary Assistance for Needy Families (TANF) program was reauthorized after three long years of contentious debate. Members of Congress had argued heatedly regarding the overall efficacy of the program, and many disagreed as to the role that postsecondary education ought to play in TANF policy. Under the 1996 guidelines, families demonstrating need could receive public assistance for up to five years as long as parents engaged in work or educational activities. The federal guidelines regarding eligible educational activities were relatively vague, thereby providing states with discretionary power to locally designate acceptable educational activities. In 2002 the Center for Women Policy Studies reported that forty-nine of fifty states had implemented some form of postsecondary educational program serving TANF participants. As a part of the reauthorization in 2005, however, Congress asked the U.S. Department of Health and Human Services (DHHS) to clarify the guidelines, particularly those regarding postsecondary education. In June 2006 the DHHS published guidelines initially stating that attending college with the intent of attaining a baccalaureate or master's degree was to be eliminated from the options that parents receiving TANF could choose from in order to satisfy program requirements. According to these proposed guidelines, TANF "was not intended to be a college scholarship program" (37460). A year and a half later, when DHHS published a revised version of the guidelines, those specific restrictions were retracted and the vague language allowing for local discretion in defining acceptable educational activities was retained (Pearson 2007). However, many local social service providers acknowledged the underlying message sent by federal lawmakers, that securing jobs ought to take precedence over pursuing a postsecondary degree. As a result, many restrictions for low-income student mothers remain in place, including limitations on college program choice and the number of months for which college attendance is allowable, and many college degree programs serving TANF-eligible women are currently at risk of being dramatically reduced or eliminated (Bill and Chinen 2009; Kates 2007).

This recent bout of challenges and retractions reveals twenty-first-century policy-makers' conflicting views regarding the appropriateness of educational provisions in contemporary welfare programs serving low-income mothers. Many of these policymakers have tended to downplay the correlation between education and income, emphasizing instead the importance of mothers' securing a job. The effects of such an emphasis were clearly documented in my interview with Nicky, a twenty-four-year old mother of one, whose educational pursuits were temporarily thwarted when she applied for public assistance:

> [The TANF application] went into this whole thing where, well, "How are you supporting your family right now? Well, why don't you get a job?" kind of thing. Well, I'm like, "I'm trying to go to school so I can get a job that I want!" But they don't see it that way. They're like, "If you've got children, you might need to get a job—like now!" Not a school kind of mentality. And, I, I was denied.

Because she found it too difficult to balance TANF's work requirements, school, and family responsibilities, Nicky subsequently dropped out of school in order to receive the TANF benefits she needed to sustain herself and her daughter. She later decided that her educational goals ought to take precedence, and once she was able to secure childcare assistance from her mother, she dropped out of the TANF program and reenrolled in school.

As cited above, numerous analysts have produced research findings that challenge recent TANF policies' emphasis on work-first solutions. Those analysts argue that while work-first solutions may fulfill a need for service-sector employers who are ever in need of low-wage labor, such jobs rarely lead to long-term self-sufficiency for mothers (see for example Hays 2003; Loprest 2001; Shaw et al. 2006). Marie, a sociology major and mother of three, was well aware of the economic instability that a lack of education can produce in the lives of individuals who are eminently dispensable due to the workings of an economic system that relies in part on an ever-ready pool of surplus labor. After cycling in and out of low-wage jobs, Marie realized she was going to need an education in order to locate a job that might provide some stability and flexibility. For several years prior, she had been receiving public assistance on and off because she had been unable to get the training necessary for her to succeed:

> *Marie*: There's going to be people that companies or employers can pay less. There's always going to be that workforce that they can pay less. So then, you lose your job that you were barely making it with anyway. Like my job at the time—I was laid off my job at the daycare center because everyone else had, well, not everyone else, but where I was, the classrooms that I taught, where I worked, the other teachers had either degrees or more years of experience, so if I don't go to school and get the education or the training I'm going to continue to be . . . [*trails off*]
> > *Fiona*: Laid off?
> > *Marie*: Yeah!

Examining these policy shifts emphasizing work over education is particularly important because their net effect is very much shaped not only by gender but by race. In 2004 the DHHS reported that approximately 90 percent of adult TANF participants were women (U.S. Department of Health and Human Services 2004: chap. 10, 7) and approximately 65 percent were members of racial ethnic minority groups (chap. 10, 2). As a result, recent changes to social welfare policy restricting educational opportunities disproportionately affect an already economically vulnerable segment of the population, African American and Latina mothers. On average, women in the United States continue to earn approximately two-thirds the income that men earn, and women of color earn less on average than white women and men of all racial/ethnic groups (U.S. Census Bureau 2004). Education is one of the few proven means by which mothers can increase their earning potential and attain economic sufficiency. As stated above, economic gain via education is particularly pronounced for African American women, whose income levels exceed those of all other racial/ethnic groups of women at the baccalaureate level (U.S. Census Bureau 2004). Higher education is clearly beneficial for all groups of women, yet the cumulative effect of recent policy and budgetary changes is likely to diminish the educational prospects of many low-income mothers seeking to empower themselves by earning a college degree.

School Bills: The Role of Financial Aid

Nearly all participants encountered difficulties meeting their financial needs and were struggling to pay their housing, food, child care, and utility bills as well as cover their educational costs for tuition and books. All seventeen TANF participants stated that they received some form of financial aid grant or scholarship to assist in the payment for their postsecondary education. Of those seventeen, at least nine had received Federal Pell Grants and six qualified for Georgia's Helping Outstanding Pupils Educationally (HOPE) scholarship. Two others qualified for campus-sponsored scholarships or fellowship programs. Students with higher educational aspirations—that is, students who hoped to attain at the very least a baccalaureate degree—tended to apply for the Pell Grant, HOPE scholarship, and other campus-sponsored scholarships. Students interested in educational programs lasting two years or less more often relied on educational opportunities funded by the welfare office or its contingent organizations.

The Federal Pell Grant Program, created in 1972 and authorized under the Higher Education Act of 1965, was designed to increase the availability of financial assistance for postsecondary institutions. The Pell Grant Program makes grants available to undergraduate postsecondary students who are attending accredited colleges or universities and have been identified as demonstrating financial need. In the 2003–2004 school year, when these interviews took place, nearly seven million students across the United States applied for and were deemed eligible to receive federal assistance via the Pell Grant program. During that same year, nearly 60 percent of the recipients of Pell Grants reported incomes of $20,000 or less. In the 2003–2004 academic year, the average grant distributed totaled $2,473, although the maximum annual grant students could receive totaled $4,050 (U.S. Department of Education 2004).

In addition, six students received Georgia's HOPE scholarship, a merit-based scholarship program created in 1993 to provide financial assistance for undergraduate students attending Georgia's public and private colleges and universities.[3] According to the Georgia Student Finance Commission (2005), the program, which is funded by revenues from the state's lottery, has awarded over $2.7 billion to nearly a million students in the state of Georgia. To qualify for the HOPE scholarship, students must be legal state-residents of Georgia at the time they start their postsecondary schooling and must have earned a 3.0 grade point average in secondary school or upon completing their first thirty semester credit hours of college or university. In 2004 the scholarship award was $1,500 per academic year for part-time students and $3,000 for full-time students.

The Pell Grant and the HOPE scholarship together often covered all if not most of the tuition and book costs for many of these students, all of whom were attending public state colleges. In 2004–2005 the full-time tuition for Georgia's public regional and state colleges was $1,161 a semester, or $2,322 a year. The full-time tuition for two-year colleges was $734 a semester, or $1,468 a year. Students hoping to attend one of the state's four public research universities, however, would find themselves harder pressed to pay the $1,684 per semester, or $3,368 per year full-time, tuition rates, particularly if they were not able to attain or maintain their HOPE scholarships (Board of Regents of the University System of Georgia 2005).

Undoubtedly, students are benefiting from the distribution of grants and scholarships available and couldn't afford to attend postsecondary school otherwise. However, both the Pell Grant and HOPE scholarship programs have steadily experienced fiscal strain as increasing numbers of students across the nation who qualify for aid have been choosing to attend postsecondary institutions. In part to deal with the program's budgetary shortfalls, the Pell Grant's maximum award remained at $4,050 from 2002 until 2006 (Brainard 2007:A23). In 2005 the Bush administration and Congressional leaders proposed a variety of changes to the program, including changing the formula used by the government to determine financial need. In May of that year, the U.S. General Accounting Office (2005) verified educational lobbyists' claims that changing the family contribution formula determining eligibility would reduce awards for 36 percent of PELL Grant recipients and would eliminate awards for 92,000 current recipients. The Bush administration and legislators eventually dropped their attempt to change the program's formula, but their very challenge demonstrates the program's vulnerability to cutbacks. Such vulnerability was revealed again in early 2007, when the Bush administration put forth proposals to offset costs of the Pell Grant by cutting other federal loan and grant programs servicing low-income students (Brainard 2007:A1). Later that same year the tide began to turn as Congress passed and President Bush signed into law H.R. 2669, the College Cost Reduction and Access Act. The act was hailed as a victory for low-income students as it increased the maximum amount available for Pell Grants and increased the amount of income students could receive before they might experience reductions in their financial aid.

Although these changes will certainly increase aid for student parents demonstrating financial need, critics argue that even with these increases to the Pell Grant program, college costs continue to surpass grant offerings. According to the College Board's 2007 report on college pricing trends, in-state tuition and fees at public four-year colleges averaged $6,185 during the 2007–8 academic year (Baum and Ma 2007:2). Between 1997 and 2007, in-state tuition and fees costs for public four-year colleges and universities increased by 7.1 percent, an average of $216 per year (Baum and Ma 2007:10). During the four years between 2002 and 2006, when the maximum amount available for Pell Grants remained steady at $4,050, college costs were soaring. If these college cost trends continue, it is clear that the benefits accrued by recent Pell Grant legislation will be negligible at best.

In July 2009 President Obama pledged to spend more than $12 billion over the next ten years to fund the American Graduation Initiative, which would provide more resources to the country's community college system. Because the community college system services many older students requiring part-time and flexible schedules, it is likely that many parents will benefit indirectly and perhaps directly, particularly if some of those funds are used to finance childcare assistance for students. At this time, however, it is unclear how those funds will be allocated.

In regards to Georgia's HOPE scholarship, legislators have sought to place limitations on the program, which in 2004 was anticipated to be running at a shortfall by 2007. In order to save the scholarship, local Congressional representatives put forth proposals to (1) increase academic eligibility requirements, (2) limit the use of scholarship monies to the payment of tuition, or (3) implement family income caps for eligibility.[4] All of these proposals were put forth with the assumption that cuts to the program were imminent and that the program was worth preserving. Although generally viewed as successful by students, legislators, and state residents, the HOPE scholarship program has received some criticism for its merit-based eligibility tactics and its reliance on lottery sales for funding. Critics arguing from an educational standpoint fear that because the scholarship is merit based, requiring students to maintain a minimum 3.0 grade point average, secondary and postsecondary faculty members sympathetic to the financial needs of their students or influenced by the pressures exerted by students or parents might resort to grade inflation in the classroom. Opponents to merit-based scholarships in general argue that need ought to trump merit, particularly for students coming from poor neighborhoods with inferior schools. Other critics of institutionalized gambling and lottery-funded programs argue that the monies used to support the HOPE scholarship disproportionately come from the pockets of the poor and the scholarships themselves disproportionately aid wealthy students. Such criticisms have been verified in studies comparing zip codes, median incomes, and lottery sales or winnings (Jones and Kempner 2003;

Samuel 2002). Despite such concerns, the program has served as a model for numerous other states and is cited regularly for its perceived successes.

As stated above, without these financial aid programs most of these parents would not have been able to pay their postsecondary educational costs. It must be noted, however, that in formulating students' financial needs, none of these financial aid programs takes into consideration the costs of child care, a service that was necessary for most of these mothers to succeed educationally. I discuss institutional supports for mothers' childcare experiences in more detail in the next section.

Childcare Facilities and Campus Regulations

Historically, postsecondary institutions were not created with the working parent in mind, instead catering to the needs of adults with few responsibilities outside of the academic realm. However, as the number of older students, many with children, populating college classrooms across the nation steadily increases, educational institutions are responding accordingly, either developing college-affiliated childcare facilities or creating policies limiting or prohibiting the presence of children on campus.

None of the students with whom I talked necessarily *wanted* to bring their children to class, but they felt that on certain occasions they had no other acceptable options available. Just over half of the nation's more than four thousand college campuses have childcare facilities available on site or near by (Boswell 2003). Yet many of those facilities, particularly those with excellent local reputations, are full, often with long waiting lists, and are costly. In 2007 the National Association of Child Care Resource and Referral Agencies reported that the average annual cost for infant care in a licensed facility in Georgia was $6,245.

To better address the needs of low-income student parents, Congress in 1998 amended the Higher Education Act of 1965. This resulted in the creation of the Child Care Access Means Parents in School (CCAMPIS) program, which was authorized to fund childcare facilities on college campuses that distributed more than $350,000 in Pell Grants per academic year. Although federal funding for the CCAMPIS program dramatically increased between 1999 and 2001, the U.S. Department of Education (2007) indicates that the program's funds have steadily decreased since that time, and in 2007 were nearly 40 percent less than they were in fiscal year 2001. This decrease in available funds occurred despite steady increases in both the demand for and cost of child care on college campuses. None of the mothers I interviewed used a childcare facility funded with

CCAMPIS dollars. In addition, none of these students was even aware of the CCAMPIS program or of any college in the vicinity that provided childcare programs receiving CCAMPIS funding. This is not surprising because, as mentioned above, the program has experienced severe cutbacks, as much as 40 percent, since 2001. In 2004 only two of the more than sixty four-year colleges and universities in Georgia received CCAMPIS grants and only eight of the more than eighty two-year community colleges and technical schools in the state received such grants. Of the ten colleges and technical schools that did receive grants, the awards ranged from $10,000 to $82,778, with an average award of $27,334, which does not come close to meeting the full-time childcare costs for student parents on Georgia's college campuses.

Undoubtedly, bringing a child, particularly a very young child, to class can potentially disturb any postsecondary learning environment, which is one reason many campuses have implemented written policies that limit or in some cases strictly prohibit the presence of children in classrooms and labs. The majority of universities and colleges do not have specific policies targeting children, but they do have "disturbance" policies that more generally allow professors discretion in determining when a student's behavior or action is interfering with the process of learning. Students are subsequently forced to make difficult choices when elementary schools or childcare centers are closed or when their children are ill.

Like several other parents interviewed, Nia stated that when an emergency arose, her professors would generally allow her to bring her child with her to class. However, she also emphasized that she rarely had to make such a request because classes were frequently offered at times—at night or on weekends—when she could more likely locate emergency care:

> The one thing that I did like about [State University], to me it was conducive to parents, to single parents. Because they seem to be more understanding of the fact that . . . every student is not the traditional eighteen-, nineteen-, twenty-year-old student and they have other issues and other experiences outside of school, so—that was definitely a major push to let me go ahead and finish school. . . . It provides—like the options of time of classes. My professors would allow me to bring my child on holidays when school would be out. It was okay for my daughter to come to class with me. Just things in that way—it made it easier for me.

For those students who could locate dependable care during nontypical school hours, such flexibility in course scheduling enabled them to balance their student, employee, and parental roles more effectively. It is for this reason that many colleges and universities have offered increasing numbers of night and weekend classes, demonstrating the institutions' responsiveness to the needs of an evolving student body who are increasingly likely to be parents and/or full-time employees.

However, many of the mothers I interviewed did not have access to dependable childcare providers, particularly during the evening or weekend hours. Lisa, a twenty-nine-year-old mother of one, had to drop out of school because she could not find anyone to watch her son in the early evening, when many of her classes were scheduled:

> I'd have no one to watch him, and I started missing days, and my grades started slipping again, and so the next semester, I was like, okay, well, I'm just gonna drop my classes, and . . . I, I, I had to drop in the middle of the semester because I couldn't come. I couldn't attend. My teachers were fairly understanding, but after awhile, it's—I mean, there's really nothing anyone can do if you're not there to get the information, so . . . I had to leave.

Like Lisa, many parent students' educational tracks were interrupted until they could once again locate reliable child care, which was not provided by the college or consistently funded by the TANF program as a result of the job requirement restraints. At the time of these interviews only three of the students interviewed received childcare assistance through the TANF program.

As stated above, to receive childcare assistance through TANF in Georgia, most mothers had to be employed for a minimum of twenty hours a week, be in class a minimum of ten hours a week, and be enrolled in a program from which they could graduate within twenty-four months. Perhaps most importantly, they had to have the support of their case manager. However, case managers' discretionary support varied widely, in part because of the pressure they experienced from upper-level administrators to reduce caseloads and increase the number of clients working paid jobs (Pearson 2007). As a result, neither the college nor the social services office provided consistent, systemic support for mothers' childcare needs, thereby limiting low-income mothers' ability to pursue a postsecondary education.

When twenty-first-century policymakers revised TANF's guidelines as a part of the program's reauthorization in 2005, they retained many restrictions on college educational options, based on their belief that the objective of TANF is to facilitate securing paid jobs and not schooling. Via their actions, these policymakers continue to communicate that paid work is simply a more pressing concern for low-income mothers than education. Such actions are troubling, given the wealth of evidence available that demonstrates that both individuals and society at large benefit when access to postsecondary education is provided to low-income mothers (Shaw et al. 2006). Further, financial aid and childcare resource programs are increasingly underfunded and have consistently been targeted for cutbacks as demand for aid has increased and programs have not been able to keep up with college costs and students' needs. Formulas used to determine the dollar amounts of Pell Grants and Georgia's HOPE scholarship do not take into consideration the financial needs of families, particularly concerning child care. Finally, the one program created to address those needs, CCAMPIS, is consistently underfunded. Because children are generally not allowed in college classrooms, with some campuses explicitly prohibiting children's presence in classes and labs, these cutbacks and TANF's increasing emphasis on securing jobs and deemphasizing college education will most certainly affect low-income mothers' attendance and retention rates.

Individual friends, family members, teachers, or case managers may step in and temporarily alleviate the negative effects of these policies and budgetary cutbacks. Faculty or staff may direct students to private scholarships or campus resources, and friends or family members may step in and provide child care when alternatives do not exist. However, these fleeting individual-based resources cannot be readily relied upon for broad-based, long-term assistance. Support from prevailing social institutions is necessary if low-income mothers are to be provided with postsecondary educational access. Currently, such support is waning and access to education is decreasing for all TANF participants.

The task for future researchers and policymakers is to determine whether the experiences described here are representative of mothers in other states and of other racial and ethnic groups across the nation. In addition, because TANF is a program that overwhelmingly services mothers of color and their children, future researchers are challenged to consider the ways that policy changes and budgetary decisions are shaped by class, gender, *and* race. When TANF policy is changed or CCAMPIS budgets are cut, low-income mothers of color are disproportionately affected; the educational future of low-income African American and Latina mothers is at stake.

Researchers have long documented the social and economic inequalities women have faced in societies in which women are generally expected to shoulder the majority of domestic and caregiving responsibilities in the family. The findings here clearly reveal national budgetary and policy trends indicating that institutional resources are not sufficiently available to ensure low-income mothers' access to a college education. If these trends continue, these mothers will find it even more difficult to attain self-sufficiency and personal empowerment as their college educational opportunities are steadily taken away. If gender and racial equity is to be achieved during the twenty-first century, researchers and policymakers must be tasked with acknowledging the complex processes linking patriarchy, inequality, motherhood, and policy; these research findings regarding the multilayered effects of social institutions on the everyday lives of low-income mothers provide a place for us to begin.

NOTES

1. In this paper, the term *welfare* refers to public assistance programs designed to assist parents and children, and more specifically refers to the now-defunct Aid for Dependent Children (AFDC) and its replacement program Temporary Aid for Needy Families (TANF).
2. All names, except for the state, are fictional in order to ensure confidentiality.
3. The Georgia HOPE scholarship differs from the federal HOPE tax credit, which was implemented in 1997. The HOPE tax credit allows students to be reimbursed 100 percent for the first $1,000 spent on tuition and fees and 50 percent of the second $1,000 spent during students' first two years of school. Because grants and scholarships, including the PELL grant and Georgia's HOPE scholarship, are subtracted from the amount of tuition eligible for the HOPE tax credit, none of the students I interviewed was eligible for the federal HOPE tax credit (U.S. Department of Education 2001).
4. At the time of this writing, HOPE scholarship monies could be applied to tuition, books, and materials. In 1993, when the program was started, only students whose family incomes did not exceed $66,000 were deemed eligible for the scholarship. In 1994 the cap was increased to $100,000, and in 1995 the income cap provision was eliminated completely (Georgia Student Finance Commission 2005).

WORKS CITED

Abramovitz, Mimi. 2000. *Under Attack, Fighting Back: Women and Welfare in the United States.* New York: Monthly Review Press.

Baum, Sandy, and Jennifer Ma. 2007. *Trends in College Pricing, 2007*. Washington, D.C.: College Board.

Bill, Teresa, and Joyce Chinen. 2009. Bridge to hope: College access for AA/PI TANF participants in Hawaii. Presented at the Society for the Study of Social Problems 59th Annual Meeting, San Francisco.

Board of Regents of the University System of Georgia. 2005. Admissions and tuition. http://www.usg.edu (accessed Aug. 28, 2005).

Boswell, Tracy. 2003. Campus child care centers. Washington, D.C.: ERIC Clearinghouse on Higher Education. http://www.eriche.org/digests/2003-3.pdf (accessed Aug. 1, 2007).

Brainard, Jeffrey. 2007. President Bush and Congress set to increase Pell Grants. *Chronicle of Higher Education*, Feb. 9, A1, A23.

Center for Women Policy Studies (CWPS). 2002. *From Poverty to Self-Sufficiency: The Role of Postsecondary Education in Welfare Reform*. Washington, D.C.: Center for Women Policy Studies.

Crosnoe, Robert, Rashmita Mistry, and Glen H. Elder. 2002. Economic disadvantage, family dynamics, and adolescent enrollment in higher education. *Journal of Marriage and Family* 64:690–702.

Ellwood, David T., and Thomas J. Kane. 2000. Who is getting a college education?: Family background and the growing gaps in enrollment. In *Securing the Future*, ed. Sheldon Danziger and Jane Walfogel. New York: Russell Sage.

Ganzglass, Evelyn. 2006. Strategies for increasing participation in TANF education and training activities. April 17. Washington, D.C.: Center for Law and Social Policy. http://www.clasp.org/publications/tanf_ed_training.pdf (accessed July 28, 2006).

Georgia Student Finance Commission. 2005. Georgia's HOPE scholarship and grant program. http://www.gsfc.org (accessed Sept. 22, 2005).

Gilens, Martin. 1999. *Why American's Hate Welfare: Race, Media, and the Politics of Antipoverty Policy*. Chicago: University of Chicago Press.

Harris, Kathleen Mullen. 1996. Life after welfare: Women, work, and repeat dependency. *American Sociological Review* 61:407–426.

Hays, Sharon. 2003. *Flat Broke with Children: Women in the Age of Welfare Reform*. New York: Oxford University Press.

Immerwahr, John. 2004. *Public Attitudes on Higher Education: A Trend Analysis, 1993 to 2000*. San Jose: National Center for Public Policy and Higher Education.

Jones, Andrea, and Matt Kempner. 2003. "Pockets of the poor" finance college dreams. *Atlanta Journal Constitution*, Nov. 9. http://www.ajc.com/metro/content/metro/hope/09lotto.htm (accessed Jan. 5, 2006).

Kane, Thomas J., and Cecilia E. Rouse. 1999. The community college: Training students at the margin between college and work. *Journal of Economic Perspectives* 13:63–84.

Kates, Erika. 2007. *Low-Income Women's Access to Education.* Boston: Center for Women in Politics and Public Policy, University of Massachusetts.

Loprest, Pamela J. 2001. How are families that left welfare doing?: A comparison of early and recent welfare leavers. Washington, D.C.: Urban Institute. http://www.urbaninstitute.org/UploadedPDF/anf_b36.pdf (accessed Jan. 8, 2004).

——. 2002. Who returns to welfare? *New Federalism: National Survey of America's Families,* no. B-49. Washington D.C.: Urban Institute. http://www.urban.org/publications/310548.html (accessed Jan. 12, 2003).

National Association of Child Care Resources and Referral Agencies. 2005. 2003–2004 ranking of cost of child care for a four-year-old. http://www.naccrra.org/randd/data/2003–2004PriceofCareFora4-YearOld.pdf (accessed Aug. 7, 2007).

National Center for Health Statistics (NCHS). 1998. *Health: United States, 1996–7.* Washington, D.C.: NCHS.

Neubeck, Kenneth J., and Noel A. Casenave. 2001. *Welfare Racism: Playing the Race Card Against America's Poor.* New York: Routledge.

Pearson, A. Fiona. 2007. The new welfare trap: Case managers, college education, and TANF policy. *Gender and Society* 21:723–748.

Polakow, Valerie, Sandra S. Butler, Luisa Stormer Deprez, and Peggy Kahn, eds. 2004. *Shut Out: Low Income Mothers and Higher Education in Post-Welfare America.* Albany: State University of New York Press.

Roberts, Dorothy. 1997. *Killing the Black Body: Race, Reproduction, and the Meaning of Liberty.* New York: Vintage Books.

Samuel, Leah. 2002. The poor play more. *Chicago Reporter,* Oct. http://www.chicagoreporter.com/2002/10-2002/lotto1/lotto1.htm (accessed Jan. 4, 2006).

Shaw, Kathleen M., Sara Goldrick-Rab, Christopher Mazzeo, and Jerry A. Jacobs. 2006. *Putting Poor People to Work: How the Work-First Idea Eroded College Access for the Poor.* New York: Russell Sage.

Smith, Dorothy. 1987. *The Everyday World as Problematic: A Feminist Sociology.* Boston: Northeastern University Press.

——. 2006. *Institutional Ethnography: A Sociology for People.* Toronto: AltaMira.

U.S. Census Bureau. 2004. Current population survey: Annual social and economic supplement. http://www.census.gov (accessed Feb. 26, 2005).

U.S. Department of Education. 2001. The HOPE scholarship and lifetime learning credits. ed.gov/offices/OPE/PPI/HOPE/index.html (accessed Sept. 8, 2007).

——. 2004. Federal Pell Grant Program end-of-year report, 2003–2004. http://ed.gov/finaid/prof/resources/data/pello304.pdf (accessed Feb. 12, 2005).

——. 2006. National Center for Educational Statistics: Fast facts. http://nces.ed.gov/fastfacts (accessed Sept. 15, 2007).

———. 2007. Child Care Access Means Parents In School program. http://www.ed.gov/programs/campisp/index.html (accessed Sept. 1, 2007).

U.S. Department of Health and Human Services. 2004. Temporary Assistance for Needy Families Program: Sixth annual report to Congress. Washington, D.C.: U.S. Government Printing Office.

———. 2006a. Reauthorization of the Temporary Assistance for Needy Families (TANF) Program; interim final rule. Washington, D.C.: U.S. Government Printing Office.

———. 2006b. Temporary Assistance for Needy Families Program: Seventh annual report to Congress. Washington, D.C.: U.S. Government Printing Office.

———. 2008. Reauthorization of the Temporary Assistance for Needy Families (TANF) Program; final rule. Washington, D.C.: U.S. Government Printing Office.

U.S. General Accounting Office. 2005. Student financial aid: Need determination could be enhanced through improvements in education's estimate of applicant's state tax payments. http://www.gao.gov/new.items/d05105.pdf (accessed Nov. 15, 2005).

Academic Life Balance for Mothers

Pipeline or Pipe Dream?

FOURTEEN

MICHELE L. VANCOUR
WILLIAM M. SHERMAN

More women, even those with children, are entering academia, but at what cost to themselves? According to researchers, some women are delaying child-bearing or removing children from their list of future aspirations altogether (Hewlett 2002; Mason and Goulden 2002). Other academic women are having children, but experience inordinate distress as they try to balance career and family (Elliot 2003; Mason and Goulden 2002; Perna 2001). As a result, some of these women are opting out of this male-oriented profession in return for greater balance, control, flexibility, and stability for their families (Mason and Goulden 2004; Spalter-Roth and Erskine 2004).

Mason and Goulden (2002) report that "babies do matter" for women who work in academia. They found that female ladder-rank faculty at the University of California (UC), Berkeley were leaving their careers to care for their children and find a better balance for their families. This is likely the result of the demands placed on tenure-track faculty, which include excessive pressures to attract grants, conduct and publish research, advise students, and implement innovative teaching methods (Ward and Wolf-Wendel 2001). Women tend to be underrepresented in tenure and tenure-track positions at UC, a trend Mason and Goulden refer to as the "leaky pipeline" (2004:87). The results of their research indicate that women with children are underrepresented at all ranks, but most dramatically at the rank of full professor (Mason and Goulden 2004).

Other researchers have emphasized the incompatibility between academic careers and motherhood as the reason women are often required to sacrifice their families to meet performance standards at work (Drago and Colbeck 2003). University life necessitates long hours that exceed the time constraints of the traditional "nine-to-five" workday, multitasking to complete the various tasks associated with an academic career, performing a multitude of service work, generating research and publications, and creating a perfect teaching record that demonstrates creativity, scholarship, and innovation. All this is synonymous with the "ideal worker norm" (a term created to describe a male work pattern), and contradictory to the motherhood norm, which involves being the primary caregiver of children and performing most of the child care and household responsibilities (Williams 2000). Academic mothers may feel pressure to be superwomen—perfect mothers and successful career women.

In addition to the approximate fifty hours per week faculty women spend working in academia (Jacobs and Winslow 2004), they spend an additional fifteen hours engaged in housework and twenty-seven hours engaged in child care, according to Mason and Goulden (2004). It has been well documented that it is mothers who make most of the sacrifices when it comes to child care, considered the work of mothering (i.e., arranging for child care, transporting their children to and from child care, changing their work schedules to accommodate their children's needs, taking time off from paid labor to provide primary care, paying for child care out of their own paychecks, declining promotions, and inevitably decreasing their total workload) (Crittenden 2001; Elliot 2003; Hattery 2000).

Academic mothers struggle to overcome obstacles, such as the "glass ceiling" and the "maternal wall" (Williams 2000), as they maneuver through the proverbial leaky pipeline (Mason and Goulden 2002) at the expense of their own health. The responsibilities of motherhood and paid work result in competing demands, which often inhibit women's participation in health-promoting behaviors (Vancour 2005). The present study was guided by the following research question: How do motherhood ideology and role balance relate to health-promoting behaviors among tenured and tenure-track academic women with preschool children?

METHOD

This study focused on academic women's experiences in balancing their careers and family lives, while examining their health behaviors. The participants were seventeen academic mothers who had a child less than five years of age (a preschool child). All of the mothers were full-time tenured or tenure-track professors at four teaching universities in New England. All of the women were married or had a partner, and most mothers' spouses were employed full-time.

In April 2005 two researchers conducted semi-structured, one-on-one audiotaped interviews. The proceedings were transcribed verbatim for analysis. Interviews lasted approximately one hour and were held in the participants' offices. Questions focused on motherhood ideology, role balance, health-promoting practices, and workplace support. Prior to the interviews four items were distributed to participants: a list of interview questions, a consent form, a questionnaire listing twenty-five items, primarily related to demographics, and an incentive. The interviews were transcribed verbatim, then analyzed and interpreted using an inductive approach informed by existing research. Common themes were identified.

KEY THEMES

Five key themes emerged in the interviews. The "good mother" explored women's identification with their mother roles, and demonstrates women's priority of caring for their children. In "tug-of-war," the relationship between work and family was depicted as a constant struggle. The third theme, "flexibility and the never-ending job," described the complexities that can be involved in an academic career and the potential for spill-over between work and home. The fourth theme, "playing professor," delineated a potentially damaging syndrome in which high-achieving women downplay their success. The last theme, "kryptonite," details women's losing struggle to balance multiple competing demands while maintaining well-being.

The Good Mother

Garey (1999) presented three ways according to which women come to be considered "good mothers" in U.S. society—by always "being there" for their children, by engaging in "family time," and by "doing things" with or for their children. In other words, being a good mother means being a child's primary caregiver, devoting herself to her children twenty-four hours a day, seven days a week (Douglas and Michaels 2004). The overwhelming majority of women in this study similarly defined being a good mother in today's society. Several women discussed the transition from academician to mother as it redefined their work and their personal lives. Motherhood became their central identity and replaced the time once available for developing their professional careers and pursuing personal interests.

Consistent with much of the literature, most of the women in this study subscribed to an intensive mothering ideology (Hays 1996). Time spent with children was demanding, according to these moms, who reportedly engaged their children in structured activities (i.e., classes and field trips), played with their children, and taught their children different age-appropriate things. If women spent a weekday at home with their children, they likely spent it teaching their children. For example, one mother said she spends her *free* weekday engaging her son in French, so that he will be bilingual.

Considering the prevalence of intensive mothers and the attention paid to academic women's struggles over the past couple of years, it was astonishing to hear what these women reported on issues related to maternity leave and child care—benefits that are essential to supporting women as responsible and engaged parents and academics. The first issue was related to time off for maternity. At the universities where the women in this study worked, accrued sick leave could be used during leave for the birth of a child, as well as unpaid leave under the Families and Medical Leave Act. As a result, there was a considerable range in time taken for maternity among the mothers in this study. One woman who was newly appointed took one day off after the birth of her child before returning to work because she had not accumulated sick time and did not want to be viewed negatively by her colleagues. This may seem like an extreme case, but another mother took one week off with her first child and two weeks off with her second child, both during her academic career. This likely was not enough time for mothers to bond with their babies, and recover from the process of delivery. It also may set the bar higher for other women new to academia.

A related issue was that most of the women worked on campuses without childcare centers. For them, high-quality, affordable, on-site child care for infants through school-age children would be beneficial, as child care was described as a time-consuming and stressful issue faced by these women, especially for sick children and children's vacation care. As a potential solution, the mothers suggested that, if universities could not provide on-site childcare centers, they could facilitate child placement in nearby centers by providing women with childcare support along with information on how to choose quality child care, what types of child care are available, and how to evaluate care.

Tug-of-War

Faculty women with children are less able to meet the demands of work and family (Mason and Goulden 2002). Often confronted with long work hours and facing "publish-or-perish" pressures, the academic mothers in this study described the combination of motherhood and academia as "stretching myself in several directions," "stressful," "good and bad," "not easy," "a tug-of-war," and "the best of both worlds." Similar to the academic mothers in Ward and Wolf-Wendel's (2004) study, most women in this study listed challenges they faced regularly as long work hours; pressures to publish, conduct research, and write grants; on-the-job time constraints and meeting schedules; fears associated with the promotion and tenure process; and guilt related to time away from their children. One mother put it this way,

> My professional life and my home life interfere with each other, and I feel guilty about both. I try to keep a foot in both worlds, but when I am at home I am with my kids and I am with them 100 percent. There is a negative relationship between work and family. The more you give to one the less there is for the other. It's a negative correlation. . . . I want to do a good job here . . . but I can't if my mind is somewhere else.

Likewise, another said,

> On one hand it's great because I have certain advantages that people with more traditional jobs perhaps don't . . . if I needed to be somewhere or would just like to be somewhere for my child during the day, probably I can swing it . . . in general, I can be more available time-wise than the average parent . . . what's bad is that I feel like I always have one foot in the work world and a foot in the home world, and sometimes it is very hard to manage that.

This "tug-of-war" is stressful, and is likely exacerbated for several mothers by the presence of a preschool child. The mother of a two-year-old says, "The last twenty-four months for me have been like academically on survival mode, where I am just trying to survive in terms of teaching my course . . . , attending to students . . . , engaging in some research, so I think I am doing just what I need to survive, not really what say my professional goals are." Another mother shared a similar scenario,

> Balancing work and home are very stressful. I feel like I am never doing anything all that well. I am never as good in my job as I was before she was born, and I feel like I am never as good a parent because of my job, and I feel like I am never as good a wife because it's like I'm always making the sacrifice. . . . I always have a foot in both worlds. I am always doing work and some home-related thing all at the same time.

Flexibility and the Never-Ending Job

Women have the opportunity to use the flexibility an academic career affords to help them meet the cultural expectations of good mothers (Fothergill and Feltey 2003). However, flexible schedules result in high role strain at work and at home for some adults, who find themselves working on home tasks at work and work tasks at home (Stanfield 1998). Work doesn't end when academic women leave the office each day. Many women are working until late at night, once they put their children to bed. Some women say that they are preparing for class right up until they run out of the door to teach.

More than one woman had chosen an academic career for the flexibility it affords mothers. However, the consequence of flexible schedules is often burdensome, especially on mothers of preschool children. One mom confessed that she sometimes fantasizes about the way many nine-to-five jobs actually end at five o'clock, whereas the flexibility of her job often *requires* her to work evenings at home. Another mother described flexibility as a system of payback—taking time one day requires paying it back on another day. She portrayed flexibility as a good tool for crisis management, i.e., sick care.

Despite the flexible hours, the demands or on-the-job constraints were often difficult for mothers to manage, especially as primary caregivers responsible for their children even when they are at work. For example, one mom said she couldn't attend meetings outside of her childcare hours. Mothers who could extend their childcare hours were unwilling to do so, because it would mean leaving their children in a day care environment for longer than they felt was appropriate and acceptable. Other mothers were unwilling to schedule meetings at night, because that would interrupt family time.

"Playing" Professor

Many women spoke about giving 100 percent of themselves to their careers and their children. This formula is problematic from a mathematical perspective, since there is only 100 percent to be disseminated. In reality, having children for the majority of women is likely correlated with lower productivity at work, since child care demands time that could have otherwise been spent on work-related responsibilities. Since this decline in productivity is not recognized by society (Fothergill and Feltey 2003), the women in this study did not lower their work expectations to accommodate motherhood. Instead they described their work performance in terms of mediocrity. Still, their "slow down" did not stop them from achieving great success and receiving accolades related to their accomplishments even though they reportedly believed that their efforts were not enough.

However, there was something more going on here than was obvious at first. Most of these women seemed to suffer from the "imposter syndrome" (Clance and Imes 1978), at least since they had become mothers. They described themselves in terms of being "good enough" to get the job done at work. The imposter syndrome is associated with high-achieving, highly successful women, and seemed strong among women in this study, as many of them discounted their successes. The public impression was that these women were highly successful academicians, but their own perception of their success did not resonate. They achieved success at work, but felt less competent than before they became mothers, thus negating the extent of their victory. They did not believe that they could "have it all"—i.e., successful home and work lives. Despite their superhuman abilities to conquer the daunting tasks associated with motherhood and their profession each day, these moms did not consciously support the super-mom ideal. Contrarily, they reportedly believed that women must choose between success at home and success in the workplace. This was where the imposter reared its head.

One mom said, "You can't do it all, and if that means that I can't be a stellar scholar . . . then I wouldn't even want that. I am much more interested in having quality time with my family than I am having thousands of articles published." Another mother said, "I just don't see how you could do a good job at both . . . I don't see that you can really have both . . . you can probably do both adequately or do one really, really well and sacrifice the other. I am at the treading water adequately stage right now."

Interestingly, moms repeatedly said that they have tended to sacrifice their research because it was the least obvious concession when time ran out and something needed to go. Despite the obvious link between research and job security, and research and salary increases through promotion and tenure, mothers in this study felt they were only hurting themselves if they did not reach their research goals. One mother said,

> I tend to be putting a lot of things on hold. I am not getting the research done that I would like to do or putting in the extra effort to make a class period better. I know that sometimes I take shortcuts because of lack of time and I would say predominantly this occurs in the area of research. . . . I know I can't cut back on taking care of my children, but I know that I can cut back on my research and I can cut back on my committees. . . . Now I pretty much go to class, come to my office, get things done as fast as I can, because I know my time is so limited.

Another mother put it this way, "If I'm going to cut anywhere in my life it's not going to be with my family, because they are my priority, so it would be to find out what's the minimal stuff I can get away with here." Having a preschool child impacts research in a way that inhibits promotion. Although she's eligible to apply for promotion to full professor next year, one woman did not believe she'd "done enough publishing and other things to be ready to apply for maybe five more years." She "let go" of her research aspirations as she tried to balance two children with her academic career. She, like several other women interviewed, did the necessary day-to-day academic work to the best of her ability in order to survive. Since she became a mother, she kept her office door closed more often, aside from mandatory office hours, so that she could complete as much schoolwork as possible with the expectation that she would bring home less schoolwork at the end of each day.

The same sentiments were true for the women in this study when it came to participation in professional conferences. All of the women said that they had not attended professional conferences as often since they became mothers. Those that did attend tried to find conferences that were local enough that they could return home the same day. A mother of two children said, "There are certainly a lot more conferences that I would like to go to but I tend to just go to one a year."

Kryptonite

Academic women encounter difficulties when it comes to health-promoting behaviors (Elliot 2003). The roles and responsibilities involved in work and motherhood compete for women's time, energy, and other resources, and inhibit women's ability to maintain a health-promoting lifestyle (Nelson 1997). Consequently, several academic mothers in this study reported that they engaged in health-damaging behaviors—e.g., coffee drinking, smoking, sedentary lifestyles—in an effort to find better balance. The following health-promoting behaviors were discussed in the interviews: physical fitness, eating habits, sleep, stress management, healthcare utilization, and nonwork interests/leisure activities. Other issues affecting women's health behaviors included social support, elder care, and lactation.

Most women reported that they did not routinely participate in physical activities. Only a couple of women reported regular exercise. One mother, previously an avid exerciser, admitted that although she still tries to prioritize exercise, she finds that she is compromising more now that her two-year-old daughter is aware of her absence. She said she also feels selfish leaving her daughter again once they get home, since she's been away from her most of the workday.

There was variation among women in terms of their eating habits. One family followed a rigid diet due to the mother's chronic health problem, and another family was vegetarian and eats mostly organic foods, while the remaining mothers seem to struggle with meal planning, and healthy eating patterns. A few moms reported skipping or forgetting to eat breakfast, while some moms eat on-the-run.

Many women said they often felt tired, but most reported getting the recommended six to eight hours of sleep each night. A couple of women engaged in doctoral studies reported working late nights on their coursework.

Many mothers reported high stress, but no stress management. One woman said, "There are some moments when I feel I can't do it. It's too hard. I need a break." However, breaks seem to seldom come for these working women. As a result, some women admitted losing themselves in the mix of work and family. Scheduling, time management, and organization seemed to be the only regular mechanisms several moms reportedly used to deal with their stress.

Although many mothers were utilizing the healthcare system for routine examinations, some mothers put their children before their own healthcare needs. Several mothers reported rescheduling their own doctors' appointments. One mom rescheduled a doctor appointment two to three times because she was "busy" with her son. One mom replied, "I am a little far behind with my physical. The last time I was checked by the doctor was, I guess, post-partum, so three years ago."

The majority of the mothers laughed when they were asked about their nonwork interests/leisure activities. Several women made similar statements that demonstrated the prominent place their children hold in their lives. One mom said, "We don't have a lot of leisure activities. . . . I just think that my kids should receive everything . . . whatever leisure activities we have, the kids are a part of them." Another mother said, "I don't have enough time in my day to have interests that don't include my children." And a third put it this way, "I have no other nonwork interests at the present time. Family takes up all of my time, and I don't mind that to a great extent. That is my focus, my energy. I have a hard time setting aside time for myself to do something that I really enjoy because I don't want to take away from my family."

Many women credited their abilities to manage their multiple roles to a strong social support system. However, the way in which women described the assistance they received from their husbands was problematic. Although several women reportedly relied heavily on their spouses for support, many described their husbands as *helpers*. For example, one mom said, "I have tremendous social support, but ultimately the responsibility falls on the mother at least in my case. I am responsible for drop-offs and pick-ups five days a week unless there is some special thing I have to be at. I make the lunches. I plan the dinners. I do the grocery shopping." This mother was juggling the demands of career and the demands of family pretty much by herself.

Other potentially damaging issues surfaced related to the universities at which these women worked. Although only a couple of women reported that they were engaged in elder care, they described their resulting stress as unbearable. One woman whose mother was very ill described her balance as "out-of-whack," and counted "losing" herself as one of the most challenging consequences. For working mothers, performing eldercare responsibilities may lead to caregiving pileup, and further sabotage their efforts to engage in health-promoting behaviors (Elliot 2003).

Almost three-quarters of the women in this study were breastfeeding when they returned to work. However, there were no lactation rooms or workplace support for breastfeeding found on any of the four universities. Women described multiple breast pumping dilemmas during the interviews, including anxiety, fear, and unsanitary options for pumping. One woman described her anxiety as she occupied the department's main bathroom for half-hour time periods to pump. Another woman described pumping in dirty bathroom stalls, waiting for milk to letdown, and feeling extremely uncomfortable and anxious that someone would enter and delay the process. One woman described suffering from engorged breasts until she got home, while another woman confessed that she pumped while driving to and from work each day. There are obvious risks to women's health and safety in all these cases.

Any assumptions that tenured and tenure-track academic mothers with pre-school children found it difficult to balance work and family were confirmed in this study. Further, motherhood ideology and role balance seemed to impact academic mothers' participation in health-promoting behaviors, and resulted in health-damaging behaviors for some mothers. Since working mothers, especially intensive mothers, are susceptible to role overload, it is critical that they make health-promoting lifestyle decisions to preserve their well-being. As academic mothers attempt to combine their multiple roles, many likely will experience stress resulting from role imbalance. Physical activity and stress management, in addition to other health-promoting behaviors, can protect mothers from the detrimental health outcomes associated with this imbalance, distress, exhaustion, and illness.

Academic mothers need structural support in order to achieve true success at home and at work (Forthergill and Feltey 2003). Five interwoven themes emerged in this analysis, and each demonstrates the intricate yet delicate balance necessary to sustain intensive motherhood, an academic career, and a healthy lifestyle. Women are pressured to meet challenges that leave them without the resources to address their health needs sufficiently.

It may be a pipe dream for women to attain success in academia without sacrificing their children or their health. The results of this study portray the old "having it all" adage as a fallacy that leaves women struggling to *do* it all without realization. As such, universities need to add more family-friendly policies and programs to their list of benefits. In addition, the academic climate needs to change, so that these offerings can be accepted and utilized by faculty. Previous reports have shown that faculty perceive stigma surrounding family-friendly policies (Drago and Colbeck 2003; Mason and Goulden 2002). Also, the demands of faculty positions need alterations to enable parents to succeed while balancing family responsibilities. Jacobs suggests that universities offer faculty family-friendly promises, such as assuring that they "value faculty as individuals, parents, and members of the academic community . . . expect[ing] faculty to work hard, but not more than fifty hours a week" (2004:22–23).

WORKS CITED

Clance, Pauline R., and Suzanne Imes. 1978. The imposter phenomenon in high-achieving women: Dynamics and therapeutic intervention. *Psychotherapy Theory, Research, and Practice* 15.3:1–8.

Crittenden, Ann. 2001. *The Price of Motherhood: Why the Most Important Job in the World Is Still the Least Valued.* New York: Holt.

Douglas, Susan J., and Meredith W. Michaels. 2004. *The Idealization of Motherhood and How It Has Undermined Women: The Myth of Motherhood.* New York: Free Press.

Drago, Robert, and Carol Colbeck. 2003. The Mapping Project: Exploring the terrain of U.S. colleges and universities for faculty and families. Final report to the Alfred P. Sloan Foundation. University Park: Pennsylvania State University.

Elliot, Marta. 2003. Work and family role strain among university employees. *Journal of Family and Economic Issues* 24.2:157–181.

Fothergill, Alice, and Kathryn Feltey. 2003. I've worked very hard and slept very little. *Journal of the Association for Research on Mothering* 5.2:7–19.

Garey, Anita Ilta. 1999. *Weaving Work and Motherhood.* Philadelphia: Temple University Press.

Hattery, Angela. 2000. *Women, Work, and Family: Balancing and Weaving.* Thousand Oaks, Calif.: Sage.

Hays, Sharon. 1996. *The Cultural Contradictions of Motherhood.* New Haven: Yale University Press.

Hewlett, Sylvia A. 2002. *Creating a Life: Professional Women and the Quest for Children.* New York: Talk Miramax.

Jacobs, Jerry. 2004. The faculty time divide. *Sociological Forum* 19:1–27.

Jacobs, Jerry A., and Sarah E. Winslow. 2004. Overworked faculty: Job stresses and family demands. *Annals of the American Academy of Political and Social Science* 596:104–129.

Mason, Mary Ann, and Marc Goulden. 2002. Do babies matter? The effect of family formation on the lifelong careers of academic men and women. *Academe* 88.6. http://www.aaup.org/publications/academe (accessed April 9, 2003).

——. 2004. Marriage and baby blues: Redefining gender equity in the academy. *Annals of the American Academy of Political and Social Sciences* 596.1:86–103.

Nelson, Martha A. 1997. Health practices and role involvement among low-income working women. *Health Care for Women International* 18.2:195–206.

Perna, Laura W. 2001. The relationship between family responsibilities and employment status among college and university faculty. *Journal of Higher Education* 72.5: 584–611.

Spalter-Roth, Roberta, and William B. Erskine. 2004. The best time to have a baby: Institutional resources and family strategies among early career sociologists. Research brief. Washington, D.C.: American Sociology Association.

Stanfield, Jacqueline B. 1998. Couples coping with dual careers: A description of flexible and rigid coping styles. *Social Science Journal* 35.1:53–65.

Vancour, Michele. 2005. "Motherhood Ideology, Role Balance, and Health-Promoting Behaviors of Academic Mothers." Ph.D. diss., New York University.

Ward, Kelly, and Lisa Wolf-Wendel. 2004. Academic motherhood: Managing complex roles in research universities. *Review of Higher Education* 27.2:233–257.

Williams, Joan. 2000. *Unbending Gender: Why Family and Work Conflict and What to Do About It*. New York: Oxford University Press.

Women's Voices/Women Vote. 2007. Fast Facts: Unmarried women. www.wvwv.org/assets/2007/10/22/fastfacts.pdf (accessed Jan. 10, 2010).

——. 2008. Greenberg Quinlan Rosner Research: "Unmarried women play critical role in historic election." HYPERLINK "http://www.wvwv.org/research/2008-election-research/unmarried-women-change-america" www.wvwv.org/research/2008-election-research/unmarried-women-change-america (accessed Jan. 10, 2010).

Exclusive Breastfeeding and Work Policies in Eldoret, Kenya

VIOLET NAANYU

Aggregate increase in education generally increases the probabilities of female employment, and women's participation in the labor force has been increasing over time (Rexroat 1992). The rapid increase in female labor force participation also leads to role conflict between motherhood and employment, especially in regards to breastfeeding patterns (Duckett 1992). Breastfeeding recommendations stress the importance of six months of exclusive breastfeeding (Lutter 1992). Exclusive breastfeeding is defined as giving the infant breast milk only, except for syrups containing vitamins and minerals (Labbok and Krasovec 1990). Breast milk is convenient and hygienic, and it has high concentration of growth and immunity factors. Breastfeeding confers health benefits on both infants and mothers (American Academy of Pediatrics 1997). Still, women rarely achieve the recommended exclusive breastfeeding period owing to structural and attitudinal conflicts. Motherhood and work roles continue to make different normative and social demands (Lindberg 1996; Roe et al. 1999). As more women join the public sphere in the twenty-first century, research undertakings on how increasing female employment influences breastfeeding trends remain important.

Figure 15.1 Workplace factors and methods involved in this study.

This paper begins with background information on women's changing roles in Kenya, followed by a discussion on the association between workplace policies and their utilization. The next section discusses the association between employment and exclusive breastfeeding. The last portion comprises study methodology, findings, discussion, promising research venues, and conclusions. This study examines duration of exclusive breastfeeding during the first five months after birth. It also investigates whether exclusive breastfeeding varies with demographic characteristics, occupation, distance to work, and work policies in Eldoret, Kenya.

WOMEN'S EMPLOYMENT AND CHANGING ROLES IN KENYA

Kenya has a population of 33.5 million; its population growth has persistently exceeded the rate of economic growth, resulting in high unemployment rates (World Bank 2006). Shifting from overdependence on localized traditional agriculture and semi-nomadic husbandry, many have joined the cash economy and industrial economies are on a slow increase. The Kenyan government has increasingly invested in the education sector (Robinson 1992), and as a result there has been a dramatic increase in literacy, especially among women. As women join the competitive labor market, they enter a sphere long dominated by male tradition and culture, and most likely lacking mother-friendly work arrangements. Indeed, gender inequality is manifested in formal employment that favors males (Kiteme 1992).

The 1999 Kenya census shows that there were 10,800,000 persons aged 15–64 in the labor force; 31 percent were engaged in paid employment, 14 percent in informal sector activities, and 49 percent on their own farms, while 6 percent were unemployed (Government of Kenya 1999). World Bank (2006) statistics indicate that, by 2004, 80.7 percent of youthful women (age 15–24 years) were literate. For men and women, the public (government) sector has been their primary employer (Hughes and Mwiria 1989). Although a growing number of educated Kenyan women are joining the labor force, there is an unresolved discourse about family-work demands. Kenyan women have to overcome gender biases held by employers (Hughes and Mwiria 1989).

WORKPLACE POLICIES: UTILIZATION AND IMPACT ON FAMILY RESPONSIBILITIES

Past workplace studies tend to focus on formal policies, giving little attention to family-supportive culture. These approaches fail to look at the effects of work policies on the entire family (Kossek and Ozeki 1999). Employment in large organized firms has been associated with fewer informal concessions to family needs, and with fewer policies that depend on supervisor cooperation (Glass and Fujimoto 1995). Family-friendly policies include maternity leave, nursing breaks, and workplace care for children. Further investigation into the relationship between policies and work-family role conflict may identify whether these policies actually serve their intended purpose (Kossek and Ozeki 1999).

Some scholars have investigated employee perception and utilization of family-friendly policies, while others have examined how employee and family characteristics relate to work outcomes and perceived attractiveness of family policies (Grover and Crooker 1995). Organizations increasingly offer employees family-friendly arrangements to help them balance work and family demands (Towers 1994). However, evidence suggests that family-friendly policies are often under-utilized, and are frequently unsupported by corporate cultures (Dodgson, Chee, and Yap 2004). Even self-employed individuals do not necessarily have improved schedule flexibility, leave benefits, or access to child care (Glass and Fujimoto 1995). Therefore, access to family-friendly policies does not necessarily result in reduced work-family conflict.

The 1919 and 1954 International Labor Organization (ILO) conventions required a six-to-twelve-week maternity protection and provision of two nursing breaks per day for industrial and agricultural settings (International Labour Organization 1997). A recent revision proposed that a working mother should be entitled to maternity leave of not less than twelve weeks and daily nursing breaks whose frequency and length should be determined by member countries. ILO also recommended provision of hygienic facilities for nursing (International Labour Organization 1999). Kenya is a member of the ILO and subscribes to ILO's recommendations; however, the recent proposed ILO revisions are yet to be fully implemented.

EXCLUSIVE BREASTFEEDING AND WORK

Exclusive breastfeeding has become increasingly complex in the twenty-first century because more women have joined the public work sphere in this new millennium. While appreciating the overwhelming value of breastfeeding, women in the new millennium have sought ways of forging new frontiers that allow for both traditional motherhood roles and new female statuses. Indeed, work outside the home presents an interesting area for research. Efforts made to balance work and motherhood roles make breastfeeding as a topic a salient persisting theme in motherhood studies.

Although exclusive breastfeeding is highly recommended, supplementary fluids are common (Davies-Adetugbo 1997) because the demands of motherhood and employment have inevitably perpetuated mixed breast- and bottle-feeding (Van Esterik and Greiner 1981). The type of work a mother engages in can affect her access to the infant and the time available to breastfeed the infant (Huffman 1984). While some argue that maternal employment has little effect on breastfeeding patterns (Van Esterik and Greiner 1981), there is evidence that maternal employment creates structural barriers and threatens breastfeeding (Duckett 1992). Compared to full-time work, part-time employment is associated with higher breastfeeding (Auerbach and Guss 1984).

Some of the factors associated with structural support in the workplace and breastfeeding success are space, time, and support of the employer (Cohen and Mrtek 1994). Adequate family-friendly policies such as maternity leave, flexible hours, and facilities for expression of breast milk in the workplace are critical for encouragement of breastfeeding (American Academy of Pediatrics 1997). While research on maternal employment and breastfeeding patterns has been ongoing, little is known about the association between various occupations and duration of exclusive breastfeeding in developing countries. Data collected in Kenya in 2002 is here used to investigate whether exclusive breastfeeding differs with occupation. Additional variables in analysis include age, education, distance to work, and access to family-friendly policies.

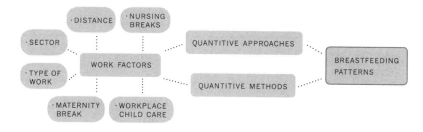

Figure 15.2 Variables of maternal employment affecting duration of breastfeeding.

METHOD AND DISCUSSION

Study Site and Design

This study was conducted in Eldoret, an urban center in Kenya. Situated 300 km northwest of Kenya's capital city, Nairobi, Eldoret is a major business and administrative center. Eldoret's general economy is characterized by primary jobs, such as farming in the outskirts of the town; secondary jobs involving factory activities; and tertiary jobs arising from educational institutions and medical care organizations. In this study, employed mothers were engaged in the public or the private sector. Typically, self-employed individuals in Eldoret run a wide range of economic projects, including retail shops, farms, schools, health facilities, cobblers, tailors/seamstresses, woodwork, food industry, service, and repair work.

The study involved face-to-face semi-structured interviews and six focus group discussions with women in Eldoret. Interviews took place in health-facility waiting bays. Two research assistants were trained prior to the pilot test, which involved thirty women from three Mother & Child Health and Family Planning (MCH/FP) clinics. This led to an improved version of the tool and development of appropriate sampling strategies. This paper presents quantitative findings with special focus on the effect of work on the duration of exclusive breastfeeding.

Sample Characteristics

Random stratified sampling was used to select participants. The selection criteria used included employed and self-employed mothers with infants aged less

Table 15.1 Descriptive Statistics of Variables in Analysis: Exclusive Breastfeeding, Demographics and Work Policies in Eldoret, Kenya (N=1,017)

Characteristics	Mean	Std. Dev.	Range	Variable Description
Dependent Variable				
Exclusive breastfeeding	2.44	1.05	0.5–5	Duration of exclusive breastfeeding (months)
Independent Variables				
Age groups				
Young mothers	0.21	0.41	0–1	1 = Mothers <20 years
Middle-aged mothers	0.69	0.46	0–1	1 = Mothers 21 to 30 years
Older mothers	0.10	0.30	0–1	1 = Mothers >31 years
Marital status	0.87	0.33	0–1	1 = Married mothers
Education	2.05	1.25	1–6	1 = Primary; 2 = 'O' Level; 3 = 'A' Level; 4 = Postsecondary certificate; 5 = Postsecondary diploma; 6 =Degree
Occupation				
Sector of employment	0.76	0.42	0–1	1 = Self-employed
Business	0.48	0.50	0–1	1 = Business mothers
Professional	0.16	0.37	0–1	1 = Professional mothers
Farmers	0.31	0.46	0–1	1 = Farming mothers
Casual	0.05	0.22	0–1	1 = Casual
Distance to work	1.43	0.89	1–5	1 = <1 km; 2 = 2–7 km; 3 = 8–13 km; 4 = 14–20 km; 5 =>20 km
Work policies				
Maternity leave	0.98	0.14	0–1	1 = Has maternity leave
Workplace child care	0.27	0.44	0–1	1 = Has workplace care
Nursing breaks	0.87	0.34	0–1	1 = Has nursing breaks

than twenty-four months old, and mothers residing in Eldoret town. Six (three private and three public) of the busiest MCH/FP clinics in Eldoret were selected. The number of respondents invited for interviewing corresponded to a third of the total number of clients seen monthly at each of the selected facilities; 1,121 mothers were successfully interviewed. Table 15.1 shows that most participants were age 21–30 years (69 percent), married (87 percent), and on average had some secondary-level education. The majority were self-employed (76 percent), with at least 48 percent participating in business activities. Only 16 percent of the sample comprised professional mothers. Mothers covered on average 1.43 (SD=.89) kilometers to get to work, with professionals covering the longest distance (1.8 kilometers, SD=.86).

Analytic Strategy

Quantitative data are examined with duration of exclusive breastfeeding being investigated in association with different occupations and work policies. STATA version 9.0 is used for all the analyses. Multivariate regression models are used to predict duration of exclusive breastfeeding. As shown in both tables, the following variables were used in the models: duration of exclusive breastfeeding (in months); age (youngest mothers as the reference category), marital status (married versus other); education (level of schooling); type of employment (self-employed versus employed mothers); sector of employment (professional mothers as the reference category), distance to work (in kilometers), and workplace policies (workplace care as the reference category).

In table 15.2 the base model (1) explores the effect of demographics on duration of exclusive breastfeeding. Occupation variables, including work distance, are introduced in model 2. In model 3, breastfeeding-friendly work benefits are added. As shown in models 2 and 3, distance to work and nursing breaks are significant, but occupation is not. Interaction models (4 and 5) then are conducted to better understand the influence of these factors.

Results

Mean duration of exclusive breastfeeding is 2.4 (SD=1.05) months. A simple bivariate look at all four occupations reveals that the mode duration of exclusive breastfeeding for each occupation is 2.5 months irrespective of diversity in family-friendly policies. At least 98 percent of all mothers in all occupations have maternity leave. About 95 percent (N=295) and 88 percent (N=431) of farmers and business mothers have access to nursing breaks respectively. Regarding casuals and professionals, 75 percent (N=39) and 71 percent (N=116) have nursing breaks respectively. Workplace child care is uncommon. Only 4 percent (N=7) of professionals and 15 percent (N=8) of casuals have policies allowing them to take their child to work. At least 33 percent (N=162) of business and 30 percent (N=94) of farming mothers have access to workplace child care.

Table 15.2 Exclusive Breastfeeding Regressed on Age Groups, Marital Status, Education, Occupation, and Family-Friendly Policies in Kenya (N=1,017)

Variables	Model 1	Model 2	Model 3	Model 4	Model 5
Age cohorts[1]					
Middle-aged mothers	0.266**	0.268**	0.254**	0.249**	0.255**
	(0.086)	(0.086)	(0.085)	(0.085)	(0.086)
Older mothers	0.240±	0.249*	0.227±	0.215±	0.219±
	(0.130)	(0.129)	(0.128)	(0.127)	(0.127)
Married mothers	-0.024	0.005	0.052	0.034	0.064
	(0.101)	(0.101)	(0.101)	(0.101)	(0.102)
Education	0.042	0.034	0.026	0.029	0.025
	(0.027)	(0.035)	(0.035)	(0.034)	(0.035)
Occupation[2]					
Self-employed[†]		-0.113	-0.091	-0.126	-0.171
		(0.138)	(0.136)	(0.137)	(0.137)
Business		0.243	0.259±	-0.103	0.372
		(0.154)	(0.153)	(0.246)	(0.234)
Farming		0.084	0.118	-0.403±	0.797*
		(0.167)	(0.166)	(0.238)	(0.329)
Casuals		0.245	0.244	-0.928**	0.973
		(0.181)	(0.180)	(0.362)	(0.330)
Distance to workplace		0.170***	0.134***	-0.144	
		(0.038)	(0.039)	(0.096)	
Work policies[3]					
Maternity leave			0.496*	0.473*	0.509*
			(0.233)	(0.231)	(0.235)
Nursing breaks			—	—	-0.218
			-0.399***	-0.449***	(0.178)
			(0.105)	(0.107)	
Interaction effects					
Distance x business				0.206±	
				(0.124)	
Distance x farming				0.329*	
				(0.107)	
Distance x casuals				0.676***	
				(0.182)	
Nursing breaks x business				-0.173	
					(0.229)
Nursing breaks x farming				-0.733*	
					(0.319)
Nursing breaks x casuals				-0.997**	
					(0.374)
Constant	2.173	1.848	1.536	2.279	1.811

Standard errors in parentheses. †Employed mothers as reference category. [1]Younger mothers omitted. [2]Professional mothers omitted. [3]Workplace childcare omitted. ±significant at p ≤.10. *significant at p ≤.05. **significant at p ≤.01. ***significant at p ≤.001 (2-tailed).

As shown in table 15.2, duration of exclusive breastfeeding increases with age. Estimates for middle-aged and older mothers are significantly higher as compared to younger mothers in all models. With regard to work factors, access to maternity leave increases exclusive breastfeeding in model 3 by a factor of .50 (t=2.13, p ≤ .05). Distance to work and nursing break variables reveal unexpected but significant results in all models: exclusive breastfeeding increases with distance to work (p ≤ .001), while access to nursing breaks decreases duration of exclusive breastfeeding (p ≤ .001), all else equal.

The first interactive model (model 4) indicates that exclusive breastfeeding does not change much with distance for business mothers. However, farmers and casual workers seem to breastfeed more with increasing distance. Consistent with these patterns, model 5 shows access to nursing breaks decreases exclusive breastfeeding among farmers and casuals.

Discussion

It is apparent in this sample that duration of exclusive breastfeeding increases with education, higher income, and greater age (Barnes, Leggett, and Durham 1993). Education, income, and age may represent differences in attitudes as well as access to different structural supports (McKinley and Hyde 2004). With increasing education, Kenyan women are gradually joining the labor force and experiencing social change (Cubins 1991). African women with seven or more years of education report shorter durations of breastfeeding than those with none (Witwer 1993). Additionally, this study's sample shows that 92 percent and 85 percent of the older and middle-aged women are married, respectively. It is therefore plausible that married participants have longer durations of exclusive breastfeeding because of spousal economic support. Indeed, spousal assistance has been positively correlated with exclusive breastfeeding (Chatman et al. 2004).

Different work environments present dissimilar structural limitations; hence, variation in duration of exclusive breastfeeding is expected since the ability to integrate work and motherhood depends on the occupation (Visness and Kennedy 1997). Structural conflicts may explain variation in breastfeeding with respect to occupation. Given its intensity and timing, breastfeeding and even breast milk expression cannot be undertaken without interfering with work schedules (Lindberg 1996).

Type of occupation and work distance seem to be central influences on exclusive breastfeeding, particularly given that many Kenyans have to walk to work or rely on undependable public transportation. Increasing distance to work lengthens exclusive breastfeeding for farmers and casuals. It is probable that farmers and casuals working far away from home may have less attachment to their work, and may have greater independence with regard to maternity leave. In this sample, 98 percent (N=305) of farmers, 92 percent (N=452) of business, and 10 percent (N=5) of casual workers are self-employed. Self-employed mothers may enjoy greater autonomy and control of their time and work conditions—hence fewer structural barriers to breastfeeding.

Unexpectedly, nursing breaks are negatively associated with exclusive breastfeeding. This is probably the result of women's fear that utilization of this benefit may jeopardize their position at work; they either stay home and breastfeed, or work and terminate exclusive breastfeeding. While self-employed women (76 percent of this study's sample) may have more control over their work conditions, their sole reliance on personal daily input may necessitate mixed feeding. Indeed the more dependent a woman is on her earnings for family support, the more rapidly she returns to work (O'Connell 1990). For the employed, absence from work may jeopardize promotion and job continuity. Therefore, family-friendly policies are underutilized by employees, and are frequently unsupported by corporate cultures (Solomon 1994). This calls for more empirical studies on utilization of family-friendly work policies.

Regarding maternity leave, there is a growing literature exploring employment, maternity leave, and breastfeeding (Lindberg 1996; Roe et al. 1999; Visness and Kennedy 1997). Women terminate breastfeeding the month they resume employment; in fact, they cannot achieve the six months of recommended breastfeeding given that maternity leave is shorter than six months (Lindberg 1996). Parental leave literature barely addresses breastfeeding issues (Galtry 2002); undeniably, more research on family-friendly work policies is needed.

Interestingly, mothers in this study have similar exclusive breastfeeding patterns irrespective of differences in family-friendly work policies. Could there be other, more prominent personal or sociocultural factors influencing breastfeeding behavior? Some researchers suggest that there is more to the breastfeeding patterns than diversity in work environments. For example, Auerbach and Guss (1984) argue that the timing of return to employment and number of daily hours worked, rather than type of occupation a mother engages in, influences breastfeeding patterns. Therefore, not all patterns of exclusive breastfeeding can be associated with work variables.

FUTURE AVENUES FOR RESEARCH

A key challenge for researchers in this century is to understand how dissimilar reforms in diverse global communities impact motherhood. For instance, we have scanty empirical work on motherhood emerging from Africa and similar developing contexts. We need studies that seek to understand African women's experiences of motherhood in changing political, social, and economic circumstances in the twenty-first century. We should strive to understand how resources are currently accessed, distributed, and used, and ultimately how that bears on women's everyday mothering decisions. This calls for more global resources and research efforts to be directed toward settings where we find the greatest burden of disease (e.g., African countries) and where resources are absent, limited, or shrinking. Specifically, future breastfeeding research would greatly benefit from studies addressing individual, cultural, and structural factors that influence breastfeeding behavior. Salient areas to consider include female employment and breastfeeding, emergent diseases (such as the HIV pandemic) and breastfeeding patterns, women's desire to (or not to) breastfeed, women's perceptions of breastfeeding, and women's personal experiences of breastfeeding.

To adequately cover the aforementioned topics, triangulation of research methods offers enormous promise (e.g., see fig. 15.1). A combination of quantitative and qualitative methods promises a constructive strategy of doing research in the twenty-first century and beyond. Such collaboration should appreciate localized meanings, as well as how social structures in which women's lives are embedded affect breastfeeding. For instance, first holding qualitative interviews with women and then using emergent themes to develop a structured tool suitably leads to a large-scale survey that appreciates diverse social experiences. This is especially important when Western research tools are applied in other contexts such as Africa.

Working mothers in Eldoret are not observing the recommended six months of exclusive breastfeeding, and generally, this sample holds a mean of 2.4 months of exclusive breastfeeding irrespective of differences in occupation and family-friendly work policies. Additionally, duration of exclusive breastfeeding seems to increase with age. Further studies should investigate utility of policies by diverse groups of workers. Type of occupation and distance to work also seem to influence duration of exclusive breastfeeding. Given the advantages of exclusive breastfeeding, strategies to promote the practice should be encouraged to keep pace with increasing maternal employment. Nevertheless, future research should also investigate women's desire to breastfeed, women's perceptions of breastfeeding, and personal experiences of breastfeeding.

This study has several limitations. First, though indicative of general patterns, the study was limited to health clinics in Eldoret and most of the sample consisted of self-employed mothers. Second, this study concentrates on work factors; however, the patterns identified could have resulted from other factors, such as the influence of psychosocial factors and forces of modernization in Kenya. Therefore, further research should include a larger sample of employed mothers, and the variables used should measure how both psychosocial and structural factors predict exclusive breastfeeding in Kenya.

Notwithstanding the caveats mentioned, this study adds to the growing literature on breastfeeding. Escalating female employment begs for a supportive social environment for working mothers who choose to breastfeed. Employees should also experience work policies as enabling role integration; they should perceive these policies as truly allowing for flexibility and schedule control before they can utilize them extensively (Kossek and Ozeki 1999). Moreover, because work factors may not be solely responsible for the patterns observed in Kenya, other individual and cultural barriers to breastfeeding require further investigation. Only then can we gain a better understanding regarding how mothers opting for exclusive breastfeeding can feasibly practice breastfeeding in this millennium.

WORKS CITED

American Academy of Pediatrics. 1997. Breastfeeding and the use of human milk (RE9729). Policy statement 100:1035–1039.

Auerbach, K. G., and E. Guss. 1984. Maternal employment and breastfeeding: A study of 567 women's experiences. *American Journal of Diseases of Children* 138.10:958–960.

Barnes, J. E., J. C. Leggett, and T. W. Durham. 1993. Breastfeeders versus bottlefeeders: Differences in femininity perceptions. *Maternal-Child Nursing Journal* 21.1:15–19.

Chatman, L. M., H. M. Salihu, M. E. A. Roofe, P. Wheatle, D. Henry, and P. E Jolly. 2004. Influence of *knowledge* and attitudes on exclusive breastfeeding practice among rural Jamaican mothers. *Birth* 31.4:265–271.

Cohen, R., and M. B. Mrtek. 1994. The impact of two corporate lactation programs on the incidence and duration of breastfeeding by employed mothers *American Journal of Health Promotion* 8.6:436–440.

Cubins, L. A. 1991. Women, men, and the division of power: A study of gender stratification in Kenya. *Social Forces* 69.4:1063–1083.

Davies-Adetugbo, A. A. 1997. Sociocultural factors and the promotion of exclusive breastfeeding in rural Yoruba communities of Osun State, Nigeria. *Social Science and Medicine* 45.1:113–125.

Dodgson, J. E., Y. O. Chee, and T. S. Yap. 2004. Workplace breastfeeding support for hospital employees. *Journal of Advanced Nursing* 47.1:91–100.

Duckett, L. 1992. Maternal employment and breastfeeding. *NAACOG Clinical Issues in Perinatal and Women's Health Nursing* 3.4:701–712.

Galtry, J. 2002. Child health: An underplayed variable in parental leave policy debates. *Community, Work, and Family* 5.3:258–278.

Glass, J., and T. Fujimoto. 1995. Employer characteristics and the provision of family responsive policies. *Work and Occupations* 22.4:380–411.

Government of Kenya. 1999. Kenya Economic Survey, Population Census, Ministry of Finance and Planning. Nairobi: Central Bureau of Statistics.

Grover, S. L., and K. J. Crooker. 1995. Who appreciates family-responsive human resource policies?: The impact of family-friendly policies on the organizational attachment of parents and non-parents. *Personnel Psychology* 48.2:271–288.

Huffman, S. L. 1984. Determinants of breastfeeding in developing countries: Overview and policy implications. *Studies in Family Planning* 15.4:170–183.

Hughes, R., and K. Mwiria. 1989. Kenyan women, higher education, and labor market. *Comparative Education* 25.2:79–195.

International Labour Organization (ILO). 1997. Maternity protection at work report. Geneva: International Labour Office V (1).

———. 1999. Maternity protection at work report. Revision of the maternity protection convention (revised), 1952 (no. 103), and Recommendation, 1952 (no. 95). Geneva: Maternity protection convention, 87th Session, International Labour Office.

Kiteme, K. 1992. The socioeconomic impact of the African market women trade in rural Kenya. *Journal of Black Studies* 23.1:135–151.

Kossek, E. E., and C. Ozeki. 1999. Bridging the work-family policy and productivity gap: A literature review. *Community, Work, and Family* 2.1:7–32.

Labbok, M., and K. Krasovec. 1990. Towards consistency in breastfeeding definitions. *Studies in Family Planning* 21.4:221–230.

Lindberg, L. D. 1996. Women's decisions about breastfeeding and maternal employment. *Journal of Marriage and the Family* 58.1:239–251.

Lutter, C. 1992. Recommended length of exclusive breastfeeding: Age of introduction of complementary foods and the weaning dilemma. Document no. WHO/CDD/EDP/92.5. Geneva: World Health Organization.

McKinley, N. M., and J. S. Hyde. 2004. Personal attitudes or structural factors? A contextual analysis of breastfeeding duration. *Psychology of Women Quarterly* 28.4: 388–399.

O'Connell, M. 1990. Maternity leave arrangements: 1961–85. In *Work and Family Patterns of American Women* (U.S. Bureau of the Census, Current Population Reports series P-23, no. 165), 11–25.

Rexroat, C. 1992. Changes in employment continuity of succeeding cohorts of young women. *Work and Occupations* 19.1:18–34.

Robinson, W. C. 1992. Kenya enters the fertility transition. *Population Studies* 46.3:445–457.

Roe, B., L. A. Whittington, S. B. Fein, and M. F. Teisl. 1999. Is there competition between breast-feeding and maternal employment? *Demography* 36.2:157–171.

Solomon, C. 1994. Work/family's failing grade: Why today's initiatives aren't enough. *Personnel Journal* 73.5:72–87.

Towers, P. 1994. Work/life programs: Supporting a new employer/employee deal. A Towers Perrin survey report. Boston: Towers Perrin.

Van Esterik, P., and T. Greiner. 1981. Breastfeeding and women's work: Constraints and opportunity. *Studies in Family Planning* 12.4:184–197.

Visness, C. M., and K. I. Kennedy. 1997. Maternal employment and breast-feeding: Findings from the 1988 National Maternal and Infant Health Survey. *American Journal of Public Health* 87.6:945–950.

Witwer, M. 1993. Mean duration of breastfeeding has risen in some developing countries, fallen in others since the 1970s. *International Family Planning Perspective* 19.1:34–35.

World Bank. 2006. Summary gender profile—Kenya. The World Bank Group. http://devdata.worldbank.org/genderstats/genderRpt (accessed Aug. 26, 2006).

Brown Bodies, White Eggs

SIXTEEN

The Politics of Cross-racial
Gestational Surrogacy

LAURA HARRISON

Reproductive technologies have become an increasingly normalized and culturally accepted component of family formation in the twenty-first-century United States. The media has been responsive to this shift—tabloids are filled with stories of the latest aging celebrity miraculously pregnant with twins, popular television shows such as *Jon and Kate Plus 8* follow plus-sized families conceived via fertility treatments, and infertility is a topic worthy of *Oprah*. While the examples that appear on television and in the media are often sensationalized, the level of intervention into the body and lives of those who employ such technologies can vary wildly, from noninvasive medication regimens to gestation by surrogates, the latter of which is the focus of this essay. For both the surrogate and the intended parent(s), difficult negotiations and complicated medical and legal maneuverings can render this a deeply fraught process. Despite the complex and seemingly private nature of this decision, surrogacy attracts a disproportionately high level of media attention in the United States today, and has been the focus of intense public debate. This fascination with surrogacy suggests that it is a repository for cultural unease surrounding race, reproduction, and the family, and is thus a vital arena for feminist critique.

This unease is in part a reaction to the rupture surrogacy creates between reproduction and socially recognized motherhood, which is counterintuitive to traditional models of the Western nuclear family, and effectively "dematernalizes" reproduction. A process of translation is therefore required in which social institutions, including popular media and the law, write cultural and moral legitimacy onto a highly commodified labor transaction. When intended parents are "white" and the surrogate is "non-white," this detachment implicates the differential value placed on the reproductive labor of "white" and "non-white" women in the United States. New reproductive technologies appear to offer an alluring promise of the deconstruction of racial difference via a postmodern explosion of possibility that includes white children borne of non-white parents. Theoretically, this mingling of "different" blood and bodies suggests that racial difference is a social construction rapidly losing cultural currency, yet the material evidence of the value placed on white and non-white labor in this reproductive arena suggests otherwise.

The contemporary reproductive market includes an increase in what I will call "cross-racial gestational surrogacy," in which the surrogate is of a different race from the child she will bear, problematizing her legibility as a potential "mother" for that child. Gestational surrogacy—particularly cross-racial—must be interrogated in and through the vexed politics of racialized gender and structural inequalities. As Anne Cheng argues in *The Melancholy of Race*, racialization operates "through the institutional process of producing a dominant, standard, white national ideal, which is sustained by the exclusion-yet-retention of racialized Others," an exclusion-yet-retention that is exemplified by the non-white surrogate who will bear, yet not raise, a white child (2000:10). As this essay will contend, the contemporary racialization of surrogacy in the United States and abroad serves the interest of white American consumers, who benefit from the naturalization of racial inequality.

Indeed, I will argue that new reproductive technologies do not serve to cast out racialized bodies, but to locate them in a way that is convenient and nonthreatening for white consumers, effectively reinforcing racialized gender hierarchies while supposedly effacing them. Meanings of racial difference in the dominant discourse of surrogacy in the United States are continuously renegotiated to benefit white consumers. Rather than exiling raced bodies, this racist discourse relies upon the economic exploitation of "Other" women as reproductive laborers. As such, racial difference must be maintained despite an outward façade of "colorblindness." Tellingly, the advent of new reproductive technologies has led white consumers not to discontinue the employment of non-white women for reproductive labor, but rather to continue constructing discourses that naturalize this relationship. As evidence, I will examine ways in which racial difference is constructed and defined in legal cases of contested surrogacy and the discourse surrounding surrogates and intended parents.

FERTILITY AND TECHNOLOGICAL ADVANCEMENT

While surrogacy is hardly a new phenomenon, technological advancements in reproductive technology have had a profound impact on the way it is accomplished. The practice of injecting sperm into a woman's cervix has been used by doctors as well as lay people to treat mild or unexplained infertility as well as cervical problems, and is crucial to the process of surrogacy because it allows for fertilization without heterosexual penetration (U.S. Department of Health and Human Services 2006). Surrogacy through artificial insemination (AI), in which the father-to-be or a donor provides sperm and the egg is biologically the surrogate's, is known as "traditional" or "complete" surrogacy (Shanley 2001). The incidence of traditional surrogacy within the United States has historically remained low in comparison to alternative means of reproduction, including adoption, in part because it arguably undermines standard notions of the biological nuclear family in which connections are based on genetic ties. Often in traditional surrogacy the prospective father remains genetically related to his son or daughter, yet the "mother-to-be" is not a legal part of the family unit because she did not give birth, necessitating her adoption of the newly born child.

This stumbling block was seemingly eradicated when in vitro fertilization (IVF) vitally and fundamentally changed the practice of surrogacy, serving as the true catalyst for the surrogacy explosion with the first successful in vitro fertilization in 1978 (Shanley 2001). In lay terms, IVF consists of fertilizing a woman's egg outside of her body and then transferring the egg into a womb. IVF is commonly used as a treatment for infertility by heterosexual couples who want to have a child that is biologically related to them, and also by lesbian couples. IVF also had a galvanizing effect on the practice of surrogacy because it allows a woman to carry and bear a child that is not genetically related to her in any way; both the egg and sperm can come from outside sources. Thus a couple can hire a surrogate, provide the sperm themselves, and then purchase an egg "donated" by a third woman if the female partner is unable to provide a viable egg. This practice, commonly known as "gestational" surrogacy, has drastically changed the landscape of surrogacy in the United States.

Although the first "test tube" baby was born through IVF in 1978, it wasn't until the mid-1980s that IVF clinics began to offer eggs for sale independent of pregnancy. Once a split had occurred between the "donation" of an egg and the use of a womb, both suppliers of eggs and surrogates became more common. By 1986, surrogacy brokers were charging couples anywhere from $25,000 to $45,000 for their services. This included a $10,000 payment to the surrogate and $15,000 for the broker and other expenses (Spar 2006). It was this transition from traditional to gestational surrogacy that drastically transformed the dynamics of surrogacy contracts, and the implications of race and socioeconomic standing for the women who were involved in such contracts.[1]

The Centers for Disease Control and Prevention, which tracks nearly 95 percent of fertility procedures in the United States, shows statistics of 1,210 attempted gestational surrogacies in 2000, double the number in 1997. They also report that gestational surrogacies now account for as many as 95 percent of all surrogacies, although less than half result in live births (Hamilton 2003:D1). The 2005 Assisted Reproductive Technology Report released by the CDC states that out of 422 reporting clinics 95 percent offer the services of a donor egg, and 77 percent offer the services of a gestational "carrier" (Centers for Disease Control and Prevention 2005). Despite what may appear to be low numbers of births attributable to surrogacy, the cultural significance of the phenomenon is indicated by its rate of increase, as well as the attention that it garners. As sociologist Susan Markens argues, surrogacy can be read as a form of "symbolic politics," or "debates that reflect underlying social tensions and concerns" (2007:8).

Part of the increase in gestational surrogacy can be attributed to cross-racial gestational surrogacy, with the most current available statistics stating that "approximately 30 percent of all gestational surrogacy arrangements at the largest program now involve surrogates and couples matched from different racial, ethnic, and cultural backgrounds" (Ragoné 2000:65).[2] Unfortunately, empirical research on the topic of surrogacy has not been produced at the same rate as ethical and legal responses to the phenomenon. Many studies that focus on surrogacy have been conducted at the "micro," ethnographic level with less focus on broader political and cultural implications. These gaps are starting to be filled but statistical research is still lacking (Markens 2007). In addition, only a fraction of the scholarship surrounding issues of surrogacy, including the substantial and contentious feminist debates, contain a "racialized" reading of this issue.[3] While many scholars examine the basic relationship between surrogate and contracting parties, there is a dearth of research on the implications of a system that is embedded within an ongoing history of class and race oppression, including the reliance of the dominant classes upon women of color as paid or coerced caregivers, whether for children, the elderly, or the home.

SURROGACY, FEMINISM, AND THE LAW

Inevitably, the rise of contracted surrogacy arrangements within the United States has led to custody battles between intended parents and both traditional and gestational surrogates. Krista Sirola (2006), in the *American University Journal of Gender, Social Policy, and the Law,* argues that the judicial response to surrogacy has primarily fallen into three standards or approaches; the genetic provider standard, the gestational motherhood standard, and the intent-based approach; I will discuss the intent-based approach.[4]

This approach stems from the case of *Johnson v. Calvert,* which was heard by the Supreme Court of California in 1993. In this case of gestational surrogacy, Crispina Calvert and husband Mark Calvert provided the genetic material, but surrogate Anna Johnson filed suit for parental rights and custody. According to the gestational motherhood standard set by the case of "Baby M," as the birth mother Johnson would be the legal mother of the child. In contrast, the courts resolved that the couple who *intended* to create the child, in this case the Calvert's, were the legal parents, but also specified that it was not intent *alone* that would decide the case. Rather, "when more than one woman has a valid claim of motherhood under California law the intent element 'breaks the tie' between the two women" (Sirola 2006). This decision suggests that both gestation *and* genetics are "valid" claims to motherhood, neither of which can trump the other, and thus intent can "break the tie."

Because of the significance of this case to the way in which this essay will conceptualize race, I will spend some time unpacking the racial identification of the three key actors. While Mark Calvert is white, and his wife Filipina, the Calverts were repeatedly referred to as a "white couple" in the press.[5] Although the Calverts are no more a "white" couple than a "non-white" one because of their interracial status, their race as a couple is read *in relation* to Johnson's blackness, marking them as white in the media and, arguably, in the courts. To reiterate, the media defined the Calverts as white *in contrast* to Johnson's blackness, which exemplifies how race is socially constructed in a way that benefits the middle-class white consumer. As defined by Michael Eric Dyson, to call race, or whiteness in his example, a social construct is to view it as having "a historically mediated cultural value that challenges the biological basis of white identity" (2004:108).

Regardless of either of the Calverts' specific racial or ethnic background, they gain a white identity in comparison to Anna Johnson.[6] Before whiteness was understood to be a social construction, according to Dyson, whiteness was in part "called into existence by blackness" to the extent that the meanings of the terms *white* and *black* were constitutive of one another (108). I would argue that the "symbolic link" that Dyson notes between racial categories continues to shape popular discourse on race. Because the concepts "white" and "non-white" are routinely defined in relation to one another, the meaning of these terms is not simply temporally, culturally, and geographically contingent—each term is also dependent upon the other for its cohesion.[7]

As such, cross-racial gestational surrogacy is a site in which definitions of race are not static; they are contingent. The case I will now turn to suggests that meanings of racial difference are also affected by national identity and the racialized hierarchies that emerge between nation-states. While this case is not one of cross-racial gestational surrogacy and both parties are Hispanic, it is significant as evidence that incommensurable difference is marked between the surrogate and intended parents in this case in ways that mimic or parallel the racial "difference" constructed in cases of cross-racial gestational surrogacy.

While many details of the case were disputed, most newspaper accounts reported that Nattie and Mario Haro, who lived in Chula Vista, California, contacted an aunt in Mexico when they discovered that Nattie Haro could not conceive. Through this aunt they came in contact with Alejandra Muñoz, Nattie's nineteen-year-old second cousin who lived in the small town of Mazatlán with her two-year-old daughter before illegally immigrating to California to become a surrogate. According to Muñoz, she was told that she would be inseminated with Mario Haro's sperm, but would only remain pregnant for a few weeks before a procedure called a "womb transfer" would occur between herself and Nattie Haro (Robertson 1987). When Muñoz realized that she had to carry the baby to term, she threatened to abort. It was then that the Haros created a contract stating that they would have full custody of the child, and Muñoz signed it. After signing the contract, Muñoz decided that she wanted to keep the baby, and a custody battle ensued (Okerblom 1986).

This case marked the first time that a California judge rendered a decision on the legality of a surrogacy contract, inciting some media scrutiny. Yet the media attention to this rather bizarre tale came nowhere close to that surrounding the Baby M case or the *Johnson v. Calvert* dispute, which is arguably reflective of a disinterest in the mainstream culture concerning the reproductive rights of immigrant women. A San Diego Superior Court judge ruled that contracting surrogacy in California was legal, and assigned shared custody between the Haros and Muñoz. Muñoz's custody was revoked a few months later when a lawyer representing the child reported that the baby was not adequately developing, a charge that the ACLU assisted Muñoz in fighting (Turegano 1987b). After extensive and repeated custody hearings, Muñoz and the Haros maintained a strained arrangement of shared custody.

The media coverage of the case, although arguably sympathetic to Muñoz, also posited the Haros and Muñoz as literally "worlds apart" despite their kinship and shared heritage. One article, discussing the child, explicitly marks the Haros and Muñoz as belonging to two different and differentially valued worlds: "One world is that of her middle-class father, Mario Haro, a junior high school teacher, and his wife Nattie, of Chula Vista. The other is that of her mother, Alejandra Arellano Munoz, a former $50-a-week janitor from El Habal, a tiny Mexican town near Mazatlan" (Okerblom 1990). Muñoz's world is pared down to her status as Mexican, poor, and single, all positioning her as the "bad," or at least less-deserving, mother, and the Haros are elevated to middle-class, cultured, and married—the "ideal" family.

Alejandra Muñoz is posited as the binary opposite of her cousin, relying on such dichotomies as First World/Third World, urban/rural, middle-class wealth/ working-class poverty, and American culture/Mexican "tradition." Numerous media stories repeat that Muñoz was living in near-poverty in Mexico, earning $40 or $50 a week as a janitor in a bank, and much was made of her grade-school education, inability to speak English, and alleged illiteracy in Spanish (Romero 1986; Peterson 1987). A *New York Times* article summed up her supposed ignorance and backwardness as evidenced in the custody trails by saying that "Miss Munoz had little education, was unclear about what city she was in, and wept frequently while testifying. She said she could not read the 'connected letters,' or longhand, in a seven-line two-sentence contract she signed for the Haros when she was two months pregnant" (Peterson 1987). Another article in the *San Diego Union* referred to Muñoz as "a Mexican national who speaks no English," and said that she was "at the center of an emotional legal battle that she does not fully comprehend" (Okerblom 1986).

What can this case tell us about the racial implications of cross-racial gestational surrogacy? First, the link between Muñoz's inability to speak English and her supposed inability to comprehend her custody trial is telling. Her status as a Spanish speaker is translated into a general incomprehension, marking Muñoz as out of place in an American context. This is exacerbated by repeated referrals to Muñoz as an "undocumented alien" in the press (Turegano 1987a). Munoz is "alien" to the United States, the English language, and the American legal system, all of which marks her as "different" from Nattie Haro. While this case involved parties that were both Hispanic, the response of the media was to demarcate the two potential "mothers" as clearly as possible, marking Muñoz as the "Other" and as arguably *more* "Other" than Nattie Haros, the legal United States resident. By citing a litany of supposed differences between Muñoz and the Haro family—in this instance citizenship and nationality stand in for race—journalists placed Nattie and Mario Haro squarely on the side of the unmarked *in relation to* Alejandra Muñoz, just as Mark and Crispina Calvert were "whitened" as a couple in relation to Anna Johnson.

In addition, Muñoz was posited as ignorant of basic biological facts (despite her previous childbirth), as well as illiterate and uneducated. This representation allows her to conform to racial stereotypes of the servant or laborer who "produces" for the upper classes. The Haros, while not uniformly portrayed in a positive light, are excused for doing what any American couple would do, which is absolutely anything to have a child. Muñoz's race, and specifically her "traditional" (read ignorant) Mexican values, combined with United States' cultural acceptance of Mexican women as illegal "domestics," help to slot her into the role of surrogate.

CONTESTED SURROGACY—
RACE AND THE LEGITIMATE MOTHER

As the previous proceedings suggest, there are reasons beyond monetary incentives for hiring women of color as gestational surrogates—reasons that white couples may or may not be conscious of, but certainly benefit from. First, the physical aspect of surrogacy is generally most appealing to women for whom paid pregnancy is economically attractive. The structural limitations placed upon black and Latina women who live below the poverty line with reduced earning potential in the mainstream workforce may increase their participation in this form of employment. Of course, American women are not the only women living in poverty. Interested parties seeking gestational surrogates also recruit poor, young mothers from developing countries. A surrogate earning $20,000 for a contract pregnancy in California is making only 40 percent above minimum wage, while this would be equivalent to twenty times as much for a woman in Mexico (Spar 2006). The disparity in cost between hiring a surrogate in the United States and finding a surrogate in a developing country creates a massive demand for the "outsourcing" of surrogacy. Both egg donation and surrogacy can be outsourced, although some couples who require egg donation find a donor in their own country, while choosing a surrogate in a developing country.

In addition, the meaning of racial difference in surrogacy discourse is contextually contingent and made renegotiable for the purposes of the white consumer. Racial differences that may go unspoken or are downplayed in cross-racial surrogacy arrangements may indeed "speak" once the child is born. When a woman of color gives birth to a white child she is visually identifiable as "Other" to the baby, weakening her potential maternal claims. The raced body of the surrogate can be read as a text that marks her liminality both socially and legally. If a surrogate's skin color can serve as a marker of the nongenetic tie between herself and the child, this can be read as "evidence" that the child does not belong to her. Indeed, Valerie Hartouni (2008), author of *Cultural Conceptions,* points out that in the custody battle between Anna Johnson and Mark and Crispina Calvert, Crispina repeatedly stressed to the media and the courts that the child "looked just like" her and her husband as evidence of their parental rights.

Cross-racial gestational surrogacy is made culturally coherent by marking the surrogate as racially "Other" from the child, and thus not a possible mother figure. This disjuncture between surrogate and child is strengthened by our cultural acceptance of the categories of non-white/white as effectively marked/unmarked. When these two categories collide, as in the birth of a white child by a non-white woman, this may strengthen the dichotomous nature of the white/non-white boundary by clarifying the surrogate's "marked" status. While this scenario could also be read as destabilizing notions of race as a biological construct and accepting its status as a social and ideological construction, race in this respect is more commonly viewed as a marker of difference, reifying the white couple's genetic "ownership" of the white child. Racial difference is brought to the forefront strategically in the racist discourse of surrogacy.

Within the American context, it is crucial to consider the specific historical and culture context that makes African American women particularly vulnerable to reproductive exploitation. The history of slavery in the United States and the unequal status of black people in American society thereafter have discursively naturalized black women as physical, paid laborers—especially reproductive laborers—while white women are lauded as the providers of valued genetic material. This reifies an ideological construct that posits white women as physically weak and unfit for heavy labor, giving credence to black women's oppression while locating them as an integral if invisibilized component of white reproduction. This concept clearly has historical precedence in the

United States; as Dorothy Roberts states in *Killing the Black Body*, during slavery the United States courts protected slave owners' control over black women's reproduction, giving the slave master ownership over the woman, her children, and any future children she might bear. Roberts argues that this created a division between black mothers and their children that did not exist for white women, a practice that "violated the prevailing ideology of female domesticity that posited mothers as the natural caretakers for their children" (1997:39) and that now contributes to the naturalization of black women in the United States as surrogates for white babies.

In addition, Patricia Hill Collins demonstrates that the cultural representation of black women "transmits clear messages about the proper links among female sexuality, fertility, and Black women's roles in the political economy" (1990:78). Part of that political economy today includes gestational surrogacy. The image of black women as purveyors of amplified sexuality and fertility, as well as their continued economic exploitation in the United States, make them appealing and seemingly "natural" candidates. The "mammy" stereotype encourages a view of black women as loving, doting, asexual caretakers of white children, while the continued portrayal of black women as "welfare mothers" and destructive matriarchs suggests that a child borne by a black woman would be better off reared by a white family. Black women are depicted as hypersexual when it conveniently allows dominant groups to blame them for their own oppression, or benefit from their bodies, while they are construed as nurturing when employed as caretakers, nannies, and surrogates. This parallels the discursive renegotiation of race in cross-racial surrogacy narratives, in which racial difference is foreground in certain circumstances and dismissed in others. Anna Johnson, for example, was often portrayed in the media as a con artist and "welfare queen," with "welfare queen" serving as shorthand for "bad black mother" (Grayson 1998). In this instance, the stereotype of the sexual, inappropriate mother sticks, while the image of the maternal caregiver is conveniently brushed aside.

The subordination of black female reproduction and sexuality to economic interests retains cultural currency today as good motherhood is tied to "the longings of the nation-state" (Lawson 2004:195). The creation of a family is defined by one's ability to produce children, which is a reflection of the power of the nation, and therefore vulnerable to state intervention. If childbearing increases the strength of the nation and is a reflection of it, then certain people will be encouraged to reproduce over others. Lawson (2004) defines these as "women who are thought to embody the physical, cultural, and mythical ideals of the nation's past, present, and future" (195), namely, white upper-class women. This analysis begs an important question: What if women who do not fall within this desirable category are (re)producing children for those who do? What if women of color are bearing the genetic children of acceptable members of the nation-state?

American culture and historical practices have institutionalized the belief that having a black ancestor, especially a black mother, makes a child black (Grayson 1998). The commonly known "one drop rule" insists that a long history of white lineage is instantly erased once a single ancestor can be identified as black. Do the children of cross-racial gestational surrogacy fall under the same rules for racial heritage and naming as their gestational "mothers" or are they subject to those of their genetic parents? Are these children white because their genetic parents are white, or does the "one drop" of their gestational "mother" relegate them to the status of mere "passing"? It is clear that the nation has a vested interest in protecting the custodial parental rights of its most valued citizens and illegitimating the parental rights of the literal "Others," while continuing to define race in ways that shore up this system.

One potential reason for this vested interest is what Lee Edelman (2004) refers to as "reproductive futurism." Reproductive futurism presupposes the absolute and inherent good of heteronormative reproduction by limiting any discourse that would counter this claim, rendering dissent unthinkable. Edelman posits queerness as necessarily oppositional to this discourse, and claims that "queer negativity" challenges the value of the social by refusing to fetishize the future. He supports the revolutionary nature of this claim by arguing, "We are no more able to conceive of a politics without a fantasy of the future than we are able to conceive of a future without the figure of the Child. The figural Child alone embodies the citizen as an ideal, entitled to claim full rights to its future share in the nation's good, though always at the cost of limiting the rights 'real' citizens are allowed" (Edelman 2004:11).

By reading Lawson and Edelman together, one can see that childbearing *by certain types of women* is necessary for shoring up the power of the nation-state as long as reproductive futurism holds political and social currency. This is reflected in the practice of gestational surrogacy. Even many critics of surrogacy argue that it should be practiced in some form, as the end result is a child. Although Debora Spar sees many pitfalls to surrogacy arrangements, she argues that the market for babies is undeniable and thus must be accepted and regulated. Even after a book-length critique of the inequities and moral complexities of all forms of surrogacy, her final claims speak to the very core of reproductive futurism, "It's hard to imagine that we could ever put this particular genie back in its bottle. Moreover, it's not at all clear that we should. For the baby business—unlike, say, the arms race or the heroin trade—produces a good that is inherently *good*" (Spar 2006:196). By comparing the "baby business" to things that many people would find inherently *bad* such as heroin and the arms race, Spar further inoculates her claim about the goodness of babies. Edelman calls claims such as this "self-evident one-sidedness—the affirmation of a value so unquestioned, because so obviously unquestionable" (Edelman 2004:2). It is this unquestioned value of the end result of gestational surrogacy that serves to elide the material and historical inequities that exist within the relationship between surrogate and contracting parties.

In *Against Race,* sociologist and race theorist Paul Gilroy concludes that contemporary medical breakthroughs such as genetic engineering, transnational organ transplants, and cross-racial surrogacy are part of a biotechnological revolution of such cultural significance that it "demands a change in our understandings of 'race', species, embodiment, and human specificity" (2000:20). Without endorsing Gilroy's call for a reconsideration of race as an organizing principle of identity, I would argue that advances in reproductive technologies do demand a shift in understandings of how racist discourse operates. As this essay has evidenced, the racism that is deployed within the practice of cross-racial gestational surrogacy is insidious in part because it does not exile the racial "Other" from the economy of reproductive labor, but rather situates non-white surrogates in a location that benefits the white consumer.

In order to mark this process as morally and ethically legitimate, the terms of racial difference must remain open for strategic redefinition. This is not to say that the *race* of women-of-color surrogates is contested by white consumers, but that the significance and the meaning of racial difference are discursively "up for grabs." Legally, racial difference may remain un(re)marked in a surrogacy contract, but suddenly "speak" if the contract is contested, as was the case with Anna Johnson. Culturally, race may be coded as "likeness" or "difference" in order to signify the preferred race of an egg or sperm donor. Nationality may stand in for race, attesting to the power of "Americanness," as it worked against Alejandra Muñoz. Racial difference is deployed strategically to benefit white consumers of surrogacy—it is foreground or it is dismissed; it is used as shorthand for injurious stereotypes or it is brushed aside. All the while, whiteness remains the unmarked category, a privilege that must be addressed in feminist critiques of surrogacy.

This essay calls for a further examination of racist discourse in surrogacy arrangements, and of how such discourses serve the interests of white American consumers. While new reproductive technologies allow possibilities for family formation that may have radical potential to minimize the stigma of infertility or create queer families of choice, these technologies are increasingly underwritten by a reliance on the bodies of women of color and poor women. Feminists who support surrogacy have rightly focused on agency and the liberatory potential of contract surrogacy for women, but before we can endorse surrogacy as yet another bastion of choice for both surrogates and intended parents, we must continue to interrogate the racialized discourse that cross-racial gestational surrogacy relies upon, and seek solutions to the inequalities from which white consumers benefit.

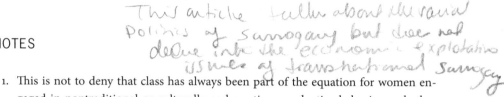

This article talks about the racial politics of surrogacy but does not delve into the economic exploitation issues of transnational surrogacy

NOTES

1. This is not to deny that class has always been part of the equation for women engaged in nontraditional or culturally aschematic reproductive behaviors, whether measured in consequences or in levels of acceptance.

2. While these statistics may appear dated, there is a dearth of research concerning the racial background of surrogates in relation to prospective parents. This information is not published by government or surrogacy centers, and has only recently begun being systematically compiled.

3. Racialization involves "attaching racial meaning to a previously racially unclassified relationship, social practice, or group" (Collins 1990:73).

4. The case that created what Sirola calls the gestational motherhood standard was quite galvanizing in feminist circles and in the general public. It was known as the Baby M case, and it was the first major custody challenge by a traditional surrogate to reach the courts. The first judge terminated the surrogate's parental rights, but on appeal, the New Jersey Supreme Court awarded parental rights to the surrogate, but custody to the intended father.

5. This is exemplified in a 1993 article in the *Los Angeles Sentinel* entitled "Surrogate Mothers: Are We Creating a Breeder Class?" (Brown 1993), which questions the legitimacy of surrogacy and its racial implications. In it the author discusses the *Johnson v. Calvert* case, simply stating that "Johnson is black and the child she bore as a surrogate is white," effectively coding Crispina Calvert as white despite her Filipino heritage.

6. In *Defining the Family*, Janet Dolgin notes that Janet Healy makes a similar point in her article "Beyond Surrogacy: Gestational Parenting Agreements Under California Law," in which Healy argues that Crispina Calvert is "ethnically unmarked *in contrast* with Anna" (1999:130; emphasis mine).

7. By making this argument, I do not mean to posit race as purely metaphor. For more on this, see, for example, Homans 1997.

WORKS CITED

Brown, Malaika. 1993. Surrogate mothers: Are we creating a new class of breeders? *Los Angeles Sentinel*, A1.

Centers for Disease Control and Prevention. 2004. Assisted Reproductive Technology (ART) Report: Commonly asked questions. http://www.cdc.gov (accessed June 5, 2007).

Cheng, Anne. 2001. *The Melancholy of Race: Psychoanalysis, Assimilation, and Hidden Grief*. New York: Oxford University Press.

Collins, Patricia Hill. 1990. Mammies, matriarchs, and other controlling images. In *Black Feminist Thought: Knowledge, Consciousness, and the Politics of Empowerment*, 69–96. Boston: Unwin Hyman.

Dolgin, Janet. 1999. *Defining the Family: Law, Technology, and Reproduction in an Uneasy Age*. New York: New York University Press.

Dyson, Michael Eric. 2004. *The Michael Eric Dyson Reader*. New York: Basic Civitas Books.

Edelman, Lee. 2004. *No Future: Queer Theory and the Death Drive*. Durham: Duke University Press.

Gilroy, Paul. 2000. *Against Race: Imagining Political Culture Beyond the Color Line*. Cambridge, Mass.: Harvard University Press.

Grayson, Deborah. 1998. Mediating intimacy: Black surrogate mothers and the law. *Critical Inquiry* 24:525–546.

Hamilton, David. 2003. She's having our baby. *Wall Street Journal*, Feb. 4, D1.

Hartouni, Valerie. 2008. *Cultural Conceptions: On Reproductive Technologies and the Remaking of Life*. Minneapolis: University of Minnesota Press.

Homans, Margaret. 1997. "Racial composition": Metaphor and the body in the writing of race. In *Female Subjects in Black and White: Race, Psychoanalysis, Feminism*, ed. Elizabeth Abel, Barbara Christian, and Helene Moglen, 77–101. Berkeley: University of California Press.

Lawson, Erica. 2004. Black women's mothering in a historical and contemporary perspective. In *Mother Outlaws: Theories and Practices of Empowered Mothering*, ed. Andrea O'Reilly. Toronto: Women's Press.

Markens, Susan. 2007. *Surrogate Motherhood and the Politics of Reproduction*. Berkeley: University of California Press.

Okerblom, Jim. 1986. Mexican surrogate mom tests baby contracts in state. *San Diego Union*, Dec. 8, B-1.

——. 1990. An uneasy shared custody. *San Diego Union*, May 27, B-1.

Peterson, Iver. 1987. Surrogates often improvise birth pacts. *New York Times*, Feb. 25, B2.

Ragoné, Helena. 2000. Of likeness and difference: How race is being transfigured by gestational surrogacy. In *Ideologies and Technologies of Motherhood: Race, Class, Sexuality, Nationalism*, ed. Helena Ragoné and Frances Winddance Twine, 56–75. New York: Routledge.

Roberts, Dorothy. 1997. *Killing the Black Body: Race, Reproduction, and the Meaning of Liberty*. New York: Vintage Books.

Robertson, Claire. 1987. Ban on surrogate motherhood urged. *Washington Post*, Sept. 1, A3.

Romero, Fernando. 1986. Happiness engulfs surrogate mom, baby during brief reunion. *Evening Tribune*, Oct. 14, B-1.

Shanley, Mary. 2001. *Making Babies, Making Families: What Matters Most in an Age of Reproductive Technologies, Surrogacy, Adoption, and Same-Sex and Unwed Parents' Rights*. Boston: Beacon.

Sirola, Krista. 2006. Are you my mother? Defending the rights of intended parents in gestational surrogacy arrangements in Pennsylvania. *American University Journal of Gender, Social Policy, and the Law* 14.1:132–161.

Spar, Debora. 2006. *The Baby Business: How Money, Science, and Politics Drive the Commerce of Conception*. Boston: Harvard Business School Press.

Turegano, Preston. 1987a. Couple, surrogate to share custody of baby. *Evening Tribune*, Feb. 24, B-1.

——. 1987b. Surrogate mom offered ACLU help over custody. *Evening Tribune*, June 5, B-3.

U.S. Department of Health and Human Services. 2006. Infertility. http://www.womenshealth.gov/faq/infertility.htm (accessed May 15, 2008).

What Will Become of Us? | **SEVENTEEN**

New Biotechnologies and the | ENOLA G. AIRD
Need for Maternal Leadership

When the children were small, our family traveled to Aspen, Colorado, nearly every summer. We would fly early in the morning from Connecticut to Denver, and take a much-anticipated four-hour drive further up into the Colorado Rockies. Steep, winding roads led us into awe-inspiring mountains and through cavernous valleys. Along the way, we would pass many runaway-truck ramps—gravelly lanes inclined upward away from the road. The ramps are typically located on the sides of long downhill slopes, to allow trucks that are losing control to swerve onto the uphill path and slow down. The deep gravel on the ramp combines with the forces of gravity to bring the truck to a safe stop. I can remember seeing a truck forced to turn up into a runaway lane only once, but as a passenger in a car riding along those often treacherous roads, I was always grateful that the lanes were there.

Developments in the fields of genetics, robotics, informatics, and nanotechnology are proceeding at breakneck speeds. This constellation of new technologies is opening the door to a future in which, for the first time in human history, human beings may be able to take control of their own evolution. In the United

States these technologies are being pioneered and developed by scientists and entrepreneurs, in an environment that is largely unregulated, by firms driven primarily by profit, with no authoritative body to say which projects should go forward and which should not. New projects are being announced at an accelerating pace with little substantive public conversation or debate, and without the active participation of citizens, of mothers and fathers and other people, who will have their lives, and their children's and grandchildren's lives, radically transformed if certain of these technologies take hold.

We will soon face profound questions about the use of "species-altering" technologies in a culture that is not used to setting limits on itself. Our deep cultural commitments to the values of individualism, choice, and free markets, together with our faith in technology, are propelling us into a future in which there may well be no boundaries at all.

About ten years ago, sociologist Barbara Katz Rothman wrote about trends in technology that, she argued, were leading to an increasing commodification of children. "Perhaps," she said, "this is one of those moments of crisis a society faces, where there are two paths that can be taken. We can focus on nurturance, caring, human relations. . . . The values and experience of motherhood could come to shape the way we live in the world. That is, I suppose, the fantasy, the truly revolutionary potential of a recreated motherhood. Or we can recreate motherhood to reflect the commodification of children" (Rothman 2000:7–8).

There is no "perhaps" about it. We are at a moment of crisis. Human beings need the cultural equivalent of runaway-truck ramps to help them come to terms with lightning-fast changes in technology that could fundamentally reshape human beings and transform human society. In this paper I argue, first, that our society must quickly find ways to grapple with the implications of these technologies and democratize the decision-making about them, so that we can make informed choices that preserve the dignity of human beings. Second, I contend that maternal values may be the last available source of "deep gravel" that can help us gain control of the biotechnological revolution—before it is too late. Implicit in the practice of mothering is a reservoir of values that can profoundly enrich public conversation, advocacy, and decision-making about these potentially transformative technologies. We are at a crossroads. We can keep going down the path toward the commodification of human beings or we can draw on values that arise from mothering to help us chart a course to preserve our humanity.

WHERE WE ARE AND HOW WE GOT HERE

In 2007 a couple from Australia ordered two babies through the Fertility Institutes, based in Los Angeles (Hellard 2007). They wanted twins and they wanted boys. They got what they paid for. In the first two months of 2008 alone, scientists at King's College and the University of Newcastle in Britain announced that they would start mixing genetic material from humans and cows to create hybrid human-animal embryos (Henderson 2008); Ray Kurzweil of the Massachusetts Institute of Technology declared that scientists will be implanting tiny robots in people's brains by 2029 (Briggs 2008); and researchers at Newcastle University created an embryo using sperm from one man and eggs from two women (BBC News 2008). The three-parent embryo experiments, the researchers tell us, will lead to techniques to ensure that women with certain genetic defects do not pass them on to their children. The small robots would be implanted into human brains, scientists say, to improve health and enhance intelligence. And the hybrid human-animal embryo experiments are designed to lead to possible treatments of diseases such as Parkinson's and spinal muscular atrophy.

In an exciting set of developments, scientists today are leading a technological revolution that could result in cures for many diseases that are now incurable. But, as so often, along with the potential for great good comes the potential for great harm. Many of the same techniques that are being used to help cure disease can also be used to create clones, make "designer babies," and ultimately produce new—and distinct—species of human beings.

Early in 1953 James Watson and Francis Crick described the structure of deoxyribonucleic acid, or DNA, the biochemical blueprint for life found at the center of each gene. Watson and Crick pinpointed the stuff of which our genes are made, and set scientists on a forty-seven-year quest to decode the information in our DNA to find out exactly how the human body works. On June 26, 2000, President Bill Clinton, in the East Room of the White House, joined with England's Prime Minister Tony Blair, by satellite, to announce that an international team of scientists had completed the first draft of the entire human genome. Building on the work done by Watson, Crick, and others, the scientists had outlined the string of nearly 3 billion base pairs of DNA. "With this profound new knowledge," Clinton said, "humankind is on the verge of gaining immense new power to heal. . . . In coming years, doctors increasingly will be able to cure diseases like Alzheimer's, Parkinson's, diabetes, and cancer by attacking their genetic roots" (The White House 2000).

DNA produces proteins that essentially tell each cell in our bodies to grow or not to grow, and what shape to take. Different pairings of DNA lead to the production of different proteins, which, in turn, account for many physical differences among people. They help determine whether a person will be short or tall, blue- or brown-eyed. They also determine whether a person will have a genetic disorder. Insights gained from the study of the human genome are helping scientists figure out how to alter and "correct" genes. With the use of a technique called somatic gene therapy, scientists are working on ways to treat genetic diseases by introducing corrective genes. But the door has now been opened to more than just corrective or therapeutic manipulations of genes.

For a long time researchers have been at work changing plant and animal genes to breed "better" plants and "better" animals. The next great scientific frontier is the human being: the exploration, manipulation, enhancement, and reshaping of human genes. The question squarely before us now as a human civilization is whether the tools of the new biotechnologies should be used to breed what might be considered "better" human beings.

One of the most worrisome potential uses of the new technologies is inheritable genetic modification (IGM), or "germ line" modification. With IGM, the genes in eggs, sperm, or early embryos would be altered so that the genetic modification would not be limited solely to the person in whom the change has been made. It would also be passed on to all succeeding generations. This technique, proponents say, would essentially allow parents to order children to their specifications. Parents could, in theory, try to determine not only their child's sex, which is already an increasingly common practice, but also his or her hair and eye color, level of intelligence, height, weight, athletic prowess, and other traits.

Using the technology in this way would represent a break with human reproduction as we have known it throughout history. IGM would employ cloning (to make multiple copies of cells) and other techniques to allow scientists to "design" children, by adding to their genetic inheritance traits not carried by their mothers or fathers. Physically, psychologically, emotionally, and spiritually, a child "enhanced" in this way would be a new, and fundamentally different, kind of human being.

SIGNS POINTING TO THE DANGER AHEAD

While I was raising my children, roughly between 1985 and 2006, cell phones and the Internet came into being as if out of thin air, swiftly took up so large a place in our lives as to become indispensable, and fundamentally changed how children relate to parents, to each other, and to the world. Technology is like that. We can easily get caught up in it. It appears suddenly in the lives of ordinary folk, and before long it changes how we live—and even who we are. Given our human tendency to let technology lead us, we ought to be especially vigilant when it comes to new biotechnologies.

An influential, well-funded, and growing constituency, led by respected scientists, scholars, and entrepreneurs, is advocating that society use the new technologies to breed enhanced human beings. Lee Silver, a molecular biologist at Princeton University, predicts that these technologies will lead to an extremely polarized society, with all people belonging to one of two classes: the "Gen-Rich," or the gene-enriched, to be distinguished from the "Naturals," i.e., people who are enhanced biotechnologically as opposed to people who are not (Silver 2007:4–5). John Harris, a bioethicist at England's University of Manchester, argues that one day soon mothers and fathers will indeed have a moral obligation to enhance their children genetically (Harris 2007:19–35).

The World Transhumanist Association is an international, nonprofit advocacy organization devoted to exploring "possibilities for the 'post-human' future created by increased merging of people and technology via bioengineering, cybernetics, and nanotechnologies." Many transhumanists believe in and are working to bring about something called the "singularity," the moment in human history, they say, when all distinctions between the natural and the technological disappear. Ray Kurzweil, the Massachusetts Institute of Technology professor working on the tiny robots to be implanted in human brains, is one of the world's leading transhumanists. He is also an entrepreneur and inventor, with a strong track record for actually bringing into being what he envisions. He is credited with helping to create the first text-to-speech synthesizer, the first optical character recognition software to transform the written word into data, and the first print-to-speech software, which reads written words to the blind.

This cutting-edge thinking and research and development is taking place in an intensely commercialized atmosphere. On the same day he announced the sequencing of the human genome, President Clinton observed that biotechnology companies are the driving forces in exploring this new scientific frontier. "[I]t is they," he said, "who will bring to the market the life-enhancing applications of the information from the human genome" (The White House 2000). Craig Venter, one of the lead scientists on the Human Genome Project and one of the strongest advocates for commercializing biotechnology and patenting human genes, was with the president at the time of the announcement. "Diabetics," he once said, "[now] have human insulin to treat their diabetes and they have that because the gene was patented and that allowed these pharmaceutical companies to develop it into a drug that you can actually buy. . . . And no company would invest that kind of money if they didn't have this short period of monopoly to guarantee them a financial return" (CNN Specials 1999). Venter, a prodigious researcher and entrepreneur, is currently at the helm of an ambitious effort to utilize the bacterium *Mycoplasma genitalium* to create the first synthetic genome, which researchers say will enable scientists to "custom-design organisms, essentially creating biological robots that can produce from scratch chemicals humans can use" (Madrigal 2008).

With business eager to profit from the new technologies, and the nation thrilled at the prospect of gaining greater control over such seemingly random forces as intelligence and inherited disease, what once seemed impossible is becoming increasingly probable. Ideas once confined to the realm of science fiction have become scientific fact. Developments are proceeding at such an extraordinary pace that it is difficult for citizens to keep up. Momentous decisions are being made every day by scientists, researchers, and the entrepreneurs and companies backing them financially—without oversight and without public input.

A CRITICAL JUNCTURE

Remember the Australian couple I mentioned earlier, who ordered the twin boys? The new parents are among a growing number of Australians turning to the Fertility Institutes, in Los Angeles, in anticipation of getting a child of the gender they choose. They turned to the Fertility Institutes because Australia prohibits sex selection for nonmedical purposes, but California does not. And so, with a steady stream of American and international customers, business is booming for the Fertility Institutes, which bills itself as "among the world's leading centers for 100% gender selection" (Fertility Institutes). Its well-produced online video infomercial declares that it offers state-of-the-art procedures for couples "wishing to assure that a first child is of a gender they pre-choose." It boasts that "for the first time in the history of mankind," parents can have a "100% guarantee that if they want a boy . . . they are going to get a boy, and if they want a girl . . . it will be a girl." Fees for the complex procedure can be high, but "flexible payment arrangements with financing are available." In fact, the Fertility Institutes offers "low interest 100% financing for gender selection procedures."

Some people call it "gender variety." Others call it "gender pre-determination." The Fertility Institutes calls it "family balancing." It is the process of using in vitro fertilization procedures not only to help couples with fertility challenges or couples concerned about passing on serious hereditary diseases, but also to help couples who simply want to select the gender of their child. As a matter of policy, the Fertility Institutes makes the procedure available to *any* couple wishing to ensure that their child is of a gender they pre-select.

Except where there is a risk of a serious hereditary sex-related disease, the Council of Europe's 1997 Convention on Human Rights and Biomedicine prohibits the use of biotechnologies to choose the sex of a future child (Council of Europe 1997). What is wrong with selecting the sex of one's child? Simply that it is a crucial step along the road to the widespread acceptance of the idea of designing children. If we can choose or pre-select the sex of our children, why not pre-select for other traits? Indeed, a growing number of couples are already doing so as they itemize with great care the characteristics they want in an egg donor—characteristics such as blond hair, blue eyes, and high SAT scores.

Couples and single people have been making personal decisions for years about the use of these new technologies in private, unregulated laboratories—as the power of individual choice has been growing. We have now reached a point at which "the power of individual choice has never been greater" (Penn 2007:xi). Women and men are making choices against the backdrop of the powerful consumerist ethic that pervades every aspect of our culture (Spar 2006). The appeal of enhancement and the quest for perfection have already taken hold. Consider the meteoric rise in prevalence of Botox treatments, plastic surgeries, and anti-aging centers, as well as increases in the sales of products to keep people looking and feeling young.

These choices are being made in a culture in which self-indulgence, insistence on instant gratification, and the quest for material things are driving values. Consider the steroid scandals that continue to shake the world of sports, and the fact that, in a recent survey, a majority of those students in grades 8 through 12 who admitted using steroids said they were "willing to take extreme risks to reach sports stardom" even if it would harm their health or shorten their lives (Stenson 2008). These individual decisions are being made in the context of a popular media that generally acts as a cheerleader for scientific and technological advances, but offers little or no critical or ethical analysis of new technologies and their implications.

For a long time now we have been bringing our culture's dominant values of self-indulgence, instant gratification, and materialism into the creation of children and we are well along the way to commodifying human life, with no logical stopping point in sight. Our cultural disposition in favor of technology, coupled with our reigning values, makes us ill-equipped to set limits. Ours is the most consumer-driven society on earth (Schor 2004:9). For nearly thirty years, corporations in the United States have been engaged in an intense, well-financed, technologically sophisticated, and relentless campaign to train children to be avid lifelong consumers (Linn 2005:5–8). Our consumer ways of thinking promote the idea that the purpose of human life is to be able to get as much as we can get of whatever it is we want. People steeped in this view of the world are more inclined to treat other people carelessly and disrespectfully. They are more likely to be willing to treat each other as objects of experiments, as means to ends, as commodities. A culture driven by that worldview has few resources to make moral and ethical decisions about—or establish boundaries on—the use of biotechnologies. It cannot readily set limits because its internal logic says "go, go, and keep going." The shallow vocabulary of our consumer-driven culture offers little basis for drawing lines. If we are to set limits, we will need access to another set of values—another way of knowing.

DEEP GRAVEL TO SLOW US DOWN

Should we embark fully on the project to "breed" our children the way we now "breed" plants and animals? Should we combine them with computers while we are at it? Do we have moral, ethical, and parental rights to change the germ line we pass on to our descendants? Do we have moral, ethical, and parental obligations to change the germ line we pass on to our descendants in the light of the possibilities offered by the new technologies? Do we have moral, ethical, and parental obligations to pass on to our children only the germ line that we inherited? Do we have the right to create children "to order," with whatever specifications we want under whatever conditions we want? If we choose to breed our descendants, how would relationships between mothers and children, between parents and children, be transformed? How would this choice affect our understanding of what it means to be human? What would it mean for human relationships? Should we set limits? How might we set limits? Who should decide? How can we get a handle on—and keep up with—these technologies in order to make informed and democratic decisions about their use before it is too late?

These are among the flood of questions that demand urgent attention, not just from scientists, entrepreneurs, and politicians, but from *all* people. They especially demand the attention of those of us who mother—those of us who assume primary responsibility for providing for the sustained care and nurture of children (Ruddick 1995:xiii).

At the core of what it means to be human is the ability to empathize with the other (Hrdy 2000:392–393). Those of us who care for and nurture children play a crucial role in the human—and humanizing—story. In doing the work of caring for and nurturing children, those of us who mother model, to varying degrees, the values of connectedness, self-restraint, and stewardship—qualities at the heart of what it means to be human. These "motherworld" values offer an alternative to the values of the money world—the worship of self-indulgence, instant gratification, and materialism that is pushing our culture onto the post-human path. Motherworld values are essential to the care, nurture, and development of the human person. They are crucial to the preservation of human relationships and human civilization.

In our culture, motherworld values are latent. They are often marginalized, even by thoughtful feminist scholars, who worry about presenting an essentialist vision of mothering by confirming a patriarchal account of what a mother does or should value. But at this moment when we urgently need to refresh our understanding of what it means to be human, we should be more concerned about making sure we are arguing from the proper set of values than making sure we are using the right name. Whether one calls them the values of the motherworld or something else, only a vision of the human person that lifts up the values of connectedness, self-restraint, and stewardship as central to our humanity can help us set limits on technology and consumerism run amuck.

And yet the term *motherworld* seems appropriate. It is by now a commonplace that the work of nurturing a child over time changes the nurturer. Much has been written in recent years about the "mommy brain," the structural and functional changes in a woman's brain brought about by acts of mothering. Research in the neurosciences has shown that during pregnancy, childbirth, and breastfeeding, the hormones progesterone, oxytocin, and prolactin play leading roles in priming mothers to welcome, care for, and make a lifetime commitment to their babies—and thus help ensure the survival of the species. Babies too arrive primed to elicit care from their mothers. A baby's smell, cooing, and touch, a baby's rooting for the breast of a mother—all send powerful signals that give rise to equally powerful maternal responses. As anthropologist Sarah Blaffer Hrdy puts it, "babies are geared to making sure that maternal care is forthcoming and ongoing. . . . Once nursing begins . . . the mother is endocrinologically, sensually, as well as neurologically transformed in ways likely to serve the infant's needs and contribute to her own posterity" (Hrdy 2000:536–537). As Hrdy argues in her most recent work, mothers are a central part, but not all, of the humanizing story. Through the care and nurture of mothers *and* others, through "cooperative breeding," humans developed uniquely human capacities to connect with and empathize with one another (Hrdy 2009).

Mothers are not the only people whose brains are changed by the work of raising children. According to neuropsychiatrist Louann Brizendine, "even fathers, adoptive parents, and women who have never been pregnant can respond maternally after close, daily contact with an infant. These physical cues from the infant forge new neurochemical pathways in the brain that create and reinforce maternal brain circuits" (Brizendine 2006:96). The act of caring for children itself, research shows, actually contributes to neurogenesis—an increase in new brain cells and new capabilities. Chief among these new capabilities is a profound sense of connectedness that, in the words of Katherine Ellison, "keeps us automatically moving *toward* the objectively annoying sound of our babies' cries, rather than running out the door" (Ellison 2006:44).

The deep need to connect with other human beings is at the heart of what it means to be human. The practice of mothering can give rise to an especially keen awareness of the connectedness of human beings, and the empathy and the sense of self-restraint and stewardship that flow from that connectedness. Nurturing a child, before and after birth, often reorients the nurturer away from self-centeredness and toward the child. Nurturing the child can give rise to a receptivity to, a sensitivity to, and an empathy for the "other"—and a willingness to put oneself on the line for, to sacrifice for, and to accept responsibility for another. The reorientation that comes with caring for the child, researchers suggest, can make those of us who care for children "smarter" emotionally—more empathetic and more inclined to exercise to self-restraint (Ellison 2006:123).

But not only does mothering make us smarter emotionally—it also gives us access to an alternative, more balanced, account of who we are as human beings. Those of us who mother tend to be so taken up by the day-to-day challenges before us that we can easily lose sight of that fact. In much of our work in raising children, we live out, to one degree or another, the values of connectedness, self-restraint, and stewardship—values that are the opposite of the culture's dominant values. These motherworld values foster the development of people capable of empathizing with other people, making sacrifices for each other, and being responsible to one another.

My point is not that mothers or those who mother live by these values any more than anyone else does. We know that not all mothers are the same and that mothers throughout history have, in the words of Hrdy, been "flexible actors whose responses were contingent on circumstances" (Hrdy 2000:535). As a black woman, I am well aware of the differences among mothers and mothers' experiences. And as the work of the psychologist Shari Thurer (Thurer 1995), among others, has suggested, the role that mothers play, even in the lives of their own children, has likely changed dramatically over time, and differs still from culture to culture—and within cultures. Even in the United States, where many people find the image of mothering so fixed, many mothers have internalized and live by the values of our dominant consumer culture. Many mothers, for example, see no problem with choosing the sex of their babies, and in an increasingly competitive world, mothers may well be among the first to want to enhance their children.

We can acknowledge mothers' differences and at the same time recognize that there may well be a core set of values that arise from the practice of mothering that can serve as an antidote to our dominant cultural values. My point is that mothering can provide a wellspring of alternative values upon which we can draw as we seek to make sense of and make decisions about the use of new technologies—values that counsel that we proceed with restraint, with empathy for the "other." The vision I am suggesting—a vision that has at its core the values of connectedness, self-restraint, and stewardship—is present almost nowhere but in the work of those who mother. No doubt we would have a better, more egalitarian culture were these values more widespread. They should be, and we should work toward the day when they are. But for now they are not. For better or worse, at this critical moment in human history, it is those of us who mother—even with all our differences—who hold these values in greatest supply. It is this "mothers' trust" that I believe we are now called upon to defend.

Sociologist Sharon Hays, in an influential exploration of the difficulties mothers face in meeting conflicting expectations in the workplace and in the home, concludes that mothers seem to see mothering as holding "a fragile but nonetheless powerful cultural position as the last best defense against what many people see as the impoverishment of social ties, communal obligations, and unremunerated commitments" (Hays 1996:xiii). Hays's point is consistent with the findings of the Motherhood Project's 2005 *Motherhood Study*, which included a representative survey of mothers in the United States, and which suggests that "many mothers are struggling to hold on to values that are being undermined by the larger culture" (Erickson and Aird 2005:42). It may just be that mothers are so willing to make themselves the "last best defense" because of our profound, albeit largely unspoken, understanding of the crucial role that mothering plays in the human—and humanizing—story.

The full and unrestricted acceptance of technologies to "design" human babies would usher in a new era of eugenics in which large numbers of people pursue their own personalized visions of "perfect" humans. In such a world, there would be an unprecedented level of experimentation on human beings. The sense of empathy and fellow-feeling that springs from the value of connectedness would reject the sort of laboratory experiments that would be required, notably on women and on unborn children—a prospect that should be chilling no matter what one's views on abortion. To do the experiments at all—and to seek the enhancements—is already to suggest that some children are more worthy than others and that it is the characteristics of human beings, not the fact of their humanity, that makes them worthy.

In such a world we would become resigned to treating children as "objects" of parental design and as manufactured "products." The manufacture of enhanced human beings would constitute a domination of the "other" in ways fundamentally at odds with the value of self-restraint. In such a world we would have countenanced the creation of distinct classes of human beings and the dissolution of the foundations of our shared humanity. The mothers' trust, I believe, calls us to preserve the understanding of the human person that has been handed down to us—an understanding that assumes a common humanity.

A culture guided by the values of the motherworld would set and maintain thoughtful limits on the use of new biotechnologies. We can carefully embrace the therapeutic aspects of the technologies, but we must work to ensure that they are not used in ways that would undermine the integrity and dignity of the human person.

There is a growing mothers' movement in the United States and around the world. The movement in the United States is currently aimed at gaining increased societal support for mothers and the work of nurturing children. The agendas of mothers' groups in the United States are focused, understandably, on issues of work and family. But with the dazzling array of technological possibilities before us, the speed at which they are appearing, and the profound implications for mothers, children, and the human future, it is imperative that mothers' organizations put the issue of the new biotechnologies on their agendas.

In 2001 leaders in the fields of science, law, health, and women's rights (including Judy Norsigian, the widely respected author of *Our Bodies, Ourselves*) gathered in Boston to call for a "global ban on genetic procedures that [would] fundamentally change the nature of the human species . . . and provide for regulations to ensure that other new human genetic and reproductive technologies are used in ways that benefit rather than harm human life and society" (Center for Genetics and Society 2001). In 2002 leading bioethicists issued a call for a global "Convention on the Preservation of the Human Species" to ban reproductive cloning and inheritable genetic modification, and to require that all countries establish national "systems of oversight to regulate facilities engaged in assisted human reproduction" (Annas, Andrews, and Isasi 2002). The authors of the proposed convention observed that "altering the human species is an issue that directly concerns all of us, and should only be decided democratically, by a body that is representative of everyone on the planet. It is the most important decision we will ever make" (Annas, Andrews, and Isasi 2002:153).

As a human race, we may ultimately decide to pursue a path that leads to the altering of the human species. But we should not let it happen without the active engagement and advocacy of those who hold the mothers' trust, of mothers and women whose bodies will be the sites for the countless experiments that will be required to bring the new technologies to fruition.

The conversation and decision-making about these technologies should not be monopolized by scientists, researchers, and people whose primary goal is profit. Those of us who mother must find ways to break the monopoly on conversation and decision-making currently held by others. We must insist on an open and vigorous international debate about these technologies, and we must make sure that the values of the motherworld are brought to the table.

Mothers across the globe have never been more able to communicate and share ideas and strategies. We are well positioned to insist on the kind of global conversation and global decision-making that this issue demands. We must act quickly. At some point soon along the road to a post-human future, there will be no turning back. While there is still time, we must find ways to come to grips with these technologies and their implications. We must insist on a democratic, public debate about which technologies to use and how to use them, so that we can decide what kind of future we want for ourselves and our children, and our children's children. And those of us who mother must lead the way.

WORKS CITED

Annas, George, Lori Andrews, and Rosario Isasi. 2002. Protecting the endangered Human: Toward an international treaty prohibiting cloning and inheritable alterations.

American Journal of Law and Medicine 28.2–3:151–178. http://geneticsandsociety. org/downloads/2002_ajlm_annasetal.pdf (accessed Dec. 3, 2008).

BBC News. 2008. Three-parent embryo formed in lab. BBC News, Feb. 5, 2008 http:// news.bbc.co.uk/2/hi/health/7227861.stm (accessed Dec. 2, 2008).

Briggs, Helen. 2008. Machines to match man by 2029. BBC News, Boston, Feb. 16, 2008. http://news.bbc.co.uk/2/hi/americas/7248875.stm (accessed Dec. 2, 2008).

Brizendine, Louann. 2006. *The Female Brain*. New York: Morgan Road Books.

Center for Genetics and Society. 2001. Health and human rights leaders call for global ban on species-altering procedures. *Genetic Crossroads*, Oct. 3, 2001. http:// geneticsandsociety.org/article.php?id=2809&&printsafe=1 (accessed Dec. 3, 2008).

CNN Specials. 1999. Blueprint of the body: Craig Venter. June 3. www.cnn.com/ SPECIALS/2000/genome/story/interviews/venter.html (accessed Dec. 2, 2008).

Council of Europe. 1997. Convention for the Protection of Human Rights and Dignity of the Human Being with Regard to the Application of Biology and Medicine: Convention on Human Rights and Biomedicine. April 4. http://conventions.coe.int/treaty/ en/treaties/html/164.htm (accessed Dec. 3, 2008).

Ellison, Katherine. 2006. *The Mommy Brain: How Motherhood Makes Us Smarter*. New York: Basic Books.

Erickson, Martha Farrell, and Aird, Enola. 2005. *The Motherhood Study: Fresh Insights on Mothers' Attitudes and Concerns*. New York: Institute for American Values.

Fertility Institutes. Sex selection and family balancing. http://www.fertility-docs.com/ fertility_gender.phtml.

Harris, John. 2007. *Enhancing Evolution: The Ethical Case for Making Better People*. Princeton: Princeton University Press.

Hays, Sharon. 1996. *The Cultural Contradictions of Motherhood*. New Haven: Yale University Press.

Hellard, Peta. 2007. Gay couple buys "designer" sons from U.S. *Daily Telegraph* (Australia), Oct. 14, 2007. http://geneticsandsociety.org/article.php?id=3731&&printsafe=1 (accessed Dec. 2, 2008).

Henderson, Mark. 2008. First animal-human embryo trials to go ahead. *The Times* (UK), Jan. 18, 2008. www.timesonline.co.uk/tol/news/uk/science/article3204128.ece (accessed Dec. 2, 2008).

Hrdy, Sarah Blaffer. 2000. *Mother Nature: Maternal Instincts and How They Shape the Human Species*. New York: Ballantine.

——. 2009. *Mothers and Others: The Evolutionary Origins of Mutual Understanding*. Cambridge, Mass.: Harvard University Press.

Linn, Susan. 2005. *Consuming Kids: Protecting Our Children from the Onslaught of Marketing and Advertising*. New York: Anchor.

Madrigal, Alexis. 2008. Scientists build first man-made genome: Synthetic life comes next. *Wired,* Jan. 24, 2008. http://www.wired.com/science/discoveries/news/2008/01/synthetic_genome (accessed Dec. 3, 2008).

Penn, Mark. 2007. *Microtrends: The Small Forces Behind Tomorrow's Big Changes.* New York: Twelve.

Rothman, Barbara Katz, 2000. *Recreating Motherhood.* New Brunswick: Rutgers University Press.

Ruddick, Sara. 1995. *Maternal Thinking: Toward a Politics of Peace.* Boston: Beacon.

Schor, Juliet. 2004. *Born to Buy: The Commercialized Child and the New Consumer Culture.* New York: Scribner.

Silver, Lee. 2007. *Remaking Eden: How Genetic Engineering and Cloning Will Transform the American Family.* New York: Harper Perennial.

Spar, Debora L. 2006. *The Baby Business: How Money, Science, and Politics Drive the Commerce of Conception.* Boston: Harvard Business School Press.

Stenson, Jacqueline. 2008. Kids on steroids willing to risk it all for success: Users say they'd takes drugs to excel even if it shortened their lives. MSNBC, March 3, 2008. http://www.msnbc.msn.com/id/22984780 (accessed Dec. 3, 2008).

Thurer, Shari L. 1995. *The Myths of Motherhood: How Culture Reinvents the Good Mother.* New York: Penguin.

The White House. 2000. Remarks made by the President, et al., on the completion of the first survey of the entire Human Genome Project. June 26, 10:19 A.M. EDT, Office of the Press Secretary. http://www.genome.gov/pfv.cfm?pageID=10001356 (accessed Dec. 2, 2008).

Agency | **PART 4**

From "Choice" to Change:

EIGHTEEN

Rewriting the Script of Motherhood   JUDITH STADTMAN TUCKER
as Maternal Activism

In her 1974 treatise on the future of motherhood, the late sociologist Jesse Bernard proposed that mothers could not be liberated from the patriarchal institution of motherhood until a new, normative "script" of mothering was securely in place (xii). Like other writers and scholars of her generation, Bernard understood the institution of motherhood as a series of related and interlocking ideologies that justify and regulate the subordination of women and create "a dangerous schism between 'private' and 'public' life" (Rich 1976:13). Bernard was especially critical of the mid-twentieth-century standard of exclusive mothering, which she recognized as historically unprecedented:

> The way we institutionalize motherhood in our society—assigning sole responsibility for child care to the mother, cutting her off from the easy help of others in an isolated household, requiring round-the-clock tender, loving care, and making such care her exclusive activity—is not only new and unique, but not even a good way for either women or—if we accept as a criterion the amount of maternal warmth shown—for children. . . . It is as though we had selected the worst features of all the

ways motherhood is structured around the world and combined them to produce our current design. (Bernard 1974:9)

More recently, reproductive justice activists and scholars such as Patricia Hill Collins (1994:46) and Evelyn Nakano Glenn have identified how dominant ideologies and representations of motherhood reinforce and complicate the oppression of women of color and others who do not exemplify the cultural ideal. As Glenn remarks, a "particular definition of mothering has so dominated popular media representations, academic discourse, and political and legal doctrine that the existence of alternative beliefs and practices among racial, ethnic, and sexual minority communities as well as non-middle class segments of society have gone unnoticed" (1994:2). Noting that the function of ideology is to tell us "who we are" and what exists, what is good, and what is possible, Angela Hattery concludes that the contemporary ideology of exclusive, or "intensive," motherhood "has the power to shape human behavior even when it does not reflect the lived experiences of most U.S. families or benefit all members of these families" (2001:20; 40).

Dominant ideologies also determine the language and concepts mothers have available to name their shared experiences, as well as the language and concepts used to label mothers as deviant or defective. As Barbara Katz Rothman writes, "An ideology can let us see things, but it can also blind us, close our eyes to our own lived reality, our own experiences. . . . The ideologies of patriarchy, technology and capitalism give us our vision of motherhood while they block our view, give us a language for some things while they silence us for others" (1994:139). Psychologist Janna Malamud Smith assigns political meaning to the missing language of motherhood: "One way to undercut the power of any group is to obscure the truth of their experience . . . it's against the interests of the dominant culture to let groups who are marginalized or oppressed own a vibrant language to describe their reality. Instead, we construct descriptions and expectations of motherhood based on ideologies and stereotypes that preserve the status quo" (Mothers Movement Online 2003). Although the present-day "script" of motherhood has evolved to acknowledge the expansion of women's opportunities and economic roles, it is invariably improvised around a critical void.

REWORKING THE SCRIPT OF EXCLUSIVE MOTHERHOOD

In the 1970s Bernard observed that middle-class mothers were giving voice to a new narrative of discontent, one that challenged the gendering of care, the ideal of selfless motherhood, and the myths of maternal instinct, maternal bliss, and maternal omnipotence.[1] "Never until this very historical moment," Bernard wrote, "have women rebelled as women are now doing against the very way we institutionalize motherhood":

> They are daring to say that although they love children, they hate motherhood. That they object to having sole responsibility for child care. That they object to having child care conceived as their only major activity. That they object to the isolation in which they must perform the role of mother, cut off from help, from one another, from the outside world. For the first time, they are protesting the false aura of romanticism with which motherhood is endowed, keeping from young women its terrible "hidden underside" which "is hardly ever talked about." (1974:14)

Bernard ventured that "rewriting the script for the role of women as mothers" would determine not only the potential for women's progress, but the future of society. "This is no side show, no minor concern that calls for a casual glance when we have time left over debating defense and the balance of trade," she wrote. "It is the heart of the matter, one of the most momentous projects relevant for the future of our species" (1974:xiii).

Bernard was confident that a convergence of economic, cultural, and environmental pressures in the final quarter of the twentieth century would result in the unraveling of motherhood as we know it, and believed lawmakers would respond by creating public policies to accommodate men's and women's changing roles (1974:337–339). She was right about some trends, such as mothers' historically high rates of attachment to the paid workforce by the end of the 1990s. But considering that mothers' litany of grievances hasn't substantially changed in the last thirty years, it's clear we have not come as far or as fast as Bernard predicted.

Although twenty-first-century mothers are less likely to raise a ruckus about "having child care conceived as their only major activity"—now, mothers are far more likely to complain about the "struggle to juggle" work and family and the exhausting "second shift" (Hochschild 2003:4)—they still object to having sole or primary responsibility for child care, resent the isolation and invisibility of motherhood, decry the lack of social and practical support for the work of mothering, and grumble about the unsympathetic attitudes of fathers, co-workers, childless adults, and other mothers who seem insensitive to the unreasonable burdens of contemporary mothering.

Today's mothers still proceed with caution when casting off the superficial "mask" of motherhood (Maushart 1999:2), and choose their words and audiences carefully when criticizing the "false aura of romanticism with which motherhood is endowed" or talking about its "terrible hidden underside" out of legitimate fear of being judged, ignored, reprimanded, or misunderstood (Fox 2005). Even so, the script of mothering has undergone significant revisions in the last three decades, and the present generation of mothers has taken the project of recording the contradictions between their expectations of motherhood and the sensations, experiences, and costs of mothering in an unsupportive society to a new level. More specifically, mothers are taking advantage of new technologies and markets to share their stories and transmit a common rhetoric.

In fact, I believe that contemporary mothers—especially those in North America—are currently participating in reworking the script of motherhood along an ideological continuum that is anchored by a robust discourse of "choice" at one end, and by an emerging discourse of "change" at the other. Across this spectrum, it's possible to understand the range of maternal narrative as organized around a set of core themes or key words—*love, care, time, work, money, men & women, what children need,* and *difference*—which underlie, explain, and connect what mothers talk about when they talk about the rewards, challenges, and conflicts of motherhood.

From a feminist perspective, we might consider the possibility of extricating the core language of *love, care, time, work, money, men & women, what children need,* and *difference* from the constraints of patriarchal and capitalistic ideologies as a way to subvert the passive discourse of choice; to increase the visibility of mothers' diverse circumstances, experiences, and needs; and to validate mothers' demands for social change. As activist mothers engage in the process of creating this new narrative, however, we must be mindful that whenever an ideology is displaced in the interest of social justice, certain language is emptied of meaning and that space must be filled with something new.

THE GROUNDWORK

Before I describe the spectrum of maternal discourse and the conceptual work of reconfiguring the script of motherhood, I should explain how I arrived at this particular theory—and it must be emphasized that if my observations here carry any weight, this will be strictly in the theoretical realm. Although much of what follows is consistent with findings and questions posed by the collection of social research and feminist analysis that informs my thinking on motherhood and society, the method I used to gather samples for this project was neither systematic nor scientifically rigorous. In order to get a rough idea of what mothers talk about when they talk about gender, work, and motherhood, I spent several weeks reviewing the content of Web sites, blogs, and message boards focused on mothers and mothering. In all, I collected over one hundred pages of posts and comments from those sources, but this sample should in no way be construed as broadly representative of contemporary mothers' attitudes or articulations of mothering and its discontents, either for mothers at large—a significant number of whom do not participate in online communities—or for those who routinely use Internet forums to communicate with other mothers.

However, within this unscientific sample, I found striking similarities in the language and logic mothers (and the occasional non-mother or father) use to construct their stories and moral positions. This suggests that a generic script of motherhood does exist, and that it influences the way mothers define and describe their feelings, problems, and social experiences. The range of entries and comments I reviewed also suggest this script is currently in the process of being both passively and actively modified. Given the remarkable volume and variety of maternal discourse taking place in the digital sphere, this subject would surely benefit from more careful and consistent analysis than I have given it. But even to an untrained eye, dominant, transitional, and dissenting patterns of maternal discourse are easily discernible.

THE CHOICE MYSTIQUE

By far, the dominant discourse in the online mother world is the *discourse of choice*. From an activist standpoint, the discourse of choice—which is primarily used to justify or explain the way things are, rather than to defend the way things ought to be—can be understood as a passive discourse. While progressive narratives try to situate mothers and their problems in a broader social context, the rhetoric of choice produces a problem-solving model of coping strategies and personal responsibility. As historian Rickie Solinger observes, the language of maternal choice is inherently problematic. By imposing market logic on the complex moral universe of social reproduction, the rhetoric of choice consistently masks the persistence and variables of women's inequality. As she writes in *Pregnancy and Power*,

> In recent decades middle-class women have typically defined their relation to child-bearing as a "choice." But federal, state, court and corporate decisions about employment policies governing family leave, health insurance, and day care, for example,

have all constrained or expanded the individual choices of even these women. Intensely private decisions about reproduction, including decisions about getting pregnant or not, staying pregnant or not, being the mother to the child one gives birth
to or not, are always shaped by public laws and policies. This may be a particularly
difficult insight to bring into focus, in part because of the way "personal choice" has
eclipsed all other ways of thinking about pregnancy and motherhood. (Solinger
2005:17)

Indeed, when the subject is women, work, and family, the typical North
American is likely to agree with the blogger who wrote, "It's all about choice"
(Jay Allen 2006).[2] The concept of fairness rarely enters the frame. In fact, an almost ubiquitous—and extremely disquieting—feature of the contemporary narrative of maternal choice is the tendency to collapse feminist principles of the
right to self-determination and freedom from oppression into the right to freedom of choice. "I do what's best for myself and my kids," declares 'geminilove' on
a Club Mom message board. "What works for me doesn't necessarily work best
for someone else. . . . I thought the whole point of female empowerment and
feminism was that we wanted the right to make these choices for ourselves based
on what we thought was right for us and for our families" (2006). In a comment
on Blogging Baby, 'mamacita' defines "True feminism" as "having the right of
'choice'" (2006) to which 'L' replies, "I'm a classic 'choice feminist,' and so are all
my peers" (2006).

The reduction of feminism to "the right to make the right choices" has a
complicated cultural history, which includes the strategic decision of reproductive rights advocates to replace the language of abortion rights with the language
of privacy and choice (Solinger 2001:5); neoliberal attacks on feminists for characterizing women as helpless victims of men and society (Sommers 1994:16); the
perception that women's equal rights and opportunities are already secure and
North American gender politics have entered a "postfeminist" phase (Douglas
and Michaels 2004:24–25); right-wing propaganda depicting the reproductive
behavior of poor mothers, teen mothers, and most mothers of color as a threat
to society (Solinger 2001:189–194); and the repackaging of feminism as a self-im-
provement movement by mass-market media such as *Ms.* magazine in the 1970s
and '80s (Farrell 1998:192).

Considering the mash-up of competing values embedded in the twenty-
first-century "choice mystique," it's unremarkable that the allegedly feminist gos-
pel of choice dovetails perfectly with the mantra of personal accountability and
self-sufficiency favored by right-wing ideologues. "I don't think it takes a village

to raise a child, I think it takes a family," remarks 'snowflake9903' on a Club Mom message board. "I don't view government as the answer to the problems of the world, but instead look to individual responsibility" (2006).

Less modulated comments demonstrate how easily the conventional wisdom of maternal choice is converted into a weapon against women. "Having a Child is a Choice," writes 'sated' in a discussion forum on paid parental leave. "It amazes me how you think you deserve all these extra perks for having kids. . . . Giving birth to a child is a priveledge [sic], not a right. You should not have [public] entitlements for the choices you make" (2006). "Remember, having a child is a CHOICE," chides a reader on a major news network blog, "If you can't afford it, don't have one!" (Christina Figiel 2006).

Even in discussions where ideological lines are less sharply drawn, the discourse of personal choice is presented as having the potential to unite as well as divide mothers. The concept of "choice" seems to contain the possibility that there is more than one right way to be a good mother—and therefore the potential to interrupt the ideology of exclusive motherhood—but having choices is also recognized as a product of privilege. Depending on the individual's social capital and access to resources, some mothers are identified as having more choices than others, and some are said to have "no choices." "I Am 8months pregnant and i already know that i have to go back to work after six weeks," writes 'babyboy21' on the Mom Talk discussion forum. "I just feel like thats not enough time to spend with a baby, but i have no choice [sic]" (2006).

Mothers are also described as "blessed" or "lucky" if they've managed to arrange their employment schedules according to their caregiving preferences, even when they've made significant economic and career sacrifices to do so. "I have a meaningful 22.5 hour/week job," writes Kay, who explains that her husband also works part time and shares parenting duties. "I also know that I am incredibly lucky to have this—it's not something that is available to everyone. . . . Most of the time the work has been okay, some of the time it has sucked, and all of the time I can say I have missed out on opportunities because of my part-time status" (2005).

Finally, the defense of maternal choice leads to tense debates between mothers who advocate for respecting other mothers' choices and those who view their own choice as a better and more responsible one. The notorious flare-up in the maternal blogosphere over Linda R. Hirshman's scathing assessment of the "opt out revolution" (Hirshman 2006) was largely a response to her claim that the "choice" of well-educated mothers who abandon their full-time careers is morally reprehensible (Hirshman 2005).

Although the framework of choice is most often applied to women's desires and options for combining work and family, it's also used to differentiate and legitimate lifestyle, parenting and consumer philosophies (Healy 2003), and—more rarely—to talk about reproductive decisions. In practice, the quasi-feminist rhetoric of maternal choice is entwined with the concept of a free-market system in which the different choices mothers make are an accurate reflection of maternal preferences, rather than an accommodation to the scarcity of viable options. In the era of postindustrial capitalism, responsible mothers are represented as conscientious consumers in an expanding marketplace of acceptable choices (Solinger 2001:6).

"ME TIME" AND MATERNAL AMBIVALENCE

Within the mainstream discourse of choice, mothers use a subset of complementary themes to define and describe their feelings, problems, and social experiences more precisely. Many of these conceptual components are used to actively negotiate, interrupt, or resist the gendering of care, the veneration of selfless motherhood, and the myths of maternal instinct, maternal bliss, and maternal omnipotence. However, the same themes and language are also used to reinforce conventional ideals of exclusive mothering.

An especially vigorous component of the discourse of choice is the *claim to identity*. As 'GypsyDiva' writes, "Being a mom doesn't mean you stop existing" (2006). On another message board, 'bensmommy2' contends, "As mothers, we should not lose ourselves. I try not to define myself by any one role I have. That makes for a very boring, and ultimately, I think, dissatisfied person" (2006). 'Angelsmommy2' takes the claim to identity a step further: "If you think being a mom means that you are only allowed to think about and be around your kids, then you misunderstood the meaning of motherhood, and you need to back track your steps and figure out where you went wrong" (2006). To which 'gacgbaker' replies, "Being a mom isn't about me, it is about my kids" (2006).

A hot topic related to the identity discourse is the maternal right to "me time" or "mommy time," which is offered as an antidote to an excess of "mommy & me time." On the message boards of mother-oriented commercial Web sites, mothers expressed a sense of entitlement to child-free time to relax or pursue their own interests and frequently sought and gave advice on how to get it. Under the heading "How to stay sane with three kids," Leslie informs her readers that "Sticking to a routine, that includes 'me time', is key" (2006).

Maternal ambivalence, which is often expressed as a laundry list of conflicting emotions, is another component of the choice discourse. "Hi. I'm struggling with motherhood," announces 'tnt1963'. "I struggle with almost every aspect of it!!! . . . I hate the fact that I have to think about & take care of two (sometimes three) other people every day non-stop!!! Just because I'm the mom! . . . Don't get me wrong. I love & adore my boys!!! . . . They're smart & funny & creative & energetic & giving & all kinds of good things. I just need a break!!!!!" (2006). Mothers who responded to this post assured 'tnt1963' that she was not the "ONLY" one—and prescribed a healthy dose of "me time." "I would suggest to you join a fitness club (work off the frustration) or some craft clubs that would get you out of the house on a regular basis if possible," advises 'momsstayhome' (2006).

Another subnarrative in the discourse of maternal choice is *the representation of motherhood as a job, project, or profession*. For example, Robin remarks, "I think moms deserve more credit. I don't know if WonderWoman could do our job!" (2004), while Debra writes, "As a mother at home with two young children, people don't think I have a real job, but my job is more lasting and real than theirs" (2007). Online forums and message boards also reveal an active conversation about men's responsibility for housework and child care, which tends to reinforces culture-bound assumptions about gender difference and is often presented in the form of complaint. As 'ragmama' observes tartly, "I think it takes men longer to switch into parent mode than it does for women, but 14 months is long enough" (2006). Sharon reports, "I am VERY lucky to have a husband who helps immensely with the housework and the kids," but adds that her partner only "helps immensely" when she writes out a to-do list. "No matter how much we want them to, often men just don't SEE the crap that needs to be taken care of the way we do" (2006).

Two discursive elements were notable due their scarcity or absence in the discussions I surveyed, although it's possible I simply did not visit enough blogs or message boards to capture them. The first was the discourse of always "putting children first," which appeared occasionally but was generally cancelled out by mothers' claim to identity and the quest for "me time." One construction that never surfaced—but which was much discussed by feminist thinkers of Jesse Bernard's generation—was the description of motherhood as a trap or insurmountable barrier to women's self-actualization and full participation in society. (This metaphor was missing even in forums dedicated to the rigors of full-time at-home mothering.) One possible explanation is that the formulation of motherhood as a trap is fundamentally incompatible with the choice mystique. While the dominant discourse of choice may primarily be an adaptation to help mothers make sense of the complexity of their desires and adjust to the multiple demands on their time—as well as a means of creating some "wiggle room" in the ideology of exclusive motherhood—it can also be understood as a reaction to second-wave critiques of marriage and motherhood as obstacles to women's liberation.

HOW TO CHANGE THE WORLD

To introduce the opposite end of the spectrum of our evolving script of motherhood, I offer this quote from a reader comment posted on *AlterNet*, a popular progressive news site. The writer is reacting to a story on women's rights and freedom of choice:

> We don't need feminism to give us "choices." That's what we already have. Being forced to "chose" between your arm and your leg, your family or your career, is just about what the patriarchy has already given us. . . . We need shorter work weeks, more vacation time, a national child care system, more male contribution to child care and housework, paid family leave, school days that go to 5.30 pm, less intra-female backbiting and competition, complete child support and paternity payment collection, larger child support awards, bigger alimony settlements, the right to return to work without undue discrimination after taking a short time off for family, credit toward Social Security for time spent raising small children, fair hiring and promotion at work, more women in power—by god, we need BETTER CHOICES!!
>
> I'll be darned if I'm going to accept a feminism so reduced and gutted that all it is about is abandoning me to "choose" or forcing me to "choose" between the rotten, unfair, split-brain, inadequate, incompatible, half-assed, not-as-good-as-man-has options I have before me today.   ('janvdb' 2006)

Compared to the typical reader commenting on the status of mothers or other contentious topics, this writer expresses her views with exceptional passion and clarity. What I wish to draw attention to is the detail of the writer's proposed solutions and the guiding concepts animating her argument. It's safe to say these did not come to her out of thin air. To the contrary, the writer's focus on a specific set of social policies, her challenge to troublesome rhetoric of "choice," and even certain elements of her phrasing are similar to articulations of the "motherhood penalty" or "motherhood problem" found in a growing collection of reports, books, magazines, blogs, online discussions, and Web sites that explore the relationship between motherhood and gender inequality.

It's also important to note that the writer's policy agenda represents an amalgam of thinking—no single book, organization, or Web site endorses an identical combination of reforms, although discussions of the individual policy solutions the writer recommends can be readily found in different sources. And it's interesting to consider how, in one way or another, this writer's summation of the motherhood problem touches on each of the core themes of *love, care, time, work, money, men & women, what children need,* and *difference* and illuminates some of the complex connections between them.

Although the two ends of our spectrum of discourse appear to be incompatible, in practice there is considerable room for movement between the two—and there are many examples of transitional narratives that combine features of the choice mystique with selective elements of the emerging discourse of change. For example, Debra, the mother of two who described her "job" of mothering as "more lasting and real" than paid employment, adds, "Our society and culture [do] not make this easy for any mother whether working, single or at home. . . . We need workplaces that are flexible, reliable childcare and healthcare for all children. A mother who wants to stay home to raise her children should be able to or if she works she should do that and be able to go to school when her child needs her" (2007). Although the maternal narrative of change is still a work in progress, its outline is already clear.

Rather than concentrating on mothers' ability to make satisfactory choices, the discourse of change aims to identify and catalogue the unique opportunity costs, economic risks, and inequalities women experience as a result of their maternal status (Williams 2000; Jacobs and Gerson 2004), brands the disproportionate "price" of motherhood as a moral and social problem (Crittenden 2001), and offers an alternative problem-solving model of cultural and policy reform through consciousness raising and collective action (Peskowitz 2005). While the discourse of choice represents motherhood as a job, project, or profession, the discourse of change positions *caregiving* as a class of labor—"care work"—and a primary *human* activity that is vital to sustaining a functional society (Tronto 1994), and recognizes motherhood as a relationship, not a job (De Marneffe 2004). The emerging discourse of change also describes people in families as socially situated individuals with legitimate and unpredictable needs, not as isolated consumers in an imaginary market of advantageous life options (Folbre 2001).

Although the language and logic of change is creeping into the mainstream discourse of motherhood, there are several rhetorical streams that remain seriously underdeveloped. To contribute to meaningful social change, our new narrative must eventually reintroduce the framework of fairness by naming cultural and structural barriers to men's full participation in home life and women's full participation in work life, and by underscoring mothers' socio-economic, racial, and cultural diversity and how difference protects or limits women's opportunities for caregiving, economic security, and family forma-tion. It must also mount a more direct challenge to beliefs about the nature and extent of biologically inscribed gender difference—especially in regard to men's capacity to care and women's desire to compete—and recognize father-hood as a relationship, not a role. While contemporary maternal discourse is focused almost exclusively on the here and now, an effective change narrative will need to be more future-focused and provide a realistic and attractive pic-ture of what the world will look like for men, women, and children once the motherhood problem is resolved.

For feminist activists and organizers, there is a strategic opportunity to gen-tly but persistently dismantle the mythology of women's empowerment through freedom of personal choice.[3] While this essay concludes that there is a permeable barrier between the dominant discourse of maternal choice and the emerging discourse of change, rewriting the motherhood script will be an ongoing project, and cannot be forced. Paying attention to the nearly infinite combination of con-ceptual links between *love, care, time, work, money, men & women, what children need,* and *difference* might be a good place to start. But if our goal is to shape the next future of motherhood, we must find an effective and respectful way to alter mothers' perceptions of the adequacy of their existing choices, and enlarge their understanding of what is possible.

NOTES

1. Although these concepts are probably familiar to maternal readers, clarification is in order. The myth of "maternal instinct" refers to the belief that good mothers in-tuitively or instinctively understand the exact nature of their children's needs and the best way to meet them, and represents this special capacity as biologically de-termined. The myth of "maternal bliss" is the fallacy that no matter how difficult or dispiriting the work of caring for small children is, good mothers always "love every minute of it." The myth of "maternal omnipotence" is the belief that children's lives are perfectible, and mothers alone have the power to perfect them.

2. Throughout this document, bloggers and message board participants are referred to by their screen names, first names, or full names, when used. Spelling, grammar,

capitalization, and punctuation are generally quoted as in the original; clarification is added only when necessary. All comments were retrieved from public message boards, discussion forums, and blogs—i.e., any Internet user may access and read the quoted comments without being pre-approved by that blog or message board owner, although in some cases free registration was required to read discussion threads (in all instances, registration is required to post a response). Many of the comments quoted in this article were sampled from message boards provided by commercial, consumer-oriented Web sites, including Club Mom (www.clubmom.com), Mom Connection (www.momconnection.com), Modern Mom (www.modernmom.com), DotMoms (www.dotmoms.com), and Blogging Baby (www.bloggingbaby.com). I favored commercial sources over personal blogs because—based on the personal information included in the online comments—message board participants appeared to be more socioeconomically diverse. The cautionary note about all online communities is that like tends to attract like; it is possible more politically conservative mothers flock to certain commercial message boards where they expect to find a sympathetic ear, while more progressive/feminist mamas favor the personality-driven communities forming in the blogosphere or discussion forums on alternative Web sites such as HipMama.com (www.hipmama.com). Also, given the virtual nature of online communication, it's possible that some of the individuals quoted here are not mothers, and/or are not women. However, all individuals quoted from online sources *represented* themselves as mothers, unless otherwise noted.

3. There are examples of personal blogs and "members only" discussion groups—such as Miriam Peskowitz's Playground Revolution blog and the Mothers & More "POWER Loop"—that combine personal storytelling with consciousness-raising about the social context of motherhood. The tenor of discourse in these online communities is markedly different from that found on popular commercial Web sites. While the reach of these forums is presently limited, I believe they offer a practical model for discursive activism—a topic that deserves a separate and more detailed discussion than I can offer here.

WORKS CITED

Bernard, Jesse. 1974. *The Future of Motherhood*. New York: Penguin.

Crittenden, Ann. 2001. *The Price of Motherhood: Why the Most Important Job in the World Is Still the Least Valued*. New York: Holt.

De Marneffe, Daphne. 2004. *Maternal Desire: On Children, Love, and the Inner Life*. New York: Little, Brown.

Douglas, Susan J., and Meredith Michaels. 2004. *The Mommy Myth*. New York: Free Press.

Farrell, Amy Erdman. 1998. *Yours in Sisterhood: Ms. Magazine and the Promise of Popular Feminism*. Chapel Hill: University of North Carolina Press.

Folbre, Nancy. 2001. *The Invisible Heart: Economics and Family Values*. New York: New Press.

Fox, Faulkner. 2005. Judging mothers. Mothers Movement Online, April. http://www .mothersmovement.org/features/05/f_fox_0504/judging_mothers_1.htm (accessed Jan. 27, 2007).

Glenn, Evelyn Nakano. 1994. Social constructions of mothering. In *Mothering: Experience, Ideology, and Agency*, ed. Evelyn Nakano Glenn, Grace Chang, and Linda Forcey, 1–29. New York: Routledge.

Hattery, Angela. 2001. *Women, Work, and Family: Balancing and Weaving*. Thousand Oaks, Calif.: Sage.

Healy, Christopher. 2003. Parenting through art direction. *Salon*, Dec. 23. http://dir .salon.com/story/mwt/feature/2003/12/23/catalog_kids/index1.html (accessed Feb. 3, 2007).

Hill Collins, Patricia. 1994. Shifting the center: Race, class, and feminist theorizing about motherhood. In *Mothering: Experience, Ideology, and Agency*, ed. Evelyn Nakano Glenn, Grace Chang, and Linda Forcey, 45–65. New York: Routledge.

Hirshman, Linda R. 2005. Homeward bound. *American Prospect*, Dec. 12, 20–26.

——. 2006. Unleashing the wrath of stay-at-home moms. *Washington Post*, June 18, B1.

Hochschild, Arlie Russell. 2003. *The Second Shift*. New York: Penguin.

Jacobs, Jerry A., and Kathleen Gerson. 2004. *The Time Divide: Work, Family, and Gender Inequality*. Cambridge, Mass.: Harvard University Press.

Maushart, Susan. 1999. *The Mask of Motherhood*. New York: Penguin.

Mothers Movement Online. 2003. An interview with Janna Malamud Smith. April. http://www.mothersmovement.org/features/JMSinterview.htm (accessed Jan. 17, 2007).

Peskowitz, Miriam. 2005. *The Truth Behind the Mommy Wars: Who Decides What Makes a Good Mother?* Emeryville, Calif.: Seal Press.

Rich, Adrienne. 1976. *Of Woman Born: Motherhood as Experiences and Institution*. New York: Norton, 1986; reissued 1995.

Rothman, Barbara Katz. 1994. Beyond mothers and fathers: Ideology in a patriarchal society. In *Mothering: Experience, Ideology, and Agency*, ed. Evelyn Nakano Glenn, Grace Chang, and Linda Forcey, 139–157. New York: Routledge.

Solinger, Rickie. 2001. *Beggars and Choosers: How the Politics of Choice Shapes Adoption, Abortion, and Welfare in the United States*. New York: Hill and Wang.

———. 2005. *Pregnancy and Power: A Short History of Reproductive Politics in America.* New York: New York University Press.

Sommers, Christina Hoff. 1994. *Who Stole Feminism?: How Women Have Been Betrayed by Women.* New York: Touchstone.

Tronto, Joan C. 1994. *Moral Boundaries: A Political Argument for an Ethic of Care.* New York: Routledge.

Williams, Joan C. 2000. *Unbending Gender: Why Family and Work Conflict and What to Do About It.* New York: Oxford University Press.

WEBLOG AND MESSAGE BOARD COMMENTS

'angelsmommy2' [screen name]. 2006. Re: Mom finds her kids boring [message board comment]. Club Mom Forum: Hot topics, Aug. 1. http://www.clubmom.com/ jforum/posts/list/10/173067.page#536608 (accessed Jan. 29, 2007).

'babyboy21' [screen name]. 2006. . . . soon to be working mom [message board post]. Mom Connection, Mom Talk forum: Work: Working outside the home, Sept. 14. http://www.momconnection.com/mbbs2/forums/thread-view.asp?tid=1734 (accessed Jan. 27, 2007).

'bensmommy2' [screen name]. 2006. Re: Mom finds her kids boring [message board comment]. Club Mom Forum: Hot topics, Aug. 12. http://www.clubmom.com/jforum/ posts/list/60/173067.page#538175 (accessed Jan. 29, 2007).

Christina Figiel [screen name]. 2006. Working mothers [Weblog comment]. MSNBC, The Daily Nightly, July 11. http://dailynightly.msnbc.com/2006/07/working_mothers.html (accessed Jan. 29, 2007).

Debra [screen name]. 2007. Give moms a break [blog comment]. Blogging Baby: Moms, by Jonathon Morgan, Jan. 2. http://www.bloggingbaby.com/2007/01/02/give-moms-a-break-experts-say-theres-too-much-pressure-on-moms/#c3029785 (accessed Feb. 3, 2007).

'gacgbaker' [screen name]. 2006. Re: Mom finds her kids boring [message board comment]. Club Mom Forum: Hot topics, Aug. 10. http://www.clubmom.com/jforum/ posts/list/20/173067.page#537047 (accessed Jan. 29, 2007).

'geminilove' [screen name]. 2006. Re: The mommy wars [message board comment]. Club Mom Forum: Hot topics, Feb. 27. http://www.clubmom.com/jforum/posts/ list/0/150477.page#423211 (accessed Jan. 15, 2007).

'GypsyDiva' [screen name]. 2006. I had a nightmare boss . . . [message board comment]. Modern Mom Forum: Balancing it all: Bad bosses, Feb. 27. http://www.modernmom .com/forum/viewtopic.php?p=303 (accessed Jan. 29, 2007).

'janvdb' [screen name]. 2006. Feminism isn't about 'choice' . . . [reader comment]. Response to Christy Burbridge, Who's co-opting feminism?, *AlterNet*, Sept. 20. http://www.alternet.org/rights/41903/#comments (accessed Oct. 18, 2006).

Jay Allen [screen name]. 2006. "Most 'moms leaving the marketplace' stories are crap"? You don't say [Weblog entry]. Blogging Baby, Jan. 4. http://www.bloggingbaby.com/2006/01/04/most-moms-leaving-the-marketplace-research-is-crap-you-dont/ (accessed Jan. 27, 2007).

Kay [screen name]. 2005. Choice or backlash? You decide [Weblog comment]. Dot Moms: About Work and Family, Oct. 9. http://roughdraft.typepad.com/dotmoms/2005/09/choice_or_backl.html#comment-10171077 (accessed Jan. 30, 2007).

'L' [screen name]. 2006. I don't think Hirshman read all of the BB profiles . . . [weblog comment]; response to Sarah Gilbert, Linda Hirshman's "Get to Work" distorts Blogging Baby readers, writers. Blogging Baby, June 23. http://www.bloggingbaby.com/2006/06/23/linda-hirshmans-get-to-work-distorts-blogging-baby-readers-w/#c1650354 (accessed Jan. 29, 2007).

Leslie [screen name]. 2006. How to stay sane with three kids [peer-to-peer advice entry]. Club Mom: Mom know-how: Finding time for yourself, March 6. http://www.clubmom.com/display/211647?fromPage=/channels/resource_center/archive.jsp(accessed Jan. 30, 2007).

'mamacita' [screen name]. 2006. She is very much mistaken . . . [Weblog comment]; response to Sarah Gilbert, Linda Hirshman's "Get to Work" distorts Blogging Baby readers, writers. Blogging Baby, June 23. http://www.bloggingbaby.com/2006/06/23/linda-hirshmans-get-to-work-distorts-blogging-baby-readers-w/#c1650540 (accessed Jan. 29, 2007).

'momsstayhome' [screen name]. 2006. Re: I really really want to know . . . am I the only one??? [message board comment]. Club Mom Forum: Stay-at-home moms, Dec. 19. http://www.clubmom.com/jforum/posts/list/0/194959.page#659989 (accessed Jan. 29, 2007).

'ragmama' [screen name]. 2006. Re: Husbands do not understand (sometimes) [message board comment]. Modern Mom Forum: Family and home, May 25. http://www.modernmom.com/forum/viewtopic.php?p=4000 (accessed Jan. 30, 2007).

Robin [screen name]. 2004. Wonder Woman [weblog comment]. Dot Moms: Work and family, April 22. http://roughdraft.typepad.com/dotmoms/2004/04/wonder_woman.html#comment-967707 (accessed Jan. 30, 2007).

'sated' [screen name]. 2006. Having a child is a choice [message board comment]. MomsRising.org: Forum: Employers, Speak UP, May 31. http://www.momsrising.org/node/287#comment-16 (accessed Jan. 15, 2007).

Sharon [screen name]. 2006. Gender equality and new motherhood [weblog comment]. Blogging Baby, July 9. http://www.bloggingbaby.com/2006/07/09/gender-equality-and-new-motherhood/ (accessed Jan. 29, 2007).

'snowflake9903' [screen name]. 2006. What is your political persuasion [message board comment]. Club Mom Forum: Hot topics, Dec. 10. http://www.clubmom.com/jforum/posts/list/0/193910.page#654729 (accessed Jan. 29, 2007).

'tnt1963' [screen name]. 2006. I really really want to know . . . am I the ONLY one??? [message board comment]. Club Mom Forum: Stay-at-home moms, Dec. 10. http://www.clubmom.com/jforum/posts/list/0/194959.page#659989 (accessed Jan. 29, 2007).

The Mothers' Movement

NINETEEN

The Challenges of Coalition Building in the Twenty-first Century

PATRICE DIQUINZIO

The turn of the twenty-first century has seen the emergence in Canada and the United States of a movement of mothers and other caregivers that is devoted to raising consciousness about the value of caregiving work and to creating social, political, and legal changes to support the work of caregiving. This movement has the potential to bring about revolutionary change both in how we think about motherhood and mothering and in law and social policy that affects motherhood. In its infancy, however, this movement faces a number of daunting challenges. Elsewhere I have argued (DiQuinzio 2006) that the most pressing of these challenges are

- Ending the so-called mommy wars;
- Ensuring a place in the mothers' movement for every kind of mother;
- Resisting the demonization of mothers socially constructed as "bad" or "deviant" mothers;
- Making alliances with other caregivers, paid and unpaid;
- Reaching out to younger women;

- Articulating an agenda for the mothers' movement consistent with women's reproductive rights.

Thinking further about how to address these challenges and bring about the changes the mothers' movement demands has lead me to at least one conclusion: the success of the mothers' movement is more likely if it explicitly considers itself a coalition and engages in the difficult work of coalition building. A number of developments that characterize the beginning of the twenty-first century suggest why coalition building will have to be central to the mothers' movement of the future. In an age of instant communication via the Internet and other new media platforms, it is increasingly easy for mothers all over the world to learn about and communicate with each other. This development appears to present a host of new opportunities to grow and strengthen the mothers' movement. But the persistent digital divide means that without specific efforts to include them, mothers lacking access to the Internet and other new media will be excluded from these conversations. And the curious phenomenon of the ever-spreading reach of the Internet combined with its tendency to create ever-smaller niches in which a few like-minded people share or dominate a specific online space means that it's easy to be misled about the potential of the Internet for large-scale organizing and mobilizing for change.

A related development is the increasing penetration of mass media images into the lives and imaginations of people everywhere. In all societies, the cultural construct of the mother and motherhood carries a great deal of symbolic weight, even when conflicting constructs of the maternal are evident. In the twenty-first century those in a position to determine mass media representations of mothers and mothering will have considerable influence on the cultural imaginary of societies across the world. What individuals, groups, and organizations will be in this position remains to be seen, though media corporations with their origins in the West are likely to continue their dominance. But struggles over mass media images of mothers and mothering are likely to increase in intensity and complexity as mass media production becomes a truly global enterprise. At the same time, however, it becomes more difficult to figure out when, how, and to what extent struggles over media representations intersect with improvements in the real lives of mothers, children, and families.

A third characteristic development of the twenty-first century is the increased movement and relocation of people around the world. Whether as workers temporarily away from their home countries, immigrants permanently relocating, or refugees forced to leave their homes, more people from different cultures of origin are living together, especially in the West, than ever before. Twenty-first century communities are increasingly multilingual and multicultural, which means that whatever concerns and goals such people might share, their cultural traditions with respect to mothering, family life, and political mobilization are more and more likely to differ among them. So all of these trends suggest that coalition building, which focuses on dealing with differences and creating bonds among different people that are both strong and flexible enough to sustain coordinated action aimed at a variety of social and political goals, ought be central to the mothers' movement of the twenty-first century.

One of the best analyses of coalition politics in a feminist context is Bernice Johnson Reagon's essay "Coalition Politics: Turning the Century" (1983), based on a talk she gave at the West Coast Women's Music Festival in California in 1981. Rereading this essay with the mothers' movement in mind, I find much that is applicable to the current situation of the mothers' movement and to its questions about activism and change in the twenty-first century.

In "Coalition Politics," Reagon looks back over her years of activism in the U.S. civil rights movement and the women's movement. On the basis of her experiences in these movements, Reagon distinguishes the space of coalition from what she calls "the little barred room." In the little barred room gather people who are alike. Often these are the people who have already made up their minds about the movement—about who the movement is for, what the problem is, who is best qualified or positioned to solve it, and how best to solve it. Reagon writes,

> Now every once in a while there is a need for people to try to clean out corners and bar the doors and check everybody who comes in the door, and check what they carry in and say, "Humph, inside this place the only thing we're going to deal with is X, or Y, or Z." And so only the Xs or the Ys or the Zs get to come in. That place can then become a nurturing place or a very destructive place. (1983:357)

Reagon recognizes that people create these little barred rooms because they need a refuge from the struggle of living in the larger spaces in which they aren't recognized or accepted, or in which they are actively persecuted and oppressed. And this need for a refuge is a legitimate need. So, she concludes, while that little barred room lasts, "it should be nurturing space where you sift out what other people are saying about you and decide who you really are." These nurturing spaces can also be spaces in which we rehearse community and learn more about what true community entails. As Reagon puts it, these spaces can be the sites of experiments in which we consider, "If I was really running it, this is the way it would be" (358).

The mothers' movement includes many such spaces where mothers define themselves, their concerns, and their interests, and nurture and empower each other. The Association for Research on Mothering, based at York University in Toronto, often functions as such a space, and it has given rise to groups, such as Mother Outlaws, that strive both to nurture and to empower their members. In the United States, the Mothers' Centers supported by the National Association of Mothers' Centers do an outstanding job of creating nurturing and support-ive spaces for mothers (I am a former member of the board of trustees of the NAMC). And it is not surprising that the mothers' movement would proliferate such spaces—after all, nurturing, supporting, and empowering others is what mothers are supposed to be especially good at.

Within these spaces, mothers can and do engage in the work of "sifting out what other people are saying" about mothers and motherhood. For example, groups within the mothers' movement work at reconceptualizing mothering as socially valuable work, rather than merely an expression of an inherent maternal instinct. Redefining mothering in terms that will support the changes that the mothers' movement advocates is an important contribution to bringing about those changes. To the extent that mothers find support for their mothering work in these nurturing spaces, these spaces also contribute to improving the lives of mothers, children, families, and society. And to the extent that these spaces en-able mothers to learn how to work together to create the kinds of communities that would truly support mothering, they do allow mothers to articulate "how it would be" if they were "really running it."

So I do not at all deny the need for and the value of such nurturing spaces. I do, however, agree with Reagon that we must be vigilant with respect to the inevi-table problems for coalition politics that these nurturing spaces create. Given that they are predicated at least to some extent on exclusion, these nurturing spaces are always at risk of becoming little barred rooms. I believe that this risk is es-pecially high in the online spaces that the mothers' movement has created, for two reasons. First, participating in an online community often and paradoxically includes physical isolation from the other members of the community. Second, online people are able to manage their self-presentation or present a persona at odds with aspects of their real identity to a degree not possible in real-life, real-time interactions. For these reasons I think that there's an even greater tendency for participants in online communities to emphasize what they have in common and to nurture each other—or believe that they are nurturing each other—without recognizing or dealing with their differences and without recognizing who is missing or whom they may have excluded from their community.

Reagon traces the creation of little barred rooms to the myth sometimes assumed by the women's movement that there is something all women have in common, some experience we all share, simply because we are women. It is this myth that suggests that we can easily define, create, and maintain "women-only" spaces, little barred rooms just for "women." But one of the pitfalls of small nurturing spaces is that those of us in them often don't notice who is not there, and so we don't ask why they aren't there. As Reagon writes, "If we are the same women from the same people in this barred room, we never notice it. . . . It does not show up until somebody walks into the room who happens to be [one of us] but really is also somebody else" (1983:361–362).

I take Reagon's point here as a warning to the mothers' movement against making the same problematic assumption of universally shared experience about mothers—which is not to deny that mothers have at least some concerns and goals in common. The realization that mothers have some concerns and goals in common alone isn't inherently useful or problematic from the point of view of coalition building. The question is what one does with and as a result of this realization. If I use this realization about another woman as a basis or means of overlooking all the ways in which she, her situation, and her experience might be different from mine, that certainly doesn't foster coalition. But if I use this realization as an opening for conversation, a beginning point for my listening to her and learning about her life, then it can be a step in coalition building. I should use our shared concerns and goals as a point of departure to enable me to focus on how her situation or experiences differ from mine and thus differently influence or determine what she can do about the concerns, what she must do or what she needs, to achieve the goals we share.

My sense is that the mothers' movement is not likely to create explicitly exclusionary groups with rigidly defined criteria for admission or participation. But I am concerned that some of our smaller groups and nurturing spaces in effect function to exclude in just the way Reagon describes, without anyone actually intending that they do so. So, at a minimum, the mothers' movement must be careful not to assume that all of our little barred rooms are automatically nurturing spaces. I fear that, as a movement of mothers, we are especially prone to make this assumption on the grounds that when and wherever mothers gather, there must be nurturing going on. We need instead to think carefully about the purposes and goals of the nurturing spaces we create and ensure that they don't become the destructive kind of spaces that operate primarily to keep other people out. We at least need to make every effort to notice who isn't there and who isn't showing up, and to ask ourselves why.

On the other hand, Reagon's analysis of coalition building indicates the ultimate impossibility of remaining within the exclusionary boundaries of the little barred room. She insists, "There is no way you can survive by staying *inside* the barred room" (1983:358). Inside the room, you're either preaching to the choir, having little or no effect outside of the room, where the real problems and threats to your agenda, even to your life, originate; or you're busy specifying and defining your group in terms of whom you let in, so that you must police the doors, checklist in hand, to make sure that only, for example, women or mothers come in. But other people come along who insist that they belong in the little barred room, too, because they are women or mothers—as they define themselves. Then, you either let them in, because you don't want to be the proprietor of an exclusionary little barred room, or you get bogged down in arguments about why they don't really belong in the room and in more strenuous efforts to keep them out, while they rush the doors. In either case, as Reagon says, "the room don't feel like the room anymore" (359). That's because the room was really meant to be only or primarily a home, or even a womb, where those inside are to be nurtured, cared for, and supported.

So, even at their very best, the small nurturing spaces alone can't launch significant change outside of that space. For these reasons, those who start out in the little barred room can cower in the room, policing its boundaries, or they can accept the challenges posed by those who want to come and in thus be propelled into coalition building, whether they're ready for it or not. When it comes to change, nurturing spaces should only be places of temporary respite from the hard work of coalition building, and we shouldn't mistake this experience of nurturing and being nurtured for the work of coalition building. "Coalition work," Reagon argues

> is not work done in your home. Coalition work has to be done in the streets. And it is some of the most dangerous work that you can do. And you shouldn't look for comfort. Some people will come to a coalition and . . . rate the success of the coalition on whether or not they feel good when they get there. They're not looking for a coalition, they're looking for a home! (359)

Having distinguished the small barred room from the space of coalition building, what does Reagon suggest about the work of coalition building? First, there is the idea of "give" implicit in Reagon's analysis of coalition politics. I see this idea of "give" in Reagon's comment that, "you don't get fed a lot in a coalition. In a coalition you have to give, and it is different from your home" (359). To elaborate on this point, I think that in a coalition you have to "give" in two senses. You have to give something of yourself—you have to contribute your ideas and your efforts—and you have to "give" in the sense of being flexible. You have to be able to or learn how to work with others who aren't just like you and who don't share all of your concerns, interests, and goals without requiring as a condition of your cooperation that they become just like you.

Reagon makes this point about "give" in a somewhat different way when she suggests, "Think about the possibilities of going for fifty years" (361). She writes,

> There are some grey-haired women I see running around occasionally, and we have to talk to those folks about how come they didn't commit suicide forty years ago. . . . Get on your agenda some old people and try to figure out what it will be like if you are a raging radical fifty years from today. . . . What would you be like if you had white hair and had not given up your principles?   (361)

I suspect that these old people are people who had and continue to have some "give." They can deal with differences and move among a number of groups and issues, they don't expect overnight success, they don't spend their time policing the borders of the movements of which they are a part, and they don't waste their energy on excluding others.

In the context of the mothers' movement, Reagon's idea of "give" raises difficult but crucial questions that we must address. How do we stretch beyond our comfortable understandings of what it means to be a mother, beyond our assumption that what it means to be a mother is what it means *to me* to be a mother? How do we ensure that our understanding of who is a mother and what it means to be a mother is flexible enough to include many different mothers? How do we ensure that mothers who aren't privileged from the perspective of race, ethnicity, sexual orientation, and socioeconomic status are not excluded from the mothers' movement?

The difficulties here are considerable. Our understanding of motherhood has to be unifying enough to allow a movement to coalesce, but not so unifying that it excludes some mothers. Perhaps, since we've done well in creating nurturing spaces for the mothers' movement, we can begin by making sure that those spaces are sufficiently inclusive. And if we take seriously Reagon's admonition not to go looking for comfort in a coalition, then we need to distinguish nurturing from comfort. If "nurturing" includes enabling someone to grow and develop—to acquire some "give"—it might require helping people get into situations in which they are *uncomfortable*, so that they can learn to deal with the source of that discomfort or at least learn to deal with their discomfort in ways that don't undermine the coalitions they are trying to create. Ultimately a goal of these nurturing spaces should be to enable each of us to connect and become more comfortable with mothers who are not like us in significant ways, without denying our differences. I also think that each of us must make a commitment not to confine our participation in the mothers' movement entirely to those nurturing spaces. I recognize that some of us need the nurturing spaces more than others, and some are better positioned to move in and out of them than others. At the very least, these spaces must prepare those in them to recognize and deal with those who are going to show up and want to come in.

Reagon also cautions against those people and groups who insist that there is and must be only one "cutting edge" of the movement and that there is only one issue the movement must address. She writes, "Watch those mono-issue people . . . watch those groups that can only deal with one issue at a time" (363). And I think she means "watch" in two senses here, too. We should watch out for those people and groups, because their insistence on one issue or cause ultimately undermines a coalition. But we should also watch them and learn what we can from them about how to prioritize and get things done. Understanding and appreciating what is valuable about their ability to focus might allow us to find the middle ground between narrow single-mindedness and acting on so many different issues that we don't accomplish anything significant on any of them. If our nurturing spaces can encompass differences, then they can be spaces in which "mono-issue people" can acquire some "give" while also teaching the rest of us something about getting things done.

On the basis of my reading of Reagon's analysis of coalition building and coalition politics, I return to some of the most important challenges that I see facing the mothers' movement at the beginning of the twenty-first century, focusing on how those challenges raise the issue of differences among mothers. First, Reagon's analysis of coalition building helps us to see more clearly the tensions implicit in these challenges. For instance, the challenge of ending the so-called mommy wars is to some extent at odds with the challenge of ensuring a place in the mothers' movement for every kind of mother. I am thoroughly committed to ending "the mommy wars" if that means repudiating the mass media's image of a war between mothers in the paid labor force and mothers working at home. I entirely support the efforts of Moms Rising and the MOTHERS (Mothers Ought To Have Equal Rights) initiative of the NAMC to bring about "a cease fire in the mommy wars" (MOTHERS 2006). And a response to the mass media's representation of the "mommy wars" may require an emphasis on unity among mothers and on what we have in common. But the goal of ensuring that different mothers have a place in the mothers' movement requires that we recognize and deal with rather than deny the real differences among us. So the mothers' movement must simultaneously highlight our shared experiences in response to mass media over-simplifications and include opportunities for mothers to talk about and deal with the real differences among us.

One important difference among mothers, a function of age and generation, arises more often in my life as I get older. It appears to me that some mothers of infants and young children today find it easier than I did to be mothers and to combine mothering with the other things they want to do. It can be difficult for us to listen to and take seriously someone in an earlier stage of an experience we have had, especially when we perceive that younger person to be benefiting from changes we fought for. Sometimes those of us who see ourselves as having contributed to the changes from which younger women benefit want to hear thanks and praise for how much we have helped them. So we're at least taken aback when instead they tell us that their lives are difficult, too. But I remember very well how I felt as a young mother when I older mothers told me how much better I had it than they did. I didn't appreciate their failure or unwillingness to see my life from my point of view, and I resented what felt like their attempts either to make me feel guilty about my advantages or to extort my appreciation of their more difficult struggles. Now that I'm on the other side of this difference, I try to remember how difficult it was for me to see beyond my own horizons when I was immersed in the day-to-day work of caring for small children and trying to make a career for myself. This recollection should help me to have some "give" in relationship to younger mothers; it should allow me to enjoy rather than resent the extent to which they benefit from the efforts of previous generations to improve women's options and supports with respect to mothering, whether or not they see or appreciate this.

Another difference among mothers that I personally have found very difficult is the difference in socioeconomic situation of those mothers who have others—primarily husbands or partners—on whom they can depend for some or all of their material support and those like myself who do not. It is easy to resent what appears to me to be these mothers' greater options, such as their real opportunity not to work for pay, to work fewer hours, or to work at a lower-paying job because they are not the sole support of themselves and their children. In the academic context in which I work, I have colleagues who are mothers and whose partners have an income sufficient to allow them to take unpaid time off from teaching and thus produce a great deal of scholarly work. But as a single mother, I've never been in a position to take unpaid leave, even though my children's father has been an entirely reliable source of half of their financial support and much of their day-to-day care. I can only imagine the constraints experienced by single mothers without any reliable source of support for their children but themselves. I confess that I often find myself saying the right thing to and about differences among mothers such as these. I say, "None of us has really great choices when it comes to being a mother and having the economic resources we need," or "Being a mother is hard work, no matter what kind of other support you have," though often I don't really feel it. But I also confess that I have never had a truly open and honest conversation about this difference with a mother whose situation appears to be better than mine in that she has a partner who provides economic support for her and their children or she has other access to financial resources that I don't have, even though I have had chances to initiate such conversations.

Reagon's concept of "give" implies that discomfort is an unavoidable component of acquiring this "give." So despite the prospect of discomfort, if we want to have some "give" in relationships among mothers, we need to initiate these difficult conversations about what appear to be some mothers' more advantaged situations. On the other hand, this same "give" is necessary for us to hear and deal with what other mothers might say about our privileges. My birth family's socioeconomic advantages, for instance, gave me the educational opportunities that allow me to now do work that I greatly enjoy and make a very comfortable living at it. From the perspective of many, many mothers these advantages are significant privileges and I need to be able to hear and deal with what other mothers might have to say to me about them. And given the complexities of our positionings—privileged in relationship to some mothers, disadvantaged in relationship to others—we may all have to live with the discrepancies between what we feel about these differences and the positions we want to take as activist participants in the mothers' movement.

Reagon's concept of "give" thus indicates that the mothers' movement must include some opportunities for honest conversation about differences like these among mothers. Without such opportunities the unity we want and need in order to move our agenda forward is too fragile, too brittle, to be sustained. A shared commitment to engage in these difficult and discomforting conversations and live with these discrepancies, however, is not possible if we insist that the only basis for unity in the mothers' movement is what we have in common. Without a willingness to endure some discomfort in order to acquire some "give," we won't be able to keep our energies focused on using whatever advantages each of us has to advance the goals of the mothers' movement rather than letting resentment get the better of our efforts.

An excellent example of the complexities of addressing the challenge of ending the "mommy wars" while also addressing economic differences among mothers begins with a story by Jackie Regales that appeared in Mothers' Movement Online in September 2006. Regales writes with passion and anger about the failure of the emerging mothers' movement to recognize the long history of activism by mothers in the welfare rights movement, largely under the umbrella of the National Welfare Rights Organization (1966–1975). She singles out Joan Blades and Kristin Rowe-Finkbeiner's *The Motherhood Manifesto* (2006), but she could just as easily have added many other publications and organizations that see themselves as important components of the mothers' movement. In an exercise that should be depressingly familiar to those of us long active in the women's movement, Regales has to teach the history lesson that those of us in more privileged positions should have taken the trouble to teach ourselves. Is it simply right to know and honor the work of women like Johnnie Tillmon, Cheri Honkala, Lillian Hanson, and Pat Gowen, the work of the Westside mothers in Las Vegas, the Kensington Welfare Rights Union in Philadelphia, and the Welfare Warriors in Milwaukee. Moreover, we can learn from and, at least to some extent, support the work of these women and groups. Regales' anger may make us uncomfortable, but this discomfort is precisely the indication of the possibility for coalition building that Bernice Johnson Reagon urges us to seize.

Regales' article prompted a good deal of thought and reflection among several of us involved in the NAMC MOTHERS Initiative, and some email exchanges and phone conversations that included Jackie Regales, Pat Gowen, NAMC executive director Linda Lisi Juergens, and Valerie Young (advocacy coordinator for the MOTHERS Initiative), among others, followed. These discussions allowed everyone involved to learn more about the work the others are doing, and, just as Reagon's analysis of coalition politics suggests, allowed us to discover some overlapping issues and concerns. We were able to recognize and respect those issues and concerns that we don't necessarily share, come up with some ideas about what we might do to support each others' work on the overlapping issues and concerns, and agree to some steps to implement those ideas. I don't want to exaggerate either the extent or the importance of what transpired here. Nor do I want to minimize the difficulty, at least for me, of hearing these criticisms of the mothers' movement or the need for us to follow through on our agreement to support each others' work whenever possible. But I am optimistic that these exchanges could be the beginning of a coalition, with all of the difficulties that coalition politics entails.

Another challenge facing the mothers' movement that I want to return to briefly is that of making alliances with other caregivers, especially paid care workers. Certainly those who do care work for pay have some different interests and concerns than mothers, who, whatever else they do, aren't paid for their work as mothers. Paid caregivers can also have interests opposed to those of mothers. For instance, child care workers' interest in better pay is at odds with mothers' interest in affordable child care. Difficult feelings of resentment about one's low wages and resentment about one's high day care costs are hard to reconcile. Differences among mothers and paid caregivers are particularly pressing when it is a mother who is paying the caregiver to care for herself or her children. Beyond fostering discussion of the difficult questions about autonomy and exploitation in this transaction (see DiQuinzio 2003), what can the mothers' movement do to ensure that this particular intersection of mothers and paid caregivers is a point at which some degree of understanding and common purpose is possible?

Reagon's analysis of the complexity and difficulty of coalition building not predicated on the denial of differences suggests the importance of the many women who do caregiving work for pay and are also mothers. Perhaps they are uniquely positioned to contribute to this goal of forging alliances among mothers and paid caregivers. What kinds of settings or spaces could the mothers' movement create to allow these women to speak of their particular experiences, to articulate their distinct concerns and needs? I for one would like to hear from women in this position about what it is like to provide care for someone else, especially someone else's children, while at the same time caring for one's own children. While there is much that we can read to learn about these mothers' experiences (e.g., Nelson 1994; Scarr 1984), I would like the opportunity to speak with mothers in this position. What could these mothers tell us about the constraints and rewards of their different caregiving experiences? How do the obstacles and advantages they face in their paid caregiving work compare to those they face in their unpaid work of mothering? What changes would improve the circumstances of their paid caregiving work and how are those changes related to improving the circumstances of their unpaid mothering work? What changes in the circumstances of their unpaid mothering work would improve their experiences of paid caregiving?

Perhaps most important: what could the mothers' movement learn about our agenda and goals from the experiences and perspectives of these mothers who also do paid caregiving work? Soliciting the input of these mothers and taking seriously what they have to say about the mothers' movement might mean that the movement will have to rethink or reprioritize its goals, reshape its agenda, and develop more nuanced approaches to achieving those goals. It might be difficult to do so, especially for those in leadership positions in the movement, who are understandably eager to capitalize on any possibilities for achieving those goals rather than devoting a lot of time and effort to rethinking them. But here, too, I believe that a unity of purpose and action that doesn't make room for the different interests and concerns of mothers in different circumstances won't really be able to sustain the forward movement we want. So we must create the spaces and take the time for discussion of these differences among mothers, despite its difficulties and despite the risk of slower movement forward that it presents.

As Bernice Johnson Reagon's analysis of coalition building makes so clear, for any movement for change, coalition building is hard work, work in which we risk painful discomfort and a stumbling, "two steps forward and one step back" path to progress. But especially when it comes to the mothers' movement, the risks of not doing coalition building are much greater. As I see it, the mothers' movement is a crucial component of a larger project, that of improving all kinds of caregiving, without which literally none of us can survive and flourish. Improvements in caregiving that benefit some at the expense of others are fundamentally inconsistent with that goal and will only undermine the achievement of that goal in the long run. Better we do the work of coalition building with all of its difficulties now, and as we pursue that goal, rather than assume or create a false unity that won't withstand the opposition we will face as we move forward and that won't sustain the movement in the long run.

WORKS CITED

Blades, Joan, and Kristin Rowe-Finkbeiner. 2006. *The Motherhood Manifesto: What America's Moms Want and What To Do About It.* New York: Nation Books.

DiQuinzio, Patrice. 2003. Mothers and other caregivers: Moral dilemmas of "distributed mothering." *American Philosophical Association Newsletter on Feminism and Philosophy* 3.1:89–92.

——. 2006. The politics of the mothers' movement in the United States: Possibilities and pitfalls. *Journal of the Association for Research on Mothering* 8.1/2:55–71.

MOTHERS (Mothers Ought to Have Equal Rights). 2006. Cease fire in the mommy wars campaign. https://www.mothersoughttohaveequalrights.org/mother-s-day-action-archives/mothers-day-2006-mommy-wars-ceasefire-campaign.html (accessed Jan. 2007).

Nelson, Margaret K. 1994. Family day care providers: Dilemmas of daily practice. In *Motherhood: Ideology, Experience, and Agency*, ed. Evelyn Nakano Glenn, Grace Chang, and Linda Rennie Forcey, 181–210. New York: Routledge.

Reagon, Bernice Johnson. 1983. Coalition politics: Turning the century. In *Home Girls: A Black Feminist Anthology*, ed. Barbara Smith, 356–368. New York: Kitchen Table–Women of Color Press.

Regales, Jackie. 2006. Learning the lessons of history. Mothers Movement Online, Sept. http://www.mothersmovement.org/features/06/09/regales_welfare_rights_1.html (accessed Jan. 2007).

Scarr, Sandra. 1984. *Mother Care/Other Care*. New York: Basic Books.

Political Labeling of Mothers

An Obstacle to Equality in Politics

TWENTY

MARSHA MAROTTA

As the twenty-first century unfolds in the United States, we have a fictional and caricatured war between mothers who work and mothers who stay home. We have myths about a gender gap in voting that puts momentary focus on women with labels such as "soccer mom" or "security mom," then blurs that focus so that women and their needs and desires are nearly invisible. We have a media that rarely quotes women in articles on politics or prints their photos with those articles. And we have the attitude exemplified by the actress Sharon Stone, who told reporters, "I think Hillary Clinton is fantastic. But I think it is too soon for her to run. This may sound odd, but a woman should be past her sexuality when she runs. Hillary still has sexual power and I don't think people will accept that. It's too threatening" (Smyth 2006).

In fact, nothing in this context sounds odd at all, but instead is consistent with the rules and regulations that define the appropriate spaces for women. In Stone's terms—since Clinton was nearly sixty at the time of the comments—women might have to be in their seventies or older before they can run for high office—especially if they follow Stone's example and the dictates of the culture and do all they can to look young and sexy. This is simply a variation on the double-standard theme, one more technique to delay mothers' entry into politics, which puts them at a distinct disadvantage.

The made-up wars, political labels, obstacles to mothers' entry into politics, and lack of attention to women voters are in harmony with the much older notion that we can keep mothers under control and keep them in what I call MotherSpace. They are soldiers for the dominant discourses of the day that help deploy the narratives that teach mothers the "rules" of motherhood, illustrating the links among culture, identities, and practices. We can see this in "soccer moms," "security moms," and more—all terms designed to focus mothers on their roles and responsibilities as mothers, to keep them in MotherSpace and out of political space. Even when mothers package themselves—for example, Mothers Against Drunk Driving and the Million Mom March—they locate themselves in that particular space in politics and society that reinforces notions of selflessness, rather than in a position that allows for equality and full participation as citizens. The message is clear: the outer boundaries of MotherSpace are to be reached only with a station wagon or minivan filled with children and their equipage.

As most of us know, this is hardly an accurate description of most mothers' lives. But it is what U.S. culture would like to be real, or to be the goal, for most women, depending on their race and class; this image is skillfully deployed through political discourse.

Establishing boundaries around mothers and claiming the power to define MotherSpace stabilizes the meaning of motherhood and reduces the potential threat mothers pose if they venture outside that space. This is one of the techniques used to persuade mothers to engage in certain practices that reflect "choices" that put the needs of others before their own—"choices" that reduce their income, benefits, time for themselves, and so on. At issue here are not just the definitions of mothers' needs and desires and how they should be satisfied— but *where* they should be satisfied. An examination of the "choices" implied in the terms "soccer moms" and "security moms" offers examples of how the ideology of the "good" mother is disseminated in political discourse so that it becomes a ubiquitous notion, a generalized narrative with which all mothers are urged to identify on at least some level.[1]

THE "MOMMY WARS" AND THE PARTY WARS

Scores of newspaper and magazine articles and several recent books have drawn attention to the "mommy wars" in the United States, despite the fact that the "battles" in those wars surfaced at least as long ago as the Reagan era, with its penchant for categorizing and splintering groups and then pitting them against each other. The split encourages us to view the prospects as a zero-sum game: what is good for at-home mothers is bad for working mothers and vice versa. This tends to be an effective way to divide and conquer, because while each side spends time trying to defend their "choices" they stay firmly ensconced in MotherSpace, obfuscating democratic politics and the road to full citizenship participation for mothers. This dilemma provides a context for looking at the gender gap and gender stereotypes in attitudes toward politics.

In fact, until they were interrupted by the need to defend themselves against party scandals, some Republicans and some news reporters called on this narrative when they labeled the Democrats the "mommy party" of the 2006 Congressional elections because of the larger than usual number of women in House races. News reports listed the priority issues for these women candidates as ethics reform, fiscal responsibility, affordable health care, and the environment—consistent with the mother's role of moral guide and caretaker. They were depicted as the perfect messengers to run as outsiders against a culture of corruption. "If you want to communicate change, honesty, cleaning up Washington, not the same old good old boys in Washington, women are very good at communicating that," Democratic pollster Celinda Lake told the *New York Times* (Toner 2006). Yet portraying women in this way made it easy for Republicans to draw out the symbolic representation of mothers as nonpolitical beings, outside political space. The message is that "Democrats are more concerned with nurturing, caring and domestic policy, while the Republicans care more about security"—with security designated as a more important issue.

As long as women candidates are represented as mothers concerned with care and help, their candidacies will reinforce MotherSpace and assumptions about women. They will be in that particular space in politics rather than politics writ large. The connotation is clear: dubbing a political party the "mommy party" is not a compliment. Instead, it is a disparagement that suggests that the party belongs in MotherSpace and not in the masculine space of political leadership. The label of "mommy party" inserts the values of the "mommy wars" into party politics.

THE DISTORTED GENDER GAP

These notions are reinforced when most of the attention in the popular press, which follows the lead of politicians and political parties, ignores the many studies showing that the gender gap in voting has been created at least as much by changes in the way men vote as by changes in the way women vote. Instead, they focus on women—presenting them as undecided and malleable (Norrander 1999; Kauffman and Petrocik 1999). In fact, women consistently have been more attracted to the Democratic Party and men consistently have been moving to the Republican Party, a change that began in the 1960s, became clear in the 1970s, and by the early 1990s was strong enough to be called a permanent pattern (Norrander 1999:567).[2] Further, some who study the gender gap have found it to be simplified and "fundamentally misportrayed in much of the literature . . . as if it were a single, coherent construct . . . [rather than] a more nuanced assessment" (Schlesinger and Heldman 2001:84).

In fact, studies have found that the differences in attitudes between women who work outside the home and those who do not can be as great as between women who work and men who work. The difference between married women and single women can be as great as between women and men. Contrary to the simplified version of the gender gap that lumps all women together, no easy explanation exists. For example, in the 2000 presidential election, the gender gap was 10 percent; that is, women were 10 percent less likely than men to vote for Bush. In the 2004 presidential election, the gender gap was 7 percentage points, but the gap was larger in unmarried voters at 8 percent, larger in college-educated voters at 9 percent, and largest of all in voters over 60 at 11 percent (Center for American Women and Politics 2005).

Moreover, the U.S. Census reports that 46 percent of all women of voting age are not married, offering them as an important target of political campaigns; and unmarried women over 18 make up 55 percent of women not registered to vote, suggesting them as an important target for voter registration campaigns. In 2004, 71 percent of married women over 18 voted and 22 percent were not registered. For unmarried women over 18, 59 percent voted and 31 percent were not registered (Women's Voices/Women Vote 2007). Unmarried women are the fastest growing electoral group, and in 2008 had an important influence on presidential election results. That is, 47 percent of married women and 70 percent of unmarried women voted for Barack Obama in the presidential election; thus, unmarried women made up 27 percent of Obama's vote—more than the 18–29-year-old group at 23 percent, than African Americans at 23 percent, and than Latinos at 11 percent (Women's Voices/Women Vote 2008). Their political interests are driven by their economic status, especially their position as the only family earner. More than half have household incomes of less than $30,000. But we don't hear much about them. They and their preferences are not present in political discourse.

The point is that, in regard to women, most of the attention from the campaigns and the media has gone to one form or another of "moms," which takes attention away from other social statuses that are at least as important to how people vote. Studies show that race, religion, and geography, for example, are key indicators of how women and men vote (Marks 2000). Religious women tend to vote Republican because of issues such as abortion and homosexuality, while black women and highly educated nonreligious women tend to vote Democratic.

This attention to mothers and neglect of other women voters seems to suggest devotion to and concern for mothers; but it appears as though the more American political discourse claims this devotion, the more mothers are ignored. Early in the 2004 election Bush claimed about his middle initial that "W stands for women," and he touted new rights and freedoms for women in Afghanistan and Iraq. Kerry promised more funding for breast and cervical cancer research. But by the summer national party conventions the focus was on hunting with reporters watching, and the candidates shifted to macho issues such as gun ownership rights. Bush promoted his military response to terrorism, while Kerry touted his military experience. They spent far more time and energy on these rather than issues that would make women's daily lives easier, such as day care, after-school care, health insurance, equal pay, raising minimum wage, and flexible workplace.

"SOCCER MOMS"

The focus on "soccer moms" offers an example of what can happen when the cultural expectations of what mothers "should" do and how they "should" conduct themselves are applied outside the home. The label of "soccer mom" surfaced in the 1996 U.S. presidential election as part of the unending effort to understand and explain swing voters. But it ended up placing mothers on the margins of politics. The consequences of this are not only political: they are social and cultural, and have long-lasting effects that shore up traditional ways of looking at mothers and their life-space. This makes it easier for political candidates to ignore the difficulties in the daily lives of mothers rather than make policy proposals to solve those problems.

In political terms, "soccer moms" were loosely defined as mothers for whom motherhood is their lives. This is the ideal with which mothers are bombarded from all types of media, but the ideal and the category it describes took on a more direct political meaning and use with that label. The category usually refers to white, middle-class women voters who have minor children and drive minivans.

Miriam-Webster defines the term "soccer mom" as "a typically suburban mother who accompanies her children to their soccer games and is considered as part of a significant voting bloc or demographic group." "Soccer mom" suggests service as she drives her kids to practices and games, and passivity as she sits by the sidelines to watch and wait. Service and passivity are requirements of MotherSpace.

"Soccer moms" may be on the move but they still are confined—if less so to kitchens, still just as much to children. The label normalizes the practices at the same time that it reinforces the notion of mother-as-other in politics (Varvus 2000:200).[3] This and other political labels represent a reinvigoration of the insistence that mothers stay in their spaces, which in turn keeps them in their place or role. Every candidate wanted to persuade mothers they were "soccer moms," in effect packaging them in an identity that he then could court for votes. The term was used seriously and yet for the most part not taken seriously—the same impossible position mothers face when American politics and culture claim that motherhood is the most important role for women yet offer more support to corporations and other countries than to mothers. This political label was part of a campaign to tell mothers what they should be concerned about at the voting booth, but like other representations it was deployed in the service of reducing every mother to the mother who devotes her life to her children, reducing women to a maternal identity.

The emergence of "soccer mom" was especially troubling because suddenly, it seemed, women were transformed from potential wielders of great political power, during the "Year of the Woman" in 1992, to the aggregate of women, all mothers, who are defined by their relationships to their children—a backlash to that potential power. In fact, not much else beyond the label "soccer moms" was said about women during the 1996 election cycle, and even "soccer moms" later were determined to have made up as little as 4–5 percent of the electorate (Leo 1996).[4] Thus the media exaggerated the importance of "soccer moms" to the outcome of the election, disempowering nearly all women by stealing attention away from the variety of their concerns (Carroll 1999). This neglect was repeated in the 2004 election, and in the midterm elections of 2006, in which work and family issues were not present on the terms American women indicated they should be.

"SECURITY MOMS"

"Soccer moms" appeared on the scene briefly in the 2000 presidential election but were absent in the months preceding the 2004 election, at first perhaps suggesting that mothers had nothing of value to contribute to debates on war and terrorism. But mothers still could not be trusted to vote properly on their own. So, taking advantage of the Sept. 11, 2001, terror attacks, the new political label of the day became "security mom." This label also tried to tell mothers how they should feel and how they should vote. The security invoked here was home(land) security, a notion consistent with the material and discursive spaces of mothers and reinforcing MotherSpace. "Security moms" would vote to keep their children safe from terrorists at home—even if they seemed less concerned with war abroad. This term continues the discourse that mothers are responsible for the safety of their children, plays on their fears and feelings of helplessness, and urges them to act on those fears at the voting booth.

U.S. Sen. Joe Biden, D-Del., said after the 2002 mid-term elections, "When I was out campaigning last fall, this was all women wanted to talk about. Not schools, not prescription drugs. It was 'What are you doing to protect my kids against terrorists?'" (Klein 2003). Biden said Democrats lost their advantage with women in that election when they blocked the then–proposed Department of Homeland Security after Republicans sought looser union rules for hiring and firing. In fact, Republicans won nearly as many women's votes in that election as Democrats for the first time in more than a decade (Tumulty and Novak 2003:38). Karl Rove, George W. Bush's top political adviser at the time, claimed that Bush's success as the first Republican president in a century to have his party gain seats in an off-year election was in great part due to the votes of women with children under 18; many voted for Bush even though they disagreed with Republicans on many issues (Tumulty and Novak 2003:39). In the 2004 presidential election, both Democrats and Republicans chased the votes of "security moms." But Republicans apparently did a better job of persuading mothers that their children were in immediate danger and that the Republicans were the party that could keep them safe.

But just as with "soccer moms," with "security moms" the question arises of whether the political parties are listening to women or influencing women. A closer look at "security moms" shows that they were not swing voters at all but firmly in the Bush camp in 2004—despite the fact that he cut after-school programs, closed the White House Office on Women's Issues, pushed tax cuts that created shortages in state budgets that in turn forced cuts to public school funding across the country, and created insecurity around the world. Polls showed that "security moms" were not really a group of their own—they were white, married women with children who responded much the same to survey questions as white, married men with children (Morin and Balz 2004). They were not the former "soccer moms"—if in fact "soccer moms" were undecided and there-fore swing voters in 1996 and 2000. But this did not stop the use of convenient, insulting, and even silly labels that do not encourage analysis or understanding about women voters and what they want. Even when news reports across the country quoted political actors such as Democratic pollster Anna Greenberg debunking the idea of "security moms," the term surfaced again and again in media coverage of the campaign.[5]

In fact, even though press accounts and analysis continued to claim women would be the key to the 2004 election, articles about real women and their policy preferences seldom made front-page news.[6] The "tough guy" tone of the 2004 presidential race further emphasized security and marginalized other issues of women's daily lives (e.g., Lawrence and Kean 2004). In the words of Katha Pollitt in *The Nation* (2004): "In the contest between real men (Republicans) and girlie men (Democrats), women don't exist."

The political labeling of mothers appeals to mainstream media's demand for the catchy and new, and its penchant for the simplistic. But the consequences are dire: Reporters rely heavily on anecdotes when they use such labels, even when the anecdotes are belied by polls. Most reporters and much of the public seem to embrace the labels, made easier by their consistency with notions of Mother-Space. Because the circumstances surrounding elections change, future elections promise to offer still other political labels to court mothers' votes.

But if labels and discourses discipline mothers in directly political ways, they also make end runs in the attempt to keep mothers from thinking of them-selves as political beings. All of this is spatial and political, with implications for the everyday, because mothers are kept busy on care work in MotherSpace, which helps keep them out of political space and especially the kind of political activism that might solve some of the structural problems mothers face. When the powerful forces demanding intensive mothering are combined with the les-son that women do not have the "natural" qualities to be political beings, the message is clear: the political sphere and especially political leadership are not appropriate or available for mothers.

MILLIONS OF MOTHERS IN PROTEST

This is one of the reasons why, when mothers do find time to enter political space, they often take MotherSpace with them—or at least keep one foot in it. When a group of mothers outraged over children killed by drunk drivers or by handguns made collective protests, they went public with their "good mother" virtues virtually intact. Although the tone of their actions often was angry and indignant, and although they left home for several hours or even days to participate, they never left MotherSpace. There is no question that these movements achieved results, but usually at the cost of their location in political space. Although Mothers Against Drunk Driving is still running strong after more than twenty-five years, it has not dramatically increased the presence of mothers in political space writ large. After the Million Mom March, modeled after MADD, the mothers went home to MotherSpace, sent postcards to their representatives in Congress, and waited for the next election to vote.

MADD started in 1980 with a loosely assembled group it termed "brokenhearted mothers." Today it boasts that it is the largest crime victims' assistance organization in the world with more than three million members and supporters. Its mission—to stop drunken driving, support victims, and prevent underage drinking—has remained consistent and yielded results in state and federal laws and in attitudes toward drunk driving. The organization claims to be responsible for reducing the percentage of traffic fatalities related to alcohol, saving more than 300,000 lives.

The original organizers, calling attention to their motherhood and their motivation of personal tragedy, presented themselves as concerned only for the safety of children. They did not compete for political power, but were moved and tried to move others by emotion to agitate for stronger laws against drunk driving and harsher sentences against violators. The focus on emotion kept them in a particular place in politics since emotions do not belong in that masculine world. Their appeal was effective, evidenced by the presence of MADD in all fifty states, Puerto Rico, Guam, and Canada, as well as by the fact that MADD is far better known than the other national organizations fighting drunk driving even though they pursue similar goals in similar ways (McCarthy and Wolfson 1996:1071).[7] But in the semi-annual MADD magazine *Driven* (Davies 2005) celebrating the twenty-five-year anniversary in 2005, mothers received no more credit than fathers and other volunteers. Although it makes much of the first grieving mother who started the organization, it does not reflect on the particular role of mothers in the success of the organization.

Twenty years after the first mother founded MADD, another group of mothers wanted to emulate that movement to fight gun deaths of children. These mothers planned a march on Washington, D.C., on Mother's Day in 2000 to call for stricter gun control laws and requirements for child-safety locks on all guns. The Million Mom March, as it came to be known, often was billed as "soccer moms" for gun control.[8] Tapping into the "soccer mom" archetype offered a connection to all the stereotypes about mothers being like tigresses fighting for their cubs. Mothers and others took to the streets in the nation's capital and more than sixty other cities to demand a political response to school and urban shootings. Their call for tougher gun laws included requirements that all handgun owners be licensed, that all handguns be registered, and that there be a waiting period between purchase and possession.

Scheduling the march on Mother's Day invoked the spirit of that day's nineteenth-century origins, recalling women's participation in organized social reform movements that took them beyond their immediate concerns at home, especially improvements in sanitation and anti-war movements (Coontz 1992:152). This was to be a celebration of motherhood as a political force. Mother's Day "became trivialized and commercialized" later, when its meaning became associated with nuclear family relations in the home—MotherSpace—rather than public activity. The speeches accompanying Congress' adoption of Mother's Day in 1914 made it clear that mothers should embrace the care of their nuclear families and reject any public role in spaces beyond their homes (Coontz 1992:152–153). Although both the Million Mom March and MADD highlight the ways in which the personal is political and emphasize collective rather than isolated individual action, they do not do much to upset traditional gender and power relations.[9] These efforts share with the temperance movement a concern with family and children, but their maternal activism is more about exercising rights to help others than claiming rights for women themselves or furthering the goal of equality for women.[10]

Today the Million Mom March claims seventy-five chapters across the country. The "mom" in the name helps provide it with recognition, and its tag line on its Web site—"sensible gun laws, safe kids"—ensures that the organization will be associated with mothers and MotherSpace. But there has been virtually no attention to the women, usually mothers, killed by gun violence. And since 2001, when Million Mom March merged with the Brady Campaign to Prevent Gun Violence, it has had a smaller public presence even though it kept its own name.

When mothers put their gender and their maternity front and center as they label themselves, they use their motherhood consciously in a way that is beneficial to their immediate reform efforts. Once they call the stereotypes of motherhood into play, however, they claim that as their identity. They tap into cultural meanings of motherhood and MotherSpace, and act according to the rules and regulations for both. They use their relationship with their children to claim a right to call for reform. But at the same time they confine themselves to those efforts; they associate themselves inextricably with children and their identity as mothers; and they exclude less privileged mothers and women who are not mothers. If they have stepped out of traditional MotherSpace, it is only with one foot and only in service to children. When they claim motherhood as their legitimacy for protest, they exclude themselves from the larger aspects of political power and do little to promote commitments to democratic politics over the long term.

This raises the question of whether the reforms mothers have called for would be valued any differently if fathers or nonparents were the ones lobbying. Because others besides mothers may also desire such reforms, other bases of protest also could be effective. Using familiar stereotypes makes protesting mothers seem less of a threat and more easily accepted, perhaps. But at the same time it limits the possibilities. In saying, "Don't be afraid of me. I'm doing this out of mother-love and care for children," mothers exclude themselves from political power. Such a narrow view of political activity does nothing to put mothers in political space on the same terms as fathers and other non-mothers, and does little to promote commitments to democratic politics over the long term. As long as political discourse focuses on generic and mythic women voters and the narratives surrounding MotherSpace, and as long as mothers box themselves in as they package themselves, the variety of mothers who are voters or potential voters will be neglected or ignored—which reinforces their inequality and their location at the margins of political power.

NOTES

1. Political discourses continue the association of the definition of "good mothering" with intensive mothering, which demands that "good" mothers personally spend as much time, energy, and money as possible to produce "good" babies and children. Sharon Hays (1998) elaborates on the notion of intensive mothers: the contradiction is between the expectations of mothers at home of nurturing and selflessness and those at work of self-interest and profit motives. Susan Douglas and Meredith Michaels (2004) seem to mean much the same thing with their term "the new momism."

2. Although women in the South also have become less Democratic and more Republican, the rate of change for southern white men is far greater, according to Norrander. Northern men changed preferences at a slower rate than southern men, and northern women have not shown a pattern of change (Norrander 1999:575).

3. Varvus analyzed seventy-four newspaper articles and seven television news programs during the 1996 election cycle. Though she acknowledges the term has consequences for public perceptions of women and politics, she finds the trope has greater force as a commercial than as a political metaphor (2000:194). See also Hulbert 1996.

4. Other labels have been used for other groups perceived as swing voters—from "angry white men" in 1994, to "wired workers" and "waitress moms" in 1998, to "NASCAR dads" in 2004 (Breslau 2000). But none of these labels has caught on as much as "soccer moms," or been adopted in a wider ranger of uses.

5. Examples abound of efforts to debunk the myth of "security moms"; for example, see Sweet 2004; Goodman 2004; Teixeira 2004. See also Greenberg 2006.

6. For example, Andrew Kohut, director of the Pew Research Center for People and the Press, said, "The way women resolve their conflicting opinions of these two candidates will be the story of this election" (Allen 2004).

7. These authors offer no gender analysis of the varying rates of success of the organizations that fight drunken driving. The other organizations are Remove Intoxicated Drivers (RID), the National Commission Against Drunk Driving, and the Century Council, which is funded by a consortium representing the liquor industry. A Gallop Poll in 2000 showed 97 percent of the public recognized the name MADD (Davies 2005).

8. For example, Newsweek headlined its national affairs coverage on May 15, 2000, "Don't mess with the moms: The 'soccer moms' are rallying for gun control—and their march on Washington will echo in November" (135.20:28).

9. Janice Nathanson (2008) uses these three standards to determine whether maternal activism is feminist by definition. Using Nathanson's litmus test, MMM and MADD make some strides in the first two but not the third.

10. Janet Zollinger Giele (1995) found that both the maternal activism of the temperance movement and the equal rights feminism of the suffrage movement arose because of the strain between traditional expectations for women and the changing realities of their lives. Both sought to change women's roles so that they would gain more freedom. Thus both movements were necessary for the gains that women achieved. The focus of today's maternal activism is protecting children and others.

WORKS CITED

Allen, Mike. 2004. Bush makes pitch to "security moms." Washington Post, Sept. 18, A14.

Breslau, Karen. 2000. National Affairs: Wooing "wired workers": Move over, soccer moms. Pollsters have discovered a class of tech-savvy suburban voters who could turn the election. Newsweek, Aug. 28, 28.

Carroll, Susan S. 1999. The disempowerment of the gender gap: Soccer moms and the 1996 elections. *PS: Political Science and Politics* 32.1:7–11.

Center for American Women and Politics (CAWP). 2005. Fact sheet: "The gender gap: Voting choices in presidential elections." Eagleton Institute of Politics, Rutgers University. http://www.cawp.rutgers.edu/research/topics/documents/GGPresVote.pdf (accessed Oct. 6, 2006).

Coontz, Stephanie. 1992. *The Way We Never Were: American Families and the Nostalgia Trap*. New York: Basic Books.

Davies, Lauria. 2005. Twenty-five years of saving lives. *Driven*. http://www.madd.org (accessed Oct. 5, 2006).

Douglas, Susan, and Meredith Michaels. 2004. *The Mommy Myth: The Idealization of Motherhood and How It Has Undermined Women*. New York: Free Press.

Giele, Janet Zollinger. 1995. *Two Paths to Women's Equality: Temperance, Suffrage, and the Origins of Modern Feminism*. New York: Twayne.

Goodman, Ellen. 2004. The myth of security moms. *Boston Globe*, Oct. 7.

Greenberg, Anna. 2006. Moving beyond the gender gap. In *Get This Party Started: How Progressives Can Fight Back and Win*, ed. Matthew Kerbe. New York: Rowman and Littlefield.

Hays, Sharon. 1998. *The Cultural Contradictions of Motherhood*. New Haven: Yale University Press.

Hulbert, Ann. 1996. Angels in the infield. *New Republic* 215.21 (Nov. 18): 16.

Kaufmann, Karen M., and John R. Petrocik. 1999. The changing politics of American men: Understanding the sources of the gender gap. *American Journal of Political Science* 43.3:864–887.

Klein, Joe. 2003. How soccer moms became security moms. *Time* 161.7 (Feb. 17): 23.

Lawrence, Jill, and Judy Keen. 2004. Election is turning into a duel of manly men. *USA Today*, Sept. 21, 1.

Leo, John. 1996. A great story never told. *U.S. News and World Report* 21.22 (Dec. 2): 24.

Marks, Alexandra. 2000. Women's vote: Elusive prize in election 2000. *Christian Science Monitor*, April 13.

McCarthy, John D., and Mark Wolfson. 1996. Resource mobilization by local social movement organizations: Agency, strategy, and organization in the movement against drinking and driving. *American Sociological Review* 61.6:1071.

Merriam-Webster Online Dictionary. http://www.m-w.com/dictionary/soccer%20mom (accessed Sept. 20, 2006).

Morin, Richard, and Dan Balz. 2004. "Security mom" bloc proves hard to find. *Washington Post*, Oct. 1, A5.

Mothers Against Drunk Driving. "MADD." http://www.madd.org (accessed Oct. 5, 2006).

Nathanson, Janice. 2008. Maternal activism: How feminist is it? In Feminist Mothering, ed. Andrea O'Reilly, 243–256. Albany: State University of New York Press

Norrander, Barbara. 1999. The evolution of the gender gap. *Public Opinion Quarterly* 63.4:566–63.4:566–576.

O'Reilly, Andrea, ed. 2008. *Feminist Mothering.* Albany: State University of New York Press.

Pollitt, Katha. 2004. The girlie vote. *The Nation,* Sept. 27.

Schlesinger, Mark, and Caroline Heldman. 2001. Gender gap or gender gaps? New perspectives on support for government action and policies. *Journal of Politics* 63.1:59–92.

Smith, Liz. 2006. Sharon Stone, Madonna share ideas on Hillary Clinton. *Baltimore Sun,* March 27.

Sweet, Lynn. 2004. Courting the ladies. *Chicago Sun-Times,* Oct. 13.

Teixeira, Ruy. 2004. The myth of the security mom. *Public Opinion Watch* (N.Y.: Century Foundation), Sept. 29.

Toner, Robin. 2006. Women wage key campaigns for Democrats. *New York Times,* March 24, A1.

Tumulty, Karen, and Viveca Novak. 2003. Goodbye, soccer mom. Hello, security mom. *Time Europe* 161.24 (June 16): 26–39.

Varvus, Mary Douglas. 2000. From women of the year to "soccer moms": The case of the incredible shrinking women. *Political Communication* 17.2:193–213.

Women's Voices, Women Vote. Women's voices, women vote. http://www.wvwv.org (accessed Oct. 6, 2006).

Racially Conscious Mothering in the "Colorblind" Century

TWENTY-ONE

CAMILLE WILSON COOPER

Implications for African American Motherwork

I am the dark girl who crossed the wide sea
Carrying in my body the seed of the free . . .
I am the one who labored as a slave,
Beaten and mistreated for the work
that I gave . . .
Three hundred years in the deepest South:
But God put a song and a prayer in
my mouth.
God put a dream like steel in my soul.
Now through my children I'm reaching
the goal . . .
Oh, my dark children, may my dreams
and my prayers
Impel you forever up the great stairs—
For I will be with you till no white brother
Dares keep down the children of the
Negro mother.
—Langston Hughes
(excerpts from "The Negro Mother," 1931)[1]

The twenty-first century is filled with paradoxes. The coexistence of racial transcendence and racial regression in U.S. social life is one such paradox that greatly affects African American mothering. African American mothers are raising children in a society that provides an unprecedented amount of social and economic opportunities, yet U.S. society remains undermined by systemic racism. Still, both elite powerholders and mainstream citizens question the salience of race and assert colorblind ideologies. In the light of this race-related paradox, this paper considers three central questions: What does the ostensibly color-blind twenty-first century, in which many African Americans experience both racial transgression and racial regression, mean for African American mothers? How may living in an era influenced by a significant amount of whites questioning the salience of race alter how African American mothers make meaning of their race-related identities and experiences? And, do colorblind ideologies and politics present opportunities for African American families to ascend the "great stairs" of equality, or do they veil racial oppression?

To address the questions above, the author will contrast the colorblind culture of the twenty-first-century United States with the racially conscious traditions of African American mothers. These traditions are closely tied to quests for racial liberation, cultural pride, and community uplift. The author will consider the extent to which these African American mothering traditions should be sustained given the contemporary milieu, and she will describe some key opportunities and dilemmas that a nation aspiring to be colorblind presents to African American mothers and their families. Patricia Hill Collins' feminist conceptualization of *motherwork* will inform the discussion, as will current events, fiction, narrative data, and Bonilla-Silva's theories of colorblind racism. The author concludes that colorblind politics project a dangerous illusion of social amelioration in the United States that counters the lived realities of African American mothers and threatens the social advancement of African American families and communities. Thus, racially conscious motherwork remains an essential approach to childrearing and political resistance.

THE PARADOX OF RACIAL TRANSCENDENCE AND RACIAL REGRESSION

The twenty-first century is remarkably unique given the widespread political, social, and educational claims that U.S. society is now "colorblind" (Paumgarten 2007; Rosenberg 2004). The new millennium has ushered in an era where whites are comfortable accusing African Americans of "playing the race card" when the topic of racism is broached. High-profile achievers like African American media mogul Oprah Winfrey are often exalted by mainstream white Americans as proof that racism is no longer a formidable obstacle—some even assert that racism no longer exists (Bell 1992; Bonilla-Silva 2003; D'Souza 1995). Most notably, Barack Obama's successful bid to become the first African American U.S. president has fueled the nation's *colorblind* debate.

President Obama's election is undoubtedly a watershed event in U.S. politics, one that signals increasing cross-cultural alliances and the shattering of many racial barriers. The United States, however, is still a nation affected by inequality and systemic racism. African American youth, for instance, face the highest rates of poverty and inadequate healthcare access: African American boys in particular are more likely to be imprisoned than university educated (Children's Defense Fund 2007). Therefore, the inescapable paradox of the United States is that while so much racial inequity has improved in recent history, so much remains unchanged. African Americans as a whole enjoy more freedom, better socioeconomic conditions, more financial resources, and greater educational opportunities in the U.S. than ever before; these are phenomenal accomplishments, gained through struggle and sacrifice (Bell 1992; Ladner 1998). Still racism is endemic and it impacts the lives of African American families in both subtle and explicit ways.

For example, in 2007 African American communities became morally outraged after learning that white youth in a Louisiana high school had hung a noose on a schoolyard tree, thereby evoking the savagery of racial lynching to intimidate African American students and deter them from socially congregating around that tree at lunchtime. The incident sparked racially motivated violence among white and black students at the school. That same year, a nationally syndicated white disc jockey publicly insulted African American female college students who were playing in the national championship game by referring to them as "nappy-headed, hard-core hos"—a racist and misogynist comment he defended by claiming it was a joke (Paumgarten 2007). Both of these incidents drew national media attention that led to public protests and vigorous dialogue about the status of race relations in the United States. Many whites characterized the schoolyard and broadcast events as offensive, but rare, racial incidents. African American communities, however, stressed that these episodes were emblematic of continued racial intolerance.

The incidents signaled to African American mothers that the children they send to public schools and universities to be educated to achieve the American dream of prosperity can still be racially degraded. So, just as African American mothers can dream of their children becoming the next Oprah Winfrey or President Barack Obama, there are steady reminders that African Americans seeking opportunity must continue to combat racism. A major paradox of the twenty-first century, therefore, is the coexistence of racial transcendence and racial regression. Despite racist realities, colorblind ideologies persist and they inevitably affect African American mothers' consciousness and meaning-making. This paradox places African American mothers in a position of cautious optimism. Hence, many mothers are hopeful for continued racial progress, yet they are also aware of lingering risks. Colorblind ideologies and politics further complicate the mothers' quandary.

QUESTIONING THE SALIENCE OF RACE AND COLORBLIND IDEOLOGIES

For more than three centuries African American mothers have upheld traditions of mothering for racial liberation, cultural pride, and community uplift in the context of both the proliferation of systemic racism and their desire to maintain the strengths of a vibrant and resilient culture. This tradition of racially conscious mothering goes against the grain of current political, social, and educational trends that promote a colorblind consciousness. Indeed, the 1990s brought about a political backlash toward corrective, race-based social and educational policies like affirmative action and mandatory school integration that aimed to advance racial equality (Bell 1992; Bonilla-Silva 2003). This trend has continued into the twenty-first century.

In 2007, for instance, the U.S. Supreme Court banned the use of racially based student assignments in voluntary desegregation plans aimed at increasing diversity and decreasing racial segregation.[2] For many, this historical decision undermined the spirit of *Brown vs. Board of Education,* the seminal U.S. Supreme Court case that mandated school desegregation in 1954. So, at the start of the twenty-first century, the nation's most esteemed political body sent a widespread message that race and racism should no longer matter in political, social, and educational spheres. As Theodore Shaw, a nationally prominent civil rights attorney, stated, "There's an ideological war going on here with respect to not only the place of race in this country, but whether we should be able to do anything to address racial inequality on a voluntary basis" (Totenburg and Kaufman 2007).

In his book *Racism Without Racists* (2003), Eduardo Bonilla-Silva explains why so much of the white majority in the United States dismisses the importance of race-related issues. Bonilla-Silva asserts that calls for colorblind consciousness and the assault on racialized discourse, policies, and political movements link back to the classic liberal ideals of autonomy, individualism, competition, and meritocracy upon which the U.S. government was founded. Bonilla-Silva also identifies four interpretive frameworks that recur as part of what he calls "colorblind racism" (2003:7). The first two are biological inferiority and cultural deviancy, interpretations of people of color that have framed the perspectives of many white Americans, and they have fueled blatantly racist ideologies and oppression. In addition, such frameworks have shaped research, policy, and popular perceptions that depict African American families and African American mothers as pathological (Moynihan 1965; Dodson 2007).

The expression of blatantly racist perspectives has declined over many decades due to the rise of sincerely held equity-oriented ideologies as well as the increase of superficially demonstrated social behavior that is deemed "politically correct." Still, Bonilla-Silva explains that the two other seemingly benign colorblind frameworks—race minimalization and abstract liberalism—are more prevalent, disguised, and insidious. He and others note that the politics of racial minimalization negate the salience of race and the prevalence of racism. This leads many whites to assert that people of color, such as African Americans, can now function on an even playing field and that they are exaggerating or being hypersensitive when they pinpoint racism's continual effects (Bell 1992; Bonilla-Silva 2003). Drawing on racial minimalization arguments, some whites openly oppose the types of race-based policies mentioned above and claim that such policies provide unwarranted and unjust preferential treatment to African Americans and other people of color. Abstract liberalism is anchored in similar individualistic ideals. Abstract liberalists reject implementing social policies that mandate methods to achieve equal opportunity, and they regard such legislation as intrusive government intervention that impinges on their freedom.

According to Bonilla-Silva, each of the four colorblind interpretive frameworks is a form of racism that whites can employ to ignore or deflect structural inequality by overemphasizing the power of self-determination. He argues that these frameworks, which infuse mainstream social norms and politics, are evidence that whites have "developed emotional attachments to whites as their primary social group and negative stereotypes about minorities, and have not developed the skills necessary to navigate multicultural situations" (2003:109). The increase of racial minimalization and abstract liberalism also reflects many whites' emotional attachment to viewing themselves as egalitarian and nonracist despite their subconscious racist ideologies and actions.

Bonilla-Silva's conceptualization of colorblind frameworks aligns with feminist educator bell hooks' contention that many whites tend to view all things related to whites as universal and normal, while seeing the " 'blackness' " of African Americans as separate, racially specific, and often deviant. She asserts that this is a form of "white supremacist thought" that perpetuates racism (2003:39). hooks further points to the interrelated and mutually influencing nature of racist ideology, individual discriminatory acts, and institutional and societal oppression that is endemic in U.S. society.

Colorblind ideologies and politics are also found in public education arenas among some well-intentioned white educators who aim to promote educational equity. These educators explain that they are hesitant to discuss race or cultural difference for fear of perpetuating stereotypes, making white students feel guilty about racism, exacerbating any negative, self-internalized views that students of color hold, and intensifying any hostile cross-cultural relationships (Evans 2007; Rosenberg 2004). Nevertheless, critical scholars assert that colorblind approaches in education, like those described by Bonilla-Silva, prove problematic. They reduce educators' ability to be responsive to the culturally specific needs of African American students and families, and they prompt educators to overlook or minimize racism and cultural difference (Evans 2007; hooks 2003; Ladson-Billings 1998). Empirical studies have also found that colorblind approaches compel educators to avoid understanding white privilege, remain unaware to the prevalence and/or effects of discriminatory practices, and perpetuate inequities that directly harm African American families and others. Consequently, many educators become unwittingly complicit in socially reproducing structural racism (Evans 2007; Rosenberg 2004).

Together, calls for colorblind ideologies and politics and the increasing passage of colorblind social policies are shaping the contextual environments in which African American mothers and families live, work, and are educated. They are also evolving into strong social forces that conflict with racially conscious African American mothering traditions. Thus, colorblind ideologies and politics complicate how African American mothers make meaning of their race-related identities and experiences.

THE RACIALLY CONSCIOUS MEANING-MAKING OF AFRICAN AMERICAN MOTHERS

The colorblind ideologies that are heavily influencing contemporary U.S. politics and popular culture implicitly call into question the need for racially conscious identities and values. Fiction, narrative data, and feminist theorizing, however, suggest that racially conscious mothering remains an important form of political resistance. Resistance is an inextricable part of African American mothers' identity, experiences, and meaning-making. Both slave narratives and novels like Lalita Tademy's *Cane River* (1998) illustrate how African American mothering became resistance when the first African slave woman birthed a baby on U.S. soil and attempted to nurture it to live in freedom versus bondage (Crew, Goodman, and Gates 2003; Davis 1983; O'Reilly 2005). Mothers' urges to counteract oppression are driven by the constant experience of having their efforts to raise self-loving, proud, independent, respected, and *free* children socially assaulted. This experience also shapes most African American mothers' maternal identity (Collins 1994; Davis 1983; Ladner 1998). Mothering in the face of racism can lead African American mothers to more intensely resist inequity or to sink into unshakeable despair. History has shown that resistance has been a much more prevalent response, and that most African American mothers are freedom fighters in addition to being bearers of culture, identity, and love (Collins 2000; Cooper 2007; Davis 1983; hooks 1981).

Feminist theorists link the liberatory and/or empowering nature of African American mothering to the positionality and ideological orientation of most African American women. Black feminist theorists particularly contend that the legacy of African Americans' social domination has fueled a culture of resistance into which most African American women are socialized. It is this culture that inspires African American women to fight for personal empowerment and social change, and this fight typically extends to their mothering. Moreover, despite the intradiversity of African American women, feminist theorists suggest that African American mothers draw upon a set of shared values and a common heritage to construct their mothering role (Collins 1994; Cooper 2005; Ladner 1998). Moreover, these mothers' values, heritage, and resistance are deeply linked to their racially conscious meaning-making.

Davis discusses African American women's roles during slavery to contextualize the resistance function of their mothering. For nearly two hundred fifty years, African American women fought to exert sovereignty over their mind, body, and children in the face of slavery. Davis notes that U.S. slave women were considered property, human breeders and sex objects for the economic gain and physical exploitation of white men and U.S. society; thus, their survival and self-care were acts of individual resistance. African American slave mothers also committed themselves to working for group survival. These women's liberatory mothering evolved into conscious strategies for building social capital and uplifting African Americans as a whole (Collins 2000; Ladner 1998). At the start of the twenty-first century, studies show that this praxis remains an essential part of African American childrearing, cultural preservation, and social advancement (Cooper 2007; Suizzo, Robinson, and Pahlke 2008). It further constitutes a form of racially conscious mothering called *motherwork*.

Collins asserts that racial/ethnic women's motherwork reflects their unique concerns about their children's survival, lack of power, and their complex racial and ethnic identities. She explains that the motherwork of women of color, in contrast to white women's mothering, responds to "the tensions inherent in trying to foster a meaningful racial identity in children within a society that denigrates people of color" (1994:57). Collins further states:

> Their children (those of racial ethnic women) must first be taught to survive in systems that oppress them. Moreover this survival must not come at the expense of self-esteem. Thus a dialectical relationship exists between systems of racial oppression designed to strip subordinated groups of a sense of personal identity and a sense of collective peoplehood, and the cultures of resistance extant in various racial ethnic groups that resist the oppression. For women of color, motherwork for identity occurs at this critical juncture. (1994:57)

Other scholars suggest that African American women's motherwork forges a mental, psychological, and spiritual space that shapes their maternal identity, which then informs their self-concept. For example, O'Reilly explains how Toni Morrison depicts motherhood as a "site of liberation and self-realization" via the African American mothering of many of her fictional characters (2005:126). She describes Morrison as illustrating the "cultural significance and political purpose" of motherwork, which "is the way by which black people are empowered to survive and resist" (125). Research further shows that African American women, including nonbiological mothers, have performed motherwork in homes, schools, communities, and civic institutions, and within political protest movements (Collins 1994; Cooper 2005, 2007; hooks 1981; Payne 1995).

One could further associate African American motherwork with O'Reilly and Porter's notion of "transformative power," which is a positive and creative force that brings about social agency (2005:4). One must be careful, however, not to over-romanticize African American mothers' power positions or empowerment processes. As Collins explains, African American mothers have tried to exert power while facing the sociopolitical bind of possessing tremendous power in the private sphere of their homes and being relatively powerless in greater society, where their voices are often muted, ignored, or denigrated, and their influence constrained. This is a reality that even well-educated African American mothers who enjoy economic privilege and professional success must face, given their racial positionalities. For instance, African American sociologist Joyce Ladner reflected on her mothering experiences and stated:

> Keeping my son alive long enough to see adulthood has been a mammoth task in and of itself, because he like many other middle-class children, has grown up in the shadow of the ghetto. He has come of age in full view of police officers who assumed that because he was black and male, he must also be ready to commit a crime. I have lain awake many nights until I finally heard the key turn in the lock. Only then did I know that he was safe—until the next time he went out. I have vacillated between protecting him like a mother hen and allowing him to grow and mature into adulthood free and unfettered. It hasn't been easy. (1998:153)

This paradox of simultaneously exerting power while experiencing powerlessness through one's mothering can injure mothers' psyches and sense of self-efficacy (Collins 1994; O'Reilly and Porter 2005). Engaging in racially conscious mothering via motherwork can also come with great struggle, fear, and sacrifice. Moreover, while racially conscious mothering is an enduring tradition, not all African American mothers pursue or succeed in such efforts. Some African American mothers are disconnected from resistance efforts, and they may lack the self-love, hope, role models, education, and/or social support that can motivate and assist them in carrying out motherwork. As hooks explains, "When people talk about the 'strength' of Black women . . . they ignore the reality that to be strong in the face of oppression is not the same as overcoming oppression, that endurance is not to be confused with transformation" (1981:6). Still, motherwork and its racial liberation, cultural pride, and community uplift objectives can be transformative. Motherwork is also a liberatory praxis, fueled by race-related meaning-making, that is countercultural to the colorblind aims of U.S. society in the twenty-first century.

MORE EQUALITY YET CONTINUED OPPRESSION IN THE UNITED STATES: IMPLICATIONS FOR AFRICAN AMERICAN MOTHERWORK

This paper opened by posing three central questions related to the future of racially conscious mothering. The first question asked how African Americans' experiences with both racial transgression and regression in the ostensibly colorblind twenty-first century influences African American mothers. The answer is mixed. On one hand, the social and political advancements of recent history, such as the election of the first African American U.S. president, mean that African American mothers can raise their children with an expanded amount of optimism and hope. On the other hand, race still matters and racism still exists. So, for many African American mothers, maintaining hope that their child can prosper without encountering defeating barriers does not mean upholding a colorblind, individualistic ethos. To the contrary, embracing communal values and promoting community uplift rather than individualism will likely remain essential mothering strategies—strategies that are steeped in racial consciousness. These strategies constitute acts of care that benefit African Americans and all others. Indeed, African American motherwork and organized freedom movements have strived to carve out the political and social space where African Americans can actualize their human potential and optimally contribute to society. So as African Americans prosper, their hope, communal bonds, and continued work toward progress remains. At the same time, lingering racial inequality prevents most African American mothers from becoming socially complacent when it comes to engaging in political resistance.

The second question asked how will many white Americans' increasing doubts about the salience of race alter the ways in which African American mothers make meaning of their race-related identity and experiences. The answer is "very little." While colorblind ideologies presume that racism can no longer prevent African Americans from attaining wealth, power, or even the U.S. presidency, social realities imply the opposite. For every middle-class, well-educated, and successful African American, there are thousands more living in poverty, lacking health care and quality education, or imprisoned (Children's Defense Fund 2007). Thus, the political resistance and liberatory mothering performed via motherwork remain a necessity in the twenty-first century. In a 2000 interview with the author, an African American mother of five reflected on how she teaches and socializes her children to learn and resist. She stated:

> It's almost like I want to say to them [her children] what the Jews say constantly to their kids, "Don't ever forget!" This is reality, this is what they're capable of (the white establishment), and they're still capable of this. They just do it in a more subtle and sophisticated way. You know, that's why you need to get your education, get as much as you can, because your education will be what will be your guard, your weapon in life, you know, they can't take that from you, get all the education, be self-sufficient, take care of yourself! (Cooper 2007:499)

This mother's statement speaks to fact that most African American mothers know that their families remain targets of racist images, discourse, and actions. Hence, African American children still need "an unshakeable basic belief in their worth" and human dignity that is not divorced from a positive racial identity (Ladner 1998:19).

The third and final question that guided this essay asked if colorblind ideologies and politics offer equal opportunities to African American families or veil racial oppression: the latter effect seems most accurate. Colorblind ideology and politics present African American mothers, and most everyone else, a luring but naïve illusion of social amelioration. Colorblind ideologies and politics of contemporary U.S. society also collide with more than four hundred years of history and the enduring truths of African American mothers. These truths reveal that racism is still prevalent in U.S. society. Twenty-first-century racism is less visible than the explicit acts of racial hate that were prominent in centuries past. Still, in many ways racism is more insidious now because of colorblind ideologies and the failure of some to see inequity. So, turning a blind eye to the culturally relevant history, attributes, resiliency, and challenges of African Americans is not a desirable option. Both scholarly notions of motherwork and conventional motherwit suggest that African American youth cannot afford to be broadsided by racism, nor can they afford to lack cultural pride (Collins 2000; Collins 1994; Ladner 1998).

Altogether, the advent of wide-sweeping and increasingly accepted colorblind politics in the twenty-first century leaves African American mothers to negotiate their history, identities, and mothering goals in new ways. Conservative cultural critics, mainstream media pundits, and even some equity-oriented advocates frame the rise of colorblind ideologies and politics as social progress (Paumgarten 2007; Bonilla-Silva 2003). But, as African American mothers confront the paradox of rearing children in an era of both prosperity and peril, they cannot risk adopting an abstract liberalist view that minimizes the saliency of race. True progress has come with the growth of cross-cultural alliances in the United States, the rise of African American leaders, and the ability of many whites to see beyond color and value the human worth, character, and achievements of African Americans and other ethnic minorities. These advancements are signs of racial transcendence, not indicators of the racial invisibility that colorblind ideologies and politics promote.

African American mothers, like all mothers, possess the power to create, influence, change, and resist. Their power, however, is distinctly exuded for liberatory purposes, given their unique history of bondage and oppression that is linked to the legacy of U.S. slavery and to the racism that still persists. Thus, inherent in the maternal motivations, practices, and meaning-making of African American mothers is the hope that despite any oppressive conditions that hinder them and their families, they can help their families and their communities become physically, socially, and emotionally free.

The assault on racially conscious discourse, identities, and politics in twenty-first-century U.S. society contradicts the tradition of racially conscious African American mothering. Whether it is the media framing a colorblind political campaign or public educators asserting colorblind perspectives in a classroom, negating the salience of race and the racially based experiences of African Americans demeans the history of a people and a nation. Furthermore, embracing colorblind politics that seek to squelch racially conscious political resistance in the face of continued racism jeopardizes the transformative power of liberatory mothering. Liberatory mothering practices known as motherwork have helped African Americans survive and reap significant social and political gains. Ironically, these are the gains that many whites pinpoint to deny racism's perniciousness. The reality and meaning-making of African American mothers, however, overwhelming suggest that race and racism still matter. It is therefore essential that African American motherwork—while more hopeful—also remain racially conscious in the twenty-first century and beyond.

NOTES

1. Taken from Rampersad and Roessel 1994.
2. This is the U.S. Supreme Court case *Parents Involved in Community Schools v. Seattle School District No. 1 et al.*, 05-908.

WORKS CITED

Bell, Derrick. 1992. *Faces at the Bottom of the Well: The Permanence of Racism*. New York: Basic Books.

Bonilla-Silva, Eduardo. 2003. *Racism Without Racists: Color-Blind Racism and the Persistence of Racial Inequality in the United States*. New York: Rowman and Littlefield.

Children's Defense Fund. 2007. *America's Cradle to Prison Pipeline: Summary Report*. Washington, D.C.: Children's Defense Fund.

Collins, Patricia Hill. 1994. Shifting the center: Race, class, and feminist theorizing about motherhood. In *Mothering: Ideology, Experience, and Agency*, ed. Evelyn Nakano Glenn, Grace Chang, and Linda R. Forcey, 45–65. New York: Routledge.

——. 2000. *Black Feminist Thought: Knowledge, Consciousness, and the Politics of Empowerment*. 2nd ed. New York: Routledge.

Cooper, Camille Wilson. 2005. School choice and the standpoint of African American mothers: Considering the power of positionality. *Journal of Negro Education* 74.2:174–189.

——. 2007. School choice as "motherwork": Valuing African American women's educational advocacy and resistance. *International Journal of Qualitative Studies in Education* 20.5:491–512.

Crew, Spencer, Cynthia Goodman, and Henry Louis Gates Jr. 2003. *Unchained Memories: Readings from the Slave Narratives*. New York: Bulfinch.

Davis, Angela Y. 1983. *Women, Race, and Class*. New York: Vintage Books.

Dodson, Jualynne E. 2007. Conceptualizations and research of African American family life in the United States: Some thoughts. In *Black Families*, ed. Harriette P. McAdoo, 51–68. Thousands Oaks, Calif.: Sage.

D'Souza, Dinesh. 1995. *The End of Racism: Principles for a Multiracial Society*. New York: Free Press.

Evans, Andrea E. 2007. Changing faces: Suburban school responses to demographic change. *Education and Urban Society* 39.3:315–348.

hooks, bell. 1981. *Ain't I a Woman?: Black Women and Feminism*. Boston: South End Press.

——. 2003. *Teaching Community: A Pedagogy of Hope*. New York: Routledge.

Ladner, Joyce A. 1998. *Timeless Values for African American Families: The Ties That Bind*. New York: Wiley.

Ladson-Billings, Gloria. 1998. Just what is critical race theory, and what is it doing in a nice field like education? *International Journal of Qualitative Studies in Education* 11.1:7–24.

Moynihan, Daniel P. 1965. *The Negro Family: The Case for National Action*. Washington, D.C.: Office of Planning and Research, Department of Labor.

O'Reilly, Andrea. 2005. (Mis)conceptions: The paradox of maternal power and loss in Toni Morrison's *The Bluest Eye* and *Paradise*. In *Motherhood: Power and Oppression*, ed. Andrea O'Reilly, Marie Porter, and Patricia Short, 125–136. Toronto: Women's Press.

O'Reilly, Andrea, and Marie Porter. 2005. Introduction. In *Motherhood: Power and Oppression*, ed. Andrea O'Reilly, Marie Porter, and Patricia Short, 1–22. Toronto: Women's Press.

Paumgarten, Nick. 2007. Imus versus Imus. *New Yorker*, April 23.

Payne, Charles M. 1995. *I've Got the Light of Freedom: The Organizing Tradition and the Mississippi Freedom Struggle.* Berkeley: University of California Press.

Rampersad, Arnold, and David Roessel, eds. 1994. *The Collected Poems of Langston Hughes.* New York: Vintage Books.

Rosenberg, Pearl M. 2004. Color blindness in teacher education: An optical delusion. In *Off White: Readings on Power, Privilege, and Resistance,* ed. Michelle Fine, Lois Wies, Linda Powell Pruitt, and April Burns, 257–272. 2nd ed. New York: Routledge.

Suizzo, Marie-Anne, Courtney Robinson, and Erin Pahlke. 2008. African American mothers' socialization beliefs and goals with young children: Themes of history, education, and collective independence. *Journal of Family Issues* 29:287–316.

Tademy, Lalita. 2001. *Cane River.* New York: Warner Books.

Totenberg, Nina, and Wendy Kaufman. 2007. Supreme Court squashes school deseg-regation. National Public Radio, June 29. http://www.npr.org/templates/story/story .php?storyId=11598422 (accessed Feb. 3, 2008).

It Takes a (Virtual) Village | **TWENTY-TWO**

Mothering on the Internet | MAY FRIEDMAN

For sheer life-changing terror, there are few experiences that rival new motherhood. At a recent baby shower, I gave a card with the message "See you on the other side." My friend called a month later, the parent of a brand-new baby, and said, "I see what you mean." What precisely is it about mothering that makes it so inaccessible to those who have not yet crossed the divide? In all the wealth of words that we write about motherhood, in all the information we share, many mothers are nonetheless hungrily seeking out more information, more support, more of a community. In the twenty-first century, many such mothers are finding this support on the World Wide Web.

Initially, the appeal of the Internet for new (and, indeed, more seasoned) mothers might appear illogical. Childbirth and early mothering are arguably the most corporeal of tasks; one cannot think, read, or rationalize a reluctant baby into eating or sleeping. Yet nonetheless, this noncorporeal realm, where words are divorced from the physical manifestations of their makers, provides tremendous solace and comfort to millions of mothers worldwide. With that support comes the potential for uglier manifestations of maternal support: the reification of patriarchal motherhood (Rich 1976); the potential for groupthink that quashes dissonant views; and the possibility of a highly skewed use of this new tool of communication in the guise of the "digital divide" (Kennedy 2007; Herring et al. 1994, among others), separating those with access to information technology from those without. Despite the very real concerns present in understanding the ways that maternity is performed on the Internet, however, such an analysis *must* take place. Regardless of what seedy underbelly is revealed in looking at the Web (and the sheer enormity of the Internet promises seediness of epic proportions), the Internet is here, and regardless of questions of both content and access, it has changed the ways that all people communicate. Perhaps anticipating an Internet age, Donna Haraway prophetically wrote, "We are all cyborgs now" (Haraway 1991:150). Harp and Tremayne suggest that "the Internet . . . should be described within the context of both its potential and its reality, and not simply romanticized for its possibilities" (Harp and Tremayne 2006:249).

Looking at the evolution of motherhood through the lens of the Web, then, is a critically important task. In this essay I will argue that in the twenty-first century the virtual frontier alters the landscape of maternity, presenting new technologies as both sites of resistance and potential bolsters to patriarchal motherhood. This analysis of contemporary motherhood online will begin by looking at the merits and limitations of maternal presence on the Internet and will go on to consider the ways that diversity, identity, community, and activism are taken up within maternal cyberspace.

THREADS OF THE WEB:
CONSIDERING THE PROS AND CONS

To ask whether the Internet is empowering or restrictive to mothers is facile: like any sort of interaction, online conversations, communities, and activities have the capacity for redemption, the ability to keep the status quo, or, on a more sinister level, the facility to create more disturbing and misogynist pictures of motherhood. To say that the Internet has the same capacity for good and evil as any other forum is not, however, to argue that ideas and themes are taken up on the Web in the same ways that interactions occur in the real world. There are multiple unique characteristics to the Internet that make interactions within this forum quite different from those in-person conversations and relationships. In considering mothering as both action and artifact online, a closer examination must be made of mothering on the Internet and its negative and positive characteristics.

The ability to transcend geographical distance has allowed communities to flourish in ways that would have been previously impossible (Drentea and Moren-Cross 2005). Self-publishing software has made it remarkably easy for an increasingly wide range of people to assume an authorial voice in the form of blogs (Kennedy 2007). Individuals can assume anonymity, which may encourage freer communication, especially in the very loaded and provocative realm of new parenting (Madge and O'Connor 2006). For women with non-normative social locations (such as same-sex parents or differently abled parents), the ability to create community independent of physical space is a tremendous boon. Furthermore, the absence of body contact minimizes common contributors to insecurity such as size and dress (Kitchin 1998a). Mothers with disabilities can use assistive technology to communicate through the Internet in ways that might be less accessible in offline contexts (Ferris 2009). The virtual nature of the Internet means that child care is not required for participation and that many women with computer access in the workplace can surreptitiously seek community while engaging in paid employment. Our easy acceptance of the Internet allows for complacency over the fact that the ability to connect worldwide is an astonishing innovation; mothers of all earlier generations were limited to finding connections only with those in their immediate vicinity.

Not all of the distinctive characteristics of the Internet, of course, are positive. Despite the theoretical opportunity of access provided by the Web, in practice women are unlikely to connect without home or work Internet access. Committed support to online communities is highly time-consuming and is unlikely to be undertaken by mothers needing to access the Web through community, library, or other public locales. As previously mentioned, the supposed global democratization of information and communication expected with the proliferation of Internet technology simply hasn't manifested. And of course, the fact that nearly all contact over the Web is via the written word (and that the majority of these words are written in English) makes the presumption of literacy a condition of contact.

Kitchin suggests that "the vast majority of social spaces on the Internet bear a remarkable resemblance to real-world locales" (Kitchin 1998b:395). Importantly, however, Kitchin goes on to state that "as such, many online interactions are in fact situated in real-world protocols undermining the potential liberating effects of being online." There is no doubt that the Internet provides a new and different context for motherhood and maternal community. As Kitchin suggests, however, it is very possible for this new context to simply replicate unempowered and regressive behaviors. In the realm of motherhood, such a replication would manifest in two respects: first, with the majority of the performance of motherhood on the Internet documenting and reproducing the conditions of patriarchal motherhood, and second, with the predominance of elitist voices on motherhood potentially erasing empowered or otherwise non-normative experiences from the lexicon of maternal behavior. While the Internet is therefore a tremendous innovation that rewrites our approach to maternal writing, community, and activism, we must recognize that its presence alone does not automatically alleviate the systemic distribution of oppression and privilege worldwide. While the Internet cannot easily demolish patriarchal capitalist oppression via a single mouse-click, there are ways in which the immediacy of this new technology allows mothers specifically to connect in creative and unprecedented ways. One of the creative opportunities afforded by the Internet is the possibility of maternal connection independent of time shared with children. I will explore this possibility in greater detail below.

UNINTERRUPTED TIME

Many of the above characteristics of the Internet are good or bad irrespective of one's use of the Internet as, say, a political blogger, a Scientologist, or an amateur mechanic. For mothers, however, there may be other reasons the Web is such an attractive form of communication. Consider the following scenario:

> Lisa calls her friend Heather. Between them, Lisa and Heather have five children under the age of six and three different paying jobs. After three weeks of emails, they manage to get together for a playdate. The following dialogue might occur:
>
> *Lisa:* "So tell me more about your job! You just switched, right?"
>
> *Heather:* "Yeah, uh, last year—Kevin! Share with Noah! Yeah, it's going well. How about you?"
>
> *Lisa:* "Things here are good, you know, hectic . . . no, honey, don't give that to her, she's too little for that toy . . . out of your mouth! Not! In! Your! Mouth! Give it to mama. Good girl."
>
> *Heather:* "Are you guys sleeping? I meant to tell you that we met with an excellent naturopath . . . "
>
> *Lisa:* "Oh—please tell! We're exhausted. Noah, in a minute. I'm visiting with Heather right now. You go play with your friend. No, I said in a minute."
>
> [*Silence.*] "What were we talking about?"
>
> *Repeat as necessary.*

Lisa and Heather's "conversation" (such as it was) might seem familiar to any mother who has attempted to reach out and connect with other mothers of young children. In arranging playdates that are ostensibly venues for connecting children, beleaguered mothers reach out for both instrumental and emotional support, only to be thwarted by the offspring that purportedly brought them together. Events without children, while cheerfully agreed upon, are harder to arrange and are dependent on reliable child care and enough flexibility to devote that child care allotment to leisure time.

On the Internet, by contrast, interruptions go generally unrecorded. Although an online conversation might take place with children nearby, the quality of an interaction can be less fragmented by their presence. More important, however: children are not invited. Only on the Internet can (some) mothers easily connect without needing the excuse of their children to provide community. Kennedy discusses this context as a form of "virtual consciousness-raising" (Kennedy 2007).

There have been thousands, if not millions, of words expended questioning why mothers are drawn to the Internet, considering the appeal of mommyblogs and parenting (which is to say, mothering) chat rooms and bulletin boards, asking why so many women are drawn in. Perhaps the answer is simple: on the Internet, mothers are free to connect without their children present. Even consciousness-raising groups of the 1960s tended to have a number of children underfoot. By contrast, the Internet provides a venue for mothers to connect without needing to mediate the contact of their children and without the very real demands of those children derailing any potential for meaningful connection. The question to ask, then, is not why mothers are drawn to the Internet, but rather why, once they get there, they are drawn to discussions of motherhood? And who is (and isn't) able to access these discussions at all?

EQUAL ACCESS?

Many theorists have documented the extreme challenges incumbent in nurturing and protecting new humans within a patriarchal society (for example, Rich 1976; Ruddick 1983; Thurer 1994; Hays 1998). For many mothers, then, new motherhood is a trip to the trenches. If many mothers crave connection, however, only certain mothers are able to seek and find this connection on the Internet. Madge and O'Connor found that at one popular British parenting Web site, 63 percent of mothers surveyed were married and the overwhelming majority (81 percent) were white; of the sample nearly 60 percent were at home with their children either full or part time (Madge and O'Connor 2006:204). A 2005 study of an American site undertaken by Drentea and Moren-Cross found similar results: although ethnicity of participants was not determined, 95 percent of participants in one chat board were married, and 52 percent self-represented as stay-at-home mothers (Drentea and Moren-Cross 2005:927).

A stroll through the blogosphere finds similar results. On the one hand, diversity is freely accessible within mommyblogs: families of every description and social location abound. On the other, the most popular mommybloggers seem to fit a very narrow picture of maternity: white, middle- to upper-class mothers who are married to their children's fathers. Concerns regarding representation do not diminish the very real difficulties that many such women experience along the rocky path of new parenthood. For example, celebrated mommyblogger Heather Armstrong of "dooce" documented her tortuous experience with postpartum depression, eventually handwriting posts, uploaded by her husband at her request, from her room in a psychiatric institution after she made the decision to commit herself ("Unlocked," Aug. 28, 2004). Armstrong's torment served a useful purpose, in exposing the problem of postpartum depression in an unromantic and very candid way. Nonetheless, a question must be asked regarding the relative homogeneity of mommybloggers who reach any type of notoriety: although many women can blog, many fewer women can create blogs that will be widely read. Harp and Tremayne state that "entering into, or having access, is only the first step in participating in a public dialogue. Voices need an audience to truly be part of a larger public conversation" (Harp and Tremayne 2006:259).

Within the realm of the mommyblog, a hierarchy is realized that is similar to the one that silences women's voices within political blogs (Trammell and Keshelashvili 2005). Arguably, readers read blogs that are well written, compelling, and entertaining. More critically, however, one must consider that it is the internalized biases that determine which blogs meet these criteria. Perhaps the same "common sense" (i.e., racist and sexist) logic that determines that women can't write astutely about politics somehow limits the ability for non-normative mothers to document their experiences in a way that becomes accessible to the mainstream. In addition, perhaps it is the mothers who mirror the demographics of popular bloggers (mothers who are white, who are in heterosexual partnerships, and who experience a reasonable level of class privilege) who have the leisure time and interest to read and comment, creating a closed loop that resists breaking down homogenous notions of motherhood. Within this vicious circle, bloggers who do represent non-normative aspects of social location may be cautious of exposing or exploring these aspects of themselves for fear of diminishing popularity or being ghettoized; the result is that, even if some high-profile bloggers deviate from the norm, they may be perceived by the larger public as nonetheless conforming. In other words, within a larger world that is fundamentally hostile to issues of race, sexuality, and identity, mothers who do not explicitly identify themselves as non-white may be perceived as white, lending credence to the perceived homogeneity of maternal Internet presence.

SITES OF RESISTANCE

With respect to parenting styles, mothers on bulletin boards and chat rooms tend to engage in more traditional and patriarchal portrayals of motherhood (Madge and O'Connor document a group interview with participants of a popular parenting site in which every participant ends her introduction with a variation of the phrase "I love being a mum!" [2006:211–212]). By contrast, many popular mommyblogs have begun unmasking motherhood (Maushart 1997). The resistance of online mothers against traditional mores about motherhood is perhaps the most notable difference between on- and offline portrayals of maternity. Nadine of "Martinis for Milk" gives the following description:

> Blogging saved me when I was drowning in my own shortcomings. I was lonely in my new role as mother, and the mommy groups weren't turning my crank. I could say Fuck and Shit and Pussy online and still talk about my kid without getting the hairy eyeball.   ("August showers bring fall flowers," Aug. 16, 2007)

Nadine points to an important characteristic of many mommyblogs. Within this context of authorial independence, many of the most popular blogs (including "dooce") feature mothers who resist saccharine and romanticized perceptions of motherhood, choosing instead to document a much more visceral and mocking overview of maternity, albeit one that still celebrates children. When Julie of "alittlepregnant" created a video explicitly satirizing the Baby Einstein videos ("The Baby Mozart effect," Dec. 8, 2005), something much closer to O'Reilly's concept of empowered mothering (O'Reilly 2004) was enacted, a version of mothering that celebrates the hard work of parenting small children while still providing a critical (and often humorous) nod toward all that is unlovely in "being a mum." Although there are therefore very real concerns about the demographic imbalances among high-ranking bloggers, it is compelling to note that some such mommyblogs may have gained notoriety precisely *because* the version of maternity that they present is unmasked. Popular mommyblogs may not be representative, then, but they are far from politically docile.

Concerns regarding the digital divide are not to be understated. Nonetheless, one of the great strengths of maternal identity on the Internet is the sheer multiplicity of its presentation. Although mainstream mothers may dominate bandwidth, it is diverse mothers who may take most advantage of new forms of connectivity. Lesbian mothers, disabled mothers, trans-parents, parents of children with special needs, and myriad other diverse families are represented on the Internet. If the condition of modern motherhood is alienating and overwhelming to parents who may see themselves represented within mainstream media, it is only more so for parents whose lives remain silenced and erased. In this respect, while Internet motherhood may still include ghettoes, at least sites exist for the maintenance and creation of community. Furthermore, connection through the Internet may create unusual connections: as I have documented elsewhere (M. Friedman 2009), infertile women may find commonality in sharing experience with lesbian mothers around the topic of assisted reproductive technology; interracial adoptive families may find comfort or support looking to biracial biological parents; and lines that are stark in the real world, such as the communication barriers between birth and adoptive mothers, may become blurred (D. Friedman 2009).

Kennedy states that

> some bloggers are even connecting across differences of race, class, ethnicity and sexuality to see the broader implications of their own positions, as well as those of other women. Blogging has the potential to help create and encourage a new form of feminism that better avoids some of the pitfalls of an earlier generation of feminist activism, those often exclusively middle-class and heterosexual consciousness-raising groups.   (Kennedy 2007)

With respect to diversity, then, the Internet is a great boon to families. If knowledge is power, then the ability to transmit and retrieve that knowledge with just a few keystrokes has the capacity to render mothers, especially those who have been systemically disenfranchised, much more powerful. Such a celebration of diversity must continue to acknowledge the limitations of online interactions; although a diversity of representation exists, it is generally mothers who are literate as well as technologically savvy who can locate these sites (since they are less present than the overwhelming picture of patriarchal motherhood that pervades the Web) while non-Western mothers may have a much harder time finding representations at all.[1] Although the dismantling of online ghettoes should un-equivocally be high on the list of tasks for activist mothers, then, it is nonetheless encouraging that some mothers who would have seen no representation of their circumstances can begin to connect with like-minded people online.

CYBER-COMMUNITY: UNEMBODIED AND IN REAL LIFE

One of the debates that characterizes discussions of Internet community considers whether interactions that occur within the virtual realm can be considered "real" interactions in the absence of embodied contact. One critique, then, of mothering communities on the Internet is that the types of support they provide cannot be comparable to those within "real-life" interactions. Yet over and over again, mothers online pay tribute to the interactions that take place within the computer as vital and enriching, providing support that is at least different from, and at best superior to, that received offline.

Kate of "Tripping the Life Unbalanced" writes that

> despite the blogging that ties us together, we are also all very different women. We've had disagreements and conflicts. We sometimes stand on different sides of arguments. And god help anybody if any of us feel backed into a corner and defensive—we are all smart fierce mamas, after all! But we respect each other and our right to disagree. We all love our children, and walk the same line of mothering and guilt, adoration and a need to bolt for the closest exit.   ("so a pregnant lady, 10 online friends and a bag of onesies walk into a bar" . . ., Aug. 10, 2007)

Kate draws attention to the challenges that exist in any community, virtual or otherwise. Diversity of opinion is exacerbated within a virtual context, where body language and physical markers cannot be used to soften argumentative language or other challenging behavior. It is precisely this similarity, however, that leads to the conclusion that mothers on the Internet represent an interconnected network, groups of women who laugh and cry together, disagree, argue vehemently, and sometimes fail to resolve those arguments—in other words, a community. A community made unique by its composition and circumstances, not a community like any other, but a community nonetheless, with all of the joy and friction that the word suggests. When blogger Julie gave birth several hours from home and several months prematurely, her friends in the computer gave her a virtual baby shower. Only two friends knew Julie's full name and location, yet after her several-month-long vigil at a nonlocal NICU, she came home to a garage full of everything required for her son's first months ("alittlepregnant," "Scattered showers," Jan. 7, 2005). When blogger Snickollet lost her partner to pancreatic cancer when her twin children were ten months old, the mamasphere put up signposts throughout, requesting Paypal donations on her behalf[2] ("Clover's Blog," "If You'd Like To Help Snickollet," April 15, 2007). There is no question that twenty-first-century cyber-moms are different from their mothers before them. In both ephemeral and instrumental ways, however, mothers on the Internet have shown themselves to be a supportive and burgeoning community.

As with all communities, some of the function is in maintaining the status quo and upholding the normativity of community members. A popular trope throughout mothering sites on the Internet (both blogs and community fora) is the idea of "Bad mom of the year" or "World's worst mother." Within this context, mothers try to outdo one another in "proving" how terrible their mothering must be (see, for example, *Redbook*'s "Mom Moment" for the entry "America's Worst Mother," Feb. 11, 2008). In many respects, this example of community connection is hugely problematic: mothers are either fishing for compliments or attention, or genuinely castigating themselves for maternal behavior that is generally reasonable and understandable (likely, some combination of the two reasons is usually the case). In some contexts, however, even this unlikely method of maternal bonding can be redemptive. Alice Bradley of "finslippy"[3] once recounted her own "bad" mothering moment and invited readers to share their own maternal mishaps ("finslippy," "Give me your worst parenting stories," Jan. 4, 2008). The two hundred comments that followed, while sharing a common theme of shame-faced apology, nonetheless provided a relatively rare glimpse into the types of days that rarely are featured in mainstream portraits of motherhood. Most notably, mothers seemed to find real connection in reading one another's comments and finding exoneration in the form of motherhood unmasked.

A different type of community exists at the site "The Shape of a Mother," which seeks to unmask motherhood in another way. The site was created to provide literal snapshots of pre- and postpartum maternal bodies. The site is nonjudgmental and consists of a widely representative range of bodies in terms of both size and response (i.e., decisions to undertake plastic surgery or other interventions versus women who are very enthusiastic about their changing bodies). Interestingly, the photographs on the site document, once again, largely white women. Obviously the social constructs that maintain a certain type of homogeneity within this site are worthy of critique, and further research is necessary to understand both the limits and the implications of this type of community. Nonetheless, it is both refreshing and somewhat ironic that only in this unembodied context can some women find representations of the corporeal realities of motherhood. The photos on the site highlight the courage born of anonymity and the redefinition of community that epitomize twenty-first-century Internet motherhood.

ARMCHAIR ACTIVISM?

Critiques of online communities include the concern that true activism is impossible within a context that doesn't allow for physically connected collective action. In the Internet age, however, perhaps the definition of activism must be as radically reunderstood as the definition of community in order to truly understand new possibilities and implications. One interesting example of maternal activism on the Internet is the BlogHers Act.[4] BlogHer is a coalition of female bloggers that began in 2005 and is characterized by an annual conference as well as an embedded advertising network. The first BlogHer conference resulted in the ghettoization of mommybloggers, characterized by suggestions that if mothers "stopped blogging about themselves they could change the world" ("Blogher," "Mommy-Blogging is a radical act!" May 20, 2006). One year later, mommybloggers were a powerful force at the 2006 conference and have proven themselves to be a strong presence within the female blogosphere. Beginning in 2007, BlogHer leaders were receiving feedback that the collective power of so many bloggers should be harnessed to take on pressing political issues. After extensive survey of their members, BlogHer revealed their issue for 2007–2008 to be maternal health.

The presence of both the BlogHers Act and the specific project selected by the more than ten thousand women who belong to this organization[5] is very interesting. On the one hand, women (both mothers and non-mothers) are banding together to take advantage of the Internet's capacity to lead to collective action; and, needless to say, maternal health is both a laudable and a necessary sphere of influence within which to act. Nonetheless, the presence of a huge number of largely white, largely middle-class women deciding to take on a global initiative to improve quality of life issues around maternity smacks of the kind of maternal feminism that characterized prohibition-era politics. The blogosphere has spoken and has done so with a loud, collective voice—yet some unease must persist at the notion, however tacitly considered, that the reason that female bloggers are so conscionable is because so many are mothers. Overall, the presence of the Act (and its sister Act in Canada) is evidence of a growing demand to use the community-building capacity of the Internet to harness a push for collective change. As that change grows and evolves, perhaps the emphasis on women as change agents might be less intimately connected to their maternal presence.

Maternal presence on the Internet is a fascinating blend of patriarchy, empowerment, therapy, and community all tangled together. Although similar to the performance of maternity within the embodied world, the unique situation of the Internet presents specific challenges in terms of both access and content; the specific repercussions of mothering within this very public space are as yet undetermined. Ultimately, the question of whether the World Wide Web is good or bad for mothers is moot: both mothers and computers are here to stay, and the embeddedness of virtual access seems likely to only increase as the twenty-first century unfolds. Committed feminist mothers at the dawn of a new age, then, must figure out how to harness this new tool in order to maximize its revolutionary potential. The Internet has the capacity to be a powerful force, but choices must be made in order to allow empowered motherhood to make gains in resisting the stranglehold of patriarchal motherhood; to allow for the greatest diversity of maternal narrative to emerge and inform; and to interrogate and resist the ghettoization (both of and by mothers) that characterizes much of the maternal presence on the Internet. As Gillian Youngs writes, "As much as the internet is about the future, it is also about opportunities to revisit the past and reconnect it with the future—for example, in relation to lesser-known, forgotten or suppressed forms of knowledge—and to do so in networks, involving growing numbers of people in that knowledge" (Youngs 2004:204). At the opening of this new age, then, let us draw lessons from the past in order to empower ourselves and other mothers in the future.

WORKS CITED

Drentea, Patricia, and Jennifer L. Moren-Cross. 2005. Social capital and social support on the Web: The case of an Internet mother site. *Sociology of Health and Illness* 27.7:920–943.

Ferris, Lisa. 2009. Kindred keyboard connections: How blogging helped a deafblind mother find a living, breathing community. *In Mothering and Blogging: The Radical Act of the Mommyblog*, ed. May Friedman and Shana Calixte, 67–73. Toronto: Demeter Press.

Friedman, Dawn. 2009. Someone else's shoes: How on-blog discourse changed a real life adoption. In *Mothering and Blogging: The Radical Act of the Mommyblog*, ed. May Friedman and Shana Calixte, 37–44. Toronto: Demeter Press.

Friedman, May. 2009. Schadenfreude for Mittelscherz? Or, why I read infertility blogs. *In Mothering and Blogging: The Radical Act of the Mommyblog*, ed. May Friedman and Shana Calixte, 171–181. Toronto: Demeter Press.

Haraway, Donna. 1995. *Simians, Cyborgs, and Women: The Reinvention of Nature*. New York: Routledge.

Harp, Dustin and Mark Tremayne. 2006. The gendered blogosphere: Examining inequality using network and feminist theory. *Journalism and Mass Communication Quarterly* 83.2:247–264.

Hays, Sharon. 1998. *The Cultural Contradictions of Motherhood*. New Haven: Yale University Press.

Herring, Susan C., Inna Kouper, Lois Ann Scheidt, and Elijah L. Wright. 2008. Women and children last: The discursive construction of Weblogs. In *Into the Blogosphere: Rhetoric, Community, and Culture of Weblogs*, ed. Laura J. Gurak, Smiljana Antonijevic, Laurie Johnson, Clancy Ratliff, and Jessica Reyman. http://blog.lib.umn.edu/blogosphere/women_and_children.html (accessed Jan. 22, 2008).

Kennedy, Tracy L. M. 2007. The personal is political: Feminist blogging and virtual consciousness-raising. *Scholar and Feminist Online* 5.2. http://www.barnard.edu/sfonline/blogs/index.htm (accessed Jan. 15, 2008).

Kim, Hosu. 2007. A flickering motherhood: Korean birthmothers' Internet community. *Scholar and Feminist Online* 5.2. http://www.barnard.edu/sfonline/blogs/index.htm.

Kitchin, Robert. 1998a. *Cyberspace: The World in the Wires*. Chichester: Wiley.

——. 1998b. Towards geographies of cyberspace. *Progress in Human Geography* 22:385–406.

Madge, Clare, and Henrietta O'Connor. 2006. Parenting gone wired: Empowerment of new mothers on the Internet? *Social and Cultural Geography* 72:199–222.

Maushart, Susan. 1997. *The Mask of Motherhood: How Becoming a Mother Changes Our Lives and Why We Never Talk About It*. New York: New Press.

O'Reilly, Andrea, ed. 2004. *Mother Outlaws: Theories and Practices of Empowered Mothering*. Toronto: Women's Press.

Rich, Adrienne. 1976. *Of Woman Born: Motherhood as Experience and Institution*. New York: Norton.

Ruddick, Sara. 1983. *Maternal Thinking: Toward a Politics of Peace*. Boston: Beacon.

Thurer, Shari. 1994. *The Myths of Motherhood: How Culture Reinvents the Good Mother*. Boston: Houghton Mifflin.

Trammell, Kaye D., and Ana Keshelashvili. 2005. Examining the new influencers: A self-presentation study of A-list blogs. *Journalism and Mass Communication Quarterly* 82.4:968–983.

Youngs, Gillian. 2004. Cyberspace: The new feminist frontier? In *Women and Media: International Perspectives*, ed. Karen Ross and Carolyn M. Byerly, 185–208. Oxford: Blackwell.

BLOGS AND WEB SITES

alittlepregnant. www.alittlepregnant.com (accessed from Jan. 2005 onward).

Armstrong, Heather. Dooce. www.dooce.com (accessed from Nov. 2003 onward).

BlogHer. www.blogher.com (accessed Feb. 10, 2008).

Bradley, Alice. Finslippy. www.finslippy.com (accessed from Nov. 2005 onward).

——. Wonderland. www.alphamom.com/wonderland (accessed from Nov. 2006 onward).

Clover's Blog. http://mymeanderings.typepad.com/clover/ (accessed Feb. 13, 2008).

Martinis for Milk. http://scarbiedoll.blogspot.com (accessed Feb. 1, 2008).

Redbook: The Mom Moment. http://www.redbookmag.com/home/mom-blog (accessed Feb. 12, 2008).

The shape of a mother. http://theshapeofamother.com (accessed Nov. 20, 2007).

Snickollet. http://snickollet.blogspot.com (accessed Jan. 20, 2008).

Tripping the life unbalanced. http://trippingthelifeunbalanced.blogspot.com (accessed Feb. 10, 2008).

Outlaw(ing) Motherhood

A Theory and Politic of Maternal
Empowerment for the Twenty-first Century

TWENTY-THREE

ANDREA O'REILLY

In her groundbreaking book, *Of Woman Born: Motherhood as Experience and Institution*, Adrienne Rich wrote, "We do not think of the power stolen from us and the power withheld from us in the name of the institution of motherhood" (1976:275). In the three-plus decades since the publication of Rich's ovarian work, the empowerment of mothers has been a central, if not defining, concern of maternal activism and scholarship. More recently, with the emergence of an international motherhood movement and the development of motherhood studies as an academic discipline, maternal scholars and activists have sought to define and develop a politic or theory of maternal empowerment. Maternal activists and researchers today agree that motherhood, as it is currently perceived and practiced in patriarchal societies, is disempowering if not oppressive for a multitude of reasons: namely, the societal devaluation of motherwork, the endless tasks of privatized mothering, and the impossible standards of idealized motherhood. Likewise, maternal activists and researchers have developed a plethora of theories of and strategies for maternal empowerment to contest, challenge, and counter patriarchal motherhood. This paper will not so much revisit these ideas and strategies as it will request that scholars and activists alike rethink received or accepted notions of how and why motherhood functions as an oppressive institution for women.

When they are asked, students, mothers, and researchers readily describe the exhaustion, guilt, boredom, anxiety, loneliness, and so forth of contemporary Western motherhood, but are less forthcoming on why this is so. Indeed, mothers in North America are overwhelmed, fatigued, and guilt-ridden because of the hard work and responsibility that they alone assume in motherhood. Yet the larger question remains: why is this so? Despite forty years of feminism, it is my view, and the argument of this paper, that modern motherhood continues to function as a patriarchal institution that is largely impervious to change because it is grounded in gender essentialism, a gender ideology that establishes a naturalized opposition between public and private spheres. This paper will argue that only by unearthing and severing the ideological underpinning of patriarchal motherhood, gender essentialism, can we develop a politic of maternal empowerment and a practice of outlaw motherhood for the twenty-first century.

THEORIZING AND DEFINING MATERNAL EMPOWERMENT

Any discussion of maternal empowerment must begin with the distinction that Rich made in *Of Woman Born* between two meanings of motherhood, one superimposed on the other: "the *potential* relationship of any woman to her powers of reproduction and to children," and "the *institution*—which aims at ensuring that that potential—and all women—shall remain under male control" (1976:13; emphasis in original). It has long been recognized among scholars of motherhood that Rich's distinction between mothering and motherhood was what enabled feminists to recognize that motherhood is not naturally, necessarily, or inevitably oppressive, a view held by some second-wave feminists. On the contrary, if freed from motherhood, mothering could be experienced as a site of empowerment and as a location of social change if, to use Rich's words, women became "outlaws from the institution of motherhood" (195).

However, while *Of Woman Born* interrupted the patriarchal narrative of motherhood and cleared a space for the development of counter-narratives of mothering, it did not generate a discourse of outlaw motherhood or maternal empowerment. Moreover, while much has been published on patriarchal motherhood since Rich's inaugural text—documenting why and how patriarchal motherhood is harmful, indeed unnatural, to mothers and children alike—little has been written on the possibility of empowered mothering or outlaw motherhood. As Fiona Green writes, "A discussion of Rich's monumental contention that even when restrained by patriarchy, motherhood can be a site of empowerment and political activism [is] still largely missing from the increasing dialogue and publication around motherhood" (2004a:31).

In my earlier work I used the term *empowered mothering* to signify nonpatriarchal maternity or outlaw motherhood; however, I now think that the term *maternal empowerment* better describes an identity and practice of outlaw motherhood. While these two concepts are certainly similar and overlapping, there are significant differences between them. *Empowered mothering*, constructed as it is from a verb, leaves both the subject and object (in both senses of the word) of the action more-or-less ambiguous. More specifically, the term fails to answer who is doing this? for whom? and why? Moreover, *empowered mothering* is not synonymous with an *empowered mother*; a mother may perform empowered mothering, say in the instance of anti-sexist childrearing or maternal activism, without herself being empowered. Anti-sexist childrearing and maternal activism are certainly significant and essential tasks of empowered mothering; however, maternal activism on behalf of children and feminist childrearing for children does not address the needs of mothers themselves in any real manner. Specifically, as I have argued elsewhere, by defining maternal empowerment in this manner it seems that we have, whether consciously or otherwise, discounted and disregarded what should be the first and primary aim of empowered mothering: the empowerment of mothers (O'Reilly 2006b). How and why patriarchal motherhood is oppressive to mothers has been well documented in feminist scholarship; however, when this same scholarship seeks to imagine an empowered mode of mothering, the focus inexplicably shifts from mothers to children (anti-sexist childrearing) and/or to a world apart from the mother (maternal activism). In the feminist critique of patriarchal motherhood the mother and her discontent was our foremost concern; however, as we endeavor to define a nonpatriarchal maternity, the mother, while still crucial, frequently becomes instrumental to larger and seemingly more important social change objectives. In other words, mothers are accorded agency to affect social change through childrearing or activism but little attention is paid to what this agency does or means for the mother herself in the context of *her own life*.

Equally as troubling is the way that the concept of empowered mothering has made possible disturbing justifications and rationalizations; too often the demand to empower mothers is recast as a strategy for more effective parenting. In her study on empowered mothering Erika Horwitz argues that this practice is characterized by women insisting on "the importance of mothers meeting their own needs," and the realization that "being a mother does not fulfill all of women's needs." However, in most instances, the mothers' demands for agency and autonomy are repositioned as requirements of the children. As one mother explained, she resisted patriarchal motherhood "to make me a better mother for my children" (Horwitz 2003:52). While I do believe that empowered mothers are more effective mothers and that anti-sexist childrearing and maternal activism are worthwhile aims, I still worry about why the rhetoric of rationalization has become the strategy of choice among feminist activists and scholars today, and wonder why our campaigns for social change center on children and not on ourselves as mothers. Why can we not simply demand that motherhood be made better for mothers themselves? Why are mothers' demands for more time, money, support, and validation only responded to when they are seen as benefiting children? I realize that this rhetoric is often employed strategically to make gains for mothers that otherwise would not be possible; in other words, patriarchal culture will accord mothers resources if they use them on behalf of children. However, whether or not one agrees with such a strategy, what becomes apparent in such is that empowered mothering does not automatically or necessarily mean or translate into a politic of empowerment for mothers or a theory of outlaw motherhood.

Thus, for the reasons noted above, the term *maternal empowerment* better defines a theory and politic of outlaw motherhood in that it positions such as a noun; that is, a state or place in which mothers are or may be empowered. But what do we mean when we theorize upon or lobby for maternal empowerment? Maternal empowerment or outlaw motherhood is best understood as an oppositional stance that seeks to counter and correct the many ways that patriarchal motherhood causes mothering to be limiting or oppressive to women. Elsewhere I have argued that contemporary Western patriarchal motherhood may be characterized by eight characteristics or rules: (1) children can be properly cared for only by the biological mother; (2) this mothering must be provided 24/7; (3) the mother must always put children's needs before her own; (4) mothers must turn to the experts for instruction; (5) the mother must be fully satisfied, fulfilled, completed, and composed in motherhood; (6) mothers must lavish excessive amounts of time, energy, and money in the rearing of their children; (7) the mother has full responsibility but no power from which to mother; (8) motherwork, child rearing specifically, is regarded as a personal, private undertaking with no political import (O'Reilly 2004a). Patriarchal motherhood causes motherwork to be oppressive to women because it necessitates the repression or denial of the mother's own selfhood; as well, it assigns mothers all the responsibility for mothering but gives them no real power. Such "powerless responsibility," to use Rich's term, denies a mother the authority and agency to determine her own experiences of mothering. As well, it results in most women mothering alone in the isolation of their home, feeling overwhelmed and exhausted. Moreover, since no mother can achieve idealized motherhood, women bring to their lived experiences of mothering self-recrimination, anxiety, doubt, and guilt. In turn, mothers who do not seek to achieve idealized motherhood, either by choice or circumstance, are labeled "unfit" mothers who will find themselves and their mothering under public scrutiny and surveillance. Finally, in defining mothering as private and nonpolitical work, patriarchal motherhood restricts the way mothers can and do affect social change through feminist child rearing and maternal activism.

Maternal empowerment, whether it be termed feminist (Gordon, Glickman, Green, O'Reilly), outlaw (O'Reilly, Rich), radical (Cooper), rebellious (Douglas and Michaels), or hip (Gore) seeks to confer to mothers the agency, authority, authenticity and autonomy denied to them in patriarchal motherhood. (O'Reilly 2004a, 2004b, 2006a, 2006b, 2007, 2009). As Fiona Green has observed, empowered or outlaw mothers "seek to live Rich's emancipatory vision of motherhood and, driven by their feminist consciousness, their intense love for their children and the need to be true to themselves, their families, and their parenting, [these] feminist mothers choose to parent in a way that challenges the status quo" (2004:130).

Erika Horwitz's study (2003) on empowered mothering reveals that the practice of outlaw motherhood may be characterized by seven themes: (1) the importance of mothers meeting their own needs; (2) being a mother does not fulfill all of a woman's needs; (3) involving others in their children's upbringing; (4) actively questioning the expectations that are placed on mothers by society; (5) challenging mainstream parenting practices; (6) not believing that mothers are solely responsible for how children turn out; and (7) challenging the idea that the only emotion mothers ever feel toward their children is love. Central to each of these themes and acts of maternal empowerment is a redefinition of motherhood from a feminist-maternal perspective. "Good" mothers in patriarchal motherhood, for example, are defined as white, middle-class, married, stay-at-home moms; "good" mothers from a politic of maternal empowerment are drawn from the full spectrum of maternal identities and include lesbian, noncustodial, poor, single, older, and "working" mothers. Likewise, patriarchal motherhood limits "family" to a patriarchal nuclear structure wherein the parents are married and are the biological parents of the children, the mother is the nurturer, and the father is the provider; the maternal empowerment perspective embraces a variety of family structures, including single, blended, step, matrifocal, same-sex, and so forth. Further, as patriarchal motherhood characterizes childrearing as a private, nonpolitical undertaking, maternal empowerment foregrounds the political-social dimension of motherwork; more specifically, it challenges traditional practices of gender socialization and performs anti-sexist childrearing practices so as to raise empowered daughters and empathetic sons. Finally, for many mothers, maternal empowerment comes to be expressed as maternal activism. Mothers, by way of maternal activism, use their position as mothers to lobby for social and political change. Whether it is in the home or in the world at large, expressed as anti-sexist childrearing or as maternal activism, from this perspective motherwork is redefined as a social and political act through which social change is made possible.

Returning to Rich's quote from the beginning of this paper: simply put, the aim of maternal empowerment is to reclaim the power denied to mothers in patriarchal motherhood.

GENDER ESSENTIALISM AND THE "NEW MOMISM" OF THE TWENTY-FIRST CENTURY

In both motherhood theory and motherhood activism the costs of patriarchal motherhood have been well examined and critiqued. I would argue, however, that this feminist criticism has been largely limited to the symptomatic manifestations of patriarchal motherhood, leaving unexamined their root cause: the gender essentialism of modern motherhood. Contemporary Western patriarchal motherhood, though nuanced in its manifestations, is ideologically quite homogeneous and unambiguous, defined by a rigid and uniform philosophy of gender essentialism and the resulting binary opposition of the public and private sphere. A central, if not defining, event in the rise of Western modernity was the emergence of the public/private dichotomy in which the work of production was assigned to the public sphere and the work of reproduction to the private sphere. This dichotomy was, of course, gender coded: a man belonged in the public realm and was to embody the valued masculine traits of the emergent capitalist and industrial society, while a woman was to remain in the home domain and serve as the ornamental wife or, in the lexicon of the day, "the angel in the house." Significantly, this gender polarity resulted in the emergence or, more accurately, the invention of full-time motherhood. While this notion of full-time motherhood was largely symbolic—and restricted to middle-class mothers—such women acquired moral superiority and cultural prestige (though of course not real societal power or respect) in and through their identity as Mother. This gendered schism converged to construct mothering as *essentially* and naturally the identity and purpose of women and the family as fundamentally a private unit separate and distinct from the larger public, political, social world.

Susan Douglas and Meredith Michaels (2004) have termed the twenty-first century manifestation of this ideology the "new momism" which, as they explain, begins with:

> The insistence that no woman is truly complete or fulfilled unless she has kids, that women remain the best primary caretakers of children, and that to be a remotely decent mother, a woman has to devote her entire physical, psychological, emotional, intellectual being, 24/7, to her children. The new momism is a highly romanticized view of motherhood in which the standards for success are impossible to meet.   (4)

Douglas and Michaels go on to explain, "The new momism involves more than just impossible ideals about women childrearing; it redefines all women, first and foremost, through their relationships to children. Thus, being a citizen, a worker, a governor [and so forth] are supposed to take a backseat to motherhood" (2004:22). "The new momism," Douglas and Michaels continue, "insists that if you want to do anything else, you'd better first prove that you're a doting, totally involved mother before proceeding. The only recourse for women who want careers, or to do anything else besides stay at home with the kids all day, is to prove they can 'do it all' " (22). This type of gender essentialism, whether it is conveyed as the "angel in the house" ideology of the nineteenth century or this century's "new momism," necessarily naturalizes mothering as "a woman's calling"; such is to be performed by the biological mother, who must be a wife and nurturer in a heterosexual family wherein the father is the provider, and thus is not expected to engage in "mothering."

What perhaps is most distributing about this naturalization of motherhood is the degree to which the notion is found in purportedly feminist writing. I recently undertook a study of the contemporary motherhood memoir only to find that most of this literature, while highly critical of patriarchal motherhood, was complicit in its gender essentialism and naturalization of motherhood through its allegiance to the new momism ideology. As I have explored elsewhere, the motherhood memoir reinscribes—or, more accurately, naturalizes and normalizes—the very patriarchal conditions of motherhood that feminists, including the motherhood memoir writers themselves, seek to dismantle (O'Reilly 2009). At the turn of the last century maternal feminists relied upon the belief in innate gender difference, particularly the alleged moral superiority of mothers, to lobby for and make legitimate their claims for female suffrage. Similarly, be it consciously or otherwise, motherhood memoir writers today draw upon the ethos of the "new momism" to value and validate a public literature on motherhood; in particular, the assumption that children are the all-consuming focus and purpose of a mother's life. This use of maternal feminism and the "new momism" did make significant gender change possible: in the form of female suffrage in the last century and a de-privatization of motherhood in this century. However, they also serve to reify gender difference and hence reinforce traditional and patriarchal notions of womanhood and motherhood—most notably, the private/public divide and the gender dichotomy between the feminine/nurturer and the masculine/producer.

In the remaining pages I will cite some examples of this genre's compliance and complicity with the gender essentialism of the "new momism" in order to demonstrate the larger argument of this paper: namely, that meaningful change becomes possible only when a theory and politic of and for maternal empowerment confronts and counters the gender essentialism of patriarchal motherhood and the feminist writing that continues to conform to it.

Memoir authors do critique the *consequences* of this patriarchal motherhood—e.g., women do all the work of mothering with little or no support—however, they do not challenge the *assumptions* themselves. Thus, their challenge remains at the level of criticism and not change. This is most evident in the authors' views on child care. Of the memoirs I have read thus far, none of the authors consider child care as a possible option for allowing women to develop a selfhood outside of motherhood. For some the reason is financial, though for most it is because they subscribe to the new momism belief in the necessity of full-time, natural, and attachment mothering. They believe that they must be at home 24/7 for the benefit of the child for at least the first three–five years, and that to do otherwise would be unwise, if not unnatural, to both child and mother. Indeed, as Ivana Brown (2006) notes in her research paper: "While some authors challenge parts of the 'natural mother' myth, all of them are the primary caregivers of their children" (56). She goes on to explain: "Mothers are the main caretakers of the children and fathers are more or less absent, appearing at the time of birth and then having a role in the background in financially supporting the family and helping the mother with certain tasks and responsibilities. The absence of fathers from the daily parenting tasks remains mostly unexplained" (56). Furthermore, as Brown notes, "this approach contributes to the categorical differentiation between men and women [in the motherhood memoir]" (45).

For me the most worrisome part of the new momism, particularly as it is manifested in the motherhood memoir, is that being a stay-at-home mother is constructed as the mother's choice. Again, to return to Douglas and Michaels (2004):

> The mythology of the new momism now insinuates that, when all is said and done, the enlightened mother chooses to stay at home with the kids. Back in the 1950s mothers stayed home because they had no choice. Today having been to the office, having tried a career, women supposedly have seen the inside of the male working world and found it be the inferior choice to staying home, especially when her kids' future is at stake. It's not that mothers can't hack it (1950s thinking). It's that progressive mothers refuse to hack it. The June Cleaver model, if taken as a *choice*, as opposed to a requirement, is the truly modern fulfilling forward-thinking version of motherhood.   (23)

While many of the authors expose the concept of choice for what it is—a fiction and a fallacy—they nonetheless see their full-time mothering as inevitable and necessary.

However, other memoir writers do deflect and disguise the very real structural and familial inequities mothers face by way of a narrative of choice. For example, a writer in the collection *Breeder* who practices attachment parenting as a college student explains why she decided to quit school when pregnant with her second child: "I was tired every day, tired all over, and the prospect of spending the next several months so impossibly tired was too much for me" (Gore and Lavender 2001:83). As she goes on to explain, "Feeling that I faced a *choice* between my future and my present, I withdrew from my classes" (84; emphasis added). She later writes, "My education has not been put on hold; on the contrary, I am a full-time student in an accelerated toddler studies program. My three-year old is experimenting with wet-on-wet watercolours, and the baby will be walking soon. Now that's what I call progress" (85). As someone who gave birth to three children in five years while an undergrad and later a grad student, I can certainly understand being "impossibly tired," but the reasons for such tiredness are as much the result of her adherence to the new momism discourse, which requires her to be the main caretaker of the children 24/7 via attachment parenting, as they are of the demands of academia. Had she used some child care, insisted upon shared parenting (her partner is mentioned only once), and renounced or reduced her "natural" and intensive mothering practices, she would have had, in all likelihood, the time and energy to combine motherhood with her studies. (This is not to minimize the real need for structural change in education and the workplace to enable women to combine work with motherhood.) But because of her adherence to the new momism philosophy of mothering, she simply cannot see these as possibilities, and thus must accept societal and familial gender inequities as both inevitable and natural. More troublesome is that all of this is narrated and justified in the language of choice and, even more problematically, as a feminist choice: i.e. when she proclaims: "now that's progress." Most motherhood memoirs, because of their identification with the new momism and its gender essentialism, cannot discern, let alone critique, the root causes of mothers' oppression, and thus the genre remains one of complaint and not change.

My observations on the motherhood memoir are echoed in the feminist sociology on the family and in everyday conversations with women; simply put, mothers are still doing the bulk of domestic labor and child care in homes around the world. The necessary work of home and community maintenance is performed by mothers, whether they work part- or full-time. Today however, with the majority of mothers in the paid labor force, we do not have full-time homemakers to do the necessary work of social reproduction; hence the family and work conflict experienced my mothers but not fathers. Although this gender inequity is well documented in feminist scholarship and well experienced in women's own lives, it is strangely absent in much of the activism and thinking on maternal empowerment, and in family and work balance discussions. In order to better illustrate this, I now turn to the following two stories.

In 2005 I attended the Canadian Labour Congress "Balancing Work and Family" conference as a delegate from my faculty union. What struck me first was the "cognitive dissonance" between the topic being discussed and those discussing it. The vast majority of the attendees—it appeared to be well over 90 percent—were women, and yet the terms used were *family* and *parents*. From the talks, workshops, and discussions at the conference, the solutions offered for work and family balance seemed to be twofold: a national childcare program and reduced work hours (with a particular emphasis on eliminating overtime). While I would agree that both would go a long way to enable families to do the essential work of social reproduction (from dentist appointments to children's field trips), startlingly absent from the discussion was the recognition that it is mothers who still do the majority of the second-shift labor, and that such is wrong and must be challenged and changed. It is not enough to ask the government for a national childcare program, and our employers for reduced work hours, if our partners are not doing their fair share. And while the women certainly complained about this during coffee breaks, not once was it brought up as an official topic of discussion in this two-day conference on family and work balance.

More recently I attended a large motherhood conference that featured talks by the prominent leaders of the North American Motherhood Movement. This conference was attended by close to two hundred mothers who lead or attended mother empowerment groups in the United States. At the close of the conference, a leader from the organization asked the mothers to email pictures of their home when they returned from the conferences to show its complete disarray—laundry undone, kids not bathed, empty pizza boxes about, and a living room littered with children's toys—as a result of their two-day absence. The women laughed uproariously and were soon bragging about and betting upon whose home would be found in the most chaos. No one in my hearing range was asking what should have been obvious questions, particularly at a conference on maternal empowerment: why should the mothers come home and find their house in such a state after a two-day conference? Should fathers not be expected and required to competently run a household in their absence? And why was their "incompetence" or "failure" to do such considered funny? Throughout the weekend, these same women spoke eloquently, passionately, and insightfully on how to empower mothers through support groups, advocacy, and activism and yet when it came to their own partners they expected and demanded so very little.

I have shared the latter story with mothers and scholars of motherhood and while they were saddened by it, they were not shocked: "after all, what do you expect?" I have spoken extensively on how mothers, even with the involved partners, are the ones who do the maternal thinking: the remembering, worrying, planning, anticipating, orchestrating, arranging, and coordinating of and for the household. It is mothers who remember to buy the milk, plan the birthday party, and worry that the daughter's recent loss of appetite may be indicative of anorexia. Although the father may sign the field trip permission form, or buy the diapers, it is the mother, in most households, who reminds him to do so. Delegation does not make equality. However, as this gender inequity may be commonplace, what must be remembered and emphasized, particularly in discussions on maternal empowerment, is that it is neither natural nor inevitable.

WHERE DO WE GO FROM HERE?
A FEMINIST ETHIC OF CARE PARADIGM AND
DEGENDERING REPRODUCTIVE LABOR

In my view, the absence of a sustained analysis on gender inequity in our homes and the ideology of gender essentialism that supports and legitimizes this inequality is the "Achilles' heel" of the contemporary maternal empowerment movement. While family-friendly government policies and workplace practices are certainly desired and needed, they will only serve to empower mothers if their progress is matched in the private sphere. As the results from my own large qualitative study on mother academics suggest, it seems that gender equity in the home is more often a determinant of employment success than family-friendly policies in the workplace. When asked what enabled them to achieve success in academia, the overwhelming majority of respondents identified not workplaces policies but the support of their partners: "I couldn't have done it without him" Or as historian Jodi Vandenberg-Davis remarked (pers. comm.): "Women who have reached full professor have shared a common characteristic: husbands who stay at home for part of the child-rearing years, work part time, or at the very least are not in jobs that require a great deal of travel." "These familial adaptations" she continues, "may prove to be more important than the rather minimal institutional adaptations."

It must be recognized that gender essentialism underpins modern motherhood and gives rise to its many oppressive practices. But what does all of this mean for a theory and politic of maternal empowerment or outlaw motherhood? The challenge, as I see it, is to determine how best to affirm the necessary work of social reproduction; it must be acknowledged that it is mothers who do this work, often to their own detriment, while insisting that culture—and that includes fathers—must likewise assume responsibility for motherwork and take on its tasks in both thought (i.e., the maternal thinking described above) and action. What is needed, in other words, is a repositioning of the word *mother* from a noun to a verb so that the work of mothering is rendered separate from the identity of mother—so that care is divested of biology. In the context of the scholarship and activism on maternal empowerment this requires that we move from a politic of maternalism to what Judith Stadtman Tucker (2008) perceptively defines as a "feminist ethic of care" framework:

> As with maternalism, feminist care ethic designates caring for others as an essential social function. But rather than valorizing maternal sensitivity and altruism as a

vital resource, feminist care ethic aims to liberate caregiving from its peripheral status and reposition it as a primary human activity.   (212)

She goes on to explain that, "for proponents of the contemporary mothers' movement, grounding the agenda in an ethic of care opens up the possibility of developing a *gender neutral* approach to social policy and an opportunity to expand the language of care as a public good beyond the maternalist paradigm" (212; emphasis added).

The feminist ethic of care perspective redefines "motherhood issues"—maternity leave, child care, flextime, workplace discrimination against mothers, and the societal devaluation of carer work, to name but a few—as parental and family concerns. In so doing, the "feminist ethic of care" paradigm displaces and dislodges the gender essentialist framework that constructs and constitutes contemporary Western motherhood and gives rise to its many oppressive practices. Perhaps this reframing will not automatically result in gender equity in our homes; however, it does make such more probable and achievable. A gender-neutral approach not only makes progressive social policy—from parental leave to flextime—available to fathers, thus allowing for their active participation in the social reproduction of households; more importantly, it makes carework for men and masculinity normative. In other words, if carework is degendered and if such is reinforced by workplace and governmental policy, not only will more men do reproductive labor, but this work, as a result, will no longer be viewed or defined as women's calling and vocation.

While the disempowerment of patriarchal motherhood is well known, in my view, what is less understood is why this institution gives rise to the oppressive practices that it does. Moreover, as I have argued in this paper, the feminist criticism of patriarchal motherhood has largely been limited to the symptomatic manifestations of patriarchal motherhood, leaving unexamined their root cause, which I contend is the gender essentialism of modern motherhood. The challenge for theorists of and activists for maternal empowerment is to affirm the necessary work of social reproduction, to acknowledge that it is mothers who do this work, often to their own detriment, while at the same time insisting that culture, which includes fathers, must likewise assume responsibility for reproductive labor.

I have suggested that in order to effectively destabilize patriarchal motherhood we must disrupt and dislodge the gender essentialism that grounds and structures it. Such can be achieved by re-envisioning and repositioning *mother* from a noun to a verb and by creating, in policy, practice, and perception, a "feminist ethic of care" paradigm. Paradoxically, as the title of this paper suggests, we must outlaw motherhood to make possible outlaw motherhood. Only then will we achieve a truly transformative theory and politic of maternal empowerment for the twenty-first century.

WORKS CITED

Brown, Ivana. 2006. Mommy memoirs: Feminism, gender, and motherhood in popular literature. *Journal of the Association for Research on Mothering* 8.1–2:200–212.

Cooper, Baba. 1987. The radical potential in lesbian mothering of daughters. In *Politics of the Heart: A Lesbian Parenting Anthology*, ed. Sandra Pollack and Jeanne Vaughn. Ithaca: Firebrand.

Douglas, Susan J., and Meredith Michaels. 2004. *The Mommy Myth: The Idealization of Motherhood and How It Has Undermined Women*. New York: Free Press.

Glickman, Rose L. 1993. *Daughters of Feminists: Young Women with Feminist Mothers Talk About Their Lives*. New York: St. Martin's Press.

Gordon, Tuula. 1990. *Feminist Mothers*. New York: New York University Press.

Gore, Ariel, and Bee Lavender. 2001. *Breeder: Real Life Stories from the New Generation of Mothers*. Seattle: Seal Press.

Green, Fiona. 2004. Feminist mothers: Successfully negotiating the tensions between motherhood and mothering. In *Mother Outlaws: Theories and Practices of Empowered Mothering*, ed. Andrea O'Reilly, 31–42. Toronto: Women's Press.

——. 2006. Developing a feminist motherline: Reflections on a decade of feminist parenting. *Journal of the Association for Research on Mothering* 8.1–2:7–20.

Horwitz, Erika. 2003. "Mothers' Resistance to the Western Dominant Discourse on Mothering." Ph.D. diss., Simon Fraser University.

——. 2004. Resistance as a site of empowerment: The journey away from maternal sacrifice. In *Mother Outlaws: Theories and Practices of Empowered Mothering*, ed. Andrea O'Reilly, 43–58. Toronto: Women's Press.

O'Reilly, Andrea, ed. 2004a. *Mother Matters: Motherhood as Discourse and Practice*. Toronto: ARM Press.

——. 2004b. *Toni Morrison and Motherhood: A Politics of the Heart*. Albany: State University of New York Press.

——. 2006a. Between the baby and the bathwater: Some thoughts on a mother-centered theory and practice of feminist mothering. *Journal of the Association for Research on Mothering* 8.1–2:323–330.

———. 2006b. *Rocking the Cradle: Thoughts on Motherhood, Feminism, and the Possibility of Empowered Mothering*. Toronto: Demeter Press.

———. 2007. *Maternal Theory: Essential Readings*. Toronto: Demeter Press.

———. 2009. *Feminist Mothering*. Albany: State University of New York Press.

Rich, Adrienne. 1976. *Of Woman Born: Motherhood as Experience and Institution*. 2nd ed. 1986. New York: Norton.

Stadtman, Judith Tucker. 2008. Rocking the boat: Feminism and the ideological grounding for the twenty-first century mothers' movement. In *Feminist Mothering*, ed. Andrea O'Reilly, 205–219. Albany: State University of New York Press.

Contributors

Enola G. Aird is an activist mother. She is the founder and director of Mothers for a Human Future, an initiative focused on fighting the commercialization of childhood and the commodification of children. She is a graduate of Barnard College and Yale Law School, and has at various times practiced corporate law, cared for her children full-time, and balanced mothering with advocacy for mothers and children. She gratefully acknowledges thoughtful comments on earlier drafts of this paper from Stephanie Robinson, Gia Interlandi, Marcy Darnovsky, Richard Hayes, Susan Linn, Stephanie Maitland, and Stephen L. Carter.

Honor Brabazon has published research on social movements, law, and global capitalism in academic and nonacademic periodicals, and she has conducted research in Sweden, India, and Venezuela. She received an Honours B.A. from Trinity College at the University of Toronto. Since writing the paper in this volume, she has completed a Master's degree in political science at York University and has begun work on a doctorate in politics at the University of Oxford. She is concurrently a visiting graduate student in law at Birkbeck College in the University of London.

Ivana Brown is a Ph.D. candidate in the Department of Sociology at Rutgers University in New Brunswick, New Jersey. In her dissertation she explores social aspects of maternal ambivalence, employing quantitative analysis of a national data set. Ivana is interested in cultural and social structural effects on motherhood experience, cultural representations of motherhood and mothering, and issues of balancing work and family. Ivana and her husband are raising two children.

Deirdre M. Condit is an associate professor of political science and women's studies at Virginia Commonwealth University, where she has been since 1994. She completed her M.A. and Ph.D. degrees in political science at Rutgers University in New Brunswick, New Jersey. Her research interests in feminist political theory and ethics broadly encompass the engagement of the public with issues of importance to women, the politics of reproduction, androgenetic theory, maternal theory and public policy, and women in elected office. She is co-editing a book with Andrea O'Reilly tentatively titled *The Palin Factor: Political Mothers and Public Motherhood in the Twenty-first Century*, scheduled for completion in summer 2010. Together with her co-author, Janet Hutchinson, she is completing a manuscript on elected women in Virginia politics, tentatively titled *Sisters Across the Aisle?: Legislating Virginia Women*, scheduled for completion in spring 2010. Her other publications include articles in *Public Administration Review, Sex Roles, Rhetoric and Public Affairs,* the *Journal of Medical Humanities,* the *American Review of Public Administration, Women and Politics,* and *Policy Sciences.* She is the ecstatic (if often exhausted!) mother of six-year-old Corbette and three-year-old Moira. Her partner is a professor of environmental politics at VCU. They are permitted to live on the premises with three ancient but wise cats, Emily, Shelley, and Byron.

Camille Wilson Cooper, Ph.D., is an associate professor in the Educational Leadership and Cultural Foundations Department at the University of North Carolina at Greensboro (USA). Her scholarship links issues of race, culture, and gender to educational equity and social justice. She specifically focuses on critical and culturally relevant approaches to school-family engagement. Feminist theories and methodologies inform her work. Dr. Cooper's research on the educational experiences, values, and choices of African American mothers has appeared in journals such as *Teacher Education Quarterly,* the *Journal of Negro Education,* and the *International Journal of Qualitative Studies in Education.* She has also presented this work at conferences throughout the United States and in Europe. Dr. Cooper earned her Ph.D. in education from the University of California, Los Angeles (USA).

Patrice DiQuinzio is associate provost for academic services at Washington College in Chestertown, Maryland. Previously she was professor of philosophy and women's studies at Muhlenberg College in Allentown, Pennsylvania, where she also directed the women's studies program. She is the author of *The Impossibility of Motherhood: Feminism, Individualism, and the Problem of Mothering* (1999) and co-editor of *Women and Children First: Feminism, Rhetoric, and Public Policy* (2005) with Sharon M. Meagher and *Feminist Ethics and Social Policy* (1987) with Iris Marion Young. She is also a former member of the board of trustees of the National Association of Mothers' Centers. She is deeply grateful to her sons, Tom and Brian Waitzman, and her daughter-in-law, Amanda Mahoney, and her companion, Tom Sandbach, for their love and support.

Andrea Doucet is professor of sociology at Carleton University, Ottawa, Canada. Her book *Do Men Mother?* was awarded the 2007 John Porter Tradition of Excellence Book Award from the Canadian Sociology Association. She is the author of more than thirty book chapters and articles and co-author of *Gender Relations: Intersectionality and Beyond* (with Janet Siltanen, Oxford University Press, 2008). She is the 2007 (and the eleventh) recipient of the Thérèse Casgrain Fellowship for research on women and social justice from the Canadian Social Sciences and Humanities Research Council; with this funding, she is currently writing a book on the narratives of Canadian and American mothers who are primary breadwinners.

Rachel Epstein has been a queer parenting activist, educator, and researcher for close to twenty years and coordinates the LGBTQ Parenting Network at the Sherbourne Health Centre in Toronto, Ontario. She has published on a wide range of queer parenting issues, including assisted human reproduction, queer spawn in schools, butch pregnancy, and the tensions between queer sexuality, radicalism, and parenting. Rachel is the 2008 winner of the Steinert & Ferreiro Award (Community One Foundation), recognizing her leadership and pivotal contributions toward the support, recognition, and inclusion of queer parents and their children in Canada, and editor of the ground-breaking anthology *Who's Your Daddy? And Other Writings on Queer Parenting* (Sumach Press, 2009).

May Friedman is a graduate student, an educator, a social worker, an activist, a partner, and a parent. She blends these multiple roles with varying degrees of grace. May is hard at work on her dissertation on the topic of mommyblogs and is the editor, with Shana Calixte, of *Mothering and Blogging: The Radical Act of the MommyBlog* (Demeter Press, 2009).

Laura Harrison is a doctoral candidate in gender studies at Indiana University. Originally from Wisconsin, Harrison received an undergraduate degree in women's studies and psychology from the University of Iowa. Her current research analyzes reproduction as a site of racialization, cultural contestation, and meaning-making through an interdisciplinary feminist framework.

Thenjiwe Magwaza, a gender and social justice activist, is an associate professor and head of the Gender Studies Department at the University of KwaZulu-Natal, South Africa. She holds a doctoral degree in oral studies from the same university. Her area of expertise, research, and teaching is cultural constructions of gender, with a special focus on the Zulu language and culture, motherhood, Durban-based refugees, and the impact of HIV/AIDS on women and home-care givers. She has published widely in national and international papers and book chapters in these areas. Her most recent publication is a co-edited book (2006) entitled *Freedom Sown in Blood: Memories of the Impi Yamakhanda, Bhambada Uprising*.

Marsha Marotta, Ph.D., is dean of undergraduate studies at Westfield State College, where she previously served as professor and chair of the Department of Political Science, and on the women's studies faculty. She is the recipient of a grant from the National Endowment for the Humanities. She is the author of several book chapters, has presented her research on feminist theory and women and politics at numerous conferences, and is at work on a book. A former newspaper reporter and city editor, she emphasizes both theory and practice in her writing.

Adrienne McCormick is associate professor and chair of the English Department at SUNY Fredonia. Her publications focus on theorizing difference and identity in contemporary American poetry, reading race and gender in contemporary American literature, and on experimental feminist film. She has published in journals such as *MELUS*, *Callaloo*, and *Hitting Critical Mass* and in several edited collections. She is editing a collection of essays on the V-Day movement, and working on a book project tentatively titled *Op/positional Poetries*. She spends the rest of her time mothering Kai, Indigo, and Rouen; watching movies; and cooking organic whole foods.

Gail Murphy-Geiss is an assistant professor of sociology and feminist and gender studies at Colorado College. She teaches courses in sociology of religion, gender, and family, and her research focuses on various topics at the intersection of these three areas, such as gender in children's religious education materials, clergy families, and sexual harassment in religious groups.

Violet Naanyu's research is based in Africa and includes topics on breastfeeding patterns, social networks, care-seeking behavior, and disease stigma. She holds a Ph.D. in sociology (Indiana University, USA), an M.A. degree in sociology (Indiana University, USA), and an M.A. in medical anthropology (University of Amsterdam, Netherlands). She is a lecturer in the Department of Behavioral Sciences, Moi University School of Medicine, Eldoret, Kenya.

Andrea O'Reilly is associate professor in the School of Women's Studies at York University. She is editor of more than twelve books, including *Textual Mothers/Maternal Texts: Motherhood in Contemporary Women's Literatures* (2010); *Feminist Mothering* (2008); and *Maternal Theory* (2007). O'Reilly is author of *Toni Morrison and Motherhood: A Politics of the Heart* (2004) and *Rocking the Cradle: Thoughts on Motherhood, Feminism, and the Possibility of Empowered Mothering* (2006). She is founder and director of the Association for Research on Mothering, the *Journal of the Association for Research on Mothering*, and Demeter Press. In 2009 she was the recipient of the university-wide "professor of the year award" at York University. She is editor of the first-ever encyclopedia of motherhood (2010).

Sarah F. Pearlman was formerly an associate professor in the doctoral program in clinical psychology at the University of Hartford and is currently associate professor emeritus. She is now an adjunct faculty member at Suffolk University and a clinical psychologist in private practice in the Boston area. She was a contributing editor and author for *Lesbian Psychologies: Explorations and Challenges*, as well as other published articles on lesbian couple relationships, psychotherapy with lesbians, and mothers of lesbian daughters and female-to-male transgender children.

A. Fiona Pearson is an assistant professor of sociology at Central Connecticut State University in New Britain. Her research and teaching interests include sociology of education, public policy, consumer culture, and social inequality. She is currently at work on a project analyzing the effects of policy and institutional culture on the experiences of college students balancing parenting and schooling responsibilities.

William M. Sherman received his Ph.D. in psychology from New York University. He is an associate professor at Southern Connecticut State University and a licensed psychologist with an interest in health psychology.

Mary Thompson is an assistant professor of American and women's literature in the English Department at James Madison University. She also co-coordinates the Women's Studies Program. Her research examines literary and popular culture representations of women's bodies and reproductive agency.

Judith Stadtman Tucker is a writer, an activist, and the founder and editor of the Mothers Movement Online (www.mothersmovement.org). She has contributed works on advocacy for mothers, maternal activism, and the formation and political grounding of the North American mothers' movement to a number of popular and scholarly collections.

Michele L. Vancour received her Ph.D. in health education from New York University. She is an associate professor of public health at Southern Connecticut State University. She teaches maternal and child health courses and supports multiple initiatives for working mothers.

Jessica M. Vasquez (Ph.D. in sociology from the University of California, Berkeley, 2007) is an assistant professor in sociology at the University of Kansas. Her research fields include race/ethnicity, Mexican Americans/Latinos, family, identity, and culture. She is currently completing a book on Mexican American racial identity formation and incorporation trajectories. Previously published articles can be found in *Ethnic and Racial Studies* and *Sociological Perspectives*.

Ana Villalobos received her Ph.D. in sociology from the University of California, Berkeley, and is currently a visiting scholar at Brandeis University. Her scholarly work focuses on mothering, and her dissertation research, a multiyear longitudinal study of the effects of societal insecurity on mothering, forms the basis of her contribution to this volume.

Index